PROTECTION OF LEGITIMATE EXPECTATIONS IN INVESTMENT TREATY ARBITRATION

This book evaluates the core of the concept of legitimate expectations from first principles in moral philosophy. It adopts an unconventional approach by examining this topic from a deep, philosophical perspective and delves into the debates on the binding nature of promise in moral philosophy. It then develops a doctrinal structure for the standard of protection. The author places the key premise of the book on the possibility of deriving firm conclusions from the debate and on creating a set of precise and prescriptive 'guidelines of the application of legitimate expectations'. The features of this book are threefold: first, a significant body of literature on moral philosophy is assimilated; second, core philosophical principles are extracted and expressed as a normative framework to resolve concrete cases; third, the author's analysis covers a vast number of investment treaty awards against the underlying framework.

TEERAWAT WONGKAEW is a legal officer at the Department of Treaties and Legal Affairs, Ministry of Foreign Affairs, Thailand. His current practices focus on treaty-making and public international laws issues, in particular, international investment law, international humanitarian law and the laws of international organisations. Previously he was Legal Adviser at the Department of International Economic Affairs of Thailand and was involved with the negotiations of bilateral and regional investment treaties as well as free trade agreements and investment treaty disputes. He also worked as a legal consultant at International Investment Agreement Division, United Nations Conference on Trade and Development (UNCTAD). He earned degrees in Law with French Law and Master of Law (LLM) from University College London. In 2016, he completed his PhD study at the Graduate Institute of International and Development Studies, Geneva.

PROTECTION OF LEGITIMATE EXPECTATIONS IN INVESTMENT TREATY ARBITRATION

A Theory of Detrimental Reliance

TEERAWAT WONGKAEW

Ministry of Foreign Affairs, Thailand

CAMBRIDGE
UNIVERSITY PRESS

CAMBRIDGE
UNIVERSITY PRESS

University Printing House, Cambridge CB2 8BS, United Kingdom

One Liberty Plaza, 20th Floor, New York, NY 10006, USA

477 Williamstown Road, Port Melbourne, VIC 3207, Australia

314–321, 3rd Floor, Plot 3, Splendor Forum, Jasola District Centre, New Delhi – 110025, India

79 Anson Road, #06–04/06, Singapore 079906

Cambridge University Press is part of the University of Cambridge.

It furthers the University's mission by disseminating knowledge in the pursuit of education, learning, and research at the highest international levels of excellence.

www.cambridge.org
Information on this title: www.cambridge.org/9781108474283
DOI: 10.1017/9781108675680

First published 2019

Printed and bound in Great Britain by Clays Ltd, Elcograf S.p.A.

A catalogue record for this publication is available from the British Library.

Library of Congress Cataloging-in-Publication Data
Names: Wongkaew, Teerawat, 1984– author.
Title: Protection of legitimate expectations in investment treaty arbitration : a theory of detrimental reliance / Teerawat Wongkaew, Ministry of Foreign Affairs, Thailand.
Description: Cambridge, United Kingdom ; New York, NY, USA : Cambridge University Press, 2018. | Based on author's thesis (doctoral – Graduate Institute of International and Development Studies (Geneva, Switzerland), 2016). | Includes bibliographical references and index.
Identifiers: LCCN 2018039850 | ISBN 9781108474283 (hardback)
Subjects: LCSH: Investments, Foreign (International law) | International commercial arbitration. | Rational expectations (Economic theory) | BISAC: LAW / International.
Classification: LCC K3830 .W66 2018 | DDC 346/.092–dc23
LC record available at https://lccn.loc.gov/2018039850

ISBN 978-1-108-47428-3 Hardback

For my parents, my brother
Saman and Prisana, Thitirat

CONTENTS

FOREWORD

Empowering international tribunals to adjudge a state's conduct by reference to a 'fair and equitable' standard of treatment was a leap of faith when investment treaties first populated the global legal space. What does it mean? A cacophony of different voices quickly filled the silence of the treaty text. Some thought it was a broad licence to do equity; others saw it as a fossilised incarnation of the international minimum standard. Still others greeted the fair and equitable treatment standard as a commitment to a specific economic programme of liberalisation and investment promotion – a rather heavy burden for a few words to bear. Individual decisions, when they started to appear, added further voices, but little by way of harmony. There was no shortage of false notes. Did states really sign up to international responsibility on the basis of a subjective judgment that their laws and regulations are not 'transparent' or 'stable' enough?

One concept emerging from the body of decisions has nonetheless struck a chord: legitimate expectations. This concept has a pedigree in comparative public law and some rudimentary soundings in general international law as well. It does not come from thin air. But it has had its fair share of controversy in these formative years of international investment law, and the big questions are still to be answered: When exactly will expectations be protected? Is the investor's conduct relevant? How is legitimacy to be assessed? What remedies should follow a breach?

As is so often the case in the life of the law, there is nothing new under the sun. Much of the hard thinking has already been done: on this occasion by analytical philosophers who may be presumed with confidence to be oblivious to investment treaties. There is in fact a vast philosophical literature providing a sophisticated and nuanced account of the different conceptions of legitimate expectations and the moral arguments underpinning them. If only this learning could be assimilated for problem solving in investment treaty arbitration.

And now it has. For those interested in and committed to the coherent development of international investment law, Dr Wongkaew's book will be the most valuable of companions, if not a revelation. He has provided the first systematic study of the concept of legitimate expectations by exploring the three principal philosophical arguments for why expectations deserve protection: the voluntarist, assurance and detrimental reliance theories. He then sets about finding the best fit for investment treaty arbitration, and his meticulous reasoning leads him to the conclusion that the detrimental reliance theory of legitimate expectations provides the most compelling justification for imposing liability on a host state in this context.

Dr Wongkaew's research and conclusions present a structure for the just and deliberative adjudication of claims for fair and equitable treatment through the prism of legitimate expectations and as such will be an indispensable tool for counsel and arbitrators alike and a first reference for scholars in this field. It is also an answer both to critics who maintain that the fair and equitable standard is infected with a fatal dose of indeterminacy (or worse) and to apologists who think nothing of converting subjective investor expectations into primary obligations of international law.

Professor Zachary Douglas QC

PREFACE

The concept of protection of legitimate expectations has provided a solution to the 'indeterminacy' problem of the vaguely worded provision of fair and equitable treatment in investment treaty. Frustration of the investor's legitimate expectations gives one possible meaning to what is regarded as an unfair or inequitable conduct of the state towards the investor. However, as the jurisprudence has revealed, the notion of 'legitimacy' or 'reasonableness' of expectations seems to be just as indeterminate as the notion of fairness to which it is supposed to give meaning. For this reason, the jurisprudential development of the concept is far from being coherent and principled, which supplies critics of the investment treaty regime with another bullet to shoot. Given the great importance of the fair and equitable treatment standard in investment treaty arbitration, the stake of resolving this indeterminacy problem is high.

This book is dedicated to demarcating the boundaries of legitimate expectations by tackling a problem in an unconventional way – namely, by drawing insights from moral philosophy to resolve a legal problem. I realise that to elucidate the concept, one cannot simply analyse conflicting awards which are repeated one after another without deep reflections. Nor is it the way forward to draw from comparative public laws because each legal system is unique and the rules thereof cannot be uncritically transplanted into the investment treaty regime. I have long been interested in the interface between law and philosophy, so I explored such interface in the context of legitimate expectations given that the concept raises several philosophical questions about promise. The approach I adopt in the book is to return to 'first principles' underlying protection of legitimate expectations – examining the fundamental question of why the law should protect legitimate expectations.

The book addresses three interrelated questions: (1) Why do we need a theory of legitimate expectations? (2) What is the theory of legitimate expectations? and (3) What is the application of the reliance theory? The examination of philosophical underpinnings of the concept results in a practical framework for adjudication of claims based on the protection of legitimate expectations.

The main idea of the book is that whilst there are three possible conceptions of legitimate expectations which focus on three different aspects of liability, the reliance theory of legitimate expectations should prevail. The reliance theory emphasises the act of detrimental reliance on the party of the investor as the basis for liability. This philosophical divide accounts for different reasoning and outcomes in the current investment treaty jurisprudence. As the chosen unifying conception, the reliance theory of legitimate expectations has three normative implications: purpose, conditions for liability and remedy. First, it underpins the concern of the law with compensation of harm suffered by the investor rather than enforcement of sovereign promise. Second, it dictates that the investor's conduct is an important normative element in the determination of state liability. Third, it provides a conceptual framework for justifying the award of reliance damages.

Whilst this book is essentially about the justification and conceptualisation of protection of legitimate expectations from the moral discourse, I hope that this book will also prove to be a useful tool for practitioners in the field, especially the Proposed Guidelines for the Application of the Reliance Theory of Legitimate Expectations.

The book was delivered to the publisher in March 2018 and takes account of the relevant awards as of that date. However, given that the book takes an analytical account of the jurisprudence, it is only possible to subject certain awards to critical analysis. Nevertheless, the book tries to incorporate references to the relevant awards which address issue of legitimate expectations.

This book is a revised version of my doctoral thesis defended in 2016 under the same title at the Graduate Institute of International and Development Studies, Switzerland. Many people have helped me in some way in the process of producing this book.

First, I owe immense gratitude to the PhD Committee composed of Professor Zachary Douglas QC, my thesis supervisor; Professor Thomas Schultz, the second reader; and Professor Stephan Schill, the external examiner, for constructive comments and suggestions which enabled me to improve the work tremendously and for words of encouragement in publishing the thesis.

I had to admit that I had never imagined spending four years thinking over one topic. But life just took its course and here I am publishing the book based on my PhD thesis! I owe immense gratitude to one special friend, Ms Anna Brinkmeier, who was the source of inspiration for taking up the PhD in the first place, which then allowed me to discover many enjoyable things of life, one of which is the joy of thinking deeply. I would like to thank friends and colleagues in Geneva and Bangkok, especially those from the Thai Ministry of Foreign Affairs, who inspired and supported me throughout these years. I remain eternally grateful to the financial support from the Royal Thai Government for the PhD study. I also appreciate the opportunity to gain insights into the policy perspectives of investment treaty arbitration whilst working as a legal consultant at UNCTAD during the PhD years.

I owe my gratitude to the entire Cambridge University Press team for the opportunity to work on this project and for continuous support throughout the process.

I am thankful for the help of Ms Sukanya Wisedsri for her research and technical assistance which proved to be essential to the completion of the book.

Above all, I am greatly indebted to my parents and brother and my partner in life, Ms Suchaya Tancharoenpol, who have given me endless love and support throughout these years.

TABLE OF CASES

Investment Treaty Cases

Decisions of International Courts

Decision of Municipal Courts

England

Australia

ABBREVIATIONS

BIT	bilateral investment treaty
BOT	build-operate-transfer
CDCA	California Desert Conservation Area
CEO	chief executive officer
DCF	discounted cash flow
EU	European Union
FET	fair and equitable treatment
ICJ	International Court of Justice
ICSID	International Centre for Settlement of Investment Disputes
ILC	International Law Commission
INECEL	Instituto Ecuatoriano de Electrificacio, Ecuador
IPO	initial public offering
NAFTA	North American Free Trade Agreement
PCIJ	Permanent Court of International Justice
PPA	purchase power agreement
SPA	share purchase agreement
UK	United Kingdom

PART I

Why Do We Need a Theory of Legitimate Expectations?

1

Introduction

'Must a name mean something?' Alice asked doubtfully.

'Of course it must,' Humpty Dumpty said with a short laugh; 'my name means the shape I am – and a good handsome shape it is, too. With a name like yours, you might be any shape, almost.'

. . . .

'When I use a word,' Humpty Dumpty said, in a rather scornful tone, 'it means just what I choose it to mean – neither more nor less.'

'The question is,' said Alice, '*whether you can make words mean so many different things.*'

'The question is,' said Humpty Dumpty, '*which is to be master – that's all.*'

Lewis Carroll, *Through the Looking Glass and What Alice Found There*[1]

1.1 Setting the Scene: Legitimate Expectations in Search of a Principled Justification

Since its inception in the decision of *Tecmed v. Mexico*,[2] the doctrine of legitimate expectations has been pervasively deployed as a legal tool to give legal protection to the investor's expectations created by the host state's representation or conduct in the assessment of the fair and equitable treatment standard. Despite the recognition that the doctrine of legitimate expectations has been embedded in investment treaty arbitration,[3] it has become part of international investment law without

[1] L Carroll, *Through the Looking-Glass and What Alice Found There* (1941), 111–12 (emphasis added), cited in C Brown, 'A Comparative and Critical Assessment of Estoppel in International Law' (1995) 50 *U Miami L Rev* 369.

[2] *Técnicas Medioambientales Tecmed, S.A. v. Mexico*, ICSID Additional Facility Case No ARB (AF)/00/02, Award (29 May 2003) 10 ICSID Rep 134.

[3] R Dolzer and C Schreuer, *Principles of International Investment Law* (Oxford: Oxford University Press, 2008) 134 ('firmly rooted in arbitral practice'); *Electrabel S.A. v. Republic of Hungary*, ICSID Case No ARB/07/19, Decision on Jurisdiction, Applicable Law and

understanding *why the law should protect legitimate expectations.*[4] What is meant by 'legitimate expectations' and what is the underlying rationale are the fundamental questions that have not been properly addressed by arbitral tribunals and legal scholars. It is pertinent to recall the acute observation on this point by F Dupuy and PM Dupuy that 'after more than ten years of intensive use of this phrase, do we really know what the doctrine of "legitimate expectations" stands for and what purpose it serves?'[5]

It is unclear why there has been little discussion on the underlying rationale of protection of legitimate expectations on the part of arbitral tribunals and legal scholars.[6] Does it seek to protect the investor from the harm caused by its reliance on the state's conduct to enforce sovereign commitments or to promote the rule of law or prevent abuse of regulatory power or arbitrary or inconsistent conduct? In the absence of such rationale, the tribunals have developed the jurisprudence in a conflicting and unstructured manner.

Nevertheless, one might suggest that the application of the principle seems *in vogue*[7] and so widely recognised in several municipal public laws[8] that it obviates the need for theoretical justification. After all, 'who could be against the protection of legitimate expectations?'[9] In investment treaty arbitration, the doctrine of legitimate expectations

Liability (30 November 2012) para 7.75 (the 'most important function' of the FET standard); *International Thunderbird Gaming Corporation v. Mexico*, UNCITRAL Case, Final Award (26 January 2006) Separate Opinion of Professor Walde, para 37 ('a self-standing subcategory and independent basis for a claim under the "fair and equitable standard" under Art. 1105 of the NAFTA').

4 Similar concern in English public law, CF Forsyth, 'Legitimate Expectations Revisited' (2011) 16(4) *JR* 429, 430 ('[I]t seems to me that the time has come to return to fundamentals. So we should ask fundamental questions about the justification and the task of the concept of legitimate expectations.').

5 F Dupuy and PM Dupuy, 'What to Expect from Legitimate Expectations? A Critical Appraisal and Look into the Future of the "Legitimate Expectations" Doctrine in International Investment Law' in NG Ziadé (ed), *Festschrift Ahmed Sadek El-Kosheri* (The Hague: Kluwer Law International 2015), 273.

6 *AWG Group v. Argentina*, UNCITRAL Case, Decision on Liability (30 July 2010) para 222 (the tribunal discussed 'the theoretical basis' of legitimate expectations and cited the work of Max Weber); R Dolzer, 'Fair and Equitable Treatment: Today's Contours' (2014) 12 *Santa Clara J Int'l L* 7, 17 (the author briefly discussed the rationale and justification for the recognition of legitimate expectations).

7 *EB (Kosovo) v. Secretary of State for the Home Department* [2008] UKHL 41 [2009] 1 AC 1159 at [31], per Lord Scot.

8 Dolzer, 'Fair and Equitable Treatment' (n 6).

9 Forsyth, 'Legitimate Expectations Revisited' (n 4) 429.

can be used to maximise protection to the investor by circumventing the high threshold test of expropriation because it allows 'a measure of subjective judgment'.[10] The tribunal in *Suez v. Argentina* considered legitimate expectations as 'an *operational method* for determining the existence or non-existence of fair and equitable treatment'.[11] It is hard to see how an abstract term such as 'legitimate expectations' could define 'fair' or 'unfair' treatment.

It is unfortunate that such metalegal understanding of protection of legitimate expectations cannot be acquired purely from the formalist approach based on the sources of law framework or the use of comparative public laws. The legal question on protection of legitimate expectations has an inherently moral dimension – namely, why a state must keep its promise or else pay compensation for the harm caused by a broken promise. The tribunals have already implicitly engaged in 'moral reasoning' in interpreting the rules on legitimate expectations. The moral philosophy of promise would offer invaluable guidance on the doctrine of legitimate expectations. This book proposes to elucidate the core of legitimate expectations from philosophical perspectives with a view to developing a coherent understanding of the doctrine and a normative framework for adjudication of cases.

This introductory chapter explains why a theory of legitimate expectations is needed in investment treaty arbitration and how such theory would improve the current state of law. It sets out the argument of the book and how it will be developed in the chapters that follow.

1.2 Three Reasons for a Theory of Legitimate Expectations

First, the questions of what is meant by legitimate expectation and why legitimate expectations should be protected have received little attention. This has resulted in the application of different conceptions of legitimate expectations, which has caused uncertainty and unpredictability in the outcome. Several practical questions have been given conflicting answers. Inconsistencies and poor reasoning are the hallmarks of arbitral decisions dealing with legitimate expectations. Second, following the lack of conceptual clarity, the doctrine of legitimate expectations has seen the so-called grey areas in adjudication of cases and lacks a clear doctrinal

[10] *Thunderbird v. Mexico* (n 3), Separate Opinion of Arbitrator Waelde, para 37.

[11] *Suez, Sociedad General de Aguas de Barcelona, S.A. and Vivendi Universal, S.A. v. Argentine Republic*, ICSID Case No ARB/03/19, Decision on Liability, Final Award, 30 July 2010, para 203.

structure. Third, inconsistent application of the principle of legitimate expectations has contributed to the level of legitimacy deficit in investment treaty regime. This problem is highlighted by the fact that arbitral tribunals have rarely engaged in the principled justification of protection of legitimate expectations.

1.2.1 Lack of Conceptual Clarity

The conceptual ambiguity of the doctrine of legitimate expectations can be illustrated with the following hypothetical situation based on the excerpt at the outset of the chapter.

Alice and Humpty Dumpty meet four distinguished investment treaty arbitrators at the International Centre for Settlement of Investment Disputes (ICSID) in Washington DC. Alice, who wants to reassure herself about Humpty Dumpty's answer from the previous conversation (in the excerpt), curiously asks the arbitrators, 'Must a word like "legitimate expectations" mean something, and can you make it mean so many different things?'

Upon reflection and recollection of the investment treaty jurisprudence, four arbitrators give four different answers. The first arbitrator tells her that 'legitimate expectations' means that the investor can expect the host state to act transparently and consistently,[12] as well as to ensure the stability of legal framework.[13] The second one explains that the doctrine of legitimate expectations is about the host state's acting in a non-arbitrary[14] or non-discriminatory[15] manner. The third displays the mastery of the obvious by suggesting that the investor can expect to be treated fairly and equitably.[16] The fourth one explains in a learned manner: 'yes, in real life, people have different expectations because they have different conceptions of present reality and the future; they are also influenced by different values, experiences and circumstances.

[12] *Tecmed v. Mexico* (n 2) para 154.

[13] *Frontier Petroleum Services Ltd v. Czech Republic*, UNCITRAL Case, Final Award (12 November 2010), para 285.

[14] *Alpha Projektholding GmbH v. Ukraine*, ICSID Case No ARB/07/16, Award (8 November 2010) para 420 ('this means, in part, that governments must avoid arbitrarily changing the rules of the game in a manner that undermines the legitimate expectations of, or the representations made to, an investor').

[15] *Saluka Investments BV (The Netherlands) v. Czech Republic*, UNCITRAL Rules, Partial Award (17 March 2006) para 321.

[16] Ibid para 446 ('the host State, in providing State aid, is clearly bound not to frustrate an investor's legitimate and reasonable expectation to be treated fairly and equitably').

The principle of legitimate expectations does not mean that every legitimate expectation should be protected. The challenge is how to decide which expectation should come under its protection. My view is that legitimate expectations must have a specific meaning – and in the context of investor–state dispute, legitimate expectations occur when the state has caused harm to the foreign investor by not keeping its promise made to that investor.[17] But I must leave the explanation for another time. Well done, Alice; you asked the question that even my colleagues or experts rarely address'. Alice is perplexed by these four answers. Humpty Dumpty comes and reminds her once more of the words of wisdom, '*which is to be master – that's all*'. The doctrine of legitimate expectations has been applied to mean different things. This book simply seeks to identify the master meaning.

1.2.2 Lack of Doctrinal Structure and the Adjudicative Problem

The law of legitimate expectations lacks a clear doctrinal structure and conceptual guidance for resolving the 'grey areas'.[18] Some issues can be mentioned: can a state create a legitimate expectation without explicit promise? Is detrimental reliance required? To what extent is the investor's own conduct relevant in the assessment of its legitimate expectations? In what circumstances can investors legitimately expect legal stability? Let us take just the first issue to illustrate that we may get different answers depending on which decision we look at. It might not be an exaggeration to characterise the doctrine of legitimate expectations as 'little more than a mechanism to dispense palm-tree justice'.[19]

Some arbitral decisions suggest that legitimate expectations can only arise where there is a specific promise or representation or certain conduct. However, even within this category, there are different views on whether expectations must derive from legal commitment or if it suffices to have a specific representation or consistent conduct.

[17] Some investment treaty decisions which suggest the reliance approach include *International Thunderbird Gaming Corporation v. Mexico*, UNCITRAL Case, Final Award (26 January 2006); *AWG Group v. Argentina*, UNCITRAL Case, Decision on Liability (30 July 2010); *Mohammad Ammar Al-Bahloul v. The Republic of Tajikistan*, SCC Case No V (064/2008), Final Award (8 June 2010).

[18] Dupuy and Dupuy, 'What to Expect from Legitimate Expectations?' (n 5) 290–93.

[19] J Watson, 'Clarity and Ambiguity: A New Approach to the Test of Legitimacy in the Law of Legitimate Expectations' (2010) 30(4) *LS* 633, 651.

The other decisions suggest that legitimate expectations can arise without assurance or the state's conduct because the law should provide protection when the investor 'could reasonably expect' it.[20] Furthermore, there are tribunals who employ the term 'legitimate expectations' in a rhetorical or tautological manner,[21] which does not add much to the legal analysis.

Some scholars have argued that the doctrine of legitimate expectations as an 'essentially contested concept'[22] cannot adjudicate the case 'as an arbiter of the controversy'[23] because there are disagreements over the exact meaning of the concept.[24] It is claimed that 'the principle of protecting reasonable expectations provides *a signpost* that points down the right road, but it does not provide *a map* to the end'.[25] However, the important premise of the book is that the underlying principles will provide invaluable guidance to resolve difficult questions regarding the extent to which the law protects the investor's legitimate expectations.[26]

1.2.3 Legitimacy Deficit and Protection of Legitimate Expectations

Arbitral tribunals have never explained why fair and equitable treatment should embrace protection of the investor's legitimate expectations. In many instances the doctrine has been applied to challenge the exercise of sovereign powers. Therefore, the continued application of the doctrine of legitimate expectations, which has no clear juridical basis or principled justification, will undermine the legitimacy of investment treaty arbitration.[27] This is not least because protection of legitimate

[20] *Saluka v. Czech Republic* (n 15) para 329.

[21] *Franck Charles Arif v. Republic of Moldova*, ICSID Case No ARB/11/23, Award (8 April 2013) para 533 (noting 'a certain easy circularity of argument' based on legitimate expectations in that an investor can postulate an expectation to condemn the sovereign conduct without articulation of the origins and scope of expectations).

[22] W Connolly, *The Terms of Political Discourse* (Princeton, NJ: Princeton University Press, 3rd edn, 1993), 10.

[23] BH Kuklin, 'The Justification for Protecting Reasonable Expectations' (2001) 29(3) *Hofstra L Rev* 863, 865.

[24] BH Kuklin, 'The Plausibility of Legally Protecting Reasonable Expectations' (1997) 32 *Val U L Rev* 19, 21.

[25] Ibid 33.

[26] P Reynolds, 'Legitimate Expectations and the Protection of Trust in Public Officials' (2011) *PL* 330; Forsyth, 'Legitimate Expectations Revisited' (n 4) 429.

[27] M Sornarajah, *Resistance and Change in the International Law on Foreign Investment* (Cambridge: Cambridge University Press, 2015), 299 ('The tribunal ceases to have

expectations has featured in almost all claims concerning the fair and equitable treatment standard. Its prominent role in the investment treaty arbitration, if misused, contributes significantly to the criticism of the investment treaty regime. Furthermore, given that the investment treaty regime has been undergoing a period of reflection and reform,[28] it is timely to rethink about the proper role and function of the doctrine of legitimate expectations.

1.3 The Argument: Protection against Detrimental Reliance as the Core of Protection of Legitimate Expectations

This book aims to develop a theory for protection of legitimate expectations in investment treaty arbitration from the philosophical perspectives based on the moral philosophy of promise. It defends a reliance conception of legitimate expectations – namely, that the fundamental purpose of the principle is to protect the investor against the harm that it has suffered from reasonably relying on the expectations created by the state's promise. In other words, the principle of legitimate expectations seeks to protect reliance interests rather than expectation interests of the investor.

Prior to setting out the discourse towards the theory of legitimate expectations, the book critically assesses the current approaches to the doctrine of legitimate expectations adopted by arbitral tribunals and legal scholars, which mainly focus on the sources of international law framework in Article 38(1) of the Statute of the International Court of Justice. The continued justification of legitimate expectations based on a general principle of law or good faith does not offer useful guidance to solve difficult cases of legitimate expectations that raise moral and political dimensions. The scholars' works take the protection of legitimate expectations as a self-evident premise and promptly proceed to enquire into *what expectations* to protect, often with the aid of comparative public laws.[29] Scholars and tribunals overlook the wisdom of the theory of

legitimacy and the law it formulates itself is not founded in authority. It is this double illegitimacy that taints the use of the rule on legitimate expectations. Its continued use will undermine investment arbitration even further'.).

[28] UNCTAD IIA Issues Note, 'Reform of the IIA Regime: Four Paths of Action and A Way Forward' (No 3, June 2014) 2.

[29] Textbooks on the doctrine of legitimate expectations in English laws include Soren Schønberg, *Legitimate Expectations in Administrative Law* (Oxford: Oxford University Press, 2000); R Thomas, *Legitimate Expectations and Proportionality in Administrative Law* (Oxford: Hart Publishing, 2000); R Moules, *Actions against Public*

judicial borrowing,[30] which cautions us that the purpose and rationale of rules should be identified before any meaningful borrowing of rules is possible. Dworkin's wisdom – 'analogy without theory is blind'[31] – confirms this.

Having set out the need for a theory of legitimate expectations and refuted the current approaches to legitimate expectations, the second part of the book develops a theory of legitimate expectations based on the alternative methodology in the moral philosophy of promise. The main argument is that protection of legitimate expectations should be based on a theory of detrimental reliance. The argument is substantiated in three steps.

First, Chapter 3 sets out the theoretical foundations for the use of moral philosophy in developing a theory of legitimate expectations. The important premise of this book is that understanding the phenomenon and reason for liability from the moral philosophy perspectives of promissory obligation will help us understand the doctrinal structure of an obligation to protect legitimate expectations. The underlying idea behind this chapter is that if we could understand how 'promise' or similar notions could create an obligation, we would be able to explain the mystery of how the state could incur an obligation from frustrating the investor's expectations.

The notion of 'promise' is at the heart of legitimate expectations cases. Investment treaty tribunals even employ the term 'promise' and other similar notions, such as 'assurance', 'commitment' and 'representation', as the 'legal' threshold for determining liability for breach of legitimate expectations, without explaining how those acts can generate an obligation. Why is an expectation based on a specific representation more 'legitimate' than a vague promise? It seems intuitively right that when the state makes a promise, which has created the expectation and is subsequently frustrated, there is something unfair or morally wrong about it. The use of these terms in laws without articulating the phenomenon of liability creates confusion and reveals ambiguity of thought.[32]

Officials: Legitimate Expectations, Misstatements and Misconduct (London: Sweet & Maxwell, 2009). One comparative law book which includes a discussion of French law is S Calmes, *Du principe de protection de la confiance légitime en droits allemand, communautaire et français* (Nouvelle bibliothèque de thèses) (Paris: Dalloz 2001).

30 The issue of judicial borrowing is discussed in Chapter 2.

31 R Dworkin, 'In Praise of Theory' (1997) 29 *Ariz St LJ* 353, 371 ('an analogy is a way of stating a conclusion, not a way of reaching one, and theory must do the real work').

32 P Millett, 'Equity's Place in the Law of Commerce' (1998) 114 *LQR* 214, 225 ('misuse of language often conceals a confusion of thought').

Second, the book draws from three main theories of promissory obligation in the philosophy literature to form the underlying framework, which results in different understandings about legitimate expectations.[33] Promise as a wilful act to undertake an obligation leads to a restrictive, state-centric view of legitimate expectations. Promise as an intention to create expectations allows the non-binding, voluntary conduct of the state as the basis for an obligation. Promise as a conduct that induces reliance offers a flexible framework for balancing the investor's conduct and the investor's expectations. The book applies these three conceptions to illustrate the important point that a philosophical divide explains different reasoning and outcomes in the current jurisprudence on protection of legitimate expectations.

Chapter 4 examines the voluntarist conception of legitimate expectations, which attributes a binding nature of promise to the will of the promisor. Therefore, expectations would only be legitimate and legally protected if they arise from a legal commitment. Chapter 5 examines the bare expectations or assurance conception, which locates the obligation in the intention to provide assurance. In effect, this is a weaker version of the voluntarist conception as there is no need to prove an intention to assume a legal obligation. Chapter 6 examines the distinct reliance theory, which does not focus on the legally binding nature of the state's conduct but rather the reasonable act of reliance by the investor upon the state's promise. This conception of legitimate expectations provides a flexible conceptual framework for considering the perspectives of both the state and the investor.

The third step in the argument is to choose the most suitable conception out of the three conceptions. Chapter 7, which concludes Part II of the book, defends the reliance conception based on the 'best-fit' criteria.

The conclusions in favour of the reliance conception are based on the assessment of the best-fit conception or the architecture of the investment treaty regime. The best-fit analysis considers both macro and micro aspects of the investment treaty regime. At the macro level, the reliance conception provides a useful framework for balancing the conflicting interests in the regulatory state paradigm. Furthermore, the reliance conception that requires relief of reliance damages is most compatible with the remedial structure of the investment treaty regime. At the micro level, only the reliance conception could overcome the issue of

[33] Chapter 3 sets out the structure and details of this analytical framework.

assimilation of contractual right and expectations. More significantly, only the reliance conception can protect non-legally binding interests which would not otherwise be protected under investment treaties. The main purpose of introducing the doctrine of legitimate expectations is to provide additional protection where other provisions are not applicable; therefore, it would defeat the purpose to choose the other two conceptions that would deny such protection.

Part III of the book offers the analysis on the practical application of the reliance theory of legitimate expectations on two dimensions: (1) substantive dimension – namely, the scope of the principle and the conditions for liability – and (2) remedial dimension – the appropriate remedy for a breach of legitimate expectations. Chapter 8 examines the substantive application of the reliance theory on three main aspects: (1) scope of application of the theory, (2) application of the theory to three main paradigms – (i) breach of contract, (ii) revocation of administrative representations and (iii) change of legislative framework – and (3) relationship with other relevant standards, such as an umbrella clause or non-arbitrary standard.

The reliance theory means the restrictive scope of protection of legitimate expectations. The over-inclusive conception as elaborated in *Tecmed v. Mexico* falls outside the proposed theory. This theory does not deny that other fundamental values such as due process, denial of justice, non-arbitrariness or non-discrimination are not 'legitimate expectations' of the investor. Those types of expectations should not come to seek refuge under the principle of legitimate expectations, but they could be protected under other specific principles. After all, the function of a legal system is to protect security of expectations because the stability of expectation is an essential condition for social interaction and personal continuity'.[34]

Chapter 9 addresses the often-neglected topic of remedy for a breach of legitimate expectations in which the reliance theory reinforces the argument for reliance damages. It revisits the issue of suitability of applying the interstate rule on remedy to the context of an investor–state dispute settlement and examines how the reliance theory can provide guidance on the issue of remedy.

In summary, the book is structured as follows. After these introductory considerations, Chapter 2 offers a critique of the sources-

[34] PJ Kelly, Utilitarianism and Distributive Justice: Jeremey Bentham and the Civil Law (Oxford: Oxford University Press, 1990) 87–88.

based conception of legitimate expectations that confines the understanding of the rules to the sources of international laws. Part II of the book begins with Chapter 3, which sets out the theoretical foundations for the use of moral philosophy as a method for developing a theory of legitimate expectations and some methodological caveats. It explains why and how we can apply insights from the moral philosophy of promise to understand the concept of legitimate expectations. Chapter 4 examines the normative implication of the voluntarist conception of legitimate expectations. This theory attributes an obligation to an intention to undertake an obligation. Chapter 5 analyses the 'bare expectations' or assurance theory of promise, which attributes liability to the intention to give assurance. Chapter 6 discusses the reliance conception of legitimate expectations, which focuses on the act of detrimental reliance by the investor on the state's promise. Each conception has been analysed and criticised on its own terms. Chapter 7, which concludes Part II, sets out the 'best-fit' criteria for choosing the most suitable conception, which focuses on the macro and micro aspects of the investment treaty regime.

Part III of the book discusses the application of the reliance theory of legitimate expectations. Chapter 8 examines the consequence on the substantive rules, whereas Chapter 9 examines the remedial consequence of the reliance theory by revisiting the question of remedy and the suitability of the current remedial regime based on the interstate rules.

1.4 Theoretical and Practical Relevance and Contribution of the Book

The book develops a reliance-based theory of legitimate expectations and articulates a normative framework for adjudication of cases for breach of the fair and equitable treatment standard. In this regard, the book has theoretical and practical relevance to the investment treaty arbitration community.

The book takes an interdisciplinary approach based on moral philosophy to the complex issue of protection of legitimate expectations, which has so far been approached mostly from a formalist perspective. The reliance theory of legitimate expectations offers penetrative insights into the doctrinal structure and assists arbitral tribunals and counsels in adjudicating complex cases for breach of fair and equitable treatment standard.[35] The proposed guidelines for application of the principle of legitimate expectations offers a concrete framework for applying the doctrine to solve practical issues, which should provide more clarity and certainty to the law over time. The reliance theory of legitimate expectations serves as a conceptual map[36] for tribunals and legal counsels in the navigation of the legal landscape of legitimate expectations.

From the policy perspective, the reliance theory of legitimate expectations should shield against those critics who would like to discard the doctrine for its superfluous and irrelevant role.

1.5 Miscellaneous Points: Scope of the Book

Even though the concept of protecting investors' legitimate expectations plays an important role in defining the term 'investment'[37] or the assessment of damages[38] or in the expropriation case,[39] the book only addresses protection of legitimate expectations under the fair and equitable treatment standard. A comparative analysis of the role of investors' expectations in those circumstances may be interesting to study, but it is beyond the scope of this book. The jurisprudence on legitimate expectations in the expropriation cases is of limited use to our discussion. This is because legitimate expectations in the context of expropriation are usually based on existing 'property' rights, whereas under the fair and equitable treatment standard, they can arise from a wider range of situations and very often are not based on a prior legal right but on the conduct of the state.

For the purpose of completeness, it should be clarified that the terms 'legitimate' and 'reasonable' are used interchangeably without any normative significance. Most investment treaty tribunals often employ

[35] Z Douglas, J Pauwelyn and JE Viñuales (eds), *The Foundations of International Investment Law – Bringing Theory into Practice* (Oxford: Oxford University Press, 2014).

[36] M Loughlin, *Political Theory and Public Law* (Oxford: Clarendon Press, 1992), 37.

[37] Z Douglas, 'Concepts of Property' in Douglas et al. (eds), 'The Foundations of International Investment Law' (n 36).

[38] *MTD Equity Sdn. Bhd. and MTD Chile S.A. v. Republic of Chile*, ICSID Case No ARB/01/7, Award (25 May 2004) para 240 (ii) (the tribunal linked the question of recoverability of pre-contract expenses to the moment of creation of legitimate expectations).

[39] S Fietta, 'Expropriation and the "Fair and Equitable" Standard: The Developing Role of Investors' "Expectations" in International Investment Arbitration' (2006) 23 *J Int'l Arb* 375.

both terms in the same context[40] whilst some tribunals use each term alone.[41] Finally, this book does not undertake a comparative analysis of legitimate expectations in municipal systems and in investment treaty arbitration.[42] The book focuses on the theoretical foundation of the doctrine of legitimate expectations.

[40] *Duke Energy Electroquil Partners & Electroquil S.A. v. Ecuador*, ICSID Case No ARB/04/19, Award (18 August 2008) para 340 ('the investor's expectations must be legitimate and reasonable'); *Electrabel S.A. v. Republic of Hungary*, ICSID Case No ARB/07/19, Decision on Jurisdiction, Applicable Law and Liability (30 November 2012) para 7.76 ('the assessment of *legitimate and reasonable expectations*'); *Grand River Enterprises Six Nations Ltd et al. v. USA*, NAFTA/UNCITRAL, Award (12 January 2011) para 140 ('the concept of *reasonable or legitimate expectations*').

[41] *Generation Ukraine v. Ukraine*, ICSID Case No ARB/00/9, Award (16 September 2003) para 20.37 ('determining the investor's legitimate expectations'); *Toto Construzioni Generali SpA v. Republic of Lebanon*, ICSID Case No ARB/07/12, Award (7 June 2012) para 159 ('*Legitimate expectations* may follow').

[42] For this subject, see F Dupuy, La protection de l'attente légitime des parties au contrat – Etude de droit international des investissements à la lumière du droit compare (Thèse: University of Paris (Panthéon-Assas) and Berlin: Humboldt Universität, 2007).

2

The Formalist Conception of Legitimate Expectations and Different Paradigms of the Investment Treaty Regime: A Critique

'No Law is an Island, Entire of Itself'.

F Baetens[1]

2.1 Introduction

From the current legal scholarship and arbitral decisions, we can deduce three main doctrinal approaches in understanding the doctrine of legitimate expectations in investment treaty arbitration. First, the doctrine of legitimate expectations is a general principle of law as recognised in municipal public laws of major legal systems. Second, it is a general principle of international law which is an expression of good faith principle. Third, the application of the doctrine of legitimate expectations is justified on the basis of arbitral decisions as subsidiary source of law. These doctrinal approaches are based on the sources of international law in Article 38 of the Statute of the International Court of Justice (ICJ), alternatively referred to as the 'formalist' framework.[2] Such divergent conceptualisation of legitimate expectations coheres with different conceptions of the investment treaty regime.[3]

This chapter examines the public law and public international law conceptions of legitimate expectations. Under the first conception, the doctrine of legitimate expectations originates from domestic laws and could be 'transplanted' into investment treaty arbitration. The rationale

[1] F Baetens, 'No Law Is an Island, Entire of Itself – How International Investment Law Interacts with Other Fields of Public International Law' in F Baetens (ed), *Investment Law within International Law: Integrationist Perspectives* (Cambridge: Cambridge University Press, 2013).

[2] Jean d'Aspremont, *Formalism and the Sources of International Law: A Theory of the Ascertainment of Legal Rules* (Oxford: Oxford University Press, 2011); H Thirlway, *The Sources of International Law* (Oxford: Oxford University Press, 2014).

[3] A Roberts, 'Clash of Paradigms: Actors and Analogies Shaping the Investment Treaty System' (2013) 107(1) *AJIL* 45.

for such transplantation is that the investment treaty regime could be conceptualised as a public law regime because these two regimes address similar concerns of abuse of regulatory powers and have similar adjudicative functions. It uses the 'general principles of law' criteria in Article 38(1)(c) of the Statute of the International Court of Justice as the conceptual framework for making the argument (Section 2.2).

Under the second conception, a legal obligation to protect legitimate expectations could be ascertained within the framework of international law sources – namely, treaty, customs, general principles of law or general principle of international law, such as principles of estoppel, unilateral declarations and good faith (Section 2.3). The most common argument in this paradigm is that protection of legitimate expectations is an expression of 'good faith' principle.

The ubiquitous justification of legitimate expectations, which does not subscribe to a particular conception of the regime, is based on the arbitral decisions, despite the absence of binding precedent system in international investment law. This approach is formalist in nature because it implicitly relies on 'judicial decisions' as subsidiary means for the determination of rules of law according to Article 38(1)(d) of the Statute of the International Court of Justice (Section 2.4).

This chapter aims to provide critical analysis of three doctrinal approaches to protection of legitimate expectations, which highlights fundamental weaknesses of each approach. For the public law approach, the assumption that the investment treaty regime and public law regime are analogous such that the rules could be transposed from one regime to another could be questioned. Furthermore, there are limits to the use of comparative public laws in elaborating the rules in investment treaty regime.[4] For the public international law approach, it is questionable that the good faith principle or other general principles, such as estoppel or doctrine of unilateral declarations, could provide a basis for developing a useful normative framework for resolving the practical issues of legitimate expectations. For instance, the questions, such as whether detrimental reliance is required or whether expectations without a specific representation can be legitimate, cannot be resolved by the interpretation of abstract principle of good faith. For the precedent-based approach to justification of legitimate expectations, the argument of consistency and

[4] V Vadi, *Analogies in International Investment Law and Arbitration* (Cambridge: Cambridge University Press, 2015).

predictability as a sufficient ground for supporting this approach will be challenged.

2.2 Public Law Conception of Protection of Legitimate Expectations

The argument for the public law conception of legitimate expectations has two important aspects. The first concerns the contention that the principle of legitimate expectations is 'a general principle of law as recognized by civilized nations' by virtue of Article 38(1)(c) of the Statute of the International Court of Justice. Protection of legitimate expectations enjoys widespread recognition in municipal public laws.[5] The emergence of substantive expectations in some domestic jurisdictions has acted as 'a catalyst' for its introduction into investment treaty arbitration.[6] The second aspect of the argument is contingent on the assumption about the functional similarity of the investment treaty regime and domestic judicial review as a basis for applying by analogy the rules in public laws to a dispute in investment treaty arbitration.

2.2.1 Legitimate Expectations as a General Principle of Law Revisited

The validity of the 'general principle of law' argument is questionable because there is no consensus amongst legal scholars[7] and the arbitral tribunals have rarely addressed this issue. The proponents of the argument essentially suggest that the principle of legitimate expectations is recognised in several major legal systems, whereby the lack of universality concerning the scope of application of the principle of legitimate

[5] C McLachlan, L Shore and M Weiniger, *International Investment Arbitration: Substantive Principles* (Oxford: Oxford University Press, 2007), 234 (the principle of legitimate expectations as applicable in investment treaty arbitration is a creation 'borrowed from [domestic] administrative law').

[6] F Vicuna, 'From Preston to Prescott: Globalizing Legitimate Expectation' in S Charnovitz, D Steger and P Van den Bossche (eds) *Law in the Service of Human Dignity: Essays in Honour of Florentino Feliciano* (Cambridge: Cambridge University Press, 2005), 307.

[7] M Potesta, 'Legitimate Expectations in Investment Treaty Law: Understanding the Roots and the Limits of a Controversial Concept' (2013) *ICSID Review* 1; F Dupuy and PM Dupuy, 'What to Expect from Legitimate Expectations? A Critical Appraisal and Look into the Future of the "Legitimate Expectations" Doctrine in International Investment Law' in Nassib G. Ziadé (ed), *Festschrift Ahmed Sadek El-Kosheri* (The Hague: Kluwer Law International, 2015) 273–98; HA Mairal, 'Legitimate Expectations and Informal Administrative Representations' in S Schill (ed) *International Investment Law and Comparative Public Law* (Oxford: Oxford University Press, 2010).

expectations does not hinder its recognition under Article 38(1)(c) of the Statute of the International Court of Justice.[8]

By contrast, some scholars argue that the lack of uniformity in the domestic laws could obstruct the recognition of the principle as a general principle.[9] Other authors take an intermediary approach by suggesting that there is an 'emerging general principle of protection of legitimate expectations'.[10]

The current jurisprudence does not provide clear support for the 'general principle of law' approach. The decision of *Tecmed v. Mexico*, which first articulated the doctrine of legitimate expectations, relied on the principle of good faith for providing its juridical basis.[11] Subsequent tribunals advanced the comparative public law argument for protection of legitimate expectations with some reluctance. They never explicitly recognise protection of legitimate expectations as 'a general principle of law' but merely recognised the use of comparative public laws as 'a point of reference'[12] or as 'a benchmark'[13] or being 'relevant'.[14] The tribunal in *Gold Reserve v. Venezuela* suggested that the legal sources of legitimate expectations are to be found in the comparative analysis of many domestic legal systems.[15] The closest point in which the tribunal recognised legitimate expectations as a general principle was when the tribunal in *Total v. Argentina* suggested that protection of legitimate expectations was based on good faith, 'one of the general principles referred to in

[8] E Snodgrass, 'Protecting Investors' Legitimate Expectations – Recognising and Delimiting a General Principle' (2006) 21 *ICSID Rev – FILJ* 1, 21; C Brown, 'The Protection of Legitimate Expectations as a "General Principle of Law": Some Preliminary Thoughts' (2009) 6(1) *TMD*.

[9] T Zeyl, 'Charting the Wrong Course: The Doctrine of Legitimate Expectations in Investment Treaty Law' (2011) 49 *Alberta L Rev* 203; see also M Sornarajah, *The International Law on Foreign Investment* (Cambridge: Cambridge University Press, 3rd edn, 2010) 355; C Campbell, 'House of Cards: The Relevance of Legitimate Expectations under Fair and Equitable Treatment Provisions in Investment Treaty Law' (2013) 30(4) *J Int'l Arb* 361.

[10] Potesta, 'Legitimate Expectations in Investment Treaty Law' (n 7) 34.

[11] *Técnicas Medioambientales Tecmed, S.A. v. Mexico*, ICSID Additional Facility Case No ARB(AF)/00/02, Award (29 May 2003) 10 *ICSID Rep* 134 para 121.

[12] *International Thunderbird Gaming Corporation v. Mexico*, UNCITRAL Case, Final Award (26 January 2006) Separate Opinion of Arbitrator Waelde para 28.

[13] *Toto Construzioni Generali SpA v. Republic of Lebanon*, ICSID Case No ARB/07/12, Award (7 June 2012) para 166.

[14] *Total S.A. v. Argentina*, ICSID Case No ARB/04/1, Decision on Liability (21 December 2010) para 128.

[15] *Gold Reserve Inc. v. Bolivarian Republic of Venezuela*, ICSID Additional Facility Case No ARB(AF)/09/1), Final Award (22 September 2014) para 576.

Article 38 (1)(c) of the Statute of the International Court of Justice as a source of international law'.[16]

These instances cannot be construed as arbitral endorsement of the principle of legitimate expectations as a general principle of law. The reason for the reluctance to clarify the juridical basis of the principle is unknown. The instrumental value of the doctrine in circumventing the high threshold test of expropriation[17] or in determining the existence or non-existence of fair and equitable treatment[18] are not sufficient to provide a theoretical foundation.

In addition to the lack of scholars' consensus and arbitral support, the general principle of law approach can be criticised on other grounds. First, the proponents did not set out the clear methodology and the threshold required for the doctrine of legitimate expectations to be recognised as a general principle of law under Article 38(1)(c). They merely relied on the legal works on comparative laws or expert opinions to make their case and insisted that the lack of unanimity in terms of the scope of protection in domestic public laws[19] should not prevent its recognition as a general principle of law.[20] However, the opponents rejected the doctrine because such lack of uniformity and universality hinders the recognition as a general principle of law. Essentially, the two sides agree on the fact of the lack of uniformity but disagree on its effect. Which side of the argument is more convincing?

The question of whether legitimate expectations are a general principle of law as recognised under Article 38(1)(c) cannot be satisfactorily answered at this stage because a convincing answer requires a thorough comparative investigation into the operation of the concept in municipal systems of law. At the moment comparative law scholarship has little influence on reflections on general principles of international law.[21] However, the interpretation of the opponents is untenable because it

[16] *Total S.A. v. Argentina* (n 14) para 128.

[17] *Thunderbird v. Mexico* (n 12) para 37.

[18] *Suez, Sociedad General de Aguas de Barcelona, S.A. and Vivendi Universal, S.A. v. Argentine Republic*, ICSID Case No ARB/03/19, Decision on Liability (30 July 2010) para 203.

[19] S Schønberg, *Legitimate Expectations in Administrative Law* (Oxford: Oxford University Press, 2000).

[20] Snodgrass, 'Protecting Investors' Legitimate Expectations' (n 8) 21–22; Brown, 'The Protection of Legitimate Expectations' (n 8) 6.

[21] J Ellis, 'General Principles and Comparative Law' (2011) 22 (4) *EJIL* 949, 950.

would render Article 38(1)(c) unworkable[22] and would contradict the general trend that many principles recognised as a general principle of law, such as good faith,[23] equity[24] or *pacta sunt servanda*[25] or the doctrine of *rebus sic stantibus*[26] have different scopes of application in domestic laws.[27] Even if the general principle of law approach is correct, the use of comparative laws to elaborate the content of any particular legal principle would still be required.[28]

2.2.2 *Argument by Analogy for the Public Law Conception of Legitimate Expectations*

The public law regime could provide an 'interpretive paradigm' for developing rules in the investment treaty arbitration.[29] The argument by analogy for the 'general principle of law' approach asserts that investment treaty arbitration is functionally analogous to domestic judicial review[30] – namely, to ensure respect for non-discrimination, the rule of law and property rights as well as to prevent an abuse of regulatory power.[31] In this regard, investment treaty arbitration is not simply a mechanism to resolve investor–state disputes but has 'a broader function in providing a legal framework for a public international economic order . . . by establishing principles of investment protection under international law that endorse the rule of law standards for the treatment of foreign investors'.[32]

22 HC Gutteridge, 'The Meaning and Scope of Article 38 (1) (c) of the Statute of the International Court of Justice' (1952) 38 *Transactions of the Grotius Society* 125.

23 I Brownlie, *Principles of Public International Law* (Oxford: Oxford University Press, 7th edn, 2008), 19.

24 M Akehurst, 'Equity and General Principles of Law' (1976) 25 *ICLQ* 801.

25 H Wehberg, 'Pacta Sunt Servanda' (1959) 53 *Am J Int'l L* 775, 786.

26 H Lauterpacht, *The Function of Law in the International Community* (Oxford: Clarendon Press, 1933), 272.

27 A McNair, 'The General Principles of Law Recognized by Civilized Nations' (1957) 33 *BYIL* 1.

28 Gutteridge, 'The Meaning and Scope of Article 38 (1) (c)' (n 22) 125, 128.

29 Roberts, 'Clash of Paradigms' (n 3).

30 G Van Harten and M Loughlin, 'Investment Treaty Arbitration as a Species of Global Administrative Law' (2006) 17 *EJIL* 121.

31 S Schill, 'Fair and Equitable Treatment, the Rule of Law and Comparative Public Law' in S Schill (ed), *International Investment Law and Comparative Public Law* (Oxford: Oxford University Press, 2010) 24.

32 Schill, 'International Investment Law and Comparative Public Law – An Introduction' (n 31) 3.

This section assesses the strength and weakness of the argument by analogy and the use of comparative laws. It essentially questions the assumption that the two regimes are analogous in terms of its underlying rationale and adjudicative functions.

2.2.2.1 The Case for the Use of Comparative Public Laws

It is hard to disagree with the learned observation by Professor Friedmann that 'the general principles formed by a comparative study of the relevant principles of the different national systems provide the principal source from which the new bodies of international law are being developed'. The proponents have advanced five reasons for the use of comparative public laws in elucidating the doctrine of legitimate expectations.

First, the public laws are more developed and therefore provide 'a method for concretizing and legitimating standards of international investment law'.[33] Comparative laws help adjudicators in interpreting and applying broad and open-ended provisions, serving as a critical tool in developing international investment law.[34] However, there might be some challenges in selecting comparative legal systems from which we draw lessons. Furthermore, there may be different views on certain issues of a legal standard in one system; this makes identification of a rule difficult. For example, for the doctrine of legitimate expectations in English law, the issue of detrimental reliance is subject to different scholarly views and court decisions.[35] Second, it seeks to balance investment protection and non-investment concerns, such as the protection of public health, cultural heritage, labour standards or the environment. Third, it ensures consistency in the interpretation and application of investment treaties because the interpretative method is uniform for all investment treaties. Fourth, the comparative public law legitimises existing arbitral jurisprudence by showing that the solutions adopted in investment treaty arbitration are analogous to the ones adopted by domestic courts or other international courts or tribunals. Fifth, it ensures cross-regime consistency and mitigates the negative effects of fragmentation by stressing commonalities and openness of international

[33] Ibid 1.

[34] S Montt, *State Liability in Investment Treaty Arbitration – Global Constitution and Administrative Law in the BIT Generation* (Portland, OR: Hart Publishing, 2009), 166.

[35] J Watson, 'Clarity and Ambiguity: A New Approach to the Test of Legitimacy in the Law of Legitimate Expectations' (2010) 30(4) *SLS* 633.

investment law towards other international regimes, such as human rights and environmental law.

2.2.2.2 A Critique of the Use of Comparative Public Laws

The use of comparative public laws should be cautioned because the investment treaty regime and public law systems are not functionally or ideologically similar. The argument in this section draws insights from the theory of judicial borrowing,[36] which essentially warns against the outright transposition of rules and a tendency for free decision-making[37] and encourages *contextual and purposive tailoring of legal rules*[38] in the process of judicial borrowing. We must account for contextual differences[39] and identify the guiding rationale behind the municipal public law of legitimate expectations rather than import 'lock, stock and barrel'.[40] This is particularly pertinent in our context when a legal concept from national law is transplanted into a different institutional framework of international law.[41] The analysis focuses on three main features: (a) the rationales or purposes of the two regimes, (b) the interpretative and remedial powers and legitimacy of arbitrators and judges and (c) the different nature of legal relationships between host state and foreign investors and public authorities and citizens.

2.2.2.2.1 Foundations of the Two Regimes: The Rule of Law in Public Law versus Protection of Investment in Investment Treaty Arbitration The rationale of the judicial review is to ensure the rule of law and to prevent abuse of power by public authorities.[42] The judiciary acts as a mechanism of checks and balance based on the constitutional principle

[36] T Wongkaew, 'The Transplantation of Legitimate Expectations in Investment Treaty Arbitration: A Critique' in S Lalani and R Polanco (eds), *The Role of the State in Investor-State Arbitration* (Leiden: Brill Nijhoff, 2015), 69.

[37] V Vadi, 'Critical Comparisons: The Role of Comparative Law in Investment Treaty Arbitration' (2010) 39(1) *Denv J Int'l L& Pol'y* 89, 182.

[38] AA Momirov and AN Fourie, 'Vertical Comparative Law Methods: Tools for Conceptualizing the International Rule of Law' (2009) 2(3) *Erasmus L Rev* 292.

[39] L Oppenheim, 'The Science of International Law: Its Tasks and Methods' (1908) 2 *AJIL* 313, 336, 338; Momirov and Fourie, 'Vertical Comparative Law Methods' (n 38) 292, 297.

[40] *International Status of South-West Africa Case*, ICJ Reports, Advisory Opinion, Judge McNair Opinion, 1950, 148.

[41] JB Wiener, 'Something Borrowed for Something Blue: Legal Transplants and the Evolution of Global Environmental Law' (2001) 27 *Ecol L Q* 1297, 1298.

[42] M Elliot, 'Judicial Review's Scope, Foundations and Purposes: Joining the Dots' (2012) *NZ L Rev* 75.

of separation of powers. This means that judges cannot substitute their own views on issues which are more suited for democratically elected bodies to decide.

The proponents of the public law conception have not adequately explained the theoretical foundations of the 'public' character of investment treaty regime, so as to justify the transplantation of public law rules. Anthea Roberts offered two possible theories: first, the 'public action theory', which suggests that disputes involving a state are public if they arise under an agreement concluded by the state in its public capacity; second, the 'public interest theory', which suggests that significant matters of public concern are involved.[43]

The views regarding the purpose of the investment treaty regime are unsettled. From one point of view, the function of investment treaty regime is not simply for resolving a dispute between an investor and a state but to foster the good governance and the rule of law.[44] There seems to be support for such view by the recent empirical study that the investment treaty arbitration has been used to impose the rule of law on non-democratic states and to strengthen the international rule of law.[45] From the other point of view, some scholars reject the rule of law-based conceptualisation as an attempt to impose the standards of Western political and economic philosophies through arbitration system.[46] It is argued that the rule of law ideal is but 'a castle in the air' and rests on 'the imaginations of arbitrators'; the investment treaty arbitration seems to undermine the rule of law for the lack of any settled rules.[47]

For a more moderate view, the fundamental purpose of investment treaties is to promote and protect investment,[48] whereby the arbitration system acts as a mechanism for resolving a dispute between an investor and a host state, and recognises that the rule of law value plays an

[43] Roberts, 'Clash of Paradigms' (n 3).

[44] Van Harten and Loughlin, 'Investment Treaty' (n 30) 121; B Kingsbury and S Schill, 'Investor–State Arbitration as Governance: Fair and Equitable Treatment, Proportionality and the Emerging Global Administrative Law' (2006) IILJ Working Paper 2009/6 24–30; R Dolzer, 'The Impact of International Investment Treaties on Domestic Administrative Law' (2005) 37 *NYU J Int'l L & Pol* 953.

[45] T Schultz and C Dupont, 'Investment Arbitration: Promoting the Rule of Law or Over-Empowering Investors? A Quantitative Empirical Study' (2014) 25(4) *EJIL* 1147.

[46] M Sornarajah, *Resistance and Change in the International Law on Foreign Investment* (Cambridge: Cambridge University Press, 2015), 294.

[47] Ibid 297.

[48] J Salacuse, 'The Emerging Global Regime for Investment' 2010 51(2) *Harv Int'l LJ* 427, 428.

important part in that process. Some provisions in investment treaties, such as the fair and equitable treatment standard, embody the rule of law values – predictability, due process of law, non-arbitrariness and non-discrimination.[49] It provides the boundary for the exercise of sovereign power, as the tribunal in *ADC v. Hungary* stated: 'while a sovereign State possesses the inherent right to regulate its domestic affairs, the right is not unlimited and must have its boundaries'; the rule of law, which includes treaty obligations, provides such boundaries'.[50]

However, the rule of law arguably serves different objectives in investment treaty arbitration and in domestic judicial reviews. The rule of law has an 'instrumental' value in facilitating the fulfilment of promotion and protection of investment in investment treaty regime, whilst it forms an inherent and core value in domestic judicial review. Therefore, a conception of the regime plays an important role in determining what types of rules should be accepted. For instance, the domestic public law, which seeks to promote the rule of law, requires the principle of legitimate expectations, which can be applied to intensively review public powers and to protect citizens against the abuse of power in a wide range of circumstances. The same type of rule or the threshold for liability cannot be uncritically transposed into the investment treaty regime, which requires greater sensitivity to sovereign powers of states.

2.2.2.2.2 Function, Authority and Powers of Investment Treaty Arbitrators and Public Law Judges The different function, authority and interpretive and remedial powers of investment treaty arbitrators and public law judges provide a significant factor for cautioning the judicial borrowing.

Functions of Judges and Arbitral Tribunals Municipal public law judges have broader functions in resolving individual disputes as well as in providing guidance to parties in future disputes, upholding the public interest and contributing to the progressive development of the law.[51] By contrast, investment treaty arbitrators lack a mandate to guide future parties, to defend the public interest or to participate in the

[49] S Schill, 'Fair and Equitable Treatment under Investment Treaties as an Embodiment of the Rule of Law', IILJ Working Paper 2006/6, Global Administrative Law Series.

[50] *ADC Affiliate Limited and ADC & ADMC Management Limited v. The Republic of Hungary*, ICSID Case No ARB/03/16, Award (2 October 2006).

[51] A Chayes, 'The Role of the Judge in Public Law Litigation', (1976) 89 *Harv L Rev* 1281; Harry Woolf, 'The Role of the English Judiciary in Developing Public Law' (1986) 27 *Wm & Mary L Rev* 669.

systematic development of jurisprudence or to promote the harmonious development of international investment law.[52] They only perform the secondary functions of adjudication. Their role is to simply resolve the dispute that is before them. The role of the tribunal ultimately depends on the type of conception of the investment treaty regime. For the proponents of the public law approach, investment treaty arbitrators perform similar functions as domestic judges.[53]

The question of authority is very important to the determination of the appropriate role of adjudicative bodies. Is the relationship between arbitrators and disputing states analogous to the relationship between judges and government? To what extent can the rationale for deference in domestic law be applied to arbitrators in investment treaty arbitration? Whilst the principle of separation of powers provides the basis for governing the relationship between the two organs in public laws, such principle is not applicable in the context of investment treaty arbitration. The consent provides the basis for authority and legitimacy for the tribunals' adjudicative role.

Consequently, investment treaty tribunals should exercise judicial restraint in performing adjudicative tasks within the terms of the applicable treaty because the authority of arbitral tribunals is based on the consent of disputing parties. There can be a strong argument for arbitral deference when measures in question are taken for the public interests. This should be appreciated in the context of the distinct roles of tribunals and municipal courts. For instance, the tribunal in *Generation Ukraine v. Ukraine* seemed to distance its role from that of the domestic court, which ensures that municipal agencies perform their tasks diligently, conscientiously or efficiently, but only confined its mandate to the scrutiny of international law.[54]

Interpretive and Remedial Powers of Judges and Arbitral Tribunals

Interpretive powers of arbitral tribunals should be constrained because their authority is derived from the consent of the disputing parties.[55] In domestic laws, especially the common law system, there is greater room for judicial creativity. One can cite the famous example of the

[52] For a theoretical overview of the arbitrator's role, G Van Harten, *Sovereign Choices and Sovereign Constraints: Judicial Restraint in Investment Treaty Arbitration* (Oxford: Oxford University Press, 2013).

[53] S Schill, 'Crafting the International Economic Order: The Public Function of Investment Treaty Arbitration and Its Significance for the Role of the Arbitrator' (2010) *LJIL* 401.

[54] *Generation Ukraine v. Ukraine*, ICSID Case No ARB/00/9, Award (16 September 2003).

[55] Sornarajah, *Resistance and Change* (n 46) 291.

provenance of the concept of legitimate expectations in English law, whereby it is recalled that the origin of the concept lies within Lord Denning's justly famed creative mind.[56] In the decision of *Tecmed v. Mexico*, the arbitrators exercised their imaginative mind, which elaborated the Utopian concept of good governance and legitimate expectations. Yet the level of tolerance for such creativity does not measure up with that for Lord Denning's creativity. Why is that the case?

Judicial activism or creativity is more tolerated in domestic law because such judicial decisions might lead towards further reform; moreover the appeal system or legislative correction makes it more acceptable.[57] Such safeguards are absent in investment treaty arbitration, though one could argue that arbitral activism has provided the catalyst for investment treaty reforms.

Judges in municipal public laws have a wider range of remedial powers than do investment treaty arbitrators. Domestic courts have flexible options of granting mandatory orders, prohibitory orders, quashing orders, substitutionary orders, declarations and recommendations.[58] However, at least in English public law, pecuniary compensation or damages are only available on limited grounds[59] because it is considered that an award of damages may have adverse impact on the function of public authorities and the public interest. This situation seems rather different under the continental systems and the EU system, whereby the award of damages is more common.[60] Nevertheless, courts do limit damages to appropriate case. Whilst investment tribunals may exercise those powers to grant primary remedies, they rarely use them for reasons of impracticality of enforcement.[61] The different extent in which judges and arbitrators can exercise their interpretive and remedial powers is

[56] Professor Forsyth recalled the incident in which he wrote to ask Lord Denning about his reasoning in *Schmidt v. Secretary of State for Home Affairs* [1969] 2 *Ch* 149, where, for the first time, legitimate expectations were introduced into English law – and without any citation of authority. Denning responded immediately to say that he felt 'sure the idea came out of my own head and not from any continental or other source': see CF Forsyth, 'Legitimate Expectations Revisited' (2011) 16(4) *JR* 429, 430.

[57] Sornarajah, *Resistance and Change* (n 46) 292.

[58] M Sunkin, 'Remedies Available in Judicial Review Proceedings', in D Feldman (ed), *English Public Law* (Oxford: Oxford University Press, 2004).

[59] T Cornford, 'Administrative Redress: The Law Commission's Consultation Paper' (2009) *PL* 70.

[60] M Fordham, 'Monetary Awards in Judicial Review' (2009) *PL* 1.

[61] C Schreuer, 'Non-pecuniary Remedies in ICSID' (2004) 20(4) *Arb Intl* 325.

a significant factor for cautioning the outright transplantation of the same type of rule in domestic public law to the investment treaty regime.

Different Natures of Legal Relationships between States and Citizens and Investor and Host States

Are the two types of relationships analogous? What role does the principle of legitimate expectations play in regulating the relationship between states and individuals in municipal public law and between states and investors in investment treaty arbitration? The relationship in the investor–state arbitration comes into existence and is regulated by the treaty terms (consent of the contracting states), whereby the investor is the direct beneficiary of the treaties entered into by two sovereign states. Therefore, treatment of foreign investors will be subject to the norms set by the relevant treaties, customary international law and relevant principles of international laws.

However, the citizen–state relationship is governed by administrative laws as well as social conventions and the underlying social contract. In other words, there is a deeper bond of trust and confidence in public law context because such trust is essential to the legitimacy and authority of the government. The basis of legal relationship in the investor–state relationship is different. Therefore, the rule which aims to regulate the relationship in the culture of public law cannot be uncritically transposed to the investor–state context, whereby the relationship between the parties is underpinned by different ideology and political theory.

Despite some similarities between the two regimes, the argument by analogy fails to recognise significant differences between the two regimes, notably different remedial powers, which should encourage the customised tailoring of legal rules. When the investment treaty tribunals have limited remedial powers, the primary rule should reflect what the tribunals can do to fulfil the goal of the rule. One scholar observes that 'the unaware use of the comparative method may determine the abuse of the same, and ultimately lead to undesirable outcomes. Arbitrators risk acting as "bricoleurs" rather than as "engineers" of legal norms'.[62]

We could ask what if, instead of borrowing the 'rules' of legitimate expectations, we borrow the *underlying rationales* of the public law concept of legitimate expectations? So far, investment arbitration scholarship or arbitral tribunals have not paid much attention to this question. One can draw very useful insights from the discussions in English

[62] Vadi, 'Critical Comparisons' (n 37).

public law regarding the underlying rationale of legitimate expectations. It is reassuring to observe that even in English law, whereby the concept of legitimate expectations was introduced more than thirty years ago, and both legal scholars and courts have attentively reflected on its underlying rationale, there is still no clear answer to it. The next section analyses the extent of which the public law rationales, such as legal certainty, abuse of law, fairness or good administration, can provide conceptual guidance in the context of investment treaty arbitration.

2.2.2.3 Transplantation of 'Rationales' for Protection of Legitimate Expectations in Public Law to the Investment Treaty Regime: A Critique

The fundamental values, such as abuse of power, good administration and fairness, have been advanced as the justificatory basis for protecting legitimate expectations. The reflections on the 'fundamentals' of legitimate expectations are scant in investment treaty arbitration literature, for which public law literature can enrich our reflection.[63] Whilst these values in public laws may provide a source of inspiration or moral impetus, they cannot provide a useful framework for solving concrete problems related to protection of legitimate expectations in investment treaty arbitration. The analysis in this section focuses on the merits and pitfalls of the four main rationales: legal certainty, fairness, abuse of power and good administration.

2.2.2.3.1 Legal Certainty and Protection of Legitimate Expectations

The essence of the legal certainty rationale is that protection of legitimate expectations is an important aspect of the rule of law,[64] which embodies the notion of predictability and certainty.[65] The principle of legitimate expectations serves to reduce unpredictable conduct by a state so that people can plan and make decisions about their future.[66] This aspect

[63] This section draws heavily from enriching discussions in legal scholarship in English administrative law on this matter mainly because there is the plenitude of materials and there is a diversity of views and opinions which will provide useful insights for considerations of the doctrine in investment treaty arbitration.

[64] H Woolf, J Jowell and A Le Sueur, *De Smith's Judicial Review* (London: Sweet & Maxwell, 6th edn, 2007) para 12-001. See also P Craig and S Schønberg, 'Substantive Legitimate Expectations after Coughlan' (2000) *PL* 684, 696–97.

[65] J Raz, 'Legal Principles and the Limits of Law' (1972) 81 *Yale LJ* 823.

[66] A Scalia, 'The Rule of Law as a Law of Rules' (1989) 56 *U Chi L Rev* 1175, 1179; J Raz, *Authority of Law* (Oxford: Clarendon Press, 1979) 215–19 (finding legal certainty, equality and stability within the rule of law).

finds support in Max Weber's theory of social and economic organisation, which suggests that 'capitalistic enterprise ... cannot do without legal security',[67] and Friedrich Hayek's theory of liberalism, which suggests that legal certainty enables people to predict the consequences of their actions.[68] In the context of EU law, the principle of legal certainty underpins the European conception of legitimate expectations.[69]

However, the conceptual distinction between the principles of legal certainty and legitimate expectations must be recognised because the rationales underlying these two principles are different.[70] In the German law context, legal certainty is based on the concept of *Rechtsscherheit*, which requires certainty of the content of law and non-retroactive application of rules.[71] The doctrine of legitimate expectations, on the other hand, is derived from the principle of *Vertrauensschutz*, which is concerned with the promotion of confidence and trust in the public administration. Furthermore, it is important to take note of the different natures of the two principles: 'legal certainty is an objective value ... whereas legitimate expectations operate in the context of a specific relationship between an individual, or a specific class, and the administration'.[72] The French courts rejected the principle of legitimate expectation as being inconsistent with the *principe de securite juridique*.[73]

In the context of investment treaty arbitration, the legal certainty rationale features in some arbitral decisions on legitimate expectations.[74] For instance, in *Suez v. Argentine Republic*, the tribunal stated that 'reasonable and legitimate expectations are important factors that influence initial investment decisions and afterwards the manner in which the investment is to be managed .... An investor's expectations, created by law of a host country, are in effect *calculations about the future*'.[75] Furthermore, the tribunal in *AWG v. Argentina* drew from

[67] M Weber, *Economy and Society*, G Roth and C Wittich (eds) (Oakland, CA: University of California Press, 1978), 883.

[68] FA Hayek, *The Constitution of Liberty* (London: Routledge, 190), 156–57.

[69] J Schwarze, *European Administrative Law* (London: Sweet & Maxwell, 1992), 872.

[70] P Craig, *EU Administrative Law* (Oxford: Oxford University Press, 2nd edn, 2012).

[71] J Lang, '*Legal Certainty and Legitimate Expectations as General Principles of Law*' in U Bernitz and J Nergelius (eds), *General Principles in European Community Law* (The Hague: Kluwer International, 2000), 163–84.

[72] R Thomas, *Legitimate Expectations and Proportionality in Administrative Law* (Oxford: Hart Publishing, 2000), 45–46.

[73] S Calmes, *Du principe de protection de la confiance légitime en droits allemand, communautaire et français*, Nouvelle bibliothèque de thèses (Paris: Dalloz, 2001).

[74] *Thunderbird v. Mexico* (n 12).

[75] *Suez v. Argentina* (n 18) para 203 (emphasis added).

the work of Max Weber on the importance of legal certainty on economic activities as the justification for protection of legitimate expectations.[76] One scholar sought to appeal to the instrumental values of legal stability and predictability as the basis for protection of legitimate expectations.[77]

Let us reflect on the promise and pitfall of this rationale. Legal certainty is a valuable and desirable objective in investment treaty arbitration even without conceptualising the investment treaty regime as a public law regime. The rules on legitimate expectations guided by this rationale capture situations in which a government's actions are inconsistent or unpredictable. This rationale can essentially justify an obligation to maintain a stable legal framework, such as in the decisions of *Occidental Exploration v. Ecuador*[78] or *Sempra v. Argentina.*[79] Furthermore, the claimant does not need to show detrimental reliance because that is not the fundamental purpose of the rule.

However, this conception of legitimate expectations is not satisfactory because legitimate expectations cannot be applied distinctively from other fundamental values such as predictability and certainty and can result in excessively vague and broad rules. Any situation which involves inconsistent or irregular application of rules will potentially fall within the ambit of the rules.

2.2.2.3.2 Fairness, Abuse of Power and Good Administration and Legitimate Expectation Fairness, abuse of power and good administration have been proposed as the justification for protection of legitimate expectations in English public law.[80]

The doctrine of legitimate expectations essentially reformulates the general principle of fairness in a more technical form.[81] This approach has a simplistic appeal to our understanding that frustration of legitimate

76 *AWG Group v. Argentina*, UNCITRAL Case, Decision on Liability (30 July 2010) para 222.

77 R Dolzer, 'Fair and Equitable Treatment: Today's Contours' (2014) 12 *Santa Clara J Int'l L* 7, 17.

78 *Occidental Exploration and Production Company v. The Republic of Ecuador*, LCIA Case No UN 3467, Final Award (1 July 2004).

79 *Sempra Energy International v. Argentine Republic*, ICSID Case No ARB/02/16, Award (28 September 2007) para 303.

80 *R (on the application of Anufrijeva) v. Secretary of State for the Home Department* [2003] UKHL 36 [30] per Lord Steyn; he suggests that fairness is 'the guiding principle of our public law'.

81 TRS Allan, *Law Liberty and Justice: The Legal Foundations of British Constitutionalism* (Oxford: Clarendon Press, 1994), 197.

expectations is simply unfair. Protection of legitimate expectation is 'rooted in fairness'.[82] The concept of abuse of power has also been developed as the underlying rationale for protection of legitimate expectation in English public law. The English courts confirm that legitimate expectations are an application of the concept of abuse of power.[83] Good administration provides the alternative justification for protection of legitimate expectations by articulating the principle that 'public bodies ought to deal straightforwardly and consistently with the public'.[84]

There have been criticisms of using these abstract and vague principles in justifying protection of legitimate expectations.[85] The doctrine of legitimate expectations simply collapses into a principle of fairness[86] because there is no real content or indication on what is lawful or unlawful.[87] The unfairness concept would not guide us regarding 'what counts as fair or unfair[88] or provide the answer to the case at hand'.[89]

There are three reasons for suggesting that the public law rationales could not provide the appropriate basis for protection of legitimate expectations in investment treaty arbitration. First, these abstract principles lack practical utility. The criticism of Professor Forsyth on those abstract principles in the context of English public law is applicable in the context of investment treaty arbitration: 'the trouble with all these overarching and traditional justifications is not that they are wrong but that they are *unhelpful*'.[90] The tribunal in *Suez v. Argentina* echoed such a view and confirmed that the principle of fairness does not 'answer a fundamental and practical question that every arbitral tribunal must answer': By what criteria, standard or test is an arbitral tribunal to determine whether the

82 *R v. Inland Revenue Commissioners, Ex p. MFK Underwriting Agents Ltd* [1990] 1 *W.L.R.* 1545, 1570 per Bingham LJ.

83 *R. v. North and East Devon HA Ex p. Coughlan* [2001] Q.B. 213, [71] per Lord Woolf M.R.; *R. (on the application of Bancoult) v. Secretary of State for Foreign and Commonwealth Affairs* [2008] UKHL 61; [2009] I A.C. 453 [135] ('the basis of the jurisdiction [of legitimate expectations] is abuse of power and unfairness to the citizen on the part of a public authority').

84 *Abdi v. Secretary of State for the Home Department* [2005] EWCA Civ 1363.

85 *P Reynolds, 'Legitimate Expectations and the Protection of Trust in Public Officials' (2011) PL* 330.

86 I Steele, 'Substantive Legitimate Expectation: Striking the Right Balance?' (2005) 121 LQR 300, 309.

87 *R. (on the application of Nadarajah) v. Secretary of State for the Home Department (2005)]* EWCA Civ J 363 [67].

88 N Bamforth, 'Fairness and Legitimate Expectation in Judicial Review' (1997) 56 *CLJ* 1.

89 CJS Knight, 'Expectations in Transition: Recent Developments in Legitimate Expectations' (2009) *PL* 15, 18.

90 Forsyth, 'Legitimate Expectations Revisited' (n 56) (emphasis added).

specific treatment accorded to the investments of a particular foreign investor in a given context is or is not 'fair and equitable'?[91] Viewed in this light, Professor Salacuse's assertion that 'when a state has created certain expectations through its laws and acts that have led the investor to invest, it is generally considered *unfair* of the state to take subsequent actions that fundamentally deny or frustrate those expectations'[92] should be dismissed as unhelpful. The recourse to fairness as the normative value goes no distance to tell us what is lawful and what is not.[93]

Second, these principles, such as good administration, can be invoked to justify both sides of the argument. The claimant may claim that reneging on a specific representation, on which it relies to its detriment, is an abuse of power or contrary to the principle of good administration. On the other side of the argument, the very same act which benefits the local community could be considered an act of good administration by a government fulfilling its duty towards its own people.[94]

Third, whilst these overarching principles form the core values of the public law,[95] the main objectives of investment treaties refer to promotion and protection of investments. It is one thing to suggest that investment treaty arbitration has an impact on good governance or promotes the rule of law;[96] it is quite another to suppose that the core value of the regime is to promote those causes.

The preceding analysis illustrates that the underlying rationales of the public law concept of legitimate expectations do not provide us with a satisfactory tool for understanding legitimate expectations in investment treaty arbitration.

2.3 Public International Law Conception of Protection of Legitimate Expectations

Under the public international law conception, the doctrine of legitimate expectations is ascertained within the sources of international law

[91] *Suez v. Argentina* (n 18) para 202.

[92] Salacuse, 'The Emerging Global Regime for Investment' (n 48) 231.

[93] Similar criticism with the concept of corrective justice includes R Posner, 'The Concept of Corrective Justice in Recent Theories of Tort Law' (1981) 10 *J Legal Stud* 187, 193.

[94] J Raz, 'Liberty and Trust' in R George (ed), *Natural Law, Liberalism and Morality: Contemporary Essays* (Oxford: Oxford University Press, 2001).

[95] *R. v North and East Devon HA Exp. Coughlan* [2001] QB 213 [71] ('abuse of power has become, or is fast becoming, the root concept which governs and conditions our general principles of public law'.).

[96] Dolzer, 'The Impact of International Investment Treaties' (n 44) 953.

framework in Article 38 of the Statute of the International Court of Justice, such as treaty, customs and general principles of international laws.

The main argument advanced here is that the public international law conception of legitimate expectations does not adequately explain an obligation to protect legitimate expectations. Mere reliance on the absence of treaty practice or custom to reject this widely recognised legal principle is too restrictive a view (Section 2.3.1). The general principles of international law, such as the good faith principle (Section 2.3.2) or estoppel (Section 2.3.3) or unilateral declarations (Section 2.3.4), cannot provide direct basis for justification or the appropriate basis for the analogous application of those principles.

It is important to clarify that the application of human rights law by analogy[97] is not considered in this part in legal scholarship. This analogy seems *prima facie* compelling given that human rights treaties are structurally similar to investment treaties in that they are instruments agreed between states which confer a right to certain protections upon individuals. However, the different nature of interests protected by the two regimes may render the analogy obsolete. Human rights are regarded as a good in their own right, whereas investor rights might be seen as instrumental for promoting foreign investment.

2.3.1 Treaty and Customary Law Basis for Protection of Legitimate Expectations

The public international law conception of legitimate expectations cannot find much support in treaty[98] and customary laws.[99] This section does not intend to analyse the North American Free Trade Agreement

[97] R Daujotas and R Audzevičius, 'The Concept of Legitimate Expectation in Investor-State Arbitration and the European Court of Human Rights' (2012) 6(2) *Bulletin of the International Commercial Arbitration* 11.

[98] See the recent EU–Canada Comprehensive Economic and Trade Agreement (EU-Canada CETA) (consolidated text), Article 8.10 Treatment of investors and of covered investments: 'when applying the above fair and equitable treatment obligation, a Tribunal may take into account whether a Party made a specific representation to an investor to induce a covered investment, that created a legitimate expectation, and upon which the investor relied in deciding to make or maintain the covered investment, but that the Party subsequently frustrated'. http://trade.ec.europa.eu/doclib/docs/2014/september/tradoc_152806.pdf (accessed on 10 June 2016)

[99] P Dumberry, 'The Protection of Investors' Legitimate Expectations and the Fair and Equitable Treatment Standard under NAFTA Article' (2014) 31 (1) *J Int'l Arb* 47.

(NAFTA) jurisprudence or carry out the investigation of state practice and *opinio juris* for the identification of customary international law; rather it draws pertinent insights and adds some critical observations.

An obligation to protect legitimate expectations has been rejected for absence of treaty provisions. For example, the Separate Opinion of Arbitrator Pedro Nikken in *Suez v. Argentina* is the best illustration of this position.[100] Similarly, Professor Sornarajah's trenchant objection to the concept of legitimate expectations is in part based on the lack of treaty basis.[101]

The prevailing scholarly views also suggest that the concept of legitimate expectations cannot find a legal basis under customary international law.[102] Nevertheless, we can draw some conclusions from the interpretation of Article 1105 of NAFTA, which reflects the international minimum standard. Most NAFTA awards affirm that the host state's failure to respect an investor's legitimate expectations does not constitute a breach of the fair and equitable treatment standard under Article 1105,[103] though legitimate expectation is only a 'factor' to be taken into account.

NAFTA jurisprudence retains a restrictive vision of the legitimate expectations principle[104] compared with a more liberal approach by non-NAFTA jurisprudence. The best explanation for the difference lies in two different conceptions of legitimate expectations which the tribunals adopted. NAFTA tribunals endorsed the reliance-based theory of legitimate expectations as expounded in *Thunderbird v. Mexico*, which requires an element of detrimental reliance as well as the 'reasonableness' assessment of expectations.[105] This is arguably a narrower conception than the public law-based conception of legitimate expectations, on which several non-NAFTA decisions are based.[106]

[100] *Suez v. Argentina* (n 18), Separate Opinion of Arbitrator Pedro Nikken, paras 3, 20, 21.
[101] Sornarajah, *Resistance and Change* (n 46) 262.
[102] M Paparinskis, *The International Minimum Standard* (Oxford: Oxford University Press, 2013) 254 ('even if general customary law does not contain a rule on legitimate expectations, a special customary rule may be created to the effect'); Campbell, 'House of Cards' (n 9) 379.
[103] Dumberry, 'The Protection of Investors' Legitimate Expectations' (n 99) 47.
[104] Ibid.
[105] *Thunderbird v. Mexico* (n 12).
[106] *AWG v. Argentina* (n 76).

2.3.2 *Failure of the Good Faith Argument to Provide the Legal Basis for Protection of Legitimate Expectations*

The principle of good faith has featured as the main justification for protection of legitimate expectations in the seminal decision of *Tecmed v. Mexico*[107] and subsequent decisions.[108] However, the learned arbitrators in those decisions did not explain how and why the good faith principle embraced protection of legitimate expectations. Whether the good faith principle should continue to serve as a justification for legitimate expectations is a reasonable question.

No one would question the importance of the good faith principle.[109] It exists widely in municipal laws and has been transplanted to international law by analogy.[110] Good faith has been given concrete meanings in different contexts to include *pacta sunt servanda*, abuse of rights, estoppel and acquiescence, and negotiations in good faith.[111] It also plays an important role in the law of treaties at different stages – from treaty formation, performance of treaty obligations and interpretations of treaty obligations.[112] In the context of investment treaty arbitration, good faith plays a significant role in legal reasoning about fair and equitable treatment.[113]

There are two fundamental concerns with relying on good faith to justify protection of legitimate expectations. First, the argument must be substantiated as to how the principle of good faith can create a legal obligation to protect legitimate expectations, especially in light of the *Border and Transborder Armed Actions* (*Nicaragua v. Honduras*) judgment, which confirmed that good faith cannot generate a legal obligation

107 *Tecmed v. Mexico* (n 11) para 121.

108 *Total v. Argentine Republic* (n 14) para 128; *Thunderbird v. Mexico* (n 12) para 25.

109 AFM Maniruzzaman, 'The Concept of Good Faith in International Investment Disputes – The Arbitrator's Dilemma', (2012) 89 *Journal of the Society for Advanced Legal Studies* 16.

110 R Kolb, 'Principles as Sources of International Law (With Special Reference to Good Faith)' (2006) 53(1) *NILR* 1.

111 S Reinhold, 'Good Faith in International Law' (2013) 2 *UCL JL and J* 40.

112 Article 31, para 1, of the Vienna Convention on the Law of Treaties establishes that '[a] treaty shall be interpreted *in good faith* in accordance with the ordinary meaning to be given to the terms of the treaty in their context and in light of its object and purpose'.

113 M Paparinskis, 'Good Faith and International Economic Law' in AD Mitchell, M Sornarajah and Tania Voon (eds), *Good Faith and International Economic Law* (Oxford: Oxford University Press, 2015), 171.

where none would otherwise exist.[114] This is different from the situation where contracting parties are required to perform their *existing* contractual duties in good faith. States do not have an existing legal obligation to protect a legitimate expectation on which good faith can direct. According to the prevailing views, good faith cannot bring such obligation into existence.[115]

Second, there is little practical value of ascertaining the rules of legitimate expectations based on the good faith principle because the highly abstract character of good faith[116] is hardly useful in clarifying the grey areas concerning legitimate expectations in investment treaty arbitration. For instance, can expectations which do not arise from a specific representation or those which do not lead to detrimental reliance be legitimate under the rationale of the good faith principle?

For the two reasons just stated, investment treaty tribunals should discontinue to justify protection of legitimate expectations based on the good faith principle because to argue that good faith alone creates the obligation is, as Alfred Rubin put it, 'to argue in support of an obvious absurdity'.[117]

2.3.3 *Estoppel as the Legal Basis for Protection of Legitimate Expectations*

Estoppel, one of the 'most powerful and flexible instruments to be found in any system of court jurisprudence',[118] is recognised as a general principle of international law.[119] The principle underlying estoppel is often expressed in the Latin maxim *allegans contraria non audiendus est*, translated as 'one should not benefit from his or her own inconsistency'.[120] Estoppel in international law is applicable when

[114] *Border and Transborder Armed Actions (Nicaragua v. Honduras) (Judgment)* [1988] ICJ Rep 69 para 94 ('the principle of good faith . . . is not in itself a source of obligation where none would otherwise exist').

[115] Paparinskis, *The International Minimum Standard* (n 102); Sornarajah, *Resistance and Change* (n 46) 260; AP Rubin, 'The International Legal Effects of Unilateral Declarations' (1977) 1 *AJIL* 1, 9. For the contrary view, see R. Kolb, 'Principles as Sources of International Law (With Special Reference to Good Faith)' (2006) 53(1) *NILR* 1, 17.

[116] Maniruzzaman, 'The Concept of Good Faith' (n 109).

[117] Rubin, 'The International Legal Effects of Unilateral Declarations' (n 115) 9.

[118] Sir Frederick Pollock, *The Expansion of the Common Law* (London: Stevens and Sons, 1904) 108.

[119] I Brownlie, *Principles of Public International Law* (Oxford: Oxford University Press, 6th edn, 2003) 616.

[120] IC MacGibbon, 'Estoppel in International Law' (1958) 7 *ICLQ* 468, 513.

a state makes a clear representation to another state, which then relies on such representation to its detriment; the state making the presentation is held responsible for such action.[121] The international law rule of estoppel, though derived from the common law and entered into international law by the mechanism of Article 38(1)(c) of the Statute of the International Court of Justice, is different from the municipal rule.[122] The international law rule of estoppel is a simple and wholly untechnical conception',[123] free from the 'manifold refinements grafted onto it by domestic legal systems'.[124] Its scope has been expanded to be a rule of substance as well as one of evidence or procedure. Due to differences between these two concepts, 'the analogy with the estoppel of municipal systems may be positively misleading'.[125]

This section examines the claim by some arbitral decisions[126] and scholars who suggest the principle of estoppel as a possible justification for protection of legitimate expectations.[127] We look at the direct application (Section 2.3.3.1) and the application by analogy (Section 2.3.3.2).

2.3.3.1 Direct Applicability of the Estoppel Principle to Situations of Legitimate Expectations

No investment treaty tribunals have explicitly applied the estoppel principle to the cases of legitimate expectations. However, such an approach would suffer from two conceivable shortcomings.

First, the interstate rule, which is based on equality of actors, cannot be directly applied, nor can it form the legal basis for protection of investors' expectations for the investor–state relationship.[128] However, one can argue that some interstate rules have been applied to the context of state–individual relationship, most notably, the international law rules on remedies, as reflected in the *Chorzow factory* case. Moreover, the

[121] *Case Concerning the Temple of Preah Vihear (Cambodia v. Thailand)*, Merits, [1962] I.C.J. Rep. 6, Dissenting Opinion of Sir Percy Spender, 143–44.

[122] Ibid 39 (Separate Opinion of Judge Alfaro) ('[t]here is a very substantial difference between the simple and clear-cut rule adopted and applied in the international field and the complicated classifications, modalities, species, sub-species and procedural features of the municipal system'.).

[123] C Brown, 'A Comparative and Critical Assessment of Estoppel in International Law' (1995) 50 *U Miami L Rev* 369, 411.

[124] A D'Amato, 'Consent, Estoppel, and Reasonableness: Three Challenges to Universal International Law' (1969) 10 *Virg JIL* 1, 8.

[125] MacGibbon, 'Estoppel in International Law' (n 120) 477.

[126] *Thunderbird v. Mexico* (n 12) 147.

[127] Paparinskis, *The International Minimum Standard* (n 102).

[128] Ibid 253.

estoppel principle has been extensively invoked as a jurisdictional matter[129] or as a defence by the state[130] against the investor's misconduct[131] in the context of investment treaty arbitration.

Second, it could be argued that the protection of legitimate expectations obligation established under this approach is separate from a breach of fair and equitable treatment, which may raise the jurisdictional issue of tribunals. Furthermore, if the estoppel provides the direct basis for liability, the recourse to legitimate expectations is merely rhetorical because it is the breach of estoppel principle which provides the normative basis for liability. A breach of legitimate expectations is merely used as a conclusion.

2.3.3.2 Application of Estoppel Rules by Analogy

Some arbitral decisions illustrate the use of estoppel language in the application of legitimate expectations. The tribunal in *EDF (Services) Ltd v. Romania* suggested that 'protection of legitimate expectations comes into consideration whenever the treatment attributable to the State is in breach of representations made by it which were said to be reasonably relied upon by the Claimant'.[132] The tribunal in *Waste v. Management* stated that in considering the fair and equitable treatment standard, 'it is relevant that the treatment is in breach of representations made by the host State which were reasonably relied on by the claimant'.[133]

On the one hand, the estoppel-based rule of legitimate expectations provides a flexible legal tool for investment treaty tribunals to resolve a dispute. The elastic nature of the estoppel principle allows arbitral tribunals to do justice to disputing parties by taking into account different factors, such as the circumstances of the host state, the specificity of representation and the conduct of the representee. The rule of estoppel is recognised to have the potential to encourage 'finality, stability and

[129] *Philippe Gruslin v. Malaysia*, ICSID Case No. ARB/99/3, Award (27 November 2000).

[130] *Canfor Corporation v. United States of America, Tembec Inc. et al. v. United States of America and Terminal Forest Products Ltd. v. United States of America*, UNCITRAL, Order of the Consolidation Tribunal (7 September 2005) para 168.

[131] In *Ioannis Kardassopoulos v. the Republic of Georgia*, ICSID Case No. ARB/05/18 (6 July 2007).

[132] *EDF (Services) Ltd v. Romania*, ICSID Case No ARB/05/13, Award (2 October 2009) para 216.

[133] *Waste Management v. Mexico*, ICSID Case No ARB (AF)/00/3, Award (30 April 2004) para 98.

predictability' in international relations[134] whilst maintaining flexibility.[135]

On the other hand, the estoppel-based rules could produce a restrictive standard of judicial protection. This restrictive approach may find its justification in the current paradigm of the investment treaty regime, which demands greater regulatory space. For instance, there would have to be a 'clear and unequivocal'[136] representation in the form of conduct or declaration.[137] There must be 'a very definite, very consistent course of conduct'.[138] Such representation must be authorised and unconditional, meaning that it is made by an organ competent to bind the state[139] and unconditional if it is not made in the course of negotiation or subject to express conditions. The key factor which limits the scope is detrimental reliance. The party must have detrimentally changed its position or suffered some prejudice.[140] However, there is also authority, which recognises that detrimental reliance is not required.[141] The presence of detrimental reliance indicates that the autonomy and liberty of the representee is more affected than when there is no reliance.

The fundamental objection to the application of estoppel by analogy is the lack of principled justification for why the estoppel principle could provide the basis for analogy. The compatibility of the rationales underlying the two principles has not been identified. This argument is buttressed by the fact that the principle of estoppel, though recognised as a general principle of law,[142] has nebulous content and no coherence,

[134] *Territorial Dispute (Libyan Arab Jamahiriya v. Chad) (Merits)* [1994] ICJ Rep 6, 78 (Separate Opinion of Judge Ajibola).

[135] Brown, 'Estoppel in International Law' (n 123), 385.

[136] *Payment of Various Serbian Loans Issued in France (France v. Serb-Croat-Slovene State)* [1929] PCIJ Series A No 20, 38.

[137] *Military and Paramilitary Activities in and against Nicaragua* case, ('estoppel may be inferred from the conduct, declarations and the like made by a State which . . . clearly and consistently evinced acceptance' of a particular state of affairs').

[138] *North Sea Continental Shelf (Federal Republic of Germany v. Denmark; Federal Republic of Germany v. Netherlands)* [1969] *ICJ Rep* 3, 26.

[139] This is similar to Article 4 of the Guiding Principle on Unilateral Declarations, which suggests that heads of State, heads of Government and ministers for foreign affairs are competent to formulate such representations.

[140] *North Sea Continental Shelf* (n 138) para 30; *Land and Maritime Boundary (Cameroon v. Nigeria: Equatorial Guinea Intervening), Preliminary Objections*, Judgment of 11 June 1998, [1998] ICJ Rep 275 para 57.

[141] *Legal Status of Eastern Greenland (Denmark v. Norway)* (Judgment) [1933] PCIJ Rep Series A/B No 53.

[142] J Crawford, *Brownlie's Principles of Public International Law* (Oxford: Oxford University Press, 8th edn, 2012), 420.

which allows for 'wild fluctuations in legal rulings'.[143] This can potentially undermine the stability it seeks to promote.

2.3.4 *Legitimate Expectations through the Lens of the Doctrine of Unilateral Acts*

Certain unilateral acts of state, which engender expectations in the investor, can create a legal obligation by virtue of the doctrine of unilateral acts. The same doctrine can justify protection of legitimate expectations. The doctrine of unilateral acts can be directly or analogously applied to cases of legitimate expectations.

The application by analogy is the preferred method given that the scope of application of the Guiding Principles Applicable to Unilateral Declarations of States is expressly limited to interstate relationship.[144] Furthermore, a tribunal may lack jurisdiction to rule on a breach of unilateral acts because the fair and equitable treatment standard or other provisions in investment treaties do not cover compliance with the rules on unilateral acts.[145]

This section examines the claim for analogous application of the unilateral acts doctrine to the paradigms of legitimate expectations (Section 2.3.4.1) and critically analyses the arbitral decisions which applied the doctrine of unilateral acts (Section 2.3.4.2).

2.3.4.1 The Doctrine of Unilateral Act and Its Application by Analogy to Protect Legitimate Expectations

A unilateral act of state is defined as an expression of will emanating from one state or states which produces legal effects in conformity with international law. The form of unilateral declarations can be oral or in writing and made publicly or made during a purely bilateral meeting.[146] The statement of principle on the doctrine of unilateral acts is summarised in the judgment in *The Nuclear Tests*:

> It is well recognized that declarations made by way of unilateral acts concerning legal or factual situations, may have the effect of creating

[143] Brown, 'Estoppel in International Law' (n 123).

[144] ILC, 'Guiding Principles Applicable to Unilateral Declarations of States Capable of Creating Legal Obligations' in *Report of the International Law Commission on the Work of Its 61st Session*, UN Doc A/61/10 367.

[145] Paparinskis, *The International Minimum Standard* (n 102) 252.

[146] ILC's 'Guiding Principles' (n 144) art 1: 'declarations publicly made and manifesting the will to be bound may have the effect of creating legal obligations'.

> legal obligations. Declarations of this kind may be, and often are, very specific. When it is the intention of the State making the declaration that it should become bound according to its terms, that intention confers on the declaration the character of a legal undertaking, the State being thenceforth legally required to follow a course of conduct consistent with the declaration. An undertaking of this kind, if given publicly, and with an intent to be bound, even though not made within the context of international negotiations, is binding.[147]

The unilateral acts-based concept of legitimate expectations has a restrictive scope of application. Three aspects are examined: (1) the obligational basis in the intention of states, (2) limited authors of representations and (3) large groups of recipients of representation.

First, the binding character of unilateral declarations is based on a manifestation of intentions to be bound[148] as well as the principle of good faith.[149] The intention must be in 'clear and specific terms'.[150] Therefore, claiming for legitimate expectations requires a proof of the intention of the state, whose identification is a delicate and difficult task; this involves taking into account all the factual circumstances.[151] Moreover, this approach disregards other important factors, such as the investor's conduct or the circumstances of the host state.

Second, the rule is too restrictive in terms of who can make representation. The requirement for the author of unilateral acts is much stricter than that for legitimate expectation. Whilst only limited categories of persons are deemed as competent to bind states under the doctrine of unilateral acts, much wider groups of authorities and officials are capable of creating state responsibility under the rules of legitimate expectations

147 *Nuclear Tests (New Zealand v. France)* [1974] ICJ Rep 457 paras 44–46.

148 *Application of the Convention on the Prevention and Punishment of the Crime of Genocide (Bosnia and Herzegovina v. Serbia)* (Judgment) [2007] ICJ Rep 43; however, in the preamble of the Guiding Principle (n 144), it seems unclear: 'it is often difficult to establish whether the legal effects stemming from the unilateral behaviour of a State are the consequence of the intent that it has expressed or depend on the expectations that its conduct has raised among other subjects of international law'. The first principle of the Guiding Principle states that 'declarations publicly made and manifesting the will to be bound may have the effect of creating legal obligations'.

149 The ILC's 'Guiding Principles' (n 144) art 1 ('the binding character of such declarations is based on good faith'); E Suy, 'Unilateral Acts of States as Source of International Law: Some New Thoughts and Frustrations' in *Droit du Pouvoir, Pouvoir du Droit. Mélanges offerts à Jean Salmon* (Brussels: Bruylant, 2007), 642.

150 The ILC's Guiding Principles (n 144) art 7.

151 Ibid art 3.

so long as the rules of attribution are met.[152] Under the doctrine of unilateral acts, authors include heads of state, heads of government and foreign affairs minister,[153] as well as other persons representing the state in specified areas falling within their competence. There might be a possibility of recognising a wider class of authors to include other persons representing a state in specific fields.[154] However, such rule is still be too narrow for the paradigms of legitimate expectations. Furthermore, one could question the applicability of the doctrine of unilateral declarations to the situations of legitimate expectations based on contract because such case cannot be considered as a unilateral act.

Third, under the doctrine of unilateral acts, specific undertaking can be interpreted as an *erga omnes* undertaking. The addressee of the unilateral acts can be the international community, one or several states or some other entities.[155] This differs from the doctrine of legitimate expectations, which requires a specific addressee. It could be argued that the coverage of representee entitled to bring a claim under the unilateral acts rule is over-inclusive.

2.3.4.2 Application of the Doctrine of Unilateral Acts in the Jurisprudence

The analogous application of the unilateral acts doctrine to the investor–state context is not a novel proposal.[156] Professors Reisman and Arsanjani articulated the rule that unilateral declarations made in the context of investor–state relationship can be a source of legal obligation as follows:

> Where a host state which seeks foreign investment *acts intentionally*, so as to create *expectations* in potential investors with respect to particular treatment or comportment, the host state should, we suggest, *be bound* by the commitments and the investor is entitled to rely upon them in instances of decision.[157]

[152] ILC, 'Articles on Responsibility of States for Internationally Wrongful Acts' in *Yearbook of the International Law Commission, 2001, vol II*, UN Doc A/CN.4/SER.A/2001/Add.1.

[153] The ILC's 'Guiding Principles' (n 144) art 4.

[154] *Case Concerning Armed Activities on the Territory of the Congo*, para 47.

[155] The ILC's 'Guiding Principles' (n 144) art 6.

[156] MM Mbengue, 'National Legislation and Unilateral Acts' in T Gazzini and E de Brabandère (eds), *The Sources of Rights and Obligations in Transnational Investment Law* (Leiden: Martinus Nijhoff Publishers, 2012) 212; D Caron, 'The Interpretation of National Foreign Investment Laws as Unilateral Acts under International Law', in MH Arsanjani et al. (eds), *Looking to the Future: Essays on International Law in Honor of W Michael Reisman* (The Netherlands: Nijhoff, 2010), 649.

[157] WM Reisman and MH Arsanjani, 'The Question of Unilateral Governmental Statements as Applicable Law in Investment Disputes' (2004) 19 *ICSID Rev – FILJ* 328.

Whilst this statement is not directly concerned with protection of legitimate expectations *per se*, it suggests that expectations could potentially have a normative value in providing the basis for liability. The ambivalence of the legal basis of unilateral acts – intention or expectation – in the quoted passage is also reflected in the preamble of the Guiding Principles on the Unilateral Act.[158] Nevertheless, the generally accepted view confirms that an intention of the state provides the basis for a legal obligation under the doctrine of unilateral acts.[159] Consequently, any recourse to 'expectations' in the context of unilateral acts is simply a rhetorical use of legitimate expectations because it is the intention of the promisor which generates an obligation.

The doctrine of unilateral acts has been considered in the context of legitimate expectations in some arbitral decisions. For instance, the tribunal in *El Paso v. Argentina* dismissed the argument by the claimant that investment-promoting road shows had strong legal value by virtue of the unilateral act doctrine, distinguishing these political and commercial incitements from unilateral declarations made before the ICJ. Even if the claim had succeeded, the investor's legitimate expectations would not have had a normative role to play because liability would be based on the intention of the state.

The tribunal in *Total v. Argentina* drew the main source of inspiration from the doctrine of unilateral acts in the determination of protection of legitimate expectations, in particular the characteristic of a unilateral declaration:

> The tribunal admits that 'the recent "Guiding Principles applicable to unilateral declarations of States capable of creating legal obligations" . . . are of interest here' The tribunal, in particular consider Article 7 of the Guidelines which states that a unilateral declaration entails obligations *only if it is stated in clear and specific terms and a restrictive interpretation of obligations must be carried out in case of doubt.*[160]

The tribunal had to consider whether a unilateral modification of legislative framework constituted a breach of the investor's legitimate expectations. The tribunal relied on the absence of promise made by Argentina on the gas tariffs laws to reject a claim for liability. In the tribunal's view, such provisions could not be construed as 'promise' but rather as an integral element of the Gas Regulatory Framework because they were not

158 The ILC's 'Guiding Principles' (n 144), the preamble.
159 Rubin, 'The International Legal Effects of Unilateral Declarations' (n 115).
160 *Total v. Argentina* (n 14) para 132 (emphasis added).

addressed directly or indirectly to Total.[161] Furthermore, the tribunal ruled that the untouchability of foreign currency peg provisions cannot be the object of legitimate expectations in such monetary and economic crisis. The relevant passage of the tribunal's reasoning is cited for further analysis:

> Under international law, unilateral acts, statements and conduct by States may be the source of legal obligations which the intended beneficiaries or addressees, or possibly any member of the international community, can invoke. *The legal basis of that binding character appears to be only in part related to the concept of legitimate expectations – being rather akin to the principle of 'estoppel'.* Both concepts may lead to the same result, namely, that of rendering the content of a unilateral declaration binding on the State that is issuing it. According to the International Court of Justice, only unilateral acts that are unconditional, definitive and 'very specific' have binding force, which derives from *the principle of good faith.* This fundamental principle requires a State to abide by its unilateral acts of such a character and to follow a line of conduct coherent with the legal obligation so created.[162]

This quoted passage calls for three critical observations. First, the tribunal implied that the concept of legitimate expectations which is characterised as 'being rather akin to the principle of "estoppel"' provides a partial legal basis for unilateral acts, statements and conduct. However, it stated that the binding force of unilateral acts derives from the 'good faith'. Therefore, justifying protection of legitimate expectations from the doctrine of unilateral acts seems somewhat circular.

Second, the tribunal suggested that the person with standing included the intended beneficiary, addressee and 'any member of the international community'. This is not compatible with the paradigms of legitimate expectations, whereby only the person to whom a specific representation is made is entitled to make the claim. If the tribunal followed through the logic of unilateral act, the tribunal would have to regard that the respondent had made an *erga omnes* promise to Total. Yet it denied the claim for the reason that it was not a promise made to the claimant.

Third, the tribunal failed to explain convincingly why the Guidelines, which are applicable in the interstate context, should be applied to the

[161] Ibid para 145.
[162] Ibid para 164 (emphasis added).

context of investor–state relationship. The tribunal's explanation that just because 'the issue before the Tribunal has to be resolved by application of international law'[163] is not convincing. In my view, a better justification for the analogous application of the rules of unilateral acts should focus on the fact that the underlying rationale may be compatible with the underlying value of protection of legitimate expectations. The ICJ in *The Nuclear Tests* enunciated the non-legal rationale of the unilateral act doctrine – namely, the maintenance of *trust and confidence* inherent in international cooperation, which supplements the good faith principle:

> Trust and confidence are inherent in international co-operation, in particular in an age when this co-operation in many fields is becoming increasingly essential. Just as the very rule of pacta sunt servanda in the law of treaties is based on good faith, *so also is the binding character of an international obligation assumed by unilateral declaration*. Thus interested States may take cognizance of unilateral declarations and place confidence in them, and are entitled to require that the obligation thus created be respected.[164]

One could argue that protection of trust and confidence for furtherance of international cooperation is relevant to the investor–state relationship. If host states fail to keep their commitments and promises, no investors will rely on their promises, and the essential social mechanism of promise would dissolve.[165] However, the impact of trust and confidence in the relationship between an investor and a host state may be limited to the two parties such that it does not affect international cooperation on a larger scale, in the same way as the interstate relation.[166] Nevertheless, the global scale of investment cooperation between states and investors may arguably impact the international cooperation. In any case, the doctrine of unilateral acts should not be uncritically applied in the different context of investor–state relationship.

[163] *Total v. Argentina* (n 14) paras 131–33.

[164] *Nuclear Tests Case (New Zealand v. France)* (Judgment) [1974] ICJ Rep 268, 473 (emphasis added).

[165] O O'Neill, *Towards Justice and Virtue: A Constructive Account of Practical Reasoning* (Cambridge: Cambridge University Press, 1966), 174–75.

[166] T Franck, 'Word Made Law: *The Decision of the ICJ in the Nuclear Test Cases*' (1975) 69 *AJIL* 616.

2.3.5 Precedent-based Approach to the Justification of Legitimate Expectations

The most frequent justification for protection of legitimate expectations is the use of precedent,[167] whereby investment treaty tribunals simply refer to previous arbitral decisions, which establish or apply the rules of legitimate expectations.[168]

Some scholars suggest that recourse to past decisions can be justified on two principal grounds. First, a consistent line of cases facilitates efficiency in decision-making and promotes certainty in the law.[169] The absence of binding precedent in international investment law would undermine the consistency of jurisprudence and the need for legal predictability.[170] Second, the deontological justification for the precedent approach is that fairness requires like cases to be treated alike.[171] How valid is the frequently cited argument for precedent based on certainty and predictability in our context?

The fundamental problem with the use of precedent is that it perpetuates the original decisions which are not analysed or wrongly decided. It could be argued that promoting certainty or consistency should not be the main objective in adjudication but rather resolving the issue at hand. Professor Schultz emphasised this point:

> Precise, consistent rules, forming a regime that meets the requirement of the rule of law, are not inherently preferable to vague, inconsistent rules forming a rule that does not meet the standards of regulative quality which partake of the rule of law, in its incarnations as formal legality . . . It is not

167 The approach is conceived as a formalist framework to legitimate expectations because arbitral decisions are a 'subsidiary means for the determination of rules of law' under Article 38(1) of the ICJ Statue.

168 Sornarajah, *Resistance and Change* (n 46) 299 ('the episode relating to legitimate expectations also illustrates the unsavoury instances of attempting to foist a law lacking authority as if it is a well-founded assumption. It is made on insufficient authority by a handful of arbitrators willing to follow each other. A course of precedent is established.').

169 G Kaufmann-Kohler, 'Is Consistency a Myth?' in E Gaillard and Yas Banifatemi, *Precedent in International Arbitration: IAI Seminar, Paris – December 14, 2007* (Huntington, NY: Juris Publishing, 2008), 147.

170 I Laird and R Askew, 'Finality versus Consistency: Does Investor-State Arbitration Need an Appellate System' (2005) 7 *Journal of Appellate Practice and Process* 285.

171 Z Douglas, 'Can a Doctrine of Precedent Be Justified in Investment Treaty Arbitration?' (2010) 25 ICSID Rev – FILJ 104.

by necessity morally valuable to increase predictability and consistency in any legal regime.[172]

Protection of legitimate expectations is the obvious paradigm of perpetuating the bad rule in the name of following the precedent. Therefore, consistency in applying rules is not intrinsically good.[173] The seminal decision of *Tecmed v. Mexico,* which first articulated the concept of legitimate expectations reflecting the Utopian vision of good governance,[174] was extensively criticised by both scholars and arbitral tribunals[175] for dubiously deriving the obligation from the good faith principle and for its thin-reasoning feature of the award.[176] Yet, the decision of *Tecmed* has been frequently cited as authority for protection of legitimate expectations, substituting any analysis of the underlying rationale or juridical basis. In fairness, some tribunals attempt to distinguish the present case from the 'precedents'.[177]

Whilst previous decisions provide a source of inspiration or add authority to a certain reasoning developed by the tribunal, the practice of precedent becomes objectionable when such practice results in the absence of engagement in argumentation.[178] Furthermore, an excessive reliance on the precedent prevents an opportunity of engaging in the task of identifying the underlying rationale for protection of legitimate expectations. The words of wisdom by Samuel Johnson sharply reinforces this point: 'the more

172 T Schultz, 'Against Consistency in Investment Arbitration' in Z Douglas, J Pauwelyn and JE Viñuales (eds), *The Foundations of International Investment Law – Bringing Theory into Practice* (Oxford: Oxford University Press, 2014), 316.

173 Ibid.

174 *El Paso Energy International Company v. The Argentine Republic,* ICSID Case No ARB/03/15, Award (31 October 2011) (the tribunal referred to 'a program of good governance'.).

175 *MTD Equity Sdn. Bhv. and MTD Chile S.A. v. Chile,* ICSID Case No ARB/01/07, Decision on Annulment (21 March 2007) 13 ICSID Rep 500 para 66; *White Industries Australia Limited v. India,* UNCITRAL Case, Final Award (30 November 2011) para 10.3.5; and *Saluka Investments BV (The Netherlands) v. Czech Republic,* UNCITRAL Rules, Partial Award (17 March 2006) para 304.

176 McLachlan, Shore and Weiniger, *International Investment Arbitration* (n 5) 325; *Saluka v. Czech Republic* (n 175) 28 ('[a] description of perfect public regulation in a perfect world, to which all states should aspire but very few (if any) will ever attain'.).

177 *Metalpar v. Argentine Republic,* ICSID Case No ARB/03/5, Award (6 June 2008) and *El Paso v. Argentina* (n 174).

178 E De Brabandere, 'Arbitral Decisions as a Source of International Investment Law' in T Gazzini and E De Brabandere (eds), *International Investment Law: The Sources of Rights and Obligations* (Leiden: Martinus Nijhoff Publishers, 2012).

precedents there are, the less occasion is there for law; that is to say, the less occasion is there for investigating principles'.[179] One may add that without the principles that Mr Johnson mentioned, tribunals risk acting as 'bricoleurs' rather than as 'engineers' of legal norms because they would apply the first thing that happens to fit the immediate problem, rather than identify the overarching conceptual framework and arrange various concepts in a coherent manner.[180]

The doctrine of legitimate expectations should not be developed out of the arbitral jurisprudence alone without articulating the underlying principle; otherwise its theoretical foundation will not be solid – to borrow the simile used by one scholar, like 'building a house of cards on a wobbly table it is undermined by the fact that it has no solid basis, no legal foundation; no amount of adding new levels will make the structure stable'.[181]

2.4 Conclusion

This chapter provides a critique of the current approaches of legal scholars and arbitral tribunals on the justifications of protection of legitimate expectations. Whilst recognising that these 'formalist' approaches are not wrong from the methodological perspective, they do not offer very useful insights for adjudicating cases on protection of legitimate expectations. Given that the issues concerning protection of legitimate expectations are imbued with a combination of legal, moral and political dimensions, the comfort of relying on the formalist framework is illusory. It is more desirable to search for the normative theory than simply rely on the sources-based approach to elucidate the doctrine of legitimate expectations.

This chapter also calls into question the long-held assumption of functional and ideological similarities of the investment treaty regime

[179] Samuel Johnson, quoted in Douglas, 'Doctrine of Precedent' (n 171).

[180] The metaphor is borrowed from Levi-Strauss and M Tushnet, 'The Possibilities of Comparative Law' (1999) 108 *Yale LJ* 1225, 1285–86 ('as engineers, they would sort through the concepts and assemble them into a constitutional design that made sense according to some overarching conceptual scheme. As bricoleurs, though, they . . . use the first thing that happens to fit the immediate problem they are facing.').

[181] Campbell, *House of Cards* (n 9) 379 ('the body of arbitral jurisprudence can perhaps offer constructive guidance as to reasoning but it cannot create law').

and public law systems, which is the basis for the use of comparative public laws. The main contention so far is that the existing conceptual framework is inadequate for the challenges faced by investment treaty tribunals in the adjudication of cases on legitimate expectations. The journey to explore the *normative hinterland* of the doctrine of legitimate expectations begins in the next chapter.

PART II

What Is the Theory of Legitimate Expectations?

3

Theoretical Foundations for the Use of Moral Philosophy of Promise and Conceptualisation of Legitimate Expectations

There's no chance of their having a conscious glimpse of the truth as long as they refuse to disturb the things they take for granted and remain incapable of explaining them. For if your starting-point is unknown, and your end-point and intermediate stages are woven together out of unknown material, there may be coherence, but knowledge is completely out of the question.

Plato, *The Republic*[1]

3.1 Introduction

This chapter sets out theoretical foundations for the use of moral philosophy as the main methodology in developing a theory of legitimate expectations. It is the important premise of this book that the moral philosophy of promise can enrich our understanding about the doctrine of legitimate expectations.[2] Despite some doubt about the affinity between law and philosophy,[3] the interbreeding between law and philosophy has seen a significant rise in legal scholarship in a wide range of legal disciplines, torts,[4] contract,[5] criminal law,[6]

[1] Plato, *Republic* (translated with introduction and notes by Robin Waterfield) (Oxford: Oxford University Press, 2008). Reproduced with permission of the Licensor through PLSclear.

[2] D Owen, 'Foreword: Why Philosophy Matters to Tort Law' in D Owen (ed), *The Philosophical Foundations of Tort Law* (Oxford: Clarendon Press, 1997), 24.

[3] PS Atiyah, *Promises, Morals and the Law* (Oxford: Oxford University Press, 1981), 2.

[4] GJ Postema, *Philosophy and the Law of Torts* (Cambridge: Cambridge University Press, 2001); J Oberdiek (ed), *Philosophical Foundations of the Law of Torts* (Oxford: Oxford University Press, 2014).

[5] G Klass, G Letsas and P Saprai (eds), *Philosophical Foundations of Contract Law* (Oxford: Oxford University Press, 2014).

[6] P Green (ed), *Philosophical Foundations of Criminal Law* (Oxford: Oxford University Press, 2011).

property and unjust enrichment[7] and various fields of international laws.[8]

This chapter has three main components. First, there is justification for the assumption that protection of legitimate expectations is based on a promissory obligation. In other words, determination of legitimate expectations is analysed in terms of whether a promise has been made (Section 3.2). Second, certain methodological caveats are addressed: (a) the implication of applying moral philosophy to elucidate a positive law concept and (b) the suitability of applying the moral philosophy which usually pertains to the relationship between individuals to the investor–state context (Section 3.3). Third, the chapter provides an overview of the three conceptions of promissory obligation and explains how those conceptions can elucidate the core of legitimate expectations (Section 3.4).

3.2 First Principles in Moral Philosophy of Promise and Protection of Legitimate Expectations

This book seeks to develop a theory of legitimate expectations – which clarifies why the law protects legitimate expectations – by returning to 'first principles'[9] in moral philosophy of promise. This helps us understand the phenomenon of liability for protection of legitimate expectations and the possible reasons for liability.[10] This section explains how philosophical insights into bindingness of promise can clarify an obligation to protect legitimate expectations.

Some scholars have considered various justifications for a generic notion of protection of legitimate expectations based on deontology,

[7] James Penner and Henry Smith (eds), *Philosophical Foundations of Property Law* (Oxford: Oxford University Press, 2013); Robert Chambers, Charles Mitchell and James Penner (eds), *Philosophical Foundations of the Law of Unjust Enrichment* (Oxford: Oxford University Press, 2009).

[8] S Besson and J Tasioulas (eds), *The Philosophy of International Law* (Oxford: Oxford University Press, 2010); Z Douglas, J Pauwelyn and JE Viñuales (eds), *The Foundations of International Investment Law – Bringing Theory into Practice* (Oxford: Oxford University Press, 2014).

[9] TRS Allan, 'First Principles: The Rule of Law and Separation of Powers' in TRS Allan, *Constitutional Justice: A Liberal Theory of the Rule of Law* (Oxford: Oxford University Press, 2003).

[10] The concept is adapted from the work of EJ Weinrib, 'Private Law and Public Right' (2011) 61(2) *UTLJ* 191.

corrective justice, distributive justice, intuitive justice or teleology.[11] However, the theory of promising, whose different conceptions embody those various moral principles, provides a more concrete and practical analytical framework than these abstract principles because the rules derived from these abstract principles may render the scope of application too expansive (Section 3.2.2). Furthermore, if we consider the current jurisprudence, the tribunals' reasoning on protection of legitimate expectations hinges on the notion of promise and similar notions. It is therefore pertinent to draw from the philosophical insights on the promissory obligation (Section 3.2.1).

3.2.1 'Promise' *as the Source of Expectations: Recognition of Arbitral Jurisprudence*

3.2.1.1 The Tribunal Already Engages in 'Moral Reasoning' for Legitimate Expectations

Considering the investment treaty jurisprudence, the investment treaty tribunals seem to be 'moralising' their reasoning on protection of legitimate expectations – that is, legitimate expectations should be protected because the state has made a promise to the investor or the investor has suffered from the detriment as a result of a breach of promise. Investment treaty tribunals have often employed the notion of 'promise' and the like, such as assurance,[12] commitment,[13] guarantee, representation or even consistent practice[14] as a threshold for distinguishing between legitimate and non-legitimate expectations.[15] For instance, in *Mobil v. Canada*, the tribunal rejected the investor's claim for legitimate expectations for the lack of promise:

[11] BH Kuklin, 'The Plausibility of Legally Protecting Reasonable Expectations' (1997) 32 *Val U L Rev* 19; B Kuklin, 'The Justification for Protecting Reasonable Expectations' (2001) 29 (3)*Hofstra L Rev* 863.

[12] *Ioan Micula, Viorel Micula, S.C. European Food S.A, S.C. Starmill S.R.L. and S.C. Multipack S.R.L. v. Romania*, ICSID Case No ARB/05/20, Final Award (11 December 2013) para 671.

[13] *El Paso Energy International Company v. The Argentine Republic*, ICSID Case No ARB/03/15, Award (31 October 2011).

[14] *Gold Reserve Inc. v. Bolivarian Republic of Venezuela*, ICSID Additional Facility Case No ARB(AF)/09/1, Final Award (22 September 2014).

[15] *Total S.A. v. Argentina*, ICSID Case No ARB/04/1, Decision on Liability (21 December 2010); *PSEG Global Inc. and Konya Ilgin Elektrik Üretim ve Ticaret Limited Sirketi v. Turkey*, ICSID Case No ARB/02/05, Award (19 January 2007).

> At the heart of these claims is an assertion that the Federal and Provincial governments, and the Board, *made a series of express promises – in the form of representations – which they then broke.* For the reasons set out below, having carefully studied the record and all the evidence *the Tribunal is unable to conclude that any such 'promises' were made, either expressly or by any pattern of behavior over a ten year period, such as to give rise to a representation that there would not be changes to the regulatory regime.*[16]

Despite the central role of the notion of promise in the determination of legitimate expectations, there has not been any attempt to define this fundamental notion and its constitutive elements. The term 'promise' in law may have a different meaning from the non-legal meaning of 'promise'. The longstanding debate amongst philosophers on what constitutes a promise attests to the complexity of the issue.[17]

The discussions in legal scholarship and the decisions of domestic courts affirm that the notion of promise is at the forefront of judicial reasoning on the scope of protection of legitimate expectations. For instance, in the English public law, one scholar observed that 'in virtually every decided case it is the conception of legitimate expectations as a promise that has been at the forefront of the judges' reasoning'.[18] For example, in *R (Niazi) v. Secretary of State for the Home Department*, Laws LJ held that the public authority must have 'distinctively promised' in order for a legitimate expectation to arise.[19] In the context of public laws, the rationale for a strict approach lies with the consequence of fettering the discretion of the decision maker, which is arguably applicable to the investor–state context, in which there is the need to regain the sovereign power of host states. In *R (Bancoult) v. Secretary of State for Foreign and Commonwealth Affairs*, the law lords seem to battle over the notion of promise in the interpretation of the Foreign Secretary's statement concerning the right to return of the residents of the Chagos Islands. The facts do not concern us here; the crucial point is that the notion of

[16] *Mobil Investments Canada Inc. and Murphy Oil Corporation v. Canada*, ICSID Case No ARB (AF)/07/4, Decision on Liability and Principles of Quantum (22 May 2012) para 156 (emphasis added).

[17] M Pratt, 'Defeating Reasonable Reliance' (1999) 18 *U Tas LR* 181, 193 ('what amounts to a promise and whether a particular act falls "short of a promise" are vexed problems that have occupied philosophers since the eighteenth century'.).

[18] J Watson, 'Clarity and Ambiguity: A New Approach to the Test of Legitimacy in the Law of Legitimate Expectations' (2010) 30(4) *LS* 633, 638, 640.

[19] *R (Niazi) v. Secretary of State for the Home Department* [2008] EWCA Civ 755.

promise underlines the reasoning of both the majority and the minority judges.[20]

It is important to note that the doctrine of legitimate expectations should only be applicable where there is a very clear promise because, in such case, there is a 'very clear moral obligation pressing on the decision maker'.[21]

3.2.1.2 Moral Philosophy Can Provide a Better Explanation for How an Obligation Comes About

Understanding how a moral obligation is created provides useful insights into a legal obligation. It is suggested that the host state assumes both a legal and a moral obligation for the individual in making a promise: '*[T]he moral, promissory obligation*, which is the necessary precursor to the legal one, can only be invoked by a clear representation. In this respect, the unequivocal representation acts as the gateway for a legitimate expectation claim.'[22] In making a promise or assurance to the investor, the host state creates 'a new moral relationship' according to Hart, who suggested that

> by promising to do or not to do something, we voluntarily incur obligations and create or confer rights on those to whom we promise; we alter the existing moral independence of the parties' freedom of choice in relation to some action and create *a new moral relationship between them*, so that it becomes morally legitimate for the person to whom the promise is given to determine how the promisor shall act.[23]

Moral philosophy of promise can enrich our understanding of legitimate expectations because philosophers and arbitrators essentially address similar issues – namely, how promise or representation made by the promisor to the promisee creates an obligation. Whereas moral philosophers have developed, over the years, different conceptions of promissory obligation, investment treaty tribunals have rarely addressed the fundamental issues. The tribunals seem content to conclude that a promise or similar acts can create obligations without explaining how such obligations have come about. Arbitrators and municipal judges alike are debating about the relevance of detrimental reliance whilst reliance theorists

[20] *R (on the application of Bancoult) v. Secretary of State for Foreign and Commonwealth Affairs* [2008] UKHL 61.

[21] Ibid 640.

[22] Watson, 'Clarity and Ambiguity' (n 18) 641 (emphasis added).

[23] HLA Hart, 'Are There any Natural Rights' (1955) 64 *Phil Rev* 175 (emphasis added).

see the clear role of detrimental reliance as the basis for an obligation. The voluntarist theorists are clear that promissory obligation is completed by the will of the promisor alone and that the promisee's disappointment of expectations is not relevant to the obligation.

3.2.2 Specific Types of Expectations Protected under the Principle of Legitimate Expectations

Human beings have all sorts of expectations in their lives,[24] which 'is in most cases determined by the assurances and engagements which we receive from others'.[25] However, our expectations can come from other sources, including our experiences, existing customs, the values of civilised society or the moral sentiment of the community.[26] Expectation fulfilment is essential to all human goals.[27] The important question is this: should the doctrine of legitimate expectations seek to protect all types of 'legitimate' expectations or keep the parameter of the doctrine unique and distinct?

If only certain expectations should be protected under the doctrine of legitimate expectations, what is special or unique about certain types of expectations that warrant legal protection under the so-called principle of legitimate expectations, as distinct from other fundamental principles?

If all types of legitimate expectations come under the doctrine of legitimate expectations, the scope of the doctrine would be over-inclusive. The term 'legitimate expectations' is used merely as a concluding label as opposed to having a normative value in forming a basis for liability. Furthermore, not every expectation should be protected because some expectations are 'too minor' or 'misplaced' or 'result of fanciful optimism'.[28] This book argues that the essence of the doctrine of legitimate expectations concerns a specific situation whereby the state's conduct or representation creates the expectations in the investor who then reasonably relies on it to its detriment.

[24] KR Popper, *Objective Knowledge: An Evolutionary Approach* (Oxford: Clarendon Press, 1972), 258–59.

[25] Rev. Edmund Paley, *The Works of William Paley, D. D. and An Account of the Life and Writings of the Author*, vol III (London: Longman and Co, 1838).

[26] R Pound, *Social Control through Law* (New Haven, CT: Yale University Press, 1942), 80.

[27] DG Owen, 'Expectations in Tort' (2011) 43 *Ariz St LJ* 1287, 1291.

[28] *Franck Charles Arif v. Republic of Moldova*, ICSID Case No ARB/11/23, Award (8 April 2013) para 532.

3.3 Methodological Caveats

This section addresses two methodological caveats. First, what is the implication of applying moral philosophy to understand the conception of law? One might question whether moral philosophy can make concrete standards of positive international law if one subscribes to the view about the independence of law and morality.

Positive law can be elucidated with recourse to principles or moral philosophy, especially if the law deals with the legal question which has moral dimension.[29] For instance, investment treaty tribunals would benefit from philosophical reflections on the notion of fairness and equity in interpreting the fair and equitable treatment standard, which embraces the notion of protection of legitimate expectations. This does not make any claim about morality as a condition for being law. The doctrine of legitimate expectations is a legal principle recognised in most legal systems; whether it is a general principle of law which can be applied in investment treaty arbitration is less of a concern than how the doctrine of legitimate expectations should be understood and interpreted.

Furthermore, this book does not assert that states have a *moral* obligation to keep their promise or protect legitimate expectations. The legal principle of legitimate expectations has a moral imperative because the legal issues surrounding protection of legitimate expectations raises an essentially moral question of how a promise creates an obligation.[30] It has been argued that 'the enforcement of a legitimate expectation is the judicial protection of a moral obligation that the public authority has freely solicited'.[31] The formalist approach, which does not delve into the 'bottom of the problem', would fail to provide a clearer understanding about the doctrine of legitimate expectations.

The second caveat relates to the usefulness of applying insights from the philosophy of interpersonal morality to the investor–state context.

[29] G Fitzmaurice, 'The General Principles of International Law Considered from the Standpoint of the Rule of Law' (1997) 11 *Collected Courses of the Hague Academy of International Law* 1, 53. Fitzmaurice suggested that the binding force of law is ultimately to be found in 'a moral principle to the effect that social life is necessary and desirable, together with a factual truth to the effect that some type of legal system . . . is an essential means to this end' (53).

[30] S Schønberg, *Legitimate Expectations in Administrative Law* (Oxford: Oxford University Press, 2000) ('departures from individual representations entail *a form of moral harm* because of the detrimental impact on individual autonomy which may be compounded by detrimental reliance, or in many instances, financial loss' [53, emphasis added]).

[31] Watson, 'Clarity and Ambiguity' (n 18) 641.

The nature of relationship does not affect the validity of the underlying moral principle. The reliance principle that one must be responsible for the loss or harm caused by one's conduct, which intentionally or knowingly induces another party's detrimental reliance is equally valid in both state–investor and private individual relationships. This does not mean that various factors should not be considered. Furthermore, trust by one individual in another individual has the same moral validity as that of the investor in the host State; personal autonomy of an investor has the same moral validity as that of an individual in public or private laws.

Moreover, State is a fictional concept for organising a relationship between people in a society, and what lies behind the notion of State is human beings.[32] Therefore, any valuable principles, which are essential to the people, should be relevant to the regulation of states' conduct. The interpersonal morality can influence the development of international law norms because legal principles come from the conscience of people. This point is reiterated by Judge Alvarez in the *Anglo-Norwegian Fisheries* case; he observed that '*many of the principles, particularly the great principles, have their origin in the legal conscience of people* . . . This conscience results from social and international life; the requirements of this social and international life naturally give rise to certain norms considered necessary to govern the conduct of States inter se'.[33]

3.4 Three Conceptions of Promissory Obligation and a Theory of Legitimate Expectations

After setting out the justification for the use of moral philosophy, it is important to clarify how to apply philosophical insights into promissory obligation to elucidate the core of legitimate expectations.

There has been a lack of attempt to identify a unified theory of promise in philosophy because philosophers disagree over the fundamental basis for promissory obligation.[34] However, the recent work by Martin Hogg sought to establish a general definition of 'promise', which postulates the following constitutive elements of promise: (i) a promise is more than merely an internal mental process: promises as speech acts demonstrate

[32] R Bilder, 'The Role of Trust in International Law' (1981); available at http://ssrn.com/abstract=912741 (accessed on 10 June 2016).

[33] *The Anglo-Norwegian Fisheries Case (United Kingdom v. Norway)* 1951 *ICJ Rep* 116, 148–49 (emphasis added).

[34] M Hogg, *Promises and Contract Law, Comparative Perspectives* (Cambridge: Cambridge University Press, 2014), 4.

commitment; (ii) a promise is a commitment to a performance of the promisor; (iii) a promise must manifest more than an illusory commitment or one which the promisor is patently unable to fulfil; (iv) a promise must relate to the future and (v) a promise must state a commitment in favour of another party.[35]

However, the preceding definition of 'promise' is not satisfactory for two reasons. First, it does not encapsulate the core element of the consequentialist conception of promise – namely, expectation or reliance as the basis for obligation.[36] Second, it cannot easily distinguish between promises and statements of intent. The notion of promise may not always be a calculated, rational or careful choice of individuals.[37]

When investment tribunals employ the term 'promise' or other similar terms without defining the constitutive conditions for liability, it is unclear whether they refer to a legally binding promise or simply a specific nonbinding promise. The moral conception of promise does not always coincide with the legal conception of promise, which '*seems to come back to something binding*, something to which the law annexes an obligation, and if this is so, promise and contract do not differ as terms, for a promise is a contract'.[38] This contrasts with the notion of promise in moral philosophy, which does not always refer to a legally binding undertaking.

Despite the absence of the unified concept of promise, close reading of moral philosophy literature on promise has revealed three strands of thinking.[39] The voluntarist conception of promise attributes liability to the will of the promisor to undertake an obligation. The assurance conception requires the promisor's intention to create the expectation.

[35] Ibid.

[36] Atiyah, *Promises, Morals and the Law* (n 3) 66.

[37] Ibid 172.

[38] C Ashley, 'What Is a Promise in Law?' 16 5 (1903) *Harv L Rev* 320 (emphasis added).

[39] A distinction between the expectation-based view of promise and the reliance-based view of promise is made in S Shiffrin, 'Promising, Intimate Relationships, and Conventionalism' (2008) 117(4) *Phil Rev* 481, 486; some scholars focus on the conventionalist and non-conventionalist aspect of promissory obligation: M Pratt, 'Promise, Contracts and Voluntary Obligations' (2007) 26(6) *L & Phil* 531 (the author analyses Raz's theory which represents a non-conventionalist aspect of normative power/voluntarist view of promise and Rawls' theory of promise which represents a conventionalist voluntarism). It is noted that whilst it is also possible to conceive a promissory obligation under the types of moral theories, such as natural law theory, contract theory, consequentialism or deontological theory, the philosophy literature on the source of promissory obligation focuses on the key element which is the basis for obligation: the will, the expectation or the reliance.

The reliance conception grounds a promissory obligation in the promisee's act of reliance. As background on the philosophical discussions, following are the key features of the three conceptions of promissory obligation.

The voluntarist conception treats an intention to undertake an obligation as the basis for promissory obligation. The essence of this conception is articulated by John Finnis:

> A promise is constituted if and only if (i) A communicates to B his intention to undertake, by that very act of communication (in conjunction with B's acceptance of it), an obligation to perform a certain action (or to see to it that certain actions are performed), and (ii) B accepts this undertaking in the interests of himself, or of A or of some third party C.[40]

The assurance or bare expectation conception identifies the intention to create expectation or assurance as the sufficient basis for obligation. Thomas Scanlon, the principal proponent of the assurance conception, articulates the principle as follows:

> If (1) A voluntarily and intentionally leads *B* to expect that *A* will do *X* (unless *B* consents to *A*'s not doing so); (2) *A* knows that *B* wants to be assured of this; (3) *A* acts with the aim of providing this assurance, and has good reason to believe that he or she has done so; (4) *B* knows that *A* has the intentions and beliefs just described; (5) *A* intends for *B* to know this, and knows that *B* does know it; (6) *B* knows that *A* has this knowledge and intent, then, in the absence of special justification, *A* must do *X* unless *B* consents to *X*'s not being done.[41]

The reliance theory attributes liability to detrimental reliance of the promisee. Professor McCormick articulated the core of this conception in the following terms:

> If one person acts in a potentially detrimental way in reliance upon beliefs about another's future conduct, and if the latter person has by some act of his intentionally or knowingly induced the former to rely upon him, then the latter has an obligation not to act in a manner which will disappoint the other's reliance.[42]

All three conceptions of promise form the analytical framework for two reasons. First, they illustrate the strengths and weaknesses of each

[40] J Finnis, *Natural Law and Natural Rights* (Oxford: Clarendon Press, 1980), 298–99.

[41] TM Scanlon, *What We Owe to Each Other* (Cambridge, MA: Harvard University Press, 1998), 304.

[42] N MacCormick, 'Voluntary Obligations and Normative Powers' (1972) 46(Annual Supplement) *Proceedings of the Aristotelian Society* 59, 68.

conception, which underline the reasoning adopted advertently or inadvertently by different investment treaty tribunals. Second, the divergent jurisprudence can be explained by different conceptions to which the tribunals subscribed.

This book does not adopt the legal realist approach, which takes law as what arbitral decisions say. The preferred approach is to identify the theoretical framework based on the relevant principles and then to analyse the doctrine of legitimate expectations accordingly. Furthermore, relevant arbitral decisions are used to illustrate each conception of legitimate expectations. The existing jurisprudence falls into three main conceptions. It is important to note that there are some decisions which do not fit with any conception. Some arbitral decisions see the application of more than one conception to different sources of expectations. We can identify certain elements for determining which arbitral decisions fall under which conception of legitimate expectations.

For the voluntarist conception, an intention to undertake a legal obligation must be present. There is usually no reference to an act of reliance by a promisee because an obligation can be completed by the act of the promisor alone. Under the assurance conception, an intention to create expectation or assurance must be present, but an act of reliance is not required. Typically, the state's intention to induce investment is the main feature of this paradigm. Arbitral decisions which require an act of reliance for legitimate expectation are presumed to fall under the reliance conception. Arbitral decisions which consider the knowledge of regulatory risk or the investor's conduct in analysing reasonableness of expectations are also deemed to fall within the reliance conception.

4

The Voluntarist Conception of Legitimate Expectations and Enforcement of Sovereign Promise

4.1 Introduction

This chapter presents the conceptual analysis of legitimate expectations from the will-based (voluntarist) theory of promise. According to this theory, the obligation to keep a promise depends on the intention of the promisor to acquire it in the first place. This will-based theory, which has been relied on to justify the contractual obligation,[1] can explain the binding nature of the voluntary act of the state. One important attribute of state sovereignty is the ability to place 'a restriction upon the exercise of the sovereign rights of the State'.[2] Therefore, the state can exercise this power to make a 'promise'[3] to a foreign investor by various means, such as conclusion of investment treaties, making of investment contract or formal or informal representations.

What is the implication of applying the voluntarist theory to justify an obligation to protect legitimate expectations? The expectation which arises as a consequence of such a promise is 'reasonable' because it is based on the legal right which is conferred by the promise.[4] The scope of the conduct capable of creating legitimate expectations is limited to a legal commitment or a binding act in the form of a contract or legislation. The 'reasonable' expectation is nothing distinct but the shadow of the legal right which the investor has already possessed

[1] Champion of the theory of promise as the basis for contract is Charles Fried. See his *Contract as Promise: A Theory of Contractual Obligation* (Cambridge, MA: Harvard University Press, 1981). However, such a view is not always shared by other scholars. See S Shiffrin, 'The Divergence of Contract and Promise' (2007) 120 *Harv L Rev* 708.

[2] *SS Wimbledon*, PCIJ Series A No 1, 17 August 1923, 25.

[3] The term 'promise' under the voluntarist conception refers to a legally binding act.

[4] It is confusing and unhelpful merely to use the term 'promise' as the threshold for determining legitimacy of expectation because 'promise' can signify a legally binding act such as a contract or the conduct which seeks to create expectation or assurance or to induce reliance.

under the contract. This conception has the beauty of clarity and respect for the state's sovereignty. But what is the added value of framing the claim in terms of a breach of legitimate expectations? To what extent should we protect the contractual right dressed up in the garment of 'legitimate expectations' under the fair and equitable treatment (FET) standard?

Drawing insights from the philosophical works on the voluntarist or normative power theory of promise, the voluntarist principle of legitimate expectations is postulated to guide the analysis of protection of legitimate expectations in investment treaty disputes (Section 4.2). The normative implication of the voluntarist principle is analysed in the paradigms of expectations created by contract, administrative representations or legislative framework (Section 4.3). The chapter concludes with the analysis of strengths and weaknesses of the voluntarist conception (Section 4.4).

4.2 Conceptual Analysis of Legitimate Expectations and the Voluntarist Theory of Promise

This section sets out the main tenets of two approaches to the voluntarist theory of promissory obligation: conventionalist and non-conventionalist.[5] The non-conventionalist theory of promise asserts that the moral force of promise is found in the validity of the general rule of promise-keeping without the need to identify social convention (Section 4.2.2). This promise-keeping norm is justified because it is desirable to give people the ability to bind themselves in order to forge a bond.[6] By contrast, the conventionalist theory contends that a promissory obligation cannot be conceived in the absence of social practice (Section 4.2.3). First, it is useful to examine the origin of the voluntarist conception and the fundamental concept of normative power, which enables a promisor to create a promissory obligation in the first place (Section 4.2.1). Based on the underlying philosophical framework, the voluntarist conception of legitimate expectations is developed (Section 4.2.4).

[5] M Pratt, 'Promise, Contracts and Voluntary Obligations' (2007) 26(6) *L & Phil* 531.

[6] J Raz, 'Promises and Obligations' in PMS Hacker and J Raz (eds), *Law, Morality and Society: Essays in Honor of H.L.A. Hart* (Oxford: Clarendon Press, 1977), 210–28 ('PO principles [the obligation conceptions of promise] can only be justified if the creation of such special relationships between people is held to be valuable').

4.2.1 Promise, Normative Power and Natural Law Thinking

4.2.1.1 Natural Law Origin

The provenance of the voluntarist conception of promise stems from the natural law tradition. The idea of promise-keeping can be traced back to Aristotle's theory of promissory obligation based on the virtues of honesty and justice[7] and Aquinas' theory based on fidelity and honesty.[8] Under this view of virtue ethics, promising is considered as a virtuous act which contributed to the ultimate end of man. The promisor is only bound under the circumstances in which he or she has committed.[9]

The views of early modern commentators also support the predominance of the will as a basis for obligation. For Pufendorf, the voluntary consent of the promisor provides the grounds for a binding nature of promise.[10] According to Grotius' conception of promissory obligation, the necessary and sufficient condition of the promissory obligation is that the act of the promisor alone and the promisee's disappointment in case of a breach are not relevant to the formation of an obligation:[11]

> Promissory obligation does not, according to the conception suggested thus far, entail an intrinsic connection between promisor and promisee since the necessary and sufficient condition of the obligation's existence is *the act of the promisor alone and the form of the obligation is inward self-consistency. It is true that the promisee may have faith in my present decision to perform the future act, but his trust is not a necessary condition of the existence of the obligation which I assume in making the promise.* That obligation is already complete and the other's faith simply reflects my obligation in the mirror of his subjectivity. The promisee's trust, with its initial hope, may end in disappointment if I breach, *but these sentiments are at most the effects produced by my promise and by its fulfillment*

[7] Aristotle, *Nicomachean Ethics* (edited by Jonathon Barnes) (Princeton, NJ: Princeton University Press, 1984).

[8] Thomas Aquinas, *The Summa Theologica of St. Thomas Aquinas* (translated by English Dominicans) (London: Burns, Oates, and Washbourne. Repr New York: Christian Classics 1981).

[9] M Hogg, *Promises and Contract Law, Comparative Perspectives* (Cambridge: Cambridge University Press, 2014), 76.

[10] S Pufendorf, *De Jure Nature et Gentium* [On the Law of Nature and Nations] 1672 (translated by CH Oldfather and WA Oldfather) (New York, NY: Hein Press, 1995) ('For, since the fulfillment of any promise and agreement is associated with some burden, there is no better reason to prevent our justly complaining about it, than the fact that we voluntarily consented to what it was evidently in our own power to avoid').

[11] H Grotius, *On the Law of War and Peace* (translated by FW Kelsey) (Oxford: Clarendon Press, 1925), para 3, 329.

or breach, and are only contingently related to the nature of the promissory obligation.[12]

The modern natural law proponents, such as Finnis, provide a similar account of promise, which requires the communication or expression of an intention to obligate oneself.[13] Based on the natural law thinking, Vattel also suggested that a promisor transfers a right to a promisee, therefore a breach of promise involves a violation of the promisee's right:

> It is a settled point in natural law, that he who has made a promise to anyone has conferred upon him *a real right to require the thing promised* – and, consequently, *that the breach of a perfect promise is a violation of another person's right*, and as evidently an act of injustice as it would be to rob a man of his property. The tranquility, the happiness, the security of the human race, wholly depend on justice, – on the obligation of paying a regard to the rights of others ... *There would no longer be any security, no longer any commerce between mankind, if they did not think themselves obliged to keep faith with each other, and to perform their promises.*[14]

Therefore, based on the expounded notion of promise, legitimate expectations means that an investor can legitimately expect an enforcement of the thing promised because it is his or her right granted by the promisor. Similar to the underlying principle in the quoted passage, Fuller and Perdue argued that 'the expectancy created by an enforceable promise should be regarded as a kind of *property right*, and breach of the promise as an injury to that property'; therefore the expectancy remedy should be awarded.[15]

[12] P Benson, '"Grotius" Contribution to the Natural Law of Contract' (1985) 6 *CJNS* 1, 7 (emphasis added).

[13] J Finnis, *Natural Law and Natural Rights* (Oxford: Clarendon Press, 1980) 298–99 ('first, what is a promise or undertaking? Being a human practice, engaged in and maintained for diverse practical purposes, promising has its central cases (its focal meaning) and its secondary or borderline cases. Centrally, then, a promise is constituted if and only if (i) A communicates to B his intention to undertake, by that very act of communication (in conjunction with B's acceptance of it), an obligation to perform a certain action (or to see to it that certain actions are performed), and (ii) B accepts this undertaking in the interests of himself, or of A or of some third party C').

[14] J Chitty (ed), *Emmerich de Vattel, The Law of Nations Or, Principles of the Law of Nature, Applied to the Conduct and Affairs of Nations and Sovereigns* (Cambridge: Cambridge University Press, 2011) (emphasis added).

[15] L Fuller and WR Perdue, 'The Reliance Interest in Contract Damage (Parts 1 and 2)' (1936–1937) 46 (52) *Yale LJ* 373 (emphasis added).

4.2.1.2 The Concept of Normative Power and the 'Sovereign Power to Promise' in Investment Treaty Arbitration

A normative power is crucial to the voluntarist theory of promise because it is through the exercise of that power that the promissory obligation is created. A normative power is defined as 'the power intentionally to shape the form of his moral world, to oblige himself to follow certain goals, or to create bonds and alliances with certain people and not others'.[16] The power to promise is justifiable because it is valuable for people to be able to forge a special relationship[17] and to provide the normative assurance to a promisee.[18] Similarly, Shiffrin suggests that the power to promise is a necessary attribute of an autonomous agent who exercises the normative power to maintain special voluntary relations with others.[19]

The theory of normative power can provide a conceptual framework for analysing the power to promise in the context of an investor–state relationship. Such power is a very important aspect of an exercise of state sovereignty in forging a special relationship between investor and state.[20] Paulson argued that the state uses the power to promise to pursue the policy goal of attracting foreign investment[21] and the power to promise or to accept legal limitations is in itself an attribute of sovereignty.[22] Therefore it has to accept the legal consequence of the exercise of this power, in particular the failure to observe its promise. Paulson's analysis of the normative power in the context of an investor–state relationship underlines the normative contention that when the state creates an

16 Raz, Promises and Obligations (n 6) 228.

17 J Raz, 'Is There a Reason to Keep Promises' (2012) No. 12–320, Research Paper Series, Columbia University Public Law & Legal Theory, Columbia Law School.

18 J Raz, 'Voluntary Obligations and Normative Powers' (1972) 46 Proceedings of the Aristotelian Society. Supplementary Volume 80, 99 ('promising is surely more than inducing reliance, by promising I bind myself and confer a right on the promisee').

19 S Shiffrin, 'Promising, Intimate Relationships, and Conventionalism' (2008) 117(4) *Phil Rev* 481, 500 ('the idea that an agent can intentionally form an obligation through the exercise and expression of her will alone (and not by first transforming the state of affairs around her) comes part and parcel with any plausible conception of an autonomous agent').

20 J Paulson, 'The Power of States to Make Meaningful Promises to Foreigners' (2010) 1(2) *JIDS* 341.

21 Ibid ('If States were incapable of giving reliable promises – because their misconceived 'sovereignty' renders them powerless to do so – the policy objective of attracting foreign investment would be illusory').

22 Ibid (he cited the passage from the Wimbledon judgment in 1923, which confirmed that 'the right of entering into international engagements is an attribute of State sovereignty').

expectation through the promise, which the state has consequently frustrated, there is a legal consequence which cannot be abrogated by the invocation of 'sovereignty'. This resonates with Joseph Raz's theory of promise, which suggests that through the exercise of the power to promise – by communicating an intention to undertake an obligation – the promisor becomes bound by it.

4.2.2 Non-conventional Voluntarist Conception of Promise

Raz's theory of promise, which is characterised as non-conventional voluntarist, states that a promise is morally binding because a promisor, through the exercise of its normative power, imposes an obligation upon itself by communicating its intention to undertake an obligation.[23] Raz clarified that 'promises are voluntary obligations not because promising is an intentional action, but because *it is the communication of an intention to undertake an obligation*, or at any rate to create for oneself a reason for action'.[24]

The key ingredient for liability is an intention to undertake an obligation which is 'both a necessary and a sufficient condition of making a promise that the promisor behave in a way which is either intended or can reasonably be taken to indicate the promise's intention to bind itself to perform an act and to give the promisee a right against the promisor'.[25] This normative power changes 'the existing moral independence' of the promisee and generates 'a new moral relationship' between the parties. HLA Hart articulated that

> [b]y promising to do or not to do something, we voluntarily incur obligations and create or *confer rights on those to whom we promise*; we alter the existing moral independence of the parties' freedom of choice in relation to some action and create a new moral relationship between them, so that it becomes morally legitimate for the person to whom the promise is given to determine how the promisor shall act.[26]

There are two important points to emphasise in the aforementioned passages from Raz and Hart. First, the promise does not only occur just when the promisor intends to bind himself but also when he 'can

[23] Raz, 'Voluntary Obligations and Normative Powers' (n 18) 98 ('promises are a source of voluntary obligations they are made by the exercise of normative powers').
[24] Raz, Promises and Obligations (n 6) 218 (emphasis added).
[25] Raz, 'Voluntary Obligations and Normative Powers' (n 18) 100.
[26] HLA Hart, 'Are There any Natural Rights' (1955) 64 *Phil Rev* 175 (emphasis added).

reasonably be taken to indicate the promise's intention to bind himself'. Second, both Raz and Hart emphasise that in making a promise, a promisor actually confers a right to a promisee.

Raz's non-conventionalist conception of promise denies the indispensability of social convention for the validity of a promissory obligation. However, the social convention may be relevant for determining what constitutes a promise – namely, what acts can reasonably be taken to express an intention to undertake an obligation and confer a right.[27]

4.2.3 *Conventionalist Voluntarist Conception of Promise*

Conventionalist voluntarist conception of promise, a voluntary act, can create an obligation *only because* it is recognised by a conventional norm. The rationale for a state's obligation to fulfil an undertaking voluntarily assumed is attributable to the existence of a social norm or convention. According to the conventionalist theorists, the social norm of promising is a *precondition of* the moral obligation of a promise but not *the basis of* that obligation. The conventionalist theorists, however, rely on different bases to justify the obligation. For instance, David Hume's theory of promise relies on the instrumental value of promising convention on the viability of society (Section 4.2.3.1). John Rawls' theory of promise derives the moral force of promise from a moral principle of fairness (Section 4.2.3.2). These two views are analysed in the following paragraphs.

4.2.3.1 Hume's Theory of Promise and Social Approval of Promise-keeping

The essential feature of Hume's conception is that a promise is an 'artificial virtue' developed from a social convention for the benefit of people living in a society.[28] His view is premised on the scepticism that we could bring a promissory obligation into existence without

[27] Raz, 'Voluntary Obligations and Normative Powers' (n 18) 100 (in our culture, communicating an intention to act in a certain way to a person who is known to be interested in the action is conventionally regarded as an act expressing an intention to undertake an obligation to act in that way and to confer a right on the person concerned).

[28] D Hume, *A Treatise of Human Nature* (edited by D Norton and M Norton) (Oxford: Oxford University Press, 2000) ('promises have no natural obligation, and are mere artificial contrivances for the convenience and advantage of society').

establishing the social convention.[29] How the promise generates an obligation is perplexing, as Hume described:

> One of the most mysterious and incomprehensible operations that can possibly be imagin'd and may even be compar'd to transubstantiation, or holy orders, where a certain form of words, along with a certain intention, changes entirely the nature of an external object, and even of a human creature'.[30]

The justification for this social norm of promising, according to Hume, is based on the instrumental function of enabling and facilitating self-interested exchange and cooperation. The institution of promise-keeping is a necessary condition of the viability of society.[31] In similar term, David Gauthier appeals to the coordinative benefits of promising as a basis for obligation.[32] In the context of investor–state relationship, this rationale seems relevant. Without the assurance or promise of a state, an investor would be reluctant to commit investment capital or resources because no investor would like to be in an uncertain situation as regards the legal stability or the business environment.

4.2.3.2 Rawls' Theory of Promissory Obligation and the Principle of Fairness

Rawls' conception of promissory obligation is rooted in the rules of social practice because 'these rules are, as in the case of institutions generally, a set of constitutive conventions'.[33] For Rawls, promising is a form of activity that is governed by a 'system of rules which define offices, roles, moves, penalties, defenses, and so on and which gives the activity its structure'.[34] The rules bind anyone who voluntarily accepts the benefit of this practice by making a promise according to the rules. As was the case with Hume's theory, the benefit of this practice lies in its cooperative benefit.[35] The existence of a conventional duty is

[29] AE Pitson, 'Hume on Promises and Their Obligation' (1988) 14(1) *Hume Studies* 176; W Vitek, 'The Humean Promise: Whence Comes Its Obligation' (1986) XII(2) *Hume Studies* 160.

[30] Hume, *Treatise* (n 28) 524.

[31] DW Hamlyn, 'The Obligation to Keep a Promise' (1961–1962) 62 *Proceedings of the Aristotelian Society New Series* 179.

[32] D Gauthier, 'Morals by Agreement' (Oxford: Oxford University Press, 1987), 167.

[33] J Rawls, 'Two Concepts of Rules' (1955) 64(1) *Phil Rev* 3.

[34] Ibid 3.

[35] J Rawls, *A Theory of Justice* (Cambridge, MA: Harvard University Press, 1971), 347 ('there may be no way of assuring the party who is to perform first except by giving

a precondition of but not an explanation for the moral obligation to keep a promise.[36]

As with other voluntarist theories of promise, Rawls regards promising as an exercise of normative power, whereby people assume an obligation to pursue their goals.[37] His analysis of the state of mind of the promisor offers useful insights on our conceptualisation of legitimate expectations. For instance, the promisor must be in conscious mind and must not be under coercion or threat when he or she makes a promise.[38]

Unlike Hume's theory, the moral basis for promissory obligation under Rawls' theory is based on the moral imperative (the principle of fairness). Rawls asserts that the duty to keep a promise is grounded in the moral principle of fidelity, 'a special case of the principle of fairness'.[39] The wrongness of promise-breaking can be explained in terms of the unfairness of free-riding – namely, that it is wrong to exploit social practice by benefiting from it and not do what one promised. Rawls explained that 'a person is under an obligation to do his part as specified by the rules of an institution whenever he has voluntarily accepted the benefits of that scheme or has taken advantage of the opportunities it offers to advance his interests, provided the institution is just or fair'.[40]

4.2.4 *A Critique of Voluntarist Theories and the Conceptual Framework of Legitimate Expectations*

This section considers some criticisms of voluntarist theories with a view to identifying whether the conventionalist or non-conventionalist theory

him a promise, that is, by putting oneself under an obligation to carry through later only in this way can the scheme be made secure so that both can gain from the benefits of their cooperation').

36 Ibid ('No moral requirements follow from the existence of institutions alone').

37 Rawls, *A Theory of Justice* (n 35) 347 ('[T]hey [moral requirements] are sometimes deliberately self-imposed for our advantage. Thus, promising is an act done with the public intention of deliberately incurring an obligation the existence of which in the circumstances will further one's ends.').

38 Ibid 303 ('[I]n order to make a binding promise, one must be fully conscious, in a rational frame of mind, and know the meaning of the operative words, their use in making promises, and so on. Furthermore, these words must be spoken freely or voluntarily, when one is not subject to threats or coercion, and in situations where one has a reasonably fair bargaining position, so to speak.').

39 Rawls, *A Theory of Justice* (n 35) ('it is essential . . . to distinguish between the rule of promising and the principle of fidelity. The rule is simply a constitutive convention, whereas the principle of fidelity is a moral principle.').

40 Rawls, 'Two Concepts of Rules' (n 33).

of promise forms the basis for the conceptualisation of legitimate expectations. From the perspective of conditions for liability, there might be no need to choose one theory over the other because the two theories, which share the common feature (namely, the voluntary nature of obligation), can provide the conceptual guidance. However, these two types of theories differ with regard to the bases of the norm of promising. Raz's theory is grounded in the *validity* of the general rule of promise-keeping justified by the desirability of the normative power, whilst the theories of Hume and Rawls emphasise the conventional character of the norm. This difference may have a practical implication, as follows.

According to the conventionalist conception of promise, the rules of 'social practice' concerning a promise by a host state and investors in international law need to be identified. The existence of such social practices could be drawn from legal practices in both private and public municipal laws or even from legal practices concerning state contracts in international law. There might be some difficulty in inferring such social practice at the level of international law from municipal laws. Is this task similar to identification of customary international law, which requires state practice and *opinio juris*? In any case, there is a more fundamental objection to the conventionalist conception, which would save us from evaluating the relevance of the 'social practice' aspect of the theory. That objection concerns the characterisation of the wrong done to the promisee.

Both Rawls' and Hume's theories are subject to this fatal flaw. Under the conventionalist theory, promise-breaking is the wrong done to the practice itself and a group of participants who participate in such practice.[41] For instance, under Rawls' theory, the harm is done to all those who participate in the 'mutually advantageous cooperative venture' of promising. This characterisation of the wrong is troublesome because it does not accord with our common sense that the harm from promise-breaking is done to the promisee.[42] One can agree with Hume's contention that promise-breaking undermines the reputation and trustworthiness of a promisor.[43] However, the characterisation of the wrong done to the community at large misrepresents the true nature of promise.

[41] TM Scanlon, 'Promises and Practices' (1990) 19(3) *Phil & Pub Aff* 199.

[42] Ibid ('to give a promise is to confer a right on the promise. It is to single out that individual and to provide him alone with a moral claim to the promised performance.').

[43] Hume, *Treatise* (n 28) 335 ('When a man says he promises anything he, ... by making use of this form of words, subjects himself to the penalty of never being trust again in case of failure.').

Related to the question of 'whom the promise-breaking wrongs' is the characterisation of the type of wrong. This criticism relates to Rawls' mischaracterisation of the wrong under the principle of fairness. It is argued that by characterising the wrong of promise-breaking to some general moral principle, such as the principle of fairness, is not appropriate because the wrong of promising is *sui generis* and should not be reducible to a general wrong.[44] Furthermore, it is argued that there are other specific values which are peculiar to promising – fidelity, commitment and assurance – that can justify the moral force of a promise.

These criticisms are significant in our context because this theory mischaracterised the type of wrong of promise-breaking done to the investor. At a conceptual level, it might be hard to justify that the investor should have a *personal* claim for the wrong done to him or her because the wrong would be done to the investment community at large. Therefore, the analytical framework in this chapter is established based on the non-conventionalist conception.

4.2.4.1 The Voluntarist Principle of Legitimate Expectations

Based on the preceding philosophical framework, the voluntarist principle of legitimate expectations can be postulated as follows:

> If the State has expressed its intention to undertake an obligation to do X, which creates the expectation in the investor, the State has an obligation to fulfill that expectation. In other words, the investor can reasonably and legitimately expect X if the State has expressed the intention, by way of its communication, to undertake the obligation to do X.

The following provision can be added to that rule: 'social convention may determine what acts can reasonably be taken to express an intention to undertake an obligation'.[45]

There are four normative elements of the voluntarist conception of legitimate expectations. First, the intention to assume a legal obligation must be identified, either by explicit undertaking or inferred from circumstances. Consequently, the clear and explicit nature of a representation by a state to a particular investor will be required. However, as pointed out by Raz, social norms or practices may be relevant for determining the existence of a promissory act.[46] Drawing insights from Rawls, such intention must be given 'willingly and freely';

[44] Pratt, 'Promise, Contracts and Voluntary Obligations' (n 5) 531.
[45] J Raz, 'Voluntary Obligations and Normative Powers' (n 18) 100.
[46] Ibid.

the speaker must be 'fully conscious, in a rational frame of mind, and know the meaning of the operative words, their use in making promises, and so on'.[47] Second, there must be full disclosure of information by the investor as the state needs to have full information or all material facts before making a binding promise. Third, such intention must be communicated to and received by the promisee. Therefore, the promisee must have the knowledge of representation. Fourth, the question of 'reasonableness' will turn on the determination of whether the state has voluntarily assumed a legal obligation.

4.3 Normative Implication of the Voluntarist Conception of Legitimate Expectations

This section assesses the normative implication of the voluntarist principle of legitimate expectations to the paradigm cases based on three sources of expectations: contract, administrative representations and laws. In case of contract breach, there is assimilation of contractual right and treaty right through the concept of reasonable expectations (Section 4.3.1). The scope of legitimate expectations arising from administrative representations is restrictive (Section 4.3.2). Protection of legitimate expectations arising from legislative framework neutralises the normative power (Section 4.3.3). The relief under the voluntarist conception of legitimate expectations seeks to protect expectation interests (Section 4.3.4).

4.3.1 Assimilation of Contractual Right and Treaty Right

Contractual arrangement is the main paradigm of the voluntarist conception of legitimate expectations because the state manifests its will to undertake a legal obligation, through a contract. It is therefore unsurprising that the voluntarist principle has underpinned a number of investment treaty decisions addressing the issues of legitimate expectations arising from contractual arrangement. The most explicit articulation of the voluntarist conception is found in the excerpt of the tribunal in *Total v. Argentina*,[48] which

[47] Rawls, *A Theory of Justice* (n 35) 345.

[48] *Total S.A. v. Argentina*, ICSID Case No ARB/04/1, Decision on Liability (21 December 2010); despite the fact that the case concerns a breach of expectations generated by the legal regime, this part of the holding is relevant to our discussion.

suggested that the legitimacy of expectations depends on a legally binding obligation of the state:

> [T]he expectation of the investor is undoubtedly 'legitimate', and hence subject to protection under the fair and equitable treatment clause *if the host State has explicitly assumed a specific legal obligation for the future*, such as by contracts, concessions or stabilization clauses on which the investor is therefore entitled to rely as a matter of law.[49]

The unsatisfactory consequence of applying the voluntarist principle is that contractual right is assimilated to treaty right, which is then protected by the application of legitimate expectations. The assimilation of contractual right with reasonable expectations in domestic contract laws reflects the legalistic view of the contract (as opposed to social and factual view) – namely, the contracting parties' expectations are only what are stipulated in the contract. The judge in that case did not resort to other values or principles to enforce the terms of the contract.[50] The assimilation is undesirable in investment treaty arbitration because the principle of legitimate expectations would convert a contract breach into a treaty breach, enforcing contractual obligations through treaty mechanism. This undesirable consequence is discussed in the paragraphs that follow, with reference to selected cases: *Alpha v. Ukraine*,[51] *MCI v. Ecuador*,[52] *Electrabel v. Hungary*,[53] *Hochtief v. Argentina*[54] and *Nordzucker v. Poland*[55] (Section 4.3.1.1). However, some tribunals view that the principle of legitimate expectations should not protect contractual expectations but only 'other expectations protected by international law' (Section 4.3.1.2).

[49] Ibid para 101 (emphasis added) (However, based on the facts of the case, Total is not a party to the concession, so the TGN Licence cannot be regarded as a source of contractual legal obligations of a specific character assumed directly by Argentina towards Total.)

[50] C Mitchell, 'Leading a Life of Its Own? The Roles of Reasonable Expectation in Contract Law' (2003) 23(4)*OJLLS* 639, 650–52.

[51] *Alpha Projektholding GmbH v. Ukraine*, ICSID Case No ARB/07/16, Award (8 November 2010).

[52] *M.C.I. Power Group L.C. and New Turbine, Inc. v. Republic of Ecuador*, ICSID Case No ARB/03/6, Award (31 July 2007).

[53] *Electrabel S.A. v. Republic of Hungary* (ICSID Case No ARB/07/19), Decision on Jurisdiction, Applicable Law and Liability (30 November 2012).

[54] *Hochtief AG v. The Argentine Republic*, ICSID Case No ARB/07/31, Decision on Liability (29 December 2014).

[55] *Nordzucker v. Poland*, UNCITRAL, Second Partial Award (Merits) (28 January 2009).

4.3.1.1 Enforcement of Contractual Obligation through Legitimate Expectations

4.3.1.1.1 ***Alpha v. Ukraine*** The case of *Alpha v. Ukraine* concerns the dispute arising from the agreement on renovation and reconstruction of a hotel. The claimant entered into an agreement with the state entity. The principal conduct which gave rise to this dispute was Ukraine's interference with the day-to-day management of the hotel, and negation of the agreements. The tribunal had to consider the claimant's claim based on two expectations of renewal of the contract and non-interference with the contract.

The tribunal explicitly endorsed 'the principle of fair and equitable treatment' to include 'the obligation not to upset an investor's legitimate expectations', which requires 'the government to avoid arbitrarily changing the rules of the game in a manner that undermines the legitimate expectations of, or the representations made, to an investor'.[56] In resolving the issue of legitimate expectations, the tribunal employed the voluntarist conception by relying on the absence of legally binding commitments as a criterion for holding expectations to be unreasonable. The tribunal dealt with two claims of expectations.

On the first expectation, the tribunal rejected the claimant's expectation to continue to work with the hotel after the contractual termination because the state did not promise to renew the contract, as shown by the absence of contractual stipulation to that effect.[57] On the second expectation of non-interference by the government and of honouring agreements, the tribunal referred to the terms of the original agreements, the terms of the amendments to those agreements and the assurances as the sources of legitimate expectations which created an internationally wrongful act.[58] The tribunal reasoned that

> Claimant did possess *a legitimate expectation that the government would not interfere with the contractual relationship* between Claimant and the Hotel, and *that the agreements would be honored*, albeit with the reformation to the payment terms necessitated by the Ukrainian law on joint activities . . . *Those expectations arose not only by the terms of the original agreements, but, for example, also by the terms of the amendments to those*

[56] *Alpha v. Ukraine* (n 51) para 420.

[57] Ibid para 421 ('No doubt Claimant hoped for a continuation of the relationship, and perhaps even the management of the Hotel harbored a similar hope. However, the contracts clearly provided for their termination in 2015, and it would be pure speculation to find that the parties would have extended the agreements further.').

[58] Ibid para 422 (emphasis added).

> *agreements negotiated during or after the corporatization, and by the assurances* given by the new management of the Hotel in June 2004 that the relationship would continue.

The tribunal's reasoning is consonant with the reformulated principle which states that 'the investor can reasonably and legitimately expect X if the State has expressed the intention, by way of its communication, to undertake the obligation to do X'. Therefore, the tribunal held that the State Administration of Affairs (SAA) by acting beyond its authority and directly interfering with daily management of the hotel undermined the claimant's legitimate expectations.[59]

4.3.1.1.2 ***MCI v. Ecuador*** *MCI v. Ecuador* involved a contractual dispute between an Ecuadorian state organ and an investor for the sale of electricity, which led to the suspension of the business operation and the termination of the contract by the state organ. The INECEL (an organ of the Ecuadorian state) signed a contract with Seacoast (owned by the claimants) for the sale of electricity for a period of six months ('Seacoast Contract'). Seacoast agreed to instal and operate two electrical power generation plants and sell that energy to INECEL. At the beginning of 1996, the parties disagreed over the execution of the Seacoast Contract relating to the date of commencement, the duration of the contract, the payment for energy under the 'Take or Pay' modality, reimbursement for the cost of fuel, and the imposition of fines and penalties. Seacoast suspended the operation of the two plants and delivery of power, invoking the non-payment by INECEL for invoiced amounts payable under the terms of the Seacoast Contract. INECEL declared the Seacoast Contract to be terminated, alleging the expiration of the agreed term of six months. The contract provided for the liquidation procedure and liquidation commission. The claimants argued that Ecuador's lack of good faith with respect to the acts and omissions of the liquidation commission led to the breach of FET standard.

It is interesting to note that the claimant's argument is not specifically framed in terms of a breach of its legitimate expectations. However, it is the tribunal who assessed the FET standard with reference to legitimate expectations. In assessing the legitimacy of investors' expectations, the tribunal paid special attention to 'the content of the enforceable obligations'. In this regard, the tribunal determined the scope of protection of claimant's legitimate expectations regarding the successful handling of

[59] Ibid para 422.

the liquidation of the contract by considering the scope and legal effects of the contractual provisions. The tribunal held that the investor's expectation is *not* part of the agreement

> as to the outcome of the negotiations in the Liquidation Commission *cannot be disassociated from the scope and legal effects of* (Clause 17 of the Contract.) *This clause does not give rise to an obligation to resolve existing disputes between the parties relating to the interpretation and application of the Contract.* The fact that the parties did not achieve a definitive settlement at the Liquidation Commission could not give rise to a breach of the fair and equitable treatment standards.[60]

Furthermore, at issue is the claimant's expectations in respect to an arbitration agreement (i.e. the allegation of Ecuador's bad faith in frustrating an arbitration process for resolving the question). The claimant argued that Ecuador broke its promise to submit the dispute to arbitration.[61] The issue is whether Ecuador can engage international responsibility for the frustration of this expectation. The tribunal resorted to the voluntarist conception by suggesting that there was no evidence of *a legally binding commitment to sign an arbitration agreement.*[62] In other words, the reasonableness of the expectation is a matter of whether the respondent had assumed a legal obligation. The tribunal's adherence to the voluntarist conception is confirmed by the suggestion that the investor's expectation should be based on 'an acquired right'.[63]

4.3.1.1.3 ***Electrabel v. Hungary*** The tribunal had to consider whether regulatory measures introduced as part of the obligation from accession to the European Union violated the investor's expectations grounded in legislative framework and contractual arrangement (power purchasing

[60] *MCI v. Ecuador* (n 52) ibid para 279 (emphasis added).

[61] Ibid para 307 ('With the failure of the Liquidation Commission, the Claimants maintain that Ecuador reneged on its promise to submit the dispute to arbitration, and then obstructed judicial proceedings before the courts of Ecuador, thereby denying the possibility of resolving the dispute in any forum.').

[62] Ibid para 324 (In the tribunal's view, the failure of the negotiations for an arbitration agreement did not violate the BIT standard of fair and equitable treatment, and hence did not engage Ecuador's responsibility for any expectations that Seacoast might have entertained for reaching such agreement.).

[63] Ibid para 322 (Seacoast's expectations with respect to signature of an arbitration agreement cannot be based on *any acquired right* to reach that agreement as a consequence of an obligation assumed by Ecuador. The Claimants did not prove the existence of the obligation on the part of the Ecuadorian authorities to reach an arbitration agreement.).

agreement).[64] The claimant, who had investment in the electricity supply sector entered into the power purchase agreement (PPA) with Hungary's state-owned enterprise. Subsequent to the accession to the European Union, Hungary had to introduce a series of measures to comply with its EU obligations, which frustrated the investor's expectations. Three main claims are analysed to show how the voluntarist conception influences the final outcome of the case on legitimate expectations.

With regard to the PPA pricing claim, the claimant alleged that Hungary interfered with the contractual relationship, especially in the pricing of electricity under its PPA as of 2006. The tribunal was not convinced that the state-enterprise's conduct was attributable to Hungary.[65] However, the tribunal proceeded to analyse the substantive question, assuming some act could be attributed to Hungary. Whilst the tribunal focused on various types of conduct of the state through legislative provisions as well as the deregulated price regime,[66] the tribunal injected a very important caveat that 'such expectations could not be isolated from the common knowledge that deregulation could not cohabit with long-term PPAs having guaranteed quantities and guaranteed prices'. In this regard, the tribunal engaged in the assessment of the reasonableness of such expectations, taking into account the change of circumstances (Hungary's accession to the European Union).[67] It concluded that it was not reasonable to expect that the negotiations for 2004 and 2005 would be the reference point in 2006. However, it did not cite the absence of legal commitment as the basis.

In contrast to the regulated pricing claim, the claimant's expectations that regulated pricing would not be reintroduced are deemed unreasonable because Hungary did not voluntarily assume such obligation. The tribunal referred to the absence of express provisions guaranteed, which guaranteed the return, and to the agreed provision that shifted various risks to the investor.[68] In addition, the explicit recognition by the tribunal of Hungary's sovereign power to introduce regulated pricing

64 *Electrabel v. Hungary* (n 53) ibid para 6.66 (The claim for the premature termination of Dunamenti's PPA, one of seven PPAs concluded by Hungarian Generators with MVM, will not be analysed because the FET standard is not discussed in terms of legitimate expectations.).

65 Ibid para 7.138.

66 Ibid para 7.139.

67 Ibid para 7.140.

68 Ibid para 8.19.

reinforces the voluntarist nature of undertaking and the need for explicit guarantee to the contrary effect.

With regard to the G1 Unit claim, the claimant alleged that the exclusion of G1 Unit (co-generation unit) from the 2002 Mandatory Off-Take Decree was contrary to the expectation that it would enjoy off-take support indefinitely. However, the tribunal held that Hungary never made any specific promise that its electricity production in the G1 Unit would be covered by off-take decrees.[69] The tribunal relied on the absence of 'any specific promise, assurance or representation' amounting to a legal obligation to deny that 'aspirations' can amount to a legitimate expectation binding on Hungary.[70]

4.3.1.1.4 ***Hochtief v. Argentina*** The *Hochtief v. Argentina* case affirmed the essential claim of the voluntarist conception of legitimate expectations that an investor has a right to legitimately expect what a state has specifically promised. The dispute arose in the background of an Argentinian economic crisis and involved the concession contract for construction, maintenance and operation of roads and bridges in Argentina.[71] The claimant made two relevant claims based on legitimate expectations:[72] the 'pesification process' and the failed renegotiation attempts.

As for the pesification process, the investor's expectations for continuity of dollar–peso parity are based on representations by the authority and the contractual arrangement. The tribunal, however, held that such expectations were not part of the contractual representation made by the state because in fact the state only promised *the maintenance of value of the revenues*; therefore, its expectations about dollar–peso parity was not reasonable:

> In these circumstances, the majority of the Tribunal considers that what Respondent promised, and what Claimant had the right to expect, was *the maintenance of the value, in dollar terms, of the revenues under the*

[69] Ibid para 9.10 ('[T]he Tribunal also determines that the G1 Unit was never the subject of *any specific promise, assurance or representation* from Hungary that its electricity production would be covered by Off-Take Decrees, effectively ensuring that Dunamenti should have available a permanent purchaser for all electricity produced by the G1 Unit at regulated prices insulated from the open market' [emphasis added]).

[70] Ibid.

[71] *Hochtief v. Argentina* (n 54).

[72] In the first claim, the claim was not explicitly framed in terms of legitimate expectations. The tribunal was not convinced that the respondent's failures to meet the contractual dates for payments of the subsidy rose to the level of a violation of the FET standard.

> *Contract.* Precisely how that value was maintained was, in the view of the majority of the Tribunal, not specified. *Claimant did not have a legal right specifically to have that value maintained by means of constant adherence to peso-dollar parity.*[73]

The quoted passage confirms that the voluntarist conception underlined this part of the tribunal's reasoning because the tribunal focused *on the congruence of what the state had actually promised and what the investor expected.* The tribunal pointed out that the state promised the maintenance of the commercial balance in the contract but not the continuation of dollar–peso parity.[74] Therefore, the claimant had only the right to expect that the resulting disruption of the commercial balance would be corrected fully and in a timely manner but not the right to expect that there would never, in any circumstances, be any departure from parity.[75]

With regard to the claim on the renegotiation process, the tribunal held that the respondent's failure to implement the promised renegotiation process in a timely manner constituted a breach of the FET standard because the renegotiation process was a necessary element in the fulfilment of the respondent's obligation after the pesification:

> Respondent's conduct amounts to more than *the disappointment of the hopes and expectations of the Project Consortium.* It crosses the line between what is merely suboptimal administration and bureaucratic delay, and it becomes a failure to remedy the adverse consequences of governmental measures that is so prolonged and so complete as to infringe the investor's rights under the Treaty.[76]

The quoted passage suggests that liability is not exclusively grounded in terms of disappointment of legitimate expectations but the failure to remedy the adverse consequences of governmental action.

4.3.1.1.5 ***Nordzucker v. Poland*** The case of *Nordzucker v. Poland* raises the issue of protection of legitimate expectations created by quasi-contractual arrangement. The tribunal relied on the bidding rules as the threshold for determining the scope of protection of legitimate

[73] *Hochtief v. Argentina* (n 54) para 238 (emphasis added).
[74] Ibid para 239 ('Neither the Bidding Terms nor the Concession Contract, nor any other instrument presented to the Tribunal, contains any specific and absolute undertaking not in any circumstances to pesify the Contract').
[75] Ibid para 241.
[76] Ibid para 282 (emphasis added).

expectation as well as taking into account the investor's knowledge of regulatory risks.[77]

This dispute arose against the background of the sugar industry's privatisation in Poland. The claimants, as the winning bidder, had the expectation, based on the bidding rules, of being able to purchase Sugar Plants in the privatisation programme. However, the progress for the sale of the plants stopped as the government considered new valuations of the sugar plants. After a series of events, the claimants failed to acquire the plants.

The tribunal denied the claimant's expectations for the reason that '*the rules were very clear that the winning bidder only meant that it could engage in negotiations and there was no guarantee for becoming the purchaser*'.[78] The tribunal emphasised that the claimant's only legitimate expectation was that there would be negotiations. The reasonableness or legitimacy of the expectations under this conception depends on whether there is a guarantee to the effect. The tribunal's considerations of the circumstances of the host state in assessing reasonableness of expectations, which is characteristic of the reliance conception, may call into question its adherence to the voluntarist conception.[79] However, one could read such circumstantial and contextual evidence as merely suggesting whether the promise had been made in accordance with the voluntarist conception framework, which would allow social practice and circumstances to be taken into account when determining whether the promise has been made.

4.3.1.2 Critique of Assimilationist Approach

Why is assimilation of contractual right and treaty right objectionable? It is a well-accepted principle of international law that a mere breach of

[77] *Nordzucker v. Poland* (n 55).

[78] Ibid para 87 (emphasis added) ('[T]he tribunal, upon review of the evidence available, comes to the conclusion that this expectation of Nordzucker was not reasonable and legitimate. The Rules were clear that being the winning bidder only meant that it could engage in negotiations, also on the price, and that upon closing of the price negotiations, the Management Board had to present its decision to the GAM which had to approve it.').

[79] Ibid para 88 ('*The expectations must be tested in relation to the circumstances and context.* Nordzucker *was or must have been aware of the threat* that a national sugar company might be created and that the groups it targeted might also be interesting for that new entity. In the political context of Poland at the time, *Nordzucker should have been aware* that political opposition could make the privatisation difficult if not impossible and it was or must have been aware that this political situation could be a reason why the consent of the Ministry in the GAM or the Sugar Holding companies might be withheld' [emphasis added]).

contract does not *per se* constitute an international responsibility because these are two distinct questions governed by two sets of applicable rules. This principle is embedded in investment treaty arbitration, as recognised by the authority case on this issue, *the Vivendi Annulment Decision*:

> As to the relation between breach of contract and breach of treaty . . . [a] state may breach a treaty without breaching a contract, and vice versa . . . In accordance with this general principle (which is undoubtedly declaratory of general international law), *whether there has been a breach of the BIT and whether there has been a breach of contract are different questions.* Each of these claims will be determined by reference to its own proper or applicable law – in the case of the BIT, by international law; in the case of the [contract], by the proper law of the contract, in other words the [municipal law].[80]

This position is supported by Professor Crawford who endorsed the view of the ad hoc annulment committee in *MTD v. Chile*, reiterating that legal obligations cannot derive from any expectations entertained by investors.[81] It should be based on the investor's dealings with the authorities.[82] The principle on the distinctiveness of contract and treaty breaches is particularly significant in light of the claim based on legitimate expectation, which seeks to override this distinction.

The objection to the assimilationist approach lies with the effect of upsetting the contractual bargain between the parties by allowing one party to enforce the contractual obligation through international law mechanism. Professor Crawford asserted that 'reference to a general and vague standard of legitimate expectations is no substitute for contractual rights. The relevance of legitimate expectations is not a license to arbitral tribunals to rewrite the freely negotiated terms of investment contracts.'[83] Similarly, Professor Douglas criticised this attempt on the

[80] *Compañiá de Aguas del Aconquija S.A. and Vivendi Universal v. Argentina*, ICSID Case No ARB/97/3, Decision on Annulment (3 July 2002) paras 95–96 (emphasis added).

[81] Ibid para 67 ('the obligations of the host State towards foreign investors derive from the terms of the applicable investment treaty and not from any set of expectations investors may have or claim to have').

[82] Ibid para 69 ('legitimate expectations generated as a result of the investor's dealings with the competent authorities of the host State may be relevant to the application of the guarantees in an investment treaty').

[83] J Crawford, 'Treaty and Contract in Investment Arbitration' (2008) 24(1) *Arbitration Int'l* 374.

ground that treaty provision should not be used to enforce contractual obligations.[84]

The previously mentioned criticsm only addressed the voluntarist conception of legitimate expectations. It will be illustrated in Chapter 5 that the reliance conception of legitimate expectations can overcome this undesirable effect because a wrong from the contract breach is not *contractual wrong* but rather *a delict*. The voluntarist principle which underlines the reasoning in the selected cases just discussed allows the tribunal to surpass the need to prove various delictual elements for establishing international responsibility from a breach of contract, such as discrimination, due process or arbitrariness. This consequence provides a strong reason to reject this conception.

4.3.1.3 The Voluntarist Principle and Non-contractual Expectations

This section discusses the decisions of *Parkerings v. Lithuania*[85] and *Hamester v. Ghana*,[86] which attempt to negate the 'assimilationist' effect of the voluntarist principle. Their different approaches confirm the same point – that contractual expectation is not protected under the principle of legitimate expectations. But is this position possible under the voluntarist principle? Are the tribunals simply applying the alternative conception of legitimate expectations?

4.3.1.3.1 *Parkerings v. Lithuania* The tribunal considered the claimant's two expectations created by the parking licensing agreement, namely (1) the expectation that the municipality of Vilnius had informed the claimant about possible amendment of the law and would protect the claimant against the potential economic impact of such modification on the agreement and (2) the expectation that the respondent would maintain legal stability.

On the first expectation, the tribunal considered whether the fact that the city of Vilnius failed to advise the claimant about possible

[84] Z Douglas, 'Nothing If Not Critical in Investment Treaty Arbitration' (2006) 22 *Arb Int'l* 27, 41–42 ('[A]nother device that has been employed to undermine the contractual bargain is to convert the provisions of a contract relied upon by the investor into "legitimate expectations" and then to enforce those expectations through the medium of a claim for FET. This device cannot be endorsed either.').

[85] *Parkerings Compagniet AS v. Lithuania*, ICSID Case No ARB/05/8, Award on Jurisdiction and Merits (14 August 2007).

[86] *Gustav F W Hamester GmbH & Co. KG v. Ghana*, ICSID Case No ARB/07/24, Award (18 June 2010).

amendments of the law, which might affect the agreement, gave rise to a breach of legitimate expectations. The key question was whether such obligation was embodied in the contractual provisions (i.e. whether the state had promised to advise the investor). The tribunal rejected the claim by introducing the distinction between 'contractual expectations' and 'other expectations protected by international law' in the following terms:

> It is evident that not every hope amounts to an expectation under international law. *The expectation a party to an agreement may have of the regular fulfilment of the obligation by the other party is not necessarily an expectation protected by international law.* In other words, *contracts involve intrinsic expectations from each party that do not amount to expectations as understood in international law.*[87]

The quoted passage calls for some critical observations. First, the tribunal concluded that the failure to disclose information regarding the change of regulatory framework might breach 'the contractual obligation to act and negotiate in good faith',[88] but that did not in itself constitute a treaty breach. The tribunal rejected that the claimant's contractual expectation of the regular fulfilment of the obligation would alleviate the contractual wrong to the level of international responsibility.

The tribunal's reliance on the distinction between 'contractual expectations' of regular fulfilment of the obligation and 'other expectations protected in international law' is understandable but unhelpful because the tribunal did not explain what the latter type of expectations might entail. However, one scholar suggests that the type of expectation protected under international law is only that the state would not breach the contract by stepping outside the contractual framework and employing extra-contractual public or governmental powers.[89]

[87] *Parkerings v. Lithuania* (n 85) para 344 (emphasis added).

[88] Ibid para 335 (It is evident that the respondent, as already mentioned, had the contractual obligation to act and negotiate in good faith prior to the conclusion of the Agreement. By failing to do so, it may have breached the agreement, but that is not a matter for this tribunal.).

[89] M Paparinskis, *The International Minimum Standard* (Oxford: Oxford University Press, 2013) 226 (he suggests that the expectation is only that the type of 'expectations protected under international law in the context of contractual arrangements seems to be the expectation as to non-interference with contractual relationship, namely that the State does not use its sovereign power to upset the contractual equilibrium').

The key question is whether the non-contractual expectation (of non-interference) which arises from the contract can be accommodated by the voluntarist principle. It could be argued that such 'obligation' might be inferred because it is necessary for the fulfilment of contractual performance. In any case, we could interpret the proviso of the voluntarist principle – 'social convention may determine what acts can reasonably be taken to express an intention to undertake an obligation' – to give effect to such non-contractual or implicit obligations.

On the second expectation of legal stability, the tribunal held that such an expectation is not reasonable because

> the legitimate expectations of the Claimant that the legal regime would remain unchanged are not based on or reinforced by *a particular behaviour* of the Respondent . . . In other words, the Republic of Lithuania did not give *any explicit or implicit promise that the legal framework of the Agreement would remain unchanged.*[90]

The tribunal set out the threshold for assessing reasonableness of expectations, which reflects the voluntarist rationale, as follows:

> The expectation is legitimate if the investor received *an explicit promise or guaranty* from the host-State, or if implicitly, the host-State made assurances or representation that the investor took into account in making the investment. Finally, in the situation where the host-State made no assurance or representation, *the circumstances surrounding the conclusion of the agreement are decisive to determine if the expectation of the investor was legitimate.* In order to determine the legitimate expectation of an investor, it is also necessary to analyse the conduct of the State at the time of the investment.[91]

Two observations can be made in relation to the reasoning in the quoted passage. First, it is unclear whether 'an explicit promise or guarantee' has to be of a legally binding character. However, in the next paragraph, the tribunal's adherence to the voluntarist conception is reflected in its confirmation that a stabilisation clause, which is an express manifestation of the will of the state in relation to legal stability, could protect the investor's legitimate expectations.[92]

[90] *Parkerings v. Lithuania* (n 85) para 334 (emphasis added).
[91] Ibid para 331 (emphasis added).
[92] Ibid para 336 ('the Claimant could (and with hindsight should) have sought to protect its legitimate expectations by introducing into the investment agreement a stabilisation clause or some other provision protecting it against unexpected and unwelcome changes').

Second, in the situation, where there was no assurance or representation, the tribunal emphasised the relevance of 'the circumstances surrounding the conclusion of the agreement'[93] as well as the conduct of the state in determining the legitimacy of expectation. How could there be legitimate expectation where there was no assurance, representation under the voluntary conception? The tribunal's reasoning could be explained by the proviso that social practice could determine which acts express an intention to undertake an obligation.

4.3.1.3.2 ***Hamester v. Ghana*** The significance of the *Hamester v. Ghana* case is that the tribunal seems to have suggested that the principle of legitimate expectations has no role to play in determining state responsibility arising from a contract breach. The claimant attempted to establish an international responsibility from a breach of the joint venture agreement between the claimant and the respondent's state entity. However, the tribunal held that the claimant's expectation as to the fulfilment of contractual obligation (delivery of the requested amount of cocoa beans) was not protected, endorsing Professor Wälde's objection to equating contractual rights with legitimate expectations (on the basis that it would endorse the umbrella clause by the back door): [94]

> It is not sufficient for a claimant to invoke contractual rights that have allegedly been infringed to sustain a claim for a violation of the FET standard. Thus, *even if attributed to Ghana, and even if the impugned acts were 'sovereign' in nature, the alleged contract violations could not have amounted to a violation of the FET standard based on a theory of 'legitimate expectations'*.[95]

Two critical observations can be made with regard to the tribunal's reasoning. First, the basis for the tribunal's objection to the theory of

[93] Ibid para 335 (As any businessman would, the claimant was aware of the risk that changes of laws would probably occur after the conclusion of the agreement. The circumstances surrounding the decision to invest in Lithuania were certainly not an indication of stability of the legal environment. Therefore, in such a situation, no expectation that the laws would remain unchanged was legitimate.).

[94] *Hamester v. Ghana* (n 86) para 336 (Schreuer also explained that contractual rights are not to be equated with legitimate expectations: 'Taken to its logical conclusion this argument would put all agreements between the investor and the host State under the protection of the FET standard. If this position were to be accepted, the FET standard would be nothing less than a broadly interpreted umbrella clause.').

[95] Ibid para 337 (emphasis added).

legitimate expectations is unclear. Is it because the theory of legitimate expectations does not add any value to the legal analysis since the general rules concerning a breach of contract and treaty could provide an adequate standard for liability? Or does the tribunal's objection lie in the fact that the theory can turn a purely contract breach into a treaty breach?

However, the tribunal stated that even 'sovereign breach' would not be adequate to trigger liability under the theory of legitimate expectations. According to the investment treaty jurisprudence, an exercise of sovereign power in breaching a contract could lead to international responsibility for the reason of misuse of power. For instance, the tribunal in *Impregilo v. Argentina* stated that

> there may be cases where a state entity which has concluded a contract with an investor performs acts which do not only constitute a breach of the contract but are at the same time a misuse of its status as part of the State organization to the detriment of the investor and thereby involve the State's responsibility as party to a BIT.

For this reason, the tribunal's reasoning is rather curious.

4.3.2 *Limited Scope of Legitimate Expectations and Administrative Representations*

These types of representations do not usually create a legal obligation though they are likely to engender certain expectations in the investors. The term 'administrative representations' generally connotes various types of representations by public officials, which are generally non-contractual and non-legislative in nature. These may include but are not limited to political statements, policy or memorandum, guidelines as well as consistent practices. Can these representations express 'an intention to undertake an obligation', such that they create legitimate expectations under the voluntarist conception?

The analysis of the following selected cases illustrates the point that administrative representations are unlikely to meet the necessary threshold under the voluntarist conception in order to create legitimate expectations because these representations are not legally binding or create any rights. The analysis concerns three types of representations: political statements, policy statements and meeting records.

4.3.2.1 Political Statements

The tribunal in *El Paso v. Argentina*[96] illustrates that political statements are unlikely to create legitimate expectations under the voluntarist principle. The tribunal refused to give effect to a political statement made jointly by the president of the republic and the minister of economy, even though such representation could induce potential investors to invest in the sector concerned. The essence of the representation was to assure that the enactment of the Electricity Law gave the legal certainty to the process of transformation of the electricity sector, thus preventing the ancient lack of stability of the rules of the game'.[97]

The tribunal confirmed that political statements might induce an economic decision, but it is not the same as claiming legal guarantees.[98] The tribunal's reasoning was implicitly guided by the voluntarist conception, which focuses on the will of the state to undertake a legal guarantee, without regard to the inducing effect of the representation. If the assurance or reliance conception were to be adopted, the tribunal *might* have upheld the claim because the focus of enquiry would no longer be on the will of the state and its legal guarantee, but other factors would be relevant, such as the effect of inducing investment or providing assurance to the investor or the detrimental reliance of the investor.

4.3.2.2 Policy Statements

The effect of legitimate expectations and policy statements is considered, amongst other cases, in *PSEG v. Turkey*.[99] The claimant was granted authorisation to conduct a feasibility study into the building of a coal-fired power plant. The dispute arose out of the background of Turkey's liberalisation of the energy sector to meet increased energy demands in the 1980s. The claimant and the Turkish Ministry of Energy and Natural

[96] *El Paso Energy International Company v. The Argentine Republic*, ICSID Case No ARB/03/15, Award (31 October 2011).

[97] Ibid para 393.

[98] Ibid para 395 ('Moreover, a declaration made by the President of the Republic clearly must be viewed by everyone as a political statement, and this Tribunal is aware, as is every individual, of the limited confidence that can be given to such political statements in all countries of the world. *It might well be that these representations contributed to inducing potential investors to invest in the sectors concerned, as many of them – including El Paso – actually did. But it is one thing to be induced by political proposals to make an economic decision, and another thing to be able to rely on these proposals to claim legal guarantees'* [emphasis added]).

[99] *PSEG Global Inc. and Konya Ilgin Elektrik Uretim ve Ticaret Limited Sirketi v. Republic of Turkey*, ICSID Case No ARB/02/5, Award (10 January 2007).

Resources failed to reach agreement on the capacity of the plant and the tariffs. In the meantime, the legal framework underwent a change with the enactment of a new law barring investors from obtaining a Treasury guarantee. The new law was subsequently quashed by the Supreme Court. The relevant issue for the tribunal was whether the foreign investment policy could generate a legitimate expectation.

In rejecting the claim for legitimate expectations, the tribunal made a distinction between 'general policy' and 'a promise made specifically to the investor' in demarcating the reasonableness of the investor's expectation in the following terms:

> [T]he whole BOT [build-operate-transfer] policy was built on the premise that foreign investments would be needed, encouraged and welcome, but this was *a matter of general policy* that did not *entail a promise* made specifically to the Claimants about the success of their proposed project.[100]

The actual meaning of the term 'promise' employed by the tribunal is unclear: whether it refers to a legally binding arrangement or a specific representation to the investor. Based on the reasoning guided by the voluntarist principle, the promise must have referred to a legal undertaking. Nevertheless, the tribunal found a breach of fair and equitable treatment based on the 'roller-coaster' effect of continuing legislative changes.[101]

The issue concerning the extent to which policy can create legitimate expectations distinguishes the scope of legitimate expectations in municipal public laws and investment treaty arbitration. There is a greater tendency for municipal public laws to recognise legitimate expectations created by policy than in investment treaty arbitration.[102] However, it is interesting to note that the concept of 'promise' is employed as the threshold for determining whether the expectation is reasonable. Let us briefly illustrate this with reference to one English case law in *R (Bancoult) v. Secretary of State for Foreign and Commonwealth Affairs*.[103]

This case illustrates the division of the English Supreme Court over the meaning of the statement made by the foreign secretary, which suggested

[100] Ibid para 243 (emphasis added).

[101] Ibid para 250.

[102] R Clayton, 'Legitimate Expectations, Policy, and the Principle of Consistency' (2003) 62(1) *CLJ* 93.

[103] *R. (on the application of Bancoult) v. Secretary of State for Foreign and Commonwealth Affairs* [2008] UKHL 61; [2009] I A.C. 453.

that the UK government accepted a court ruling that the inhabitants of the island in the British Indian Ocean Territory had been unlawfully removed to make way for a US air base. Lord Hoffman held that the statement did not contain any unambiguous promise with respect to the right to return. On the other hand, Lord Mance considered that

> these statements are only consistent with a clear policy decision taken by the United Kingdom to recognise and give legal effect to a right to return on the part of the Chagossians, while continuing the feasibility study which had already been started, in order to assess the feasibility of any resettlement programme which the Government might or might not in due course support.

4.3.2.3 Meeting Records and Letters of Correspondence

The tribunal in *GEA v. Ukraine* had to consider whether the claimant's expectations concerning their entitlement to compensation money for property wrongfully taken by the government are legitimate.[104] Such expectations were based mostly on records of meeting and letter of correspondence. For instance, the claimant relied on the representation that Ukraine would promptly 'work out' the amount of misappropriated property and the repayment timetable, especially the Parties' indication that they would 'make a final decision on this problem'.[105] The tribunal dismissed the claim because

> the Tribunal struggles to see how Ukraine's promise to 'work out' the amount of misappropriated property and a payment timetable could amount to *a promise to pay*, particularly in light of the Parties' indication that they would 'make a final decision on this problem' at a later date.[106]

The claimant also relied on the letter from the Ministry of Economy, which recommended the preparation of an inventory record and a promise to 'take control of the missing quantities'.[107]

Similarly, the tribunal did not view that the recommendation to prepare an inventory and a promise to 'take control of the missing quantities' could constitute 'a promise on the part of Ukraine to make any sort of payment to GEA'.

[104] *GEA Group Aktiengesellschaft v. Ukraine,* ICSID Case No ARB/08/16, Award (31 March 2011).
[105] Ibid para 278.
[106] Ibid.
[107] Ibid para 279.

The claimant further relied on the recording of a meeting which suggested 'specific obligations of the State, including an express undertaking that the Ministry of Industrial Policy would ensure that the provisions of the protocol would be fulfilled by the Ukrainian party'.[108] The tribunal dismissed that such promises were related to the payment for the lost products.

The tribunal dismissed the claim based on the vice prime minister's statement that 'Ukraine will do its part to resolve the problem' because it could not be interpreted as *a promise* by Ukraine to pay for lost products.[109]

Similarly, with regard to the claimant's expectations about the debt recovery in the bankruptcy, the claimant relied on a series of letters – for instance, the letter from the Ministry of Industrial Policy which stated that 'the Cabinet of Ministers of Ukraine will pass a document which [. . .] will cancel these bankruptcy proceedings', the protocols of meetings, which stated that 'the Ukrainian party shall carry out all acts permitted by applicable legislation of Ukraine in order to terminate the bankruptcy proceedings pending against JSC Oriana'.[110] The tribunal held that these statements could not be considered *unconditional promises* for payment. Rather, they suggested that best efforts would be made to assist in bringing the bankruptcy proceedings to an end according to Ukrainian law.[111]

From the analysis of the *GEA v. Ukraine* case, it is interesting to see how the tribunal employed the term 'promise' as a banner to reject the claims for legitimate expectations. Like many other decisions, the tribunal did not clarify whether the promise refers to a legally binding act. The context seems to indicate such conception.

Furthermore, a distinction between 'promise' and 'unconditional promise' in the two claims is rather curious. The term 'unconditional promise' refers to a representation, which may be specific in content but does not contain a legal commitment. On this point, it is interesting

108 Ibid para 281.

109 Ibid para 282.

110 Ibid para 288 ('a letter dated 31 July 1998 from the Ukrainian Ministry of Industrial Policy, which states that "the Cabinet of Ministers of Ukraine will pass a document which, under current Ukrainian law, will cancel these bankruptcy proceedings"').

111 Ibid para 291 ('the Tribunal agrees with the Respondent. In the Tribunal's view, the statements made by the Respondent cannot be read as unconditional promises for payment. At most, these statements, taken together, may be read as Ukraine engaging to use its best efforts to assist in bringing the bankruptcy proceedings to an end within the scope of Ukrainian law.').

to recall what the tribunal in *El Paso* stated in relation to the notion of 'specific commitment':

> [T]here can indeed exist *specific commitments directly made to the investor* – for example in a contract or in a letter of intent, or even through a specific promise in a person-to-person business meeting. The important aspect of the commitment is not so much that it is legally binding . . . but that it contains a specific commitment directly made to the investor, on which the latter has relied.[112]

One possible explanation for this divergence is that the tribunal in *GEA* subscribed to the voluntarist conception as it implicitly used the term 'promise' in a legally binding sense, contrary to the reliance conception of promise in *El Paso*.

4.3.3 'Neutralization of the Normative Power of States': Legal Stability and Voluntarist Conception of Legitimate Expectations

This section considers the implication of the voluntarist conception on the investor's expectation of legal stability. The main questions are (1) under what circumstances can the investor legitimately expect legal stability under the voluntarist conception and (2) can a legislative framework constitute 'a promise'?

Under the voluntarist conception, the investor's expectations of legal stability have a high threshold. Two main sources of expectations are considered: the legislative framework and (contractual) stabilisation clause. In the first scenario, the law must be specific in terms of entitlement and beneficiary (a particular investor or a specific group of investors) so that 'an intention to undertake an obligation' can be inferred. In the second scenario, states may undertake a specific commitment not to change the law through contractual provision (stabilisation clause).

These two instances can be characterised as, in the term used by the French arbitrator Pierre Mayer, 'neutralization of the normative power of States'.[113] In essence, the state exercises its own sovereign power to 'neutralize' or 'limit' its future action for its benefit of attracting foreign investment by giving normative assurance. The following selected cases illustrate the two instances of this phenomenon, which has some normative implication for our understanding of legitimate expectations.

112 *El Paso v. Argentina* (n 96) para 376 (emphasis added).

113 P Mayer, 'La neutralisation du pouvoir normatif de l'Etat en matière de contrats d'Etat' (1986) *J Droit Int'l* 5, cited in Paulson, 'The Power of States' (n 20).

4.3.3.1 Legislative Neutralisation of the Normative Power

The specificity of the legislative framework in question is the key element to determining the reasonableness of the expectations which the law generates. The implication of the voluntarist theory of legitimate expectations can be stated as follows: in order for the legislative framework to give rise to legitimate expectations, the law must be a specific 'promise' made to a particular group of investors about a specific benefit. It is the legally binding nature of the law, which provides the basis for an obligation to protect legitimate expectations. The essence of the decision of *Total v. Argentina* endorses this view.[114]

In this case, the tribunal examined the nature of legislative framework in considering whether the relevant legislative framework (the Gas Law and the Gas Decree of 1992) invoked by Total constitute 'a set of promises and commitments' towards Total, whose unilateral modifications entail a breach of the legitimate expectations.[115] The respondent argued that it did not breach any promise or guarantee because it did not execute any contract with the claimant nor did it induce the claimant to make an investment. The legislative provisions invoked by the claimant only constituted 'the totality of the regulatory framework'.

The tribunal held that the legal regime in force was not automatically subject to a 'guarantee' of stability. The tribunal made it clear that expectations engendered by legislation or regulation of a *unilateral and general* character could not give rise to a legitimate expectation because it is not specifically addressed to the relevant investor.[116] Consequently, the tribunal held that the Gas Regulatory Framework did not contain specific promises with regard to the calculation of the gas tariffs in US dollars and the automatic adjustment of the tariffs according to the US PPI because they were not addressed directly or indirectly to Total.[117] Therefore, the currency peg provisions were susceptible to subsequent amendment in the absence of specific stabilisation promise.[118] It is important to note

[114] *Total v. Argentina* (n 48).

[115] Ibid para 99.

[116] The similar reasoning is adopted in *TECO Guatemala Holdings, LLC v. Republic of Guatemala,* ICSID Case No ARB/10/23, Award (19 December 2013) para 617 ('In the Arbitral Tribunal's view, in a regulatory context, a distinction needs to be made between the expectations arising from a specific representation that the legal framework will not change in all or in part, and the general expectation that the legal framework will not be applied arbitrarily.').

[117] Ibid paras 145 and 149.

[118] *Total v. Argentina* (n 48) para 164 ('Such changes to general legislation, in the absence of specific stabilization promises to the foreign investor, reflect a legitimate exercise of the

that Total did not enter into a contractual relationship with Argentina's authorities when it acquired an indirect share in the concessionaire (TGN). Total could not rely on TGN's licence as a contractual commitment undertaken by Argentina which set out the rights and obligations of the parties, because Total was not a party to the concession.

On the whole, the tribunal's reasoning on legitimate expectations was consistent with the voluntarist principle, which emphasises a legally binding character of the representation. Two important observations can be stated. First, legislation or regulation of a unilateral and general character can hardly generate legitimate expectations and will not be shielded from subsequent changes under the applicable law.[119] Second, the tribunal's exposition of the concept of legitimate expectations causes some confusion as to the underlying basis for an obligation to protect legitimate expectations: Is it a legally binding promise or a detrimental reliance upon that promise? The tribunal confusingly referred to both elements without articulating normative values of each element. On the close reading of the tribunal's reasoning, it can be argued that this case is underlined by the voluntarist conception of legitimate expectations, predominantly with reference to the following passages:

> The expectation of the investor is undoubtedly 'legitimate', and hence subject to protection under the fair and equitable treatment clause, *if the host State has explicitly assumed a specific legal obligation for the future, such as by contracts, concessions or stabilisation clauses on which the investor is therefore entitled to rely as a matter of law.*[120] . . . *No less relevant is the clarity with which the authorities have expressed their intention to bind themselves for the future.*[121]

4.3.3.2 Contractual Neutralisation of the Normative Power

There is considerable support in the jurisprudence for the contention that the stabilisation clause could protect the investor's expectation of legal immutability.[122] These investment decisions endorse the voluntarist

host State's governmental powers that are not prevented by a BIT's fair and equitable treatment standard and are not in breach of the same.').

119 Ibid para 122.

120 Ibid para 117 (emphasis added).

121 Ibid para 121 (emphasis added).

122 *AES Summit Generation Limited and AES–Tisza Erömü Kft. v. Hungary*, ICSID Case No ARB/07/22, Award (23 September 2010) (2011) 50 *ILM* 186 para 9.3.29 ('It is also common ground that the 2001 Settlement Agreement does not contain a so-called "stabilization clause" – i.e. a covenant not to change the relevant law [. . .] 81. In these circumstances, the Tribunal concludes that Claimants cannot legitimately

conception of legitimate expectations because the stabilisation clause represents a manifestation of the will to guarantee legal stability. However, the legal effect of the stabilisation clause is that states have to compensate an investor for changing the law rather than being prohibited to do so.[123]

This view resonates with the position adopted by the tribunal in *EDF v. Romania*, which suggested that in normal circumstances, an expectation as to the stability of the legal and business framework is neither legitimate nor reasonable because the virtual freezing of the legal regulation would be contrary to sovereign power.[124] However, the tribunal confirmed that 'where *specific promises or representations* are made by the State to the investor',[125] such expectation will be reasonable.

It should be explained that under the voluntarist conception, the specificity of the undertaking indicates the level of voluntariness, which provides the obligation basis. This rationale explains why political statements, which do not represent a legal commitment, create no legitimate expectations.[126] General legislative statements tend to be more specific, but no particular commitment is made to a particular promisee, therefore 'engender reduced expectations'. Contractual undertakings, which are promissory in nature and often addressed to a particular investor about a specific benefit, can create more legitimate expectations.

The decision of *Metalpar v. Argentina*[127] illustrates that the investor's expectations of legal stability have to be based on contractual

have been led by Hungary to expect that a regime of administrative pricing would not be reintroduced.'); *Parkerings v. Lithuania* (n 85) para 332.

123 M Hirsch, 'Between Fair and Equitable Treatment and Stabilization Clause: Stable Legal Environment and Regulatory Change in International Investment Law' (2011) 12 *JWIT* 783 ('The sensitive issue relates to the question of whether such contractual clauses do indeed impose a blanket prohibition on the host state to change its domestic legislation under international law; or whether they only bind the host government to compensate the investor for deviating from the stabilization provisions.').

124 *EDF (Services) Ltd v. Romania*, ICSID Case No ARB/05/13, Award (2 October 2009) para 217 ('the idea that legitimate expectations, and therefore FET, imply the stability of the legal and business framework, may not be correct if stated in an overly-broad and unqualified formulation. The FET might then mean the virtual freezing of the legal regulation of economic activities, in contrast with the State's normal regulatory power and the evolutionary character of economic life.').

125 Ibid ('*Except where specific promises or representations are made by the State to the investor,* the latter may not rely on a bilateral investment treaty as a kind of insurance policy against the risk of any changes in the host State's legal and economic framework. Such expectation would be neither legitimate nor reasonable' [emphasis added]).

126 Ibid para 378.

127 *Metalpar v. Argentine Republic*, ICSID Case No ARB/03/5, Award (6 June 2008).

relationship. Distinguishing the present case from the precedents,[128] the tribunal rejected the claim on the ground that '*there was no bid, license, permit or contract of any kind between Argentina and Claimants, and the Tribunal considers that there were no legitimate expectations entertained by Claimants that were breached by Argentina*'.[129]

However, the tribunal's fidelity to the voluntarist conception was cast in doubt when the tribunal examined the foreseeability of regulatory risks as well as the experience of the claimants and the actual knowledge of bad conditions in the business sector to support its conclusion on the unreasonableness of expectations.[130] Based on the voluntarist theory, those factors would not be necessary because the basis of the obligation is the intention of the state to undertake an obligation. Analysing the conduct of the investor at the level of the liability stage obscures the true basis of liability.

The *Perenco v. Ecuador* decision affirmed the voluntarist principle by reiterating the necessity of including a stabilisation clause against a change of regulatory framework. Thus, the tribunal denied protection of legitimate expectations of legal stability for lack of a stabilisation clause against future legislative or other change.[131] The tribunal reasoned that 'without a full stabilisation clause in the contracts, the contractor could not reasonably expect that the contracts would be completely immunised from future legislative or other measures.[132]

[128] Ibid para 185 ('However, in all of them, the conflict arose out of a state of facts different to the one under analysis in this case: in some of them, the relevant governments had *invited* the foreign investors to participate in a bidding process that was awarded to each of those investors and ended with the signing of a contract. In other cases, there were other types of *contractual relations* which created legitimate expectations; in all of them, the Government refused to renew or to comply with the contract, license or permit.').

[129] Ibid para 186 (emphasis added).

[130] Ibid para 187 ('Therefore, the Tribunal considers that it is unlikely that Claimants legitimately expected that their investments would not be subject to the ups and downs of the country in which they were made or that the crisis that could already be foreseen would not make it necessary to issue legal measures to cope with it'.).

[131] *Perenco Ecuador Ltd. v. The Republic of Ecuador and Empresa Estatal Petróleos del Ecuador (Petroecuador),* ICSID Case No ARB/08/6, Decision on Remaining Issues of Jurisdiction and on Liability (12 September 2014) para 593 ('Insofar as this aspect of the fair and equitable treatment claim is concerned, given the precise expression of the parties' contractual rights and obligations, Perenco has not proven that resort to the taxation modification process would have been futile. Therefore, the Tribunal declines to find the Respondent in breach for enacting and applying Law.').

[132] Ibid para 569.

4.3.3.3 Normative Implication of Neutralisation of Normative Power

This section briefly analyses the normative implication of viewing the legitimate expectations of legal stability through the 'neutralization of normative power' perspective. In the determination of the investor's expectations, the question is often characterised in terms of the conflict of the sovereign right to regulate and the investor's legitimate expectations.[133] Is the conflict real? Or is it just a matter of 'self-imposed' or voluntary neutralisation of normative power?

It can be argued that the second perspective is more compatible with the voluntarist principle. Signing a stabilisation clause or making a promise through specific laws addressed to specific investor is an exercise of normative power, an attribute of state sovereignty. Therefore, the legitimate expectations based on those representations cannot be seen as a conflict with or an affront to state sovereignty from the voluntarist principle. These two elements should be seen as two sides of the same conceptual coin.[134] This contrasts with the paradigm under the reliance conception, whereby the duty to compensate is based on the harm caused to the investor and not the voluntary undertaking of the state.

The concept of 'neutralization of normative power' finds its clearest articulation in the passage of the decision of *Parkerings v. Lithuania*, which states that

> [i]t is each State's undeniable right and privilege to exercise its sovereign legislative power. A State has the right to enact, modify or cancel a law at its own discretion. *Save for the existence of an agreement, in the form of a stabilisation clause or otherwise*, there is nothing objectionable about the amendment brought to the regulatory framework existing at the time an investor made its investment.[135]

[133] F Vicuna, 'Regulatory Authority and Legitimate Expectations: Balancing the Rights of the State and the Individual under International Law in a Global Society' (2003) 5 *Int'l LFD Int'l* 188; M Potesta, 'Legitimate Expectations in Investment Treaty Law: Understanding the Roots and the Limits of a Controversial Concept' (2013) *ICSID Review* 1, 26 ('the crucial question becomes the right balance between the stability and legitimate expectations on the one hand, and the host State's right to amend the regulatory framework on the other').

[134] *Saluka Investments BV (The Netherlands) v. Czech Republic*, UNCITRAL Rules, Partial Award (17 March 2006) 305 ('No investor may reasonably expect that the circumstances prevailing at the time the investment is made remain totally unchanged. In order to determine whether frustration of the foreign investor's expectations was justified and reasonable, the host State's legitimate right subsequently to regulate domestic matters in the public interest must be taken into consideration as well.').

[135] *Parkerings v. Lithuania* (n 85) para 332 (emphasis added).

Other tribunals also confirmed that the right of states to legislate and regulate domestic affairs has the limits defined by reference to non-arbitrary and non-discriminatory treatment and due process of law[136] as well as its own contractual commitment.[137]

The interesting question is if there should be a limit to neutralisation of normative power. In other words, can states self-impose the limit such that it can no longer change the law? Some tribunals see no limit when they suggest that 'the Tribunal would have little difficulty holding that a fully stabilised contract that did not admit of any future legislative or other change cannot be changed unilaterally'.[138] This contrasts with the 'conscionability' limit of exercise of normative power implied in *Continental Casualty v. Argentina*, where the tribunal stated that

> it would be *unconscionable* for a country to promise not to change its legislation as time and needs change, or even more to tie its hands by such a kind of stipulation in case a crisis of any type or origin arose . . . reliance on such an implication by a foreign investor would be misplaced and, indeed, unreasonable.[139]

Whilst the tribunal's conclusion might be intuitively right, the principled justification is more likely to be found in the political philosophy than in legal principle.

4.4 Critical Reflections on the Voluntarist Conception of Legitimate Expectations

The analysis so far has illustrated that the voluntarist principle of legitimate expectations is both over-inclusive and under-inclusive. The essence of the voluntarist principle suggests that an obligation to protect legitimate expectation is completed by the act of a state

136 Ibid ('what is prohibited however is for a State to act unfairly, unreasonably or inequitably in the exercise of its legislative power'). The procedural aspect of the exercise of sovereign power is stressed in *Franck Charles Arif v. Republic of Moldova*, ICSID Case No ARB/11/23, Award (8 April 2013) para 538 ('accordingly, an investor's legitimate expectations might be breached not only by a substantive change in policy, but also by the treatment of the investor during the process of the change of policy').

137 *Perenco v. Ecuador* (n 131) para 562; ibid para 563 ('Consequently, any contractor could reasonably expect that the contracts' structure would not be altered by Petroecuador unilaterally or undone by subsequent State action external to the contract except in accordance with their terms and the State's law.').

138 *Perenco v. Ecuador* (n 131) 593.

139 *Continental Casualty v. Argentina*, ICSID Case No ARB/03/9, Award (5 September 2008) para 258.

expressing its intention to undertake an obligation; therefore, the reasonableness of the investor's expectation is determined exclusively with reference to this element.

As far as the 'contractual expectation' is concerned, the principle is over-inclusive because contractual expectation is assimilated to contractual right, which is protected in the vocabulary of legitimate expectations. This consequence can circumvent the rule that a contract breach does not *per se* constitute a treaty breach. It is not the task of international law to provide a mechanism for enforcing contractual obligations governed by the relevant municipal laws.

The principle is under-inclusive in the domain of administrative representations and legislative framework. Administrative representations are unlikely to create legitimate expectations because, by their nature, they do not exhibit a legal undertaking. On the question of legal stability, the state has to undertake a specific obligation, usually in the form of a stabilisation clause (contractual) or a specific stabilisation law (legislative).

The voluntarist conception of legitimate expectations functions in a similar way as the doctrine of unilateral acts, which finds its legal basis in the intention of the state. This means that the voluntarist conception of legitimate expectations focuses exclusively on the promisor's perspective and pay no attention to the impact on the promisee in the determination of liability. This conception arguably deprives adjudicators of a conceptual tool in achieving flexibility to do justice to the parties. There are two fundamental problems with this principle. There is also an important challenge of the identification of the intent of state, especially the question of who has the authority or power to manifest an intention to undertake an obligation on behalf of the state.

A significant objection to the voluntarist conception is the remedial consequence of enforcement of expectations. The strict threshold for liability should be appreciated in light of the remedial consequence. According to the voluntarist conception, enforcing promises has the objective of protecting the practice of undertaking voluntary obligations as well as protecting individuals from abuse of the practice. Let us reflect on the philosophical insights on the remedy for a breach of promissory obligation under the voluntarist theory.

Charles Fried's theory of promise relies on the freedom of an individual as a basis for promissory obligation and categorically endorses the expectation damages. He stated:

> If I make a promise to you, I should do as I promise; and if I fail to keep my promise it is fair that I should be made to hand over the equivalent of the promised performance ... *The expectation standard gives the victim of a breach no more or less than he would have had had there been no breach-in other words, he gets the benefit of his bargain.*[140]

However, we should note Craswell's powerful criticism of Fried's theory by doubting that the notion of individual autonomy, which is relied on as the justificatory basis in the first place, would necessarily favour the expectation measure over any other type of damages.[141] At a general level, Craswell questions the relevance of philosophical account for the rules on remedies. He attacked Fried's theory and others, which ground *the enforceability of promises* on considerations of individual freedom and autonomy, or on the principle of fidelity to one's prior statements or commitments. His reasoning was that people should be able to choose the default rule of remedy:

> The principle of individual freedom is ... unhelpful, for it implies only that individuals should be left free to change whatever default rule the law adopts as a starting point ... [S]ome other value must be invoked to explain why one starting point ought to be picked by the law in preference to another.[142]

Craswell's argument might have a point in light of Raz's suggestion that reliance damages may provide an alternative way to compensate promisees for harm caused by reliance on the undertaking:

> Compensating individuals for harm resulting from *reliance on voluntary obligations* is, on the other hand, a proper goal for the law. As far as this argument goes, supporters of the harm principle should favor reliance damages rather than expectation damages as a standard legal remedy for breach of contract. *Contrary to often expressed views, the belief that the proper role of contract law is the protection of the practice of undertaking voluntary obligations does not necessarily lead*

140 Fried, *Contract as Promise* (n 1) (emphasis added).

141 R Craswell, 'Contract Law, Default Rules, and the Philosophy of Promising' (1989) 88 *Mich L Rev* 489, 518 ('almost any remedy – reliance damages, punitive damages, specific performance, etc – makes the promised course of conduct non-optional to some degree, depending on the severity of the threatened penalty. There is surely nothing in the idea of individual autonomy that requires the exact degree of non-optionality provided by the expectation measure ... [N]othing in the notion of individual autonomy gives any reason for favoring the expectation measure over any of the others.').

142 Ibid.

to endorsement of an expectation-value measure of the legal protection of contracts.[143]

Whether we agree with Craswell's argument or not, given that the voluntarist conception seeks to protect the expectations of the promisee, the tribunals *could* award expectation damages in reliance on the voluntarist principle as the justification. This issue of remedy will be dealt with in Chapter 8. For now, it suffices to conclude that however faithful the voluntarist principle is to the preservation of state sovereignty, the voluntarist theory of legitimate expectations produces the rules which are both over-inclusive and under-inclusive, which are not distinguishable from the doctrine of unilateral acts or the umbrella clause. Moreover, the relief for protection of legitimate expectations will undermine a state's sovereignty. Therefore, the search for principle on this normative hinterland journey must continue if the legitimate expectations are to remain a useful legal concept.

[143] J Raz, 'Book Review: Promises in Morality and Law' (1982) 95 *Harv L Rev* 916, 934 (emphasis added).

5

Letting Investors Down

Protection of Trust and the Assurance Conception of Legitimate Expectations

5.1 Introduction

Imagine the following situation: a country called 'Hopeland' has a wealth of natural resources, including oil and gas, but lacks both the technology and adequate capacity to explore its vast reserves of those resources. Like any sensible government with a fairly liberal economic policy, the government of Hopeland wishes to attract foreign investors. Therefore, the government has introduced a variety of specific legislative and regulatory framework offering tax incentives as well as safeguards for investment security and protection. The government through its state-owned oil enterprise has entered into some typical contractual arrangement for this industry. CEOs of potential companies have meetings with the highest-ranking officials of the government to discuss specific arrangements for forthcoming projects.

However, just *before* the investors start putting much needed capital in the projects, the country faced an unprecedented economic turmoil, which caused the government to review its policy towards foreign investment projects. In light of the changing circumstances, it decided to pursue a protectionist policy and cancelled all its contractual and non-contractual commitments with foreign investors.

Could we accord any legal protection to the investors' created expectations in the absence of reliance? For the purpose of the discussion, let us assume that the argument in the previous chapter – the voluntarist conception of legitimate expectations as a conceptual framework should not be endorsed – is sustained.

This chapter examines an alternative conception of promise, known as the assurance or expectation theory as propounded by Thomas Scanlon.[1] The essence of his theory is that if one intentionally or voluntarily creates

[1] TM Scanlon, 'Promises and Practices' (1990) 19(3) *Phil & Pub Aff* 199.

the expectations or assurance in another person, one has the obligation to fulfil the expectation, under the principle of fidelity.

According to Scanlon, promise-breaking is an instance of a moral wrong concerned with 'what we owe to other people when we have led them to form expectations about our future conduct'.[2] The notable feature of this theory is that responsibility can be established by demonstrating the volitional act of the promisor to create expectations in the mutual knowledge of both parties *without requiring the proof of detrimental reliance.*[3] This theory is in effect an attempt 'to marry the volitional character of promissory obligations with their harm-based justifications, without invoking a special norm of promise-keeping'.[4]

Nevertheless, the theory would have to provide an answer to this question: why is a promise binding when there has been no reliance on the promise? If this theory is sustained, the investors in the hypothetical situation, who suffer no detriment, might have a claim for the fulfilment of their expectations.

This theory is different from the voluntarist conception in that the promisor has to 'intentionally and voluntarily create the expectation in the representee' as opposed to having 'an intention to undertake an *obligation*'.[5] Unlike the reliance conception, it does not require detriment or reliance as the basis for obligation. If it is not the intention of the promisor to undertake a legal obligation nor the detrimental reliance of the promisee, what is the basis for obligation?

Scanlon affirms that it is 'the value of assurance', which explains how giving assurance can create an obligation. The reason is that expectations lead to actions and reliance. To what extent can we derive an obligation from the theory that seeks to establish responsibility out of the two incommensurable values – expectations and reliance[6] – which are

[2] TM Scanlon, *What We Owe to Each Other* (Cambridge, MA: Harvard University Press, 1998), 296.

[3] Scanlon, 'Promises and Practices'. According to Scanlon, 'obligations arising from promises are generally thought to bind even when the promisee will suffer no loss as a result of relying on the promise' (205).

[4] M Pratt, 'Scanlon on Promising' (2001) 14 *Can J L & Jur* 143, 145.

[5] Under Raz's classification of promise theory, this will fall under 'intention' conception as opposed to 'obligation' conception; see J Raz, 'Promises and Obligations' in PMS Hacker and J Raz (eds), *Law, Morality and Society: Essays in Honor of H.L.A. Hart* (Oxford: Clarendon Press, 1977), 210–28 (emphasis added).

[6] The main critique of Scanlon's theory is that it conflates the two values, which are not commensurable. It is either expectation or reliance but not both, which explains the binding nature of promise. D Patterson, 'The Value of a Promise' (1992) 11(4) *L & Phil* 38.

inherent in the notion of 'the value of assurance'? The normative implication of this theory of promise for the conceptualisation of legitimate expectations is analysed in the following paragraphs.

Some philosophers, out of discontent with Scanlon's theory of promise, proposed an alternative trust view of promise, which suggests that promising involves inviting trust in the promisor. The 'protection of trust' has provided the underlying rationale for protection of legitimate expectations in municipal public laws. It is illuminating to apply this analytical framework to the context of investment treaty arbitration.

This chapter is organised into three main parts. The first analyses the key tenets of the assurance conception of Scanlon and its normative implication of the assurance conception with reference to selected investment treaty decisions (Section 5.2) The second part presents the analysis of the trust view of promise based on philosophy literature and public law scholarship and assesses the feasibility and desirability of transposing such conception to the context of investor–state dispute (Section 5.3). The third part concludes the chapter with some critical reflections (Section 5.4).

5.2 Constructing the Analytical Framework Based on the Assurance Theory of Promise

The assurance (also known as 'expectation') conception of promise asserts that a promissory obligation derives from the fact that the promisor intentionally creates the assurance and raises the expectations in the promisee.[7] To give someone assurance means to create in that person an expectation that something will happen: 'in making the promise, the promisor creates an expectation that the promisee cares about'.[8] Paul Ardal suggested that when a promise is made, 'the promisee expects a certain thing from the promiser'.[9] Jan Narveson similarly stated that 'in promising, I give you to *expect* that I will do the promised thing'.[10] Essential to the expectation conception is an intention to excite expectations, as articulated by the English philosopher William Paley, as follows:

[7] Scanlon, *What We Owe to Each Other* (n 2); P Ardal, 'And That's a Promise' (1968) 18(72)*Phil Q* 225, 234 ('since the promiser raises the expectations in the promisee by the promise, and in most cases intentionally does this, he is responsible if he fails to do what he has promised to do. The evil or deprivation coming to the promisee is due to the promiser').

[8] Scanlon, 'Promises and Practices' (n 1).

[9] Ardal, 'And That's a Promise' (n 7).

[10] J Narveson, 'Promising, Expecting and Utility' (1971) 1 *Can J Phil* 207 (emphasis added).

> This obligation depends upon the *expectations which we knowingly and voluntarily excite*. Consequently, any action or conduct towards another, which we are sensible excites expectations in that other, is as much a promise, and creates as strict an obligation, as the most express assurances.[11]

The next section explains how the creation of an expectation in a promisee generates an obligation. The principle of fidelity as proposed by Scanlon provides the moral basis for promissory obligation (Section 5.2.1), which has important consequences on our conceptualisation of legitimate expectations (Section 5.2.2).

5.2.1 *The Principle of Fidelity and Promissory Obligation*

Scanlon's theory of promise explains a promissory obligation without reference to any actual practice of promising, contrary to the views of Hume or Rawls.[12] His theory seeks to underplay rather than reject the relevance of social practice in the understanding of promissory obligation.[13] Scanlon's objections to the social practice account of promise are based on two main reasons.

First, the social practice theory violates the intuitive feeling that the obligation to keep a promise is an obligation owed specifically to the promisee. According to the social practice view, when one breaks a promise, one wrongs participants in this practice collectively by depriving them of an important benefit (Hume) or by free-riding (Rawls) on their contributions to the social practice.[14]

Second, the wrong of breaking a promise can be instead explained as an instance of 'a more general family of moral wrongs',[15] which occurs as a result of our intentional act of creating expectations in another person. According to Scanlon, this family of wrongs can be defined by many principles, but mainly the principle of fidelity, which imposes a duty to

[11] Rev. E Paley, *The Works of William Paley, D. D. and An Account of the Life and Writings of the Author*, Volume III (London: Longman and Co, 1838) 58–68 (emphasis added).

[12] See the discussion in Chapter 4.

[13] Scanlon, 'Promises and Practices' (n 1) 200 ('social practices of agreement-making, when they exist, may provide the means for creating such expectations' but 'these practices play no essential role in explaining why these actions are wrong').

[14] Ibid 210–13.

[15] Scanlon, *What We Owe to Each Other* (n 2) 296 ('the wrong of breaking a promise and the wrong of making a lying promise are instances of a more general family of moral wrongs which are concerned . . . with what we owe to other people when we have led them to form expectations about our future conduct').

ensure that the expectations we create in others are not disappointed. These principles are examined in the following paragraphs.

Scanlon outlined various principles which address different situations in which the expectations of others can be wrongfully disappointed. In the investor–state context, the state can promise something that it never intends to deliver (a violation of the principle against unjust manipulation) (Principle of Non-Manipulation). The state can also negligently create expectations which turn out to be false (Principle of Due Care). If the state creates the expectation in the investor and subsequently changes its mind, it has the duty to prevent the loss to the investor (Principle of Loss Prevention).

The core of Scanlon's theory is the principle of fidelity, which comes into play when the state intentionally and voluntarily creates the expectations in the investor with the mutual knowledge of such intention (Principle of Fidelity). Let us examine how these principles may be relevant to our context.

Under the principle of non-manipulation, the state is prohibited from manipulating the investor by intentionally but deceitfully leading the investor to believe that the state will perform a certain act, though in fact it has no intention to do so. This instance of wrong is similar to Kant's famous example of the lying promise.[16] The principle is stated as follows:

> In the absence of special justification, it is not permissible for one person, A, in order to get another person, B, to do some act, *x* (which A wants B to do and which B is morally free to do or not do but would otherwise not do), to lead B to expect that if he or she does *x* then A will do *y* (which B wants but believes that A will otherwise not do), when in fact A has no intention of doing *y* if B does *x*, and A can reasonably foresee that B will suffer significant loss if he or she does *x* and A does does not do *y*.[17]

It is submitted that this principle is under-inclusive in the context of typical cases of legitimate expectations, in which states often have the intention to perform an act at the time of making a promise but are obliged to renege on their undertakings due to prevailing public interests or changing circumstances. Therefore, this principle would not serve as a useful rationale for the paradigm of legitimate expectations because the scope of the rules would be too narrow.

Similarly, the application of the principle of due care only requires the state to exercise its due care not to form false expectations. The principle

[16] I Kant, 'Groundwork of the Metaphysics of Morals' (edited by M. Gregor) (Cambridge: Cambridge University Press, 1996).

[17] Scanlon, 'Promises and Practices' (n 1) 203.

of due care states that 'one must exercise due care not to lead others to form reasonable but false expectations about what one will do when one has good reason to believe that he or she would suffer significant loss as a result of relying on these expectations'.[18]

The practical application of this principle is of limited use because the principle does not state specifically what actions it requires; the exact nature and extent of the 'due care' is unknown. In any case, this principle does not adequately address the paradigm cases of legitimate expectations, which do not involve just mere care not to create false expectations, but those in which states give assurances to induce investors and suffer consequential damages.

Therefore, the more stringent principle of loss prevention seems more relevant to the paradigm situations of legitimate expectations, according to which, 'if one has intentionally or negligently led someone to expect that one is going to follow a certain course of action, X, and one has *good reason* to believe that that person will suffer significant loss as a result of this expectation if one does not follow X, then one must take *reasonable steps* to prevent that loss'.[19]

The application of this principle requires a promisor (state) to take reasonable steps to *prevent* potential loss to an investor if it will not pursue a conduct promised to an investor. The idea of 'reasonable steps' refers to proportionality between the steps taken and the magnitude of the threatened loss, and the degree of negligence involved in creating the expectation.[20] No particular course of action to prevent others from suffering loss is prescribed, though such acts as warning, fulfilment of representation and compensation will suffice for this purpose.[21]

The normative implication of the principle of loss prevention is that legitimate expectations would be a loss-prevention obligation. Under this conception, legitimate expectations based on this principle can be fulfilled by merely giving the warning to the investor before he has taken any action or passed up any valuable opportunity. Its key weakness is that this principle cannot support the expectation that the assurance will be fulfilled.

If Scanlon's theory only sought to defend the principle of fidelity as a moral basis for promissory obligation at the level of reliance upon

[18] Ibid 204.

[19] Ibid 204 (emphasis added).

[20] Scanlon, *What We Owe to Each Other* (n 2) 301.

[21] Scanlon, 'Promises and Practices' (n 1) 204 ('the choice of means is left open: the principle is neutral between warning, fulfillment and compensation'); 205 (it is suggested however that the warning should be done 'at a time early enough to prevent the loss from occurring').

representations, it would be sustained by the application of the previously mentioned principles. However, his aim is more ambitious in justifying an obligation arising from promises and other instances of explicit and intentional expectation-creation, including when the promisee suffers no loss as a result of relying on the promise.[22]

Scanlon's theory could provide justification for why the state should be obligated to fulfil its promise to the investor without any detrimental reliance. The proposed principles so far would not be adequate to justify such obligation. Scanlon therefore proposed the principle of fidelity to explain such duty. The principle of fidelity can be stated as follows:

> If (1) *A* voluntarily and intentionally leads *B* to expect that *A* will do *X* (unless *B* consents to *A*'s not doing so); (2) *A* knows that *B* wants to be assured of this; (3) *A* acts with the aim of providing this assurance, and has good reason to believe that he or she has done so; (4) *B* knows that *A* has the intentions and beliefs just described; (5) *A* intends for *B* to know this, and knows that *B* does know it; (6) *B* knows that *A* has this knowledge and intent, then, in the absence of special justification, *A* must do *X* unless *B* consents to *X*'s not being done.[23]

Scanlon justified the principle of fidelity on the non-utilitarian and contractualist moral premises, which are based on the idea that 'an act is wrong if its performance under the circumstances would be disallowed by any set of principles for the general regulation of behaviour that no one could reasonably reject as a basis for informed, unforced general agreement'.[24] Scanlon suggested that the fact that both promisor and promisee want 'assurance' is sufficient to establish a duty unless it would be reasonable for potential promisors to reject such a principle.[25] Given that the obligation of a promise is founded on the protection of the 'value of assurance', it is important to clarify the notion.

The value of assurance can be understood in three different ways.[26] First, there is the 'experiential value' of avoiding the disappointment of

[22] Ibid 205.

[23] Scanlon, *What We Owe to Each Other* (n 2) 304.

[24] Ibid 153.

[25] Ibid 302–03 ('given the reasons that potential promisees have for wanting assurance, potential promisers have reasons to want to be able to provide it. From the point of view of both potential promisees and potential promisers, then, it is reasonable to want a principle of fidelity that requires performance rather than compensation.').

[26] This exposition of three ways of understanding the value of assurance is set out in N Southwood and D Friedrich, 'Promises beyond Assurance' (2009) 144(2) *Philosophical Studies: An International Journal for Philosophy in the Analytic Tradition* 261, 265–66.

having one's expectation frustrated. Narveson suggested: '[I]n promising, I give you reason to expect that I will do the promised thing. And in defaulting, I disappoint this expectation, a disappointment which is additional to the loss of the promised benefit, whatever it may have been.'[27]

Second, there is the 'agential value' of being able to make plans in reliance on others' performance of certain acts. On this point, Niko Kolodny and R Jay Wallace explained the value of assurance for planning our lives.[28] Protecting the assurance seeks to protect the stability and continuity of personal life. There exists 'a strong generic reason to want to be able to direct one's efforts and resources towards aims one has chosen and not to have one's planning co-opted' in the way that promise-breaking does.[29] Therefore, for both promisees and promisors, it is reasonable to want a principle of fidelity that requires performance rather than compensation.

Third, there is the 'transpirational' value, which refers to reasons for wanting it to be the case that the assuror will deliver the assured performance to the assuree. Scanlon suggests that 'what people . . . reasonably want is not mere freedom from worry; they also want certain things to happen ... [O]ne reason for caring is that they may rely on these assurances in deciding what to do. This is not, however, the only reason'.[30]

It is logical to assume that in the context of the investor–state relationship, both host state and investor want this assurance in order to facilitate their relationship. The next section assesses how this theory provides a conceptual guidance on thinking about the issues of legitimate expectations.

5.2.2 *Normative Implication of the Principle of Fidelity on Conceptualisation of Legitimate Expectation*

The reformulated principle based on the principle of fidelity in the context of the investor–state relationship can be stated as follows: if the

[27] Narveson, 'Promising, Expecting and Utility' (n 10) 214.

[28] N Kolodny and RJ Wallace, 'Promises and Practices Revisited' (2003) 31(1) *Phil & Pub Aff* 119, 128 ('[T]his [assurance] typically matters to us because of its manifold effects on our capacity to learn our activities through time and to execute our plans in action . . . I can take that as a fixed point in my deliberations about what to do myself, in ways that greatly facilitate my goals and values in the conduct of my life.').

[29] Scanlon, *What We Owe to Each Other* (n 2) 298.

[30] Ibid 303.

state voluntarily and intentionally leads the investor to expect that the state will do *x*, in their mutual knowledge of each other's intention and desire for assurance, in the absence of special justification, the state must do *x* unless the investor gives consent to do otherwise. Based on this principle, there are four conditions for establishing liability for a breach of legitimate expectations.

First, the expectation involves future conduct of the state.[31] This means that the state assures the investor that it will perform or refrain from doing a certain act. Second, the expectation involves a state of affairs that the investor desires or values. Third, the act of the state under consideration is the one which *voluntarily and intentionally* creates assurance and expectation in the investor about a benefit. This means that any assurance given under conditions of coercion or duress will not be valid. Fourth, the fact that the state has the intention must be a matter of common knowledge to both the state and the investor. Creating assurance which incurs the obligation of fulfilment is a highly transparent matter.[32] This requirement would exclude cases where an investor is not aware of a representation made by a state. The significant advantage of the assurance conception is that it allows the obligation to be established without proving detrimental reliance.[33]

5.2.2.1 The Normative Meaning of 'Assurance'

The first fundamental point to emphasise is that in investment treaty decisions, the term 'assurance' employed by tribunals is not determinative of the adoption of the assurance conception of legitimate expectations. The term 'assurance' is often used interchangeably with other similar terms, such as 'promise' or 'commitment'. It is crucial to identify principal conditions for liability, as outlined in the preceding section. For instance, the tribunal in *Duke Energy v. Ecuador* employed the term 'assurance' in the reliance conception because the detrimental act of the investor provided the basis in that case:

[31] This restriction is reflected in Scanlon's proviso: 'where the assurer A leads B to expect that A will do X'.

[32] Friedrich and Southwood, 'Promises beyond Assurance' (n 26) 264.

[33] S Stoljar, 'Promise, Expectation and Agreement' (1988) 47 *CLJ* 93 (The author makes a similar point in the contractual context: 'the whole point of recognising an expectation [as enforceable] is to enable the promisee to wait for the performance of a promise without having to "act on it" (such as starting his own performance or incurring expenses in preparation of the exchange), for the simple reason that in many situations the promisee cannot so rely, actively rely, on the other's promise; all he can do is wait.').

> The Tribunal does not believe that this expectation can be viewed as reasonable when one bears in mind the manner in which payments were handled and the opacity that prevailed in the administration of the contract prior to Duke Energy's investment. In view of the contract history, the expectation could only have been deemed reasonable if it had been based on clear *assurances* from the Government.[34]

5.2.2.2 'Voluntary and Intention Creation of Expectations' and the Requisite Specificity of Representation

The second implication concerns the requisite specificity of a representation. It is clear that under this conception a legally binding act is not required.[35] Nevertheless, only a specific and explicit act is likely to satisfy the third requirement in the proposed principle – namely, 'voluntary and intentional act'.

The distinct paradigm case under this conception of legitimate expectations involves a situation where the state intentionally creates the expectation in the investor but there is no requirement for detrimental reliance. Such a case is relatively rare in the investment treaty decisions because the investor usually has suffered from some type of harm prior to bringing the claim.

This section analyses some selected cases – *White Industries v. India*,[36] *Glamis v. USA*[37] and *Merrill v. Canada*[38] – that illustrate the 'voluntary creation of legitimate expectations'. Reasoning of the tribunals in these cases focuses on the volitional act of the state in creating expectations of the investor as the basis for liability for a breach of legitimate expectations. The reason for applying the assurance conception as opposed to the reliance conception may be explained by the motivation for the fulfilment of expectations remedy. In such cases, the prevailing basis is on the volitional conduct of the state, whilst reliance merely serves as an evidence of the created expectation.

34 *Duke Energy Electroquil Partners & Electroquil S.A. v. Ecuador*, ICSID Case No ARB/04/19, Award (18 August 2008) para 351.

35 Scanlon made it clear in the exposition of his thesis that the same analysis (for mutual promises and their analogues) 'can be extended to unilateral promises and other cases in which expectations are created with no reciprocation': Scanlon, 'Promises and Practices' (n 1) 206.

36 *White Industries Australia Limited v. India*, UNCITRAL Case, Final Award (30 November 2011).

37 *Glamis Gold, Ltd v. United States of America*, NAFTA/UNCITRAL, Award (8 June 2009).

38 *Merrill & Ring Forestry L.P. v. The Government of Canada*, UNCITRAL Case, ICSID Administered Case, Award (31 March 2010).

5.2.2.2.1 ***White Industries v. India*** This case of *White Industries v. India* confirms that the lack of specific representation justifies the rejection of legitimate expectations on the grounds of the assurance conception. The tribunal did not reject the case for the reason that the expectation was not based on a legally binding act (voluntarist conception) nor the absence of detrimental reliance (reliance conception). In focusing on the specificity of the representation, which is not a legal undertaking, the tribunal's reasoning was guided by the assurance conception.

The tribunal had to consider the claim based on a breach of legitimate expectations stemming from representations by officials regarding the investment climate in India. The representations were 'to the effect that: it was safe for White to invest in India; that the Indian legal system was, to all intents and purposes, the same as the Australian Legal system; and, accordingly, it could expect fair treatment'. The claimant's expectations related to the application of the laws on the enforcement of the arbitral award – namely, that (a) India, as a party to the New York Convention, would apply the convention properly and in accordance with international standards and (b) Indian courts would enforce the award in a fair and reasonably timely manner.[39]

In effect, the tribunal rejected two claims on similar grounds – that the representation lacked specificity: 'representations suffer from vagueness and generality, such that they are not capable of giving rise to reasonable legitimate expectations that are amenable to protection under the fair and equitable treatment standard'.[40]

> Quite apart from the point that an investor must generally take a host State (including its court system) as it finds it, on these facts, and *absent an express assurance from India that any award would be enforced in a particular manner or time frame, it is simply not possible for White, legitimately, to have had the expectation as to the timely enforcement of the Award* that it now asserts.[41]

From this analysis, it is possible to conclude that the concept of representation is different under the voluntarist conception and the assurance conception. The voluntarist conception requires an intention to undertake an obligation, whilst any volitional act to create the expectation will suffice under the assurance conception. Nevertheless, the 'mutual

[39] *White Industries v. India* (n 36).
[40] Ibid para 10.3.17
[41] Ibid para 10.3.15 (emphasis added).

knowledge' requirement, as stated in the fourth element, limits the scope of application to situations where a proximate interpersonal relationship exists.

5.2.2.2.1 *Glamis v. USA* The notable feature of *Glamis v. USA* is the high threshold requirement for the conduct, which creates legitimate expectations – namely, 'the active inducement of a quasi-contractual expectation as a prerequisite for a breach of Article 1105 under NAFTA'.[42]

This dispute concerns a goal mining operation located on US federal lands within the California Desert Conservation Area (CDCA). The project was first approved by the federal government agency, but approval was later withdrawn based on the subsequent legal opinion. Simultaneously, California's State Mining and Geology Board passed regulations which required backfilling and grading for mining operations in the vicinity of Native American sacred sites. The effect of these measures was to prevent the approval of its investment project. The claimant argued that these measures by the state of California and the US federal government were arbitrary and discriminatory and violated its legitimate expectations that the project would be approved based on the mining regime that existed at the time the plan was submitted.[43]

The tribunal identified the legal question under Article 1105 as follows: 'whether a lengthy, reasoned legal opinion violates customary international law because it changes, in an arguably dramatic way, a previous law or prior legal interpretation upon which an investor has based its reasonable, investment-backed expectations'.[44]

The tribunal set out the important principle as follows: 'a violation of Article 1105 based on the unsettling of reasonable, investment-backed expectation requires, as a threshold circumstance, at least *a quasi-contractual relationship* between the State and the investor, whereby *the State has purposely and specifically induced the investment*'.[45] Applying the statement of principle, the tribunal found no breach of legitimate expectations because the US federal government had never made any specific commitment. The government did not guarantee approval of the claimant's claims, nor did it offer the claimant any benefits to pursuing

[42] *Glamis v. USA* (n 37) para 799.
[43] *Glamis v. USA* (n 37).
[44] Ibid para 761.
[45] Ibid para 766 (emphasis added).

such claims beyond the customary chance to exploit federal land for possible profit.[46]

In a similar manner, with regard to the acts of the state of California, the tribunal concluded that the obligation under Article 1105 'arises only when the State has *induced these expectations in a quasi-contractual manner*'. The tribunal suggested that 'a State may be tied to the objective expectations that it creates in order to induce investment. Such an upset of expectations thus requires something greater than mere disappointment; it requires, as a threshold condition, *the active inducement of a quasi-contractual expectation*'.[47]

The tribunal's reasoning in this case is underlined by the assurance conception of legitimate expectations because the tribunal did not characterise an obligation in terms of a legally binding entitlement; rather it focused on the specific assurance to induce investment. In this case, the tribunal required that 'definitive, unambiguous and repeated' assurances had to be 'purposely and specifically' made to induce the investment.

The tribunal's adherence to the assurance conception is further reflected in the confirmation that whether the investor's expectations were 'reasonable or not is not an inquiry that the Tribunal need make but rather the relevant inquiry was 'solely whether California, or the federal government, made specific assurances to Claimant that such a requirement would not be instituted in order to induce Claimant's investment in the Imperial Project'.[48]

The tribunal's refusal to engage in the assessment of reasonableness of expectations as well as the absence of detrimental reliance, which is characteristic of the reliance conception, indicates its stance towards the assurance conception. However, the tribunal's endorsement of the reasoning in the case of *International Thunderbird* (the reliance conception) is confusing.

Furthermore, the tribunal contended that mere frustration of hopes is an illustration of the 'mastery of the obvious'. The threshold of the 'active inducement of a quasi-contractual expectation' was criticised for its lack of clarity and incoherence with the fundamental idea of investment-protection treaties. The notion of 'quasi-contract' was not a term known to international law, or indeed to many national legal systems.[49]

[46] Ibid para 767.
[47] Ibid para 799 (emphasis added).
[48] Ibid para 811.
[49] A critique of this notion is in J Paulsson, 'Can "Legitimate Expectations" Ever Be "Rights"?' *JOTWELL* (19 April 2016).

Moreover, as one scholar points out, the requirement for a contractual foundation for causes of actions represents 'a reversion to a past epoch' with instances of claims under 'state contracts'.

5.2.2.2.2 *Merrill v. Canada* The *Merrill v. Canada* decision illustrates the difficulty of establishing the legitimate expectations claim arising from the general legislative framework because it is unlikely to meet the threshold criteria. In this case, the investor claimed that the Log Export Control Regime violated the claimant's expectations under the fair and equitable treatment standard in Article 1105(1). The tribunal came to the view that there was no legitimate expectation because there was no evidence of representation made by Canada to induce the investor to make a particular decision. Based on the established analytical framework, the third element was not fulfilled because there was an absence of evidence of any representation by Canada to the investor which might be said to have induced or even encouraged its investment.[50]

5.2.2.3 Voluntary Creation of Expectations and Subsidiary Role of Reliance

Under the assurance conception, detrimental reliance merely plays an evidential role. The decision of *LG&E v. Argentina*[51] demonstrates the difficulty of conceptually distinguishing expectations and reliance as the basis for liability. The tribunal set out relevant conditions under the reliance conception for considering legitimate expectations but emphasised the expectation created as the basis for liability. The existence of detrimental reliance should not preclude an assurance-based characterisation of legitimate expectations if the prevailing basis is the intentional creation of expectations.

The dispute arose from the background of the Argentinian government's privatisation of gas transportation and distribution. Specific representations were made to public utilities licensees (in particular the gas distribution licensees) in the form of legislative framework. The Gas Law was enacted to offer certain benefits, such as calculation of transport and distribution tariffs in US dollars, and the government could not rescind or modify the licences without the consent of the licensees. The Basic Rules of the License obligated the government to compensate

[50] *Merrill v. Canada* (n 38) para 242.

[51] *LG & E Energy Corp. v. Argentine Republic*, ICSID Case No ARB/02/1, Decision on Liability (3 October 2006).

the licensees fully for any losses resulting from changes to the guaranteed tariff system. It is important to note that the government issued the Information Memorandum, which summarised the legal framework governing the privatisation, the terms and conditions for the bidding, the bidding process and the legal and regulatory framework that would apply to the new industry after privatisation. The tribunal emphasised the effect of the guarantee made by the government in the form of regulatory framework on the creation of expectations in investors as the basis for liability.

At first sight, this case should be characterised as the reliance-based conception as there is evidence of the investor's reliance upon the guaranteed protections.[52] Furthermore, the conception outlined by the tribunal includes consideration of relevant factors, such as business risk or an industry's regular patterns, which are important elements in the reliance conception. Nevertheless, based on the close reading of the tribunal's reasoning, there is a compelling argument to interpret this case as endorsing the assurance conception because the tribunal emphasised the creation of specific expectations as the basis for conferring a legal obligation, whereas the act of reliance might play an evidentiary role:

> *Having created specific expectations among investors, Argentina was bound by its obligations concerning the investment guarantees vis-à-vis public utility licensees*, and in particular, the gas distribution licensees. The abrogation of these specific guarantees violates the stability and predictability underlying the standard of fair and equitable treatment.[53]

One might argue that whilst the reference to stability and predictability might serve to reinforce the conclusion on the breach of the FET standard, it became difficult to determine whether the expectations element was a determinative factor for the breach.

The important issue raised in this decision underscores the critique of Scanlon's theory, which mainly concerns protection of the 'value of assurance'. The value of assurance embraces both expectation and reliance.[54] Yet some scholars contend that these two values are

[52] Ibid para 127.

[53] Ibid para 133 (emphasis added).

[54] Scanlon admitted that in the following excerpt: 'what people . . . reasonably want is not mere freedom from worry; they also want certain things to happen . . . they want to be given assurances, and they care about whether these assurances are genuine. One reason for caring is that they may rely on these assurances in deciding what to do.' Scanlon, 'Promises and Practices' (n 1) 208.

incommensurable. Promise is binding either because of what it leads the promisee to expect or because of what it leads the promisee to do. It is impossible to rely on these two values to complement each other. If expectation is the ground of promissory obligation, then reliance is superfluous. If reliance is the ground, then the expectation cannot be normatively relevant and the binding character of a promise cannot be explained.[55]

The incommensurability of these two values became more evident from the remedial perspective. On this point, one scholar puts the following question: 'what is it that we are protecting when we decide what one is entitled to when one is the recipient of a morally binding promise?'[56] Scanlon's theory, which seeks to occupy the common ground between intention and reliance, is faced with the challenge: 'either the reliance or the expectation interest is being protected, but not both'.[57]

It could be argued that one possible way out of this conundrum is to admit that reliance plays only an evidentiary as opposed to normative role in the determination of obligation, as the analysis of the preceding decisions has shown. This issue is significant for our context because this philosophical and 'intellectual' (theoretical)[58] quarrel goes deep into the foundation of the theory upon which the conceptualisation of legitimate expectations is based.

Another intellectual criticism of Scanlon's theory, which may have a practical implication on our reflection, suggests that the assurance conception of promissory obligation seems to be fraught with the 'circularity argument'.[59] The essence of the criticism is how the binding force should derive from the 'assurance' effect, which in turn should be

[55] D Patterson, 'The Value of a Promise' (1992) 11(4) *L & Phil* 385, 398–400.

[56] Ibid 400.

[57] Ibid.

[58] One example of this intellectual/theoretical critique of the assurance theory is that even though Scanlon's theory bases its normative justification on a non-consequentialist ground, it cannot escape the teleological argument based on the value of assurance. M Smith, 'The Value of Making and Keeping Promise' in H Sheinman (ed), *Promises and Agreements: Philosophical Essays* (New York: Oxford University Press, 2011) 214 ('far from Principle F's being a nonconsequentialist principle, then it turn out that Principle F is itself an implicitly consequentialist principle ... because the facts about obligation that it describes are all ultimately grounded in, and thus reduced to, facts about the relative value of agents meeting the reasonable expectations that they knowingly create'). One might argue that this does not bear any practical significance on the conceptualisation of legitimate expectations.

[59] GEM Anscombe, 'Rules, Rights, and Promises' in *The Collected Philosophical Papers of G.E.M. Anscombe*, Volume 3, *Ethics, Religion, and Politics* (Oxford: Basil Blackwell, 1981).

brought about by a binding representation.[60] Before the promisee can expect the promisor's performance, the promisor must be first bound (by a binding commitment of some sort). However, in order for the promise to be binding, under the assurance theory, the promisee must be first assured. There seems to be an illogical impasse.

Scanlon, in reply, proposes that such reason can be found in other moral principles (the weaker principles – non-manupulation, due care and loss prevention – previously discussed). Let us take the principle of due care as an example to show how it can give the promisor a distinctively moral reason to perform. In our context, the principle of due care would require a state to exercise due care not to lead an investor to form reasonable but false expectations about what the state will do when it believes that the investor would suffer significant loss as a result of reliance on those expectations. In essence, the adherence to the principle of due care means the state would not attempt to induce the investor to believe that it would do a certain thing, if the state does not believe it itself. Therefore, this explains how the investor's assurance can be generated in the first place. The real question must be whether an appeal to these weaker moral principles is sufficient for the investor's being assured that the state will do what it promises, in the same way, which engages the principle of fidelity.[61]

This remedy to the circularity problem is not wholeheartedly accepted by some scholars, such as Kolodny and Wallace who propose a hybrid theory of promise which draws on the conventional character of promising to rescue the assurance theory. The assurance-generating obligation is a convention-based obligation not to undermine or free-ride on the socially valuable practice of promising.[62] Under this hybrid conception, the reason for the performance by the promisor need not rely on Scanlon's weaker moral principles but on the social practice-based obligation not to exploit just social practices.[63] In this way, the promisee can gain the appropriate assurance required to trigger the principle of fidelity because the promisee believes that the promisor will perform, otherwise the promisor would be exploiting a just social practice. The consequence

[60] Friedrich and Southwood, 'Promises beyond Assurance' (n 26).

[61] This point is articulated in NA Tognazzini, 'The Hybrid Nature of Promissory Obligation' (2007) 35(3) *Phil & Pub Aff* 203.

[62] Kolodny and Wallace, 'Promises and Practices Revisited' (n 28) 149.

[63] Ibid 152 ('there is one obligation to keep a promise that is to be explained in terms of the wrongness of exploiting or undermining the practice, and that is thus owed to everyone who plays their part in or stands to gain from the practice').

of this hybrid conception is that breaking a promise means two wrongs being committed – namely, the wrong of exploiting a just social practice and the wrong of violating the principle of fidelity. Scanlon seems to have sympathy with this reformulation of the principle of fidelity.[64]

The hybrid theory has the virtues of preserving the strength of Scanlon's theory in explaining the nature of wrong specifically done to the promisee in a way that a pure social practice view cannot, whilst overcoming the logical impasse reflected in the circularity argument.

5.2.2.4 Undesirable Consequence of the Principle of Fidelity in Case of Contract Breach

The fourth implication relates to the effect of applying the reformulated principle of fidelity to the case of contract breach. Like the voluntarist conception, a breach of contractual expectation would constitute international responsibility by the application of the principle of fidelity. Therefore, it is objectionable for the same reason as the voluntarist conception. The intention to create expectations can be easily established with reference to contractual stipulations. The implication of this conception on the contractual expectation can be highlighted in the discussion of *Exxon Mobil v. Venezuela*.[65]

In this case, the tribunal found a breach of the FET standard by determining the frustration of the investor's legitimate expectations, as a result of the breach of contractual arrangement. At the heart of the issue is the breach of contractual obligations under the Framework of Conditions of the Association Agreement for the exploitation, upgrading and marketing of extra-heavy crude oil in the Cerro Negro Project, which was approved by the Congress of Venezuela in 1997, as a result of production and export curtailments on the Cerro Negro Project.[66]

[64] TM Scanlon, 'Reasons, Responsibility, and Reliance: Replies to Wallace, Dworkin, and Deigh', Symposium on TM Scanlon's *What We Owe to Each Other* (2002) 112 (3) *Ethics* 507, 523–24 ('it could well be true that a person who promises to do something commonly incurs two kinds of obligation to do it: one of these an obligation to abide by and support a useful practice, the other an obligation of the kind Principle F describes. The first of these obligations would in fact support the second, since the practice would provide a way of creating expectations of the kind that are central to Principle F.')

[65] *Venezuela Holdings, B.V., et al. (case formerly known as Mobil Corporation, Venezuela Holdings, B.V., Mobil Cerro Negro Holding, Ltd., Mobil Venezolana de Petróleos Holdings, Inc., Mobil Cerro Negro, Ltd., and Mobil Venezolana de Petróleos, Inc.) v. Bolivarian Republic of Venezuela,* ICSID Case No ARB/07/27, Award (9 October 2014).

[66] Ibid; the tribunal analysed the claimants' FET claims with respect to the (1) Extraction Tax, (2) production and export curtailments, (3) coercion and the expropriation

The tribunal employed the concept of legitimate expectations, underlined by the assurance conception, as a tool for converting a contract breach into a treaty breach.

The notable feature of this case is the threshold for the breach of the FET standard by frustrating the expectations that the investor may have legitimately taken into account when making the investment. Legitimate expectations may result from specific formal assurances given by the host state in order to induce investment.[67]

The tribunal applied this standard to the facts of the case and identified the claimant's reasonable expectations with reference to the terms of the agreement by considering the measures by Venezuela in 2006 and 2007 on the production and export curtailments from November 2006[68] to be incompatible with claimants' reasonable expectations (production of at least 120,000 barrels per day) and thus breached the FET standard.[69]

The tribunal's reasoning is underlined by the assurance conception despite references to the investor's investment decision based on the agreement and the inducement of investment. The tribunal placed emphasis on the specific assurance (in the form of the contractual agreement), which seeks to create expectation (induce investment) without pointing out the detrimental effect of the breach.

This case might have been read as falling within the voluntarist conception given that the contractual representation gave rise to the expectation. However, the tribunal did not emphasise a legally binding character of 'formal assurance' (the key feature of the voluntarist conception) but focused on the effect of such representation.

The advantage of the assurance conception is twofold. First, it avoids an articulation of the reliance aspect, which might lead to the consideration of reliance damages. Second, the tribunal avoided conflating a contract breach and a treaty breach by seeking refuge with the concept of 'formal assurance to induce investment'. That advantage cannot be accepted for the similar reason that the voluntarist conception is

measures and (4) severance payments. However, only the second claim, which raises the issue of legitimate expectations, is analysed.

67 Ibid para 273. ('The Tribunal does not consider it necessary to separately examine whether the Respondent's conduct was also arbitrary and/or discriminatory. Indeed, the Claimants would not be entitled to greater relief even if the Tribunal were to establish a breach of these BIT protections.')

68 Ibid para 260.

69 Ibid para 264.

criticised for collapsing the distinction between a contract and treaty breach; therefore, this aspect of the reasoning cannot be endorsed.

5.2.3 *Conclusion: Rejection of the Assurance Conception of Legitimate Expectations*

In conclusion, as a philosophical account of promise, the assurance view may be appealing to those who do not find the social practice view of promise convincing because Scanlon's theory captures a specific wrong done by promise-breaking, when it suggests that the obligation to keep a promise is owed to a specific individual who may or may not have contributed to the practice of promising. The simple conceptualisation of the wrong done from breaking a principle of fidelity offers an appealing ground of responsibility because one can appreciate the value of assurance to both promisors and promisees. It seems difficult to refute the contractualist logic that if both parties desire assurance, there is no reason to reject it.

From the claimant's perspective, this conception offers the advantage of securing protection of expectations without proving the intention of the state to undertake a legal obligation before relying on the promise to its detriment. However, from the perspective of implementing this conception in the investor–state context, the assurance conception should not be endorsed for the following reason. The preceding analysis illustrates the unjustifiable effect of using legitimate expectations as vehicle to convert a contract breach into a treaty breach. It also shows the failure of marrying the two incommensurable values of expectation and reliance.

The fundamental objection to this conception lies with its remedial effect. The undesirable consequence of this conception is that the investor would receive the performance of the promised act or the expectation damages, even though, as discussed, his or her reliance interest might provide the basis for the obligation. The rationale for these remedies is stated by Scanlon in the following terms:

> If one fails to fulfill a promise, one should compensate the promisee if one can, but the obligation one undertakes when one makes a promise is *an obligation to do the thing promised, not simply to do it or to compensate the promisee accordingly* ... In other words, having failed to do what one promised to do, one cannot bring it about that one has, nonetheless, fulfilled the obligation incurred by one's promise by compensating the promisee.[70]

[70] Scanlon, *What We Owe to Each Other* (n 2) 301 (emphasis added).

Closely related to the notion of assurance is trust.[71] In the philosophy literature, the concept of trust has been developed by some philosophers to construct the theory of promise. This alternative framework has penetrative insights for our understanding of legitimate expectations, which merit some reflections.

5.3 Variant Conception: Trust Theory of Promise and Legitimate Expectations

The notions of trust and promise are intimately linked, as suggested by many philosophers. Gary Watson speaks of promising as 'entitling others to take one's utterance as trustworthy'.[72] David Hume suggests that by breaking a promise, 'the promiser subjects himself to the penalty of never being trusted again'.[73] Dori Kimmel argues that by keeping a promise, 'a promiser can rehabilitate her reputation as a trustworthy person'.[74] Charles Fried observes that 'the device that gives trust its sharpest, most palpable form is promise'.[75]

The main enquiry in this section is to consider the extent to which the concept of protecting trust can provide a useful analytical framework for understanding protection of legitimate expectations in investment treaty arbitration (Section 5.3.3). The analysis draws insights from the philosophical works of Friedrich and Southwood on trust view of promise[76] (Section 5.3.1), as well as the English public law scholarship on trust-based concept of legitimate expectations[77] (Section 5.3.2).

[71] Pratt characterised Scanlon's obligation of a promise in terms of a general principle of wrongdoing, according to which it is wrong to let those down whom you have invited to trust. Pratt, 'Scanlon on Promising' (n 4) 148.

[72] G Watson, 'Asserting and Promising' (2004) 117 *Phil Stud* 57, 61.

[73] D Hume, *A Treatise of Human Nature* (Oxford: Oxford University Press, 2000), 335 ('when a man says he promises anything he, by making use of this form of words, subjects himself to the penalty of never being trusted again in case of failure').

[74] D Kimel, *From Promise to Contract: Towards a Liberal Theory of Contract* (Oxford: Hart Publishing, 2003).

[75] C Fried, *Contract as Promise: A Theory of Contractual Obligation* (Cambridge, MA: Harvard University Press, 1981), 16.

[76] Friedrich and Southwood, 'Promises beyond Assurance' (n 26) 276–80; D Friedrich and N Southwood, 'Promises and Trust' in H Sheinman (ed), *Promises and Agreements: Philosophical Essays* (Oxford: Oxford University Press, 2011).

[77] CF Forsyth, 'The Provenance and Protection of Legitimate Expectations' (1988) 47 *CLJ* 238; P Reynolds, 'Legitimate Expectations and the Protection of Trust in Public Officials' (2011) *PL* 330; CF Forsyth, 'Legitimate Expectations Revisited' (2011) 16(4) *JR* 429.

5.3.1 Conceptual Foundations of Trust View of Promise

Daniel Friedrich and Nicholas Southwood assert that under the trust view, a promise involves inviting another individual to trust one to do something; therefore the wrong in breaking a promise involves a betrayal of *trust reposed* in the promisor. The core principle of the trust theory is articulated in the following terms:

> Trusting one to do something . . . [']involves a form of *faith or optimism* that is more limited, since it is tie to the performance of some particular action or actions'. Moreover, the performance of such action has the importance for the promisee. Under the trust view, 'the performance of the very action that one is trusting another individual to perform is required to express adequate *fidelity* to the relationship'. The timely warning of nonfulfillment or compensation is not adequate.[78]

From the aforementioned statement of principle, two points can be made. First, the underlying justification for explaining the moral wrong from breaching the trust is absent. One can draw from Charles Fried's conception of trust that justifies the wrong based on the Kantian deontological imperative – namely, respect for individual autonomy.[79] Promise as a social convention involves bringing into existence a special kind of relationship between a promisor and a promisee. Based on the Kantian principles of trust and respect, it is wrong to invoke that convention in order to make a promise, and then to break it.[80] Therefore, in breaking a promise, the promisor betrays the trust held in him or her by the promisee. Such betrayal of trust affects the liberty and moral independence of the promisee.[81] Fried asserts:

> An individual is morally bound to keep his promises because he has intentionally invoked a convention whose function it is to give grounds – moral grounds – for another to expect the promised performance. To renege is to abuse a confidence he was free to invite or not, and which he intentionally did invite.[82]

78 Friedrich and Southwood, 'Promises and Trust' (n 76) 279 (emphasis added).

79 Fried, *Contract as Promise* (n 75) 16 ('the obligation to keep a promise is grounded not in arguments of utility but in respect for individual autonomy and in trust').

80 Ibid 17.

81 T Pink, 'Promising and Obligations' (2009) 23(1) *Phil Per* 389 (he argued that 'deliberately to invite trust, and then to betray that trust for no good reason, and to do so in circumstances where one's trustworthiness clearly matters to the person betrayed, is to show them contempt. And it is that contempt that explains the peculiar sense of wrong felt by the victims of broken promises.').

82 Ibid 16.

Second, there are two important concepts which need clarifications in the statement of principle. The first concept of 'inviting someone to trust one to do something' entails that 'for someone to trust one to do something she must have *a certain faith or optimism* in one's character insofar as one's doing it is concerned'.[83] The authors also make a distinction between *trust simpliciter* which 'requires a relatively all-encompassing faith or optimism in one's character' and 'trusting one to do something', which 'involves a form of faith or optimism that is more limited, since it is tie to the performance of some particular action or actions'.[84] It is also important that the trusted thing has a certain importance for him or her.[85]

The second notion of 'inviting' implies 'in effect, signaling to the other individual one's recognition of the importance that the relevant action has for him or her, and one's willingness to be moved on that basis, to license him or her to have the requisite faith or optimism in one's character with regard to the performance of that action'.[86] In other words, it is 'a kind of overture to the other individual to be party to a certain kind of relationship'.

Based on the proposed trust view of promise, in the investor–state context, by promising, the state makes an overture to the investor, displaying its willingness to be a party to the special relationship with the investor, in which the investor has a certain faith or optimism in the state's character that it will perform some action that is important to the investor.

5.3.2 Trust-based Conception of Legitimate Expectation as Applied in English Public Law

Trust has been considered as a very important normative basis for protection of legitimate expectations in domestic public laws, notably in the German[87] and English laws.[88] It is argued that protection of trust

[83] Friedrich and Southwood, 'Promises and Trust' (n 76) 280 (emphasis added).

[84] Ibid 279.

[85] Ibid.

[86] Ibid.

[87] M Schroeder, 'Administrative Law in Germany' in R Seerden and F Stroink (eds), *Administrative Law of the European Union, Its Members and the United States* (Gronigen: Intersentia, 2002), 119 (the principle of Vertrauensschutz ensures that 'everyone who trusts the legality of a public administrative decision should be protected').

[88] S Schønberg, *Legitimate Expectations in Administrative Law* (Oxford: Oxford University Press, 2000), 30 (he suggests that fairness as a basis for protection of legitimate expectation is supplemented by two practical considerations, 'protection of legitimate

held by a citizen in the public authority enhances the authority and legitimacy of the government. In the context of English public law, Professor Forsyth relied on the importance of trust and the authority of public officials as the justificatory basis for protection of legitimate expectations:

> The justification for the protection of legitimate expectations is the simple idea that *the law should protect the trust that has been reposed in the promise made by an official.* Good government depends upon trust between the governed and the governor. Unless that trust is sustained and protected officials will not be believed and individuals will not order their affairs on that assumption.[89]

By contrast, the lack of trust would impair the reputation and credibility of the government and compromise administrative efficiency because people would be reluctant to lend full support and cooperation.[90] One scholar highlighted the justification of legitimate expectations from this perspective:

> The theoretical underpinnings of the concept [legitimate expectations] are well-documented and need not be rehearsed at length. *If an individual is informed by an official that he will receive a particular benefit and that representation is subsequently resiled from, trust in government is impaired.* A general tendency for promises to be broken may damage the reputation of the administration as a whole. The willingness of individuals to participate in the decision-making process and to comply with decisions may consequently diminish.[91]

The problem with the trust rationale of legitimate expectations is not that its premise about the value of protecting trust is questionable; rather how

expectations will in the long term promote *trust in public authorities* and thereby also their perceived legitimacy and efficacy' [emphasis added]).

89 Forsyth, 'Legitimate Expectations Revisited' (n 77) 430 (emphasis added); a similar position has been expressed by Forsyth in his earlier work: CF Forsyth, 'The Provenance and Protection of Legitimate Expectations' (1988) 47 *CLJ* 238 ('the judicial motivation for seeking to protect such expectations is plain: if the executive undertakes, expressly or by past practice, to behave in a particular way the subject expects that undertaking to be complied with. *That is surely fundamental to good government and it would be monstrous if the executive could freely renege on its undertakings. Public trust in the government should not be left unprotected*' [emphasis added]).

90 The role of trust in public authorities is clarified by P Craig and S Schønberg, 'Substantive Legitimate Expectations after Coughlan' (2000) *PL* 684, 697 ('Trust is highly valuable because individuals are more likely to participate in decision-making process, to co-operate with initiatives, and to comply with regulations devised by authorities which are perceived as trustworthy.').

91 I Steele, 'Substantive Legitimate Expectations: Striking the Right Balance?' (2005) 121 *LQR* 300, 309 (emphasis added).

it can offer concrete guidance when deciding cases of legitimate expectations is a mystery. Paul Reynolds, English public law scholar, offers an attempt to implement the trust rationale, the analysis of which offers useful reflections for our discussion.

The exposition of the Reynolds' central thesis – legitimate expectations should be protected so as to promote specific trust reposed in the administration – could be summarised in four steps.[92] First, he criticised other traditional justifications advanced by courts and legal scholars, such as fairness, abuse of power, good administration and legal certainty. The main argument is that those values may provide moral impetus but they do not provide concrete guidance.

Second, the author made a distinction between 'general trust' and 'specific trust' and argued that the doctrine of legitimate expectations only protects the specific trust for the following reason: if the doctrine protects all public trust, the level of generality 'collapses the doctrine into a general plea to fairness. It fails to recognise the doctrine's distinct role in offering protection'.[93] This, in effect, unnecessarily overextends the scope of the doctrine.

Third, the author clarified that a 'specific trust' is present 'where there has been a representation, or something sufficiently proximate, by the relevant public authority directed to the claimant individually or as a member of a class'.[94] In other words, there is a rebuttable presumption that the claimant *trusts* the public authority to comply with that representation.[95] Such rebuttable presumption could be justified on three main grounds. First, it is normal for an individual to trust in a decision-maker. Second, trust in public officials is essential to a proper political system. Third, it is important to secure public trust in political actors by institutionalisation of public trust, whereby public institutions assume the responsibility of protecting trust.[96]

Fourth, the author confirmed that actual reliance is not required in order to establish trust, but 'if reliance (pursuant to a representation) happens to be present the case is very clear, since trust must have been reposed'. Beyond its evidential usefulness, Reynolds suggests that 'such reliance is not relevant to actually establishing that a legitimate

92 Reynolds, 'Legitimate Expectations and the Protection of Trust in Public Officials' (n 77) 332–41.
93 Ibid 343.
94 Ibid 344.
95 Ibid 346.
96 Ibid 347.

expectation exists'.[97] This view is consistent with the philosophical view that trust and reliance are not the same concepts. Friedrich and Southwood explained that 'inviting someone to rely on one to do something does not entail inviting her to trust one to do it . . . nor does inviting someone to trust one to do something entail inviting her to rely on one to do it'.[98] Therefore, inducing reliance without corresponding trust cannot create a promissory obligation.[99]

Reynolds' analysis can be commended on two accounts. First, it exposes the weaknesses of traditional justifications of legitimate expectations based on fairness, abuse of power or good administration. Second, it attempts to clarify how the trust rationale could resolve concrete cases of legitimate expectations. For instance, situations in which expectations are not based on a promise or a representation fall outside the scope of the proposed framework because claimants cannot have been said to repose specific trust on public authorities. In this way, the principle of legitimate expectation plays a distinct role.

This analytical framework cannot provide the model for thinking about trust rationale in our context because of two main problems. The first problem lies with its presumption that upon a specific representation, there is a specific trust, as stated: 'when a public official makes an express representation that something will happen the recipient would be unusual if he did not place trust in that representation and expect it to be fulfilled'.[100]

The presumption of trust based on specific representation provides a convenient and easy way to avoid defining the fundamental concept of trust. A specific representation is merely used as a substitute for specific trust. If one takes the notion of trust as elaborated in the work of Friedrich and Southwood as having 'a certain faith or optimism in one's character and integrity', one will have a narrower conception of legitimate expectations. That may not be the most appropriate definition to adopt. The main criticism is that the theory of legitimate expectations based on trust rationale cannot be a valid one without defining the core 'trust' notion.

[97] Ibid 346.
[98] Friedrich and Southwood, 'Promises and Trust' (n 76) 285.
[99] Ibid 285 ('invitations to rely that are not accompanied by corresponding invitations to trust do not suffice to create the kind of obligation that is involved in making a promise').
[100] Reynolds, 'Legitimate Expectations and the Protection of Trust in Public Officials' (n 77) 347.

The second problem is the undesirable consequence of the presumptive notion of trust, which leads to legitimate expectations being applicable to a wide range of situations. For instance, Reynolds suggests that 'it is entirely possible for a representation made by way of a policy statement to incite specific trust that that public official will stick to her word'.[101] This outcome may be considered as reasonable from the public law rationale, which ensures a consistent and predictable conduct of the state. It could be argued that such extensive scope would unduly fetter the sovereign right to regulate in the investment treaty context. Furthermore, the fact that the proposed trust-based conception does not require detrimental reliance further expands the scope of legitimate expectations.

5.3.3 Assessing the Transposition of the Trust Conception of Legitimate Expectations to Investment Treaty Context

Trust encourages participation of individuals, cooperation with the government and compliance with the laws. In the context of domestic law, based on John Locke's political theory, legitimacy of political authority must be based on 'a structure of well-founded trust', therefore trust is essential for social and political order, because individuals are more likely to participate in decision-making processes, to cooperate with initiatives and to comply with regulations devised by authorities which are perceived as trustworthy. However, 'trust' in the context of public law may well differ from that in the investment treaty context. The investor's trust is concerned more with economic interest than the legitimacy or authority of the government, as is the case with the trust of the citizens in the government.

Is the importance of trust in the investor–state relationship sufficient justification for applying the trust rationale? The main argument in this section is that trust rationale should remain as a moral aspiration as opposed to a justification for protection of legitimate expectations because such account of legitimate expectations will be uncertain depending on different conceptions of trust.

Nevertheless, the value of trust in the investor–host state relationship is uncontested because investors usually develop trust and confidence in the host state before committing their capital in an investment project.[102]

[101] Ibid 348.

[102] This may be understood in terms of trust conception as an encapsulated interest proposed by Russell Hardin. See R Hardin, *Trust and Trustworthiness* (New York, NY: Russell Sage Foundation, 2002) 1 ('on this account, I trust you because I think it

It is unquestionable that when foreign investors repose trust in host states, they are more inclined to participate and make investments in pursuit of mutually beneficial interests.[103]

The trust conception of promise seems particularly appealing in the context of investor–host state relationship, in which an investor is often induced into making investments following the state's assurance and trust that their investments will be fairly treated or the state will comply with its promise. The role of promising under the trust view is to modify the investor's relations with the host state by 'licensing investors to have faith and optimism' in the state's character with regard to the performance of actions which are important to investors. Therefore, if one of the purposes of an investment treaty is to serve as a cooperative instrument between investors and host states, the law should promote trust in the host state.[104]

The concept of trust has featured in some arbitral awards concerning legitimate expectations. But none of these arbitral decisions relied on protection of trust as a conceptual guidance in resolving cases or as an underlying rationale of legitimate expectations. For instance, the tribunal in *Total v. Argentina* stated that the degree of specificity of declaration made by a host state to the addressee affects the entitlement to rely on it 'in a context of reciprocal trust and good faith'.[105] The tribunal in *Franc Charles v. Moldova* confirmed that factors, such as time and effort, affect how much an investor can 'trust' that the government would comply with its contractual obligation; the open, transparent and continuous performance of his or her investment contributed to 'building legitimate trust' in the validity of his or her position.[106] The tribunal in *Tecmed v. Mexico* affirmed that the fair and equitable treatment provision reflected the parties' intention to 'strengthen and increase the *security and trust of*

is in your interest to take my interests in the relevant matter seriously in the following sense: You value the continuation of our relationship, and you therefore have your own interests in taking my interests into account. That is, you encapsulate my interests in your own interests.').

[103] J Dunn, 'The Concept of "Trust" in the Politics of John Locke' in R Rorty, JB Schneewind and Q Skinner (eds), *Philosophy in History: Essays in the Historiography of Philosophy* (Cambridge: Cambridge University Press, 1984).

[104] CF Forsyth, 'Wednesbury Protection of Substantive Legitimate Expectations' (1997) *PL* 375–73 ('[citizens] who have placed their trust in the promises of officials, should not find, when that trust is betrayed, that the law can give no remedy').

[105] *Total S.A. v. Argentina*, ICSID Case No ARB/04/1, Decision on Liability (21 December 2010) para 121.

[106] *Franck Charles Arif v. Republic of Moldova*, ICSID Case No ARB/11/23, Award (8 April 2013) para 544.

foreign investors that invest in the member States, thus maximising the use of the economic resources . . . by facilitating the economic contributions of their economic operators'.[107]

The main challenge of applying the trust conception of promise as the underlying rationale is the lack of clarity and uncertainty. Trust is a highly abstract and amorphous notion.[108] However, we could formulate the trust rationale of legitimate expectations based on the trust view of promise proposed by Friedrich and Southwood. The postulate could be: *when the state, through its representation or conduct, has invited the investor to put trust in its conduct or action, the state should be responsible for the (harmful) consequence of that breach of trust.*[109]

The proposed postulate may leave some interpretive challenges. For instance, how can a tribunal ascertain that an investor *trusts* as opposed to merely *relies on* a host state, especially proving a form of 'faith or optimism' that the investor has in the host state? Reliance and trust may be, arguably, very closely connected and difficult to distinguish.[110] Trusting usually concerns a *character and integrity* of a promisor.[111] How can one identify a character and integrity of a state as an entity? It could be possible to imagine that the justification of legitimate expectations could be based on a theory of trust properly developed in the context of investor–state relationship. Such theory of trust would have to address how inviting trust can create an obligation in the context of investor–state relationship. Is it because the breach of trust involves causing harm to the other person or that it constitutes a disrespect for the person's dignity and autonomy?[112]

107 *Técnicas Medioambientales Tecmed, S.A. v. Mexico*, ICSID Additional Facility Case No ARB(AF)/00/02, Award (29 May 2003) para 156 (emphasis added).

108 There is considerable disagreement among philosophers about just what trust involves. See PJ Nickel, 'Trust and Obligation-Ascription' (2007) 10(3) *Ethical Theory Moral Pract* 309.

109 Adopting the terms used by Friedrich and Southwood: by promising, the state makes an overture to the investor, displaying its willingness to be a party to the special relationship with the investor, in which the investor has a certain faith or optimism in the state's character that it will perform some action that is important to the investor.

110 A Baler, 'Trust and Antitrust' (1986) 96 *Ethics* 231 ('trust must be distinguished from reliance. It is a special kind of reliance: reliance on a person's goodwill towards one.').

111 P Hieronymi, 'The Reasons of Trust' (2008) 86 (2) *Aus J Phil* 213 ('the reasons for which one trusts a particular person on a particular occasion concern, not the value, importance, or necessity of trust itself, but rather *the trustworthiness of the person in question* in the matter at hand' [emphasis added]).

112 Fried, *Contract as Promise* (n 75).

5.4 Conclusion

Both assurance and trust conceptions of promise offer an appealing alternative framework to the voluntarist conception. Those two conceptions do not require an expectation to stem from *a legally binding* commitment but rather from the intentional act of creating expectations in the promisee. Like the voluntarist conception, the assurance conception does not offer a sophisticated framework for distinguishing between the contract breach and the treaty breach. Furthermore, it does not take into account the promisee's conduct in the assessment of liability. Above all, the theory has to choose where it puts its heart – the expectation created or the act of detrimental reliance. The trust conception of promise offers useful insights because it anchors an obligation to protect legitimate expectations in the intimate and proximate relationship created between the promisee and the promisor. However, this highly abstract notion may lead to some difficulties of implementing the rules. The search for a more suitable rationale for protection of legitimate expectations continues in Chapter 6.

6

Protecting against Investor's Detrimental Reliance

Reliance Conception of Legitimate Expectations

6.1 Introduction

This chapter seeks to elucidate the doctrine of legitimate expectations from the reliance theory of promise which attributes an obligation to protect legitimate expectations to the act of detrimental reliance by the investor on the state's promise. The investor's 'bare expectations' should not be protected because without the act of reliance, there would be no harm to compensate for. The core of the reliance theory finds its expression in the passage of the investment treaty decision in *AWG v. Argentina*, which confirms that the expectations alone are insufficient as a basis for obligation:

> This Tribunal finds that an important element of such cases has not been sufficiently emphasized: that investors, deriving their expectations from the laws and regulations adopted by the host country, *acted in reliance upon* those laws and regulations and changed their economic position as a result. *Thus it was not the investor's legitimate expectations alone that led tribunals to find a denial of fair and equitable treatment. It was the existence of such expectations created by host country laws, coupled with the act of investing their capital in reliance on them*, and a subsequent, sudden change in those laws that led to a determination that the host country had not treated the investors fair and equitably.[1]

This passage raises some fundamental questions concerning the reliance theory. First, does reliance have to be intentionally induced or it is sufficient that the state has the knowledge of the investor's probable reliance? Second, what is the relationship between the state's conduct and the investor's act of reliance for supplying predicates for liability? Is it the reliance or the intention to induce such reliance or both which

[1] *AWG Group v. Argentina*, UNCITRAL Case, Decision on Liability (30 July 2010) para 226 (emphasis added).

explains the liability? Is there any difference in each case? These questions have practical implications on whether the tribunals should focus on the state's conduct or the investor's reliance or both, and how are they conceptually related.

The tribunal seemed to focus on the state's deliberate and active act of creating expectations[2] and the investor's perspectives by asking the following question: 'what would have been the legitimate and reasonable expectations of a reasonable investor in the position of the Claimants, at the time they made their investment in 1993 [in light of the relevant circumstances]?'[3]

This chapter develops the reliance theory of legitimate expectations based on the reliance theory of promissory obligation in three main parts. First, it extracts the core principles from the reliance theory of promissory obligation and articulates the reformulated reliance principle for protection of legitimate expectations (Section 6.2). Second, it examines the key elements – namely, conduct, reliance and reasonableness of expectations – by reference to investment treaty decisions, theories and relevant legal practices (Section 6.3). Third, it offers a critical analysis of the reliance conception of legitimate expectations (Section 6.4).

6.2 The Reliance Theory of Promise and Conceptualisation of Legitimate Expectations

6.2.1 The Underlying Philosophical Framework Based on MacCormick's and Atiyah's Theories of Promise

The reliance theory of promise states that when the promisor induces the promisee to rely on his or her representation and the promisee does rely on it to his or her detriment, the promisor will be responsible for rectifying that harm. It is the law's duty to intervene to protect against detrimental harm.[4] Detrimental reliance is the underpinning basis for an obligation under this theory.[5]

[2] Ibid ('[The investors' expectations] did not suddenly and surprisingly come into their minds the way Athena sprang from the head of Zeus. Argentina through its laws, the treaties it signed, its government statements, and especially the elaborate legal framework which it designed and enacted, deliberately and actively sought to create those expectations in the Claimants').

[3] Ibid para 228.

[4] P Ardal, 'And That's a Promise' (1968) 18(72) *Phil Q* 225.

[5] J Mill, *On Liberty, Utilitarianism and Other Essays* (edited by M Philip and F Rosen) (Oxford: Oxford University Press, 2nd edn, 2015).

The reliance conception derives its justification from the harm principle[6] – namely, that there is a general obligation not to cause preventable harm to others.[7] This obligation derives from both utilitarian and non-utilitarian grounds. The utilitarian justification concerns social cooperation and social arrangement. Leaving people's reliance unprotected may discourage them to be willing to cooperate with each other, which will leave society as a whole worse off.[8] The non-utilitarian justification rests on Kantian moral imperative – namely, respect for individual autonomy.[9] Breaking the promise on which the promisee relies causes harm, which should be prevented or compensated. The duty to prevent or compensate harm is rooted in the principle of corrective justice.[10]

This chapter draws insights from Neil MacCormick's and PS Atiyah's theories of promissory obligation to formulate a specific principle applicable to the investment treaty arbitration.

MacCormick articulated a specific principle as a justification for the binding nature of promise based on a general duty not to cause preventable harm – namely, the wrongness of disappointing people whom we have wilfully induced to take action on the faith of our assurance about present facts or future acts:

> If one person acts in a potentially detrimental way in reliance upon beliefs about another's future conduct, and if the latter person has by some act of his *intentionally or knowingly* induced the former to rely upon him, then the latter has an obligation not to act in a manner which will disappoint the other's reliance.[11]

Based on MacCormick's theory of promise, two main elements would be required to establish an obligation: (1) the fact that the state intended the investor to rely upon it, or knew or thought it likely that the investor would so rely, and (2) the fact that the investor has taken detrimental

[6] Ibid ('that principle is, that the sole end for which mankind are warranted, individually or collectively, in interfering with the liberty of action of any of their number, is self-protection. That the only purpose for which power can be rightfully exercised over any member of a civilized community, against his will, is to prevent harm to others.').

[7] N MacCormick, 'Voluntary Obligations and Normative Powers' (1972) 46(Supplement) *Proceedings of the Aristotelian Society* 59.

[8] D Barak-Erez, 'The Doctrine of Legitimate Expectations and the Distinction between the Reliance and Expectation Interests' (2005) 11(4) *EPL* 583, 588.

[9] Ibid.

[10] E Weinrib 'Toward a Moral Theory of Negligence Law' (1983) 2 *L & Phil* 38.

[11] MacCormick, 'Voluntary Obligations and Normative Powers' (n 7) 68 (emphasis added).

action in the belief that the state will take certain action in the future.[12] This approach may be construed as a modified version of the will theory,[13] but it can be distinguished on the basis that the object on which the promisor wills is not the obligation but the reliance of the promisee.[14]

It is important to note how MacCormick's reliance principle has been reformulated in the context of the public law doctrine of legitimate expectations:

> A public authority's freedom to take action in the public interest is limited to the extent that it causes harm to particular individuals. *If a public authority has induced a person to rely upon its representations or conduct, realizing that such reliance was a real possibility, it is under a prima facie duty to act in such a way that the reliance will not be detrimental to the representee.* The authority must honour the expectations created by its representation or, at least, compensate the person affected for his reliance loss.[15]

The reformulated principle is notable for three aspects. First, the reiteration of the public authority's freedom to exercise its discretion finds the equivalent expression in the notion of state sovereignty in the context of investment treaty arbitration. However, the freedom of regulatory power may be limited to the extent that its exercise causes harm to others. Second, the volitional element in MacCormick's principle is omitted and only the 'knowledge' element is maintained in the reformulated version. This may be explained by the fact that the public authority's intention may be difficult to prove. Third, adding a reference to 'prima facie' duty is significant in the context of public law[16] because it implies that such duty may be defeated by the overriding public interest.

[12] N MacCormick, 'Voluntary Obligations' in N MacCormick (ed), *Legal Right and Social Democracy: Essays in Legal and Political Philosophy* (Oxford: Clarendon Press, 1982), 205 ('it is wrong in that the promisor thereby harms the promisee in a way for which he is responsible . . . a negative utilitarian morality (which gives priority to not harming people, as against failing to benefit them) can account for the bindingness of such promises'.).

[13] J Raz, 'Reply to MacCormick' (1972) 46(Supplement) *Proceedings of the Aristotelian Society* 80, 99.

[14] M Hogg, *Promises and Contract Law, Comparative Perspectives* (Cambridge: Cambridge University Press, 2014), 99.

[15] S Schønberg, *Legitimate Expectations in Administrative Law* (Oxford: Oxford University Press, 2000) 10 (emphasis added).

[16] D Ross, *Foundations of Ethics* (Oxford: Blackwell Philosophy Anthologies, 1939) 83–86; F Snare, 'The Definition of Prima Facie Duties' (1974) 24(96) *Phil Q* 235.

Nevertheless, Schønberg rejected the reliance principle as the justificatory basis for protection of legitimate expectations in the public law context because its scope of application is too narrow. He argued that detriment reliance should not be a precondition for protection of legitimate expectations[17] because this would render many situations outside the scope of the principle. For instance, procedural protection of legitimate expectations should be available in the absence of reliance. One can support his argument in the public law area,[18] where legitimate expectation seeks to protect against a wide range of situations, such as abuse of power, inconsistent conduct or legal uncertainty.[19]

The more sophisticated version of the reliance theory should also take into account the promisee's conduct. Atiyah's theory of promise suggests that reliance can be induced intentionally or knowingly but asserts that such intentionally induced reliance *alone* is insufficient to generate an obligation.[20] The crucial element of his theory is that such reliance must conform to some socially accepted values.[21]

It is important to note that Atiyah's approach does not primarily focus on whether one party intentionally makes a promise or a specific representation to induce reliance but whether such reliance is reasonable. Justification for this requirement is essentially based on the need for 'allocation of entitlements'.[22] The promisee who voluntarily relies on the assumption or expectation created is required to exercise this autonomous decision-making power responsibly. The challenge of applying Atiyah's reliance theory lies with the lack of clarification on the notion of 'socially accepted values'. However, it is suggested that laws should be the starting point for determining these values.[23]

17 Schønberg, *Legitimate Expectations* (n 15) 10.

18 However, some authors advocate for a more distinct and restricted scope of legitimate expectations: P Reynolds, 'Legitimate Expectations and the Protection of Trust in Public Officials' (2011) *PL* 330.

19 It was already argued in Chapter 3 that these values are not the core values in investment treaty arbitration.

20 PS Atiyah, *Promises, Morals and the Law* (Oxford: Oxford University Press, 1981) ('it fails to explain … why the harm which is suffered by the promisee from his disappointed expectations or reliance should be ascribed to the promisor. The mere fact that he has these expectations or has acted upon them cannot alone justify that ascription.').

21 Ibid 68.

22 Ibid.

23 Ibid 69 ('Even a moral code must surely start with the law of contrac, just as moral wrongs relating to theft must start with the law of property').

6.2.2 *Reformulated Reliance Principle and Protection of Legitimate Expectations*

Guided by the underlying philosophical framework just discussed, the reformulated reliance principle for protection of legitimate expectations can be stated as follows: a host state's sovereign power to regulate in the public interest is limited to the extent that it causes harm to particular investors. Where a host state has, through its representation or conduct, created or induced expectations on the part of an investor, upon which the investor has reasonably relied, the host state has a duty to prevent the detriment from such reliance, the failure of which incurs a duty to compensate the investor for his reliance loss.

There are five preliminary remarks about the reformulated principle. First, the theory of detrimental reliance underlines protection of the investor's legitimate expectations. This means that the fundamental purpose of the principle of legitimate expectations is to protect or prevent against detriment that investor who has suffered from its reasonable reliance on the state's promise.[24] Given that detrimental or injurious reliance is at the heart of the principle of legitimate expectations, the principle should operate by reference to the position of the investor, whilst paying regard to the state's conduct. The reformulated principle confirms that protection of legitimate expectations does not concern with enforcement of sovereign promise or protection of expectation interests. Nor does it seek to promote the rule of law, good administration or protection of trust reposed in the public authority. However, this does not deny the positive impact of correcting injustice caused by the state's conduct on the fulfilment of the public law objectives.

Second, the reliance conception of legitimate expectations underlines the reasoning of many investment treaty decisions.[25] Selected passages from two decisions will suffice to make the point. Detrimental reliance

[24] H Collins, *The Law of Contracts* (London: Weidenfeld & Nicolson, 1986) 38 ('the real meat of the reliance model lies in the requirement that the reliance must have been reasonable').

[25] *Mobil Investments Canada Inc. and Murphy Oil Corporation v. Canada*, ICSID Case No ARB(AF)/07/4, Decision on Liability and on Principles of Quantum (22 May 2012) para 156; *Southern Pacific Properties (Middle East) Ltd v. Arab Republic of Egypt*, ICSID Case No ARB/84/3, Award (20 May 1992); *CME v. Czech Republic*, UNCITRAL Case, Partial Award (13 September 2001) 9 ICSID Rep 121; *Mohammad Ammar Al-Bahloul v. The Republic of Tajikistan*, SCC Case No V (064/2008), Final Award (8 June 2010) para 210.

forms an important basis for the obligation to protect legitimate expectations. The tribunal in *AWG v. Argentina* stated:

> [I]nvestors, deriving their expectations from the laws and regulations adopted by the host country, *acted in reliance upon those laws and regulations and changed their economic position as a result. Thus it was not the investor's legitimate expectations alone* that led tribunals to find a denial of fair and equitable treatment.[26]

The tribunal in *Thunderbird v. Mexico* articulated the concept of legitimate expectations, in the context of the NAFTA framework to mean:

> [A] situation where a Contracting Party's conduct creates reasonable and justifiable expectations on the part of an investor (or investment) to act in reliance on said conduct, such that a failure by the NAFTA Party to honour those expectations could cause the investor (or investment) to suffer damages.[27]

Third, the proposed principle of legitimate expectations is conceptually more aligned with principles in domestic laws, such as equitable estoppel,[28] the law of negligence[29] and the public law of torts,[30] which are fundamentally concerned with compensation for loss. It is beyond the scope of this book to consider how the relevant insights can be drawn from those sources to enrich our understanding of legitimate expectations (bearing in mind of contextual and ideological differences).

Fourth, the appropriate remedy for a breach of legitimate expectations should be reliance damages rather than expectation damages[31] because remedy should aim to meet the primary objective of preventing or compensating the investor's reliance losses.

Fifth, at the heart of the reformulated principle is the balancing of two interests – the right to regulate, inherent in the fundamental principle of state sovereignty, and the right of the aggrieved investor protected by the moral principle of detrimental reliance. The reformulated principle provides a conceptual framework for balancing the two interests in a fair and

[26] *AWG v. Argentina* (n 1) para 226 (emphasis added).

[27] *International Thunderbird Gaming Corporation v. Mexico*, UNCITRAL Case, Final Award (26 January 2006) para 147.

[28] A Robertson, 'Towards a Unifying Purpose for Estoppel' (1996) 22(1) *Mon LR* 1.

[29] J Gardner, 'What Is Tort Law For? Part 1. The Place of Corrective Justice' (2011) 30(1) *L & Phil* 33.

[30] M Geoff, 'What Are We to Do with the Public Law of Torts?' (2009) 7 *NZJPIL*, Victoria University of Wellington Legal Research Paper No 16/2012.

[31] This issue will be discussed in detail in Chapter 9.

equitable manner, which is consistent with the rationale of investment treaties in promoting mutually beneficial relationships.

6.3 Normative Implications of the Reliance Conception of Legitimate Expectations

This section analyses three normative components of the reliance principle – namely, the conduct capable of creating legitimate expectations (Section 6.3.1), detrimental reliance (Section 6.3.2) and reasonableness of expectations (Section 6.3.3). The analysis will be based on investment treaty decisions, political theories and legal practices.

6.3.1 *The 'Conduct' Capable of Creating Legitimate Expectations*

In the current jurisprudence, there seem to be two different approaches to understanding the conduct which gives rise to legitimate expectations. The first approach focuses on the effect of state conduct on the creation of expectation (investor-based approach). For instance, the tribunal in *Thunderbird v. Mexico* asked 'whether the State's conduct creates reasonable and justifiable expectations on the part of an investor'. Similarly, the tribunal in *Micula v. Romania* focused on 'whether the state, through statements or conduct, has contributed to *the creation of a reasonable expectation*'.[32] The second approach ascertains whether the state made 'clear and explicit representations made by or attributable to' the host state[33] (state-based approach).

Before examining which types of conduct can create legitimate expectations under the reliance conception, I briefly examine two characteristics of representation – namely, 'specificity' (Section 6.3.1.1) and 'intentionality' (Section 6.3.1.2).

6.3.1.1 Specificity of Representation

Why is it that a specific representation is required for a claim in legitimate expectations? In what way is it relevant under the reliance conception? In the case of estoppel, unconscionability is hard to establish when the representation is ambiguous.[34] In the context of public law, some

[32] *Thunderbird v. Mexico* (n 27) para 669; *Ioan Micula, Viorel Micula, S.C. European Food S. A, S.C. Starmill S.R.L. and S.C. Multipack S.R.L. v. Romania*, ICSID Case No ARB/05/20, Final Award (11 December 2013) (emphasis added).

[33] *Mobil v. Canada* (n 25) para 154.

[34] *Australian Crime Commission v. Gray* [2003] NSWCA 318 para 200.

scholars suggest that specific representation assumes special weight for imposing a duty of care on the public authority.[35]

Viewed under the reliance theory, specificity of representation should be appreciated in terms of its impact on creating the expectations and inducing reliance. The clearer representation means that it is more likely to induce detrimental reliance and interfere more with a decision-making autonomy of the investor.[36] On this point, the tribunal in *Total v. Argentina* suggested that the investor's entitlement to rely on the state depends on the nature of the state's undertaking: 'the more specific the declaration to the addressee(s), the more credible the claim that such an addressee (the foreign investor concerned) *was entitled to rely on it* for the future in a context of reciprocal trust and good faith'.[37] Therefore, a specific representation is more likely to create more legitimate expectations, but it is not a sufficient ground for an obligation to occur. This contrasts with the voluntarist conception, whereby a specific representation exhibits 'an intention to undertake an obligation'.[38]

6.3.1.2 Intentionality of Representation

Does the state have to intentionally create expectation or induce reliance? For instance, the tribunal in *AWG v. Argentina* characterised the state's act as a 'deliberate and active' creation of expectations. An intention of the state to induce reliance could be inferred.[39] However, if detrimental reliance is treated as the basis of the obligation, it is hard to defend the argument that the investor's reliance must always be knowingly or intentionally induced.[40]

[35] P Sales and K Steyn, 'Legitimate Expectations in English Law: An Analysis' (2004) *PL* 564 ('short of a clear and unequivocal assurance by the public authority, the individual's interest does not assume special weight so as to impose upon the public authority a duty of particular care (beyond the usual public law duties) in relation to decision-making affecting that individual').

[36] J Conison, 'Assurance, Reliance, and Expectation' (1998) 6 *S Cal Interdis LJ* 335, 396.

[37] *Total S.A. v. Argentina*, ICSID Case No ARB/04/1, Decision on Liability (21 December 2010) para 121 (emphasis added).

[38] Collins, *The Law of Contracts* (n 24) 38 ('an express promise [will suffice], but also actions short of a promise which amount to the deliberate creation or encouragement of an expectation of future action').

[39] *Pierson v. Altrincham Urban Council* (1917) 86 LJ KB 969, 972, per Lord Reading CJ; 973, per Lush J ('an intention to induce reliance may be inferred as a fact if the representation was such as would reasonably have the effect of inducing the representee to believe and act upon it as true').

[40] Atiyah, *Promises, Morals and the Law* (n 20) 40.

The current jurisprudence confirms that both legally binding and non-legally binding representation can give rise to a legal obligation to protect legitimate expectations under the reliance conception. The analysis of the following selected decisions illustrates the required characteristics of the state's conduct under the reliance conception, such as contractual arrangement (Section 6.3.1.2.1), legislative framework (Section 6.3.1.2.2) and non-legally binding representation, such as administrative representation made by public officials or consistent conduct (Section 6.3.1.2.3).

6.3.1.2.1 Contractual Arrangement and Legitimate Expectations

Under the reliance theory, a contract does not function as a voluntary undertaking but as 'instruments of particular species of harm'.[41] The law's intervention in the case of relied-upon promises is to protect against harm resulting from reliance on the conduct of the promisee.[42] The clarity of the contractual term was important but not essential to establishing liability. The essential element is the fact that the contractual representation created the expectations in the investor and the investor acted on that representation to its detriment. The decision of *Duke Energy v. Ecuador* illustrates this point.[43]

The tribunal had to consider investors' expectations arising from the contractual arrangement in the assessment of the FET standard. This dispute involved several contracts in electricity supply arrangement (PPAs) entered into between power generator companies and the state-owned entity. The dispute arose in the political and economic context of Ecuador's energy crisis and national shortage. The two main issues concerning legitimate expectations relate to the penalties under the PPAs and poor implementation of the payment guarantee.

On the first issue, the tribunal had to consider whether Duke Energy had reasonable expectations that there would be no outstanding penalties under the PPAs when it made its investment in Electroquil. The tribunal held that the claimant's expectation that there would be no outstanding penalties under the PPAs, incurred by Electroquil's non-performance, was unreasonable because of the absence of clear assurances from the government[44] and the knowledge of the regulatory risk on the part of the investor. The tribunal reasoned that:

[41] M Pratt, 'Defeating Reasonable Reliance' (1999) 18 *U Tas LR* 181.

[42] A Robertson 'Reliance and Expectation in Estoppel Remedies' (1998) 18 *Leg Stud* 360, 365.

[43] *Duke Energy Electroquil Partners & Electroquil S.A. v. Ecuador*, ICSID Case No ARB/04/19, Award (18 August 2008).

[44] Ibid para 352.

> Duke Energy was thus aware of the risk that Electroquil could be fined for nonperformance and it assumed the related business risk. It appears, however, to have expected that no fines were yet to be imposed on account of facts that predated the investment. *The Tribunal does not believe that this expectation can be viewed as reasonable when one bears in mind the manner in which payments were handled and the opacity that prevailed in the administration of the contract prior to Duke Energy's investment.* In view of the contract history, the expectation could only have been deemed reasonable if it had been based on clear assurances from the Government.[45]

The tribunal's reasoning is underpinned by the reliance conception, which took into account the circumstances as well as the clarity of assurance to determine the reasonableness of expectations. The tribunal did not regard the absence of assurance as the lack of voluntary undertaking but as a relevant factor in assessing the reasonableness of the claimant's expectation. In any case, the tribunal held that there was no use of sovereign power in imposing sanctions/penalties; therefore such a contract breach does not rise to the level of a violation of fair and equitable treatment.[46]

On the second issue of the non-implementation of payment guarantee, the tribunal held that Electroquil's expectations embodied in the 1995 PPA did not contain any undertaking of a payment guarantee on the part of the Ministry of Finance, and the establishment of the Payment Trust did not imply the exercise of sovereign power, so Electroquil's expectations under such agreement were regarded as mere contractual expectations.[47]

[45] Ibid para 351 (emphasis added).

[46] Ibid para 354.

[47] Ibid para 358. *Philip Morris v. Uruguay* confirms that the investor's legitimate expectations of the host country's legal stability cannot be based on *provisions of general legislation applicable to a plurality of persons.* The dispute arose out of the enactment of a certain ordinance by the Uruguayan Ministry of Public Health and the enactment of a presidential decree prohibiting different packaging for cigarettes sold under a given brand and mandating graphic images showing the adverse health effects of smoking. It concerned the formulation of general regulations for the protection of public health. The tribunal had to consider whether the claimant could have a legitimate expectation that the regulatory framework would not be changed.

The tribunal seemed to adhere to the reliance conception. The tribunal stated that 'legitimate expectations depend on specific undertakings and representations made by the host State to induce investors to make an investment'. Furthermore, the tribunal showed that it had taken into account the conduct of the investor when it emphasised that the investor should exercise due diligence in inquiring about the prospects of a change in the regulatory framework and the surrounding circumstances. In this case, the tribunal held that the claimants had no legitimate expectations that the respondent would not take measures to protect the health of its citizens, especially in the absence of specific undertaking to that effect.

The 1996 PPA led to a different outcome because Electroquil entered into the 1996 PPA with the expectation that the Ministry of Finance would comply with the payment mechanism. Given that the guarantee entailed the exercise of sovereign power,[48] the failure to implement the payment guarantee constituted a breach of the fair and equitable treatment. Similarly, the tribunal's reasoning is framed in terms of the reasonableness of the investor's reliance on the state's representation.[49]

With regard to Duke Energy's expectations about the payment guarantee, Duke Energy requested certain guarantees from the state as a condition precedent to its investment, notably the Payment Decree and the establishment of the Payment Trusts. The tribunal held that the failure to implement the payment guarantee by the respondent frustrated Duke Energy's reasonable expectations and thus breached the FET standard:

> When seeking to determine whether these expectations were reasonable in the circumstances, one might ask *whether an experienced investor such as Duke Energy should not have paid closer attention to the procedure set up to implement the payment guarantee. In light of the clear terms of the Payment Trust Agreements and of the Payment Decree, which Duke Energy considered as conditions precedent to its investment, the Tribunal finds that the latter was reasonably entitled to rely on the commitment of the Government.* In other words, Duke Energy's expectations must be deemed reasonable.[50]

The tribunal's reasoning calls for two observations. First, the liability focuses on the assessment of the act of reliance by the investor on the state's promise rather than whether the state made the specific commitment. Second, the terms of the agreement as well as the experience of the investor play a significant factor in the assessment of the investor's expectations. The tribunal's reasoning which framed the analysis in terms of the investor's entitlement of reliance could be endorsed under the reliance conception.

6.3.1.2.2 Expectations Created by Legislative Framework Under the reliance conception, the threshold for establishing legitimate expectations arising from the legislative framework focuses on whether the laws have created the expectations which result in the promisee's detrimental

[48] Ibid para 360.
[49] Ibid para 361.
[50] Ibid para 363 (emphasis added).

reliance. Therefore, the context and the manner in which the laws have induced the investor's expectations are relevant for determining the liability. The selected cases under the analysis – *Enron v. Argentina*,[51] *National Grid v. Argentina*[52] and *AWG v. Argentina*[53] – emphasise this point.

In *Enron v. Argentina*, in determining the basis for liability for a breach of the fair and equitable treatment, the tribunal relied on two important elements: (1) the seducing effect of the guarantees of the tariff regime specifically addressed to the investors in the gas sectors[54] and (2) the actual reliance on the conditions established by the regulatory framework by the investor.[55] The tribunal held the state to be liable because the claimant suffered from harm as a result of 'substantial change of the legal and business framework'[56] that induced its investment and which was no longer in place.[57]

Similarly, in *National Grid v. Argentina*, the key issue is whether the change of regulatory framework for the electricity industry privatisation, which frustrated the investor's legitimate expectation, constituted a breach of the FET standard. The tribunal focused on the state's act of inducing the claimant[58] by 'offering a different image of the country with a severe economic crisis to investors' based on the BITs and the regulatory framework and the claimant's reliance on the key elements of the Regulatory Framework in its decision to invest in Argentina.[59]

The tribunal held that there was a breach of the FET standard because 'it fundamentally changed the legal framework on the basis of which the Respondent itself had solicited investments and the Claimant had made them'.[60] The combination of the act of inducing and the result of detriment reliance provides the basis for the state's responsibility.

The decision of *AWG v. Argentina*[61] also confirms that the effect of the state's conduct in creating expectations, as well as the reliance on the part

[51] *Enron Corporation & Ponderosa Assets, L.P. v. Argentina*, ICSID Case No ARB/01/3, Award (22 May 2007).
[52] *National Grid v. Argentina*, UNCITRAL Case, Award (3 November 2008).
[53] *AWG v. Argentina* (n 1).
[54] Ibid para 266.
[55] Ibid para 265.
[56] Ibid para 264.
[57] Ibid paras 267–68.
[58] Ibid para 177.
[59] Ibid para 178.
[60] Ibid.
[61] *AWG v. Argentina* (n 1).

of the investor, form the essential basis for the liability. The tribunal considered an alleged breach of the FET standard because the respondent's failure to adjust tariffs for services as required by the concession contract and the regulatory framework frustrated the expectations created by its prior undertakings. The tribunal reasoned that:

> [i]n the instant cases, it should be emphasized that *the expectations of the Claimants* with respect to their investment in the water and sewage system of Buenos Aires did not *suddenly and surprisingly come into their minds the way Athena sprang from the head of Zeus.* Argentina through its laws, the treaties it signed, its government statements, and especially the elaborate legal framework which it designed and enacted, *deliberately and actively sought to create those expectations* in the Claimants and other potential investors in order to obtain the capital and technology that it needed to revitalize and expand the Buenos Aires water and sewage system.[62]

It is important to highlight that the tribunal gave weighty consideration to the deliberate and active effort of the state as well as 'the care and attention' in creating expectations in the investor. The significant part of the excerpt is the clear articulation that the investor's legitimate expectation alone is not sufficient, but the 'change of economic position' is a requisite component for establishing liability.[63] The tribunal stated:

> *Thus it was not the investor's legitimate expectations alone* that led tribunals to find a denial of fair and equitable treatment. It was the existence of such expectations created by host country laws, *coupled with the act of investing their capital in reliance on them*, and a subsequent, sudden change in those laws that led to a determination that the host country had not treated the investors fair and equitably.[64]

This decision underpinned by the reliance conception is one of a few decisions[65] whereby the tribunal explicitly separated the notions of expectations and reliance upon such expectations. This confirms that it is not sufficient to show that the state's conduct has created the

[62] Ibid para 227 (emphasis added).

[63] The reasoning in this case clearly rejects the assurance conception as proposed by Scanlon, which does not require detrimental reliance for liability, and categorically endorses the reliance conception.

[64] Ibid para 226 (emphasis added); a similar view is adopted by the tribunal in *Suez, Sociedad General de Aguas de Barcelona, S.A. and Vivendi Universal, S.A. v. Argentine Republic*, ICSID Case No ARB/03/19, Decision on Liability, Final Award (30 July 2010) para 226.

[65] *Mohammad Al-Bahloul v. Tajikistan* (n 25).

expectations, but the investor must prove that it has relied on such expectation by changing its economic position or it has suffered some detriment.

Nevertheless, some tribunals attach importance to specificity of a legislative provision when considering the investor's expectation of legal stability. In *Philip Morris v. Uruguay*,[66] the tribunal confirmed that the investor's legitimate expectations of the host country's legal stability cannot be based on provisions of *general* legislation applicable to a plurality of persons.[67] The dispute arose out of the enactment of certain ordinance by the Uruguayan Ministry of Public Health and a presidential decree prohibiting different packaging for cigarettes sold under a given brand and mandating images showing the adverse health effects of smoking. The tribunal had to consider whether the claimant had a legitimate expectation that the regulatory framework would not be changed.

The tribunal held that 'legitimate expectations depend on specific undertakings and representations made by the host State to induce investors to make an investment'.[68] Nevertheless, the tribunal took into account the conduct of the investor by emphasising that the investor should exercise due diligence in inquiring about the prospects of a change in the regulatory framework[69] and the surrounding circumstances. In this case, the tribunal held that the claimants had no legitimate expectations that the respondent would not take measures to protect the health of its citizens, especially in the absence of specific undertakings to that effect.[70]

6.3.1.2.3 Expectation through Administrative Representation and Consistent Conduct The paradigm of expectations based on administrative representations and consistent conduct distinguishes the reliance conception and the voluntarist conception of legitimate expectations. It is

66 *Philip Morris Brands Sàrl, Philip Morris Products S.A. and Abal Hermanos S.A. v. Oriental Republic of Uruguay*, ICSID Case No ARB/10/7 (formerly *FTR Holding SA, Philip Morris Products S.A. and Abal Hermanos S.A. v. Oriental Republic of Uruguay*), Award (8 July 2016).

67 Ibid para 426.

68 Ibid para 426; para 429 ('the present case concerns the formulation of general regulations for the protection of public health. There is no question of any specific commitment of the State or of any legitimate expectation of the Claimants vis-à-vis Uruguayan tobacco control regulations.').

69 Ibid para 427.

70 Ibid para 434.

unlikely that a non-legally binding representation, such as policy statements or representations of officials or repeated and consistent practice, creates legitimate expectations under the voluntarist conception. By contrast, the threshold under the reliance conception is more plausible to protect such expectations. The threshold is that such representation or conduct creates or induces expectations on the part of the investor, upon which the investor has reasonably relied to its detriment. The analysis of the following selected decisions illustrates this point.

Frontier Petroleum v. Czech Republic

The *Frontieer Petroleum v. Czech Republic*[71] decision illustrates that the expectations based on official letters which contain no specific representation could not give rise to legitimate expectations. The tribunal had to address whether the claimant's expectations that the state would assist the claimant in the dispute with another private party were legitimate, given that the expectations were based on the letters issued by the government's ministry. The first letter suggested that it 'had no possibility to intervene' and that 'the state would have the possibility to enter into negotiations with the claimant's disputing party'. The second letter merely mentioned the arrangement for direct negotiation.[72]

The tribunal denied that the claim for representation lacked sufficient specificity.[73] However, it is submitted that the tribunal's reasoning could have been articulated in a more consistent manner under the reliance conception by clarifying the reasoning, as follows: these statements might have created the expectations in the investor, but such reliance was not reasonable because it was not a specific 'implicit undertaking'. Furthermore, the tribunal relied on the lack of reliance on the part of the claimant because the statements were made after the claimant's original investment; therefore, the investor could not have relied on those statements.[74]

Crystallex v. Venezuela

The decision for *Crystallex v. Venezuela*[75] confirmed that specific official correspondence could give rise to legitimate expectations if it fulfilled the requisite characteristics of a specific promise. This case concerns

[71] *Frontier Petroleum Services Ltd v. Czech Republic*, UNCITRAL Case, Final Award (12 November 2010).
[72] Ibid para 466.
[73] Ibid para 468.
[74] Ibid.
[75] *Crystallex International Corporation v. Bolivarian Republic of Venezuela*, ICSID Case No ARB(AF)/11/2, Award (4 April 2016).

a dispute arising from the denial of a mining permit and termination of the concession contract. The claimant contends that the respondent violated its obligation to treat the claimant fairly and equitably. The claimant had legitimate expectations that it would operate the mining project over the life of the contract. These expectations were created by a contract and legal framework as well as multiple approvals from government agencies and assurances by government officials.[76] The respondent took the view that its regulatory framework could not have given rise to any legitimate expectations, and there was no specific promise or commitment to provide the permit.[77]

In considering the claimant's claim on legitimate expectations, the tribunal adhered to the reliance conception of legitimate expectations[78] as the tribunal accorded importance to the investor's reliance: 'it is *the investor's reliance on a promise* which may prompt, or contribute to, its decision to invest and proceed with that investment, and which *makes in turn the expectation worthy of legal protection*'.[79] The tribunal recognised a specific representation pertaining to a substantive benefit frustrated to be an essential element. For this reason, the tribunal rejected the legitimate expectations based on the regulatory framework[80] as well as the political statement expressed by the government official or the statements reported in the minutes of the National Assembly.[81] However, the tribunal considered the 16 May 2007 letter from the Office of Permission of the Ministry of Environment sent to the claimant to be a specific representation with clear and precise terms that the permit would be granted.[82] The claimant's reliance upon the representation was the payment of the bond, and the stamp taxes made the expectations reasonable and legitimate.[83] Therefore, the tribunal held that the said letter could create the type of legitimate expectation that, if later frustrated, was protected under the FET standard.

Bilcon v. Canada

Although protection of the investor's reasonable expectations is just a factor to be taken into account in the determination of a breach of the international minimum standard under Article 1105 of NAFTA, the

[76] Ibid para 487.
[77] Ibid para 507 (emphasis added).
[78] Ibid para 547.
[79] Ibid para 557.
[80] Ibid para 552 ('laws are general and impersonal in nature').
[81] Ibid paras 554–55.
[82] Ibid para 563.
[83] Ibid para 564.

Bilcon v. Canada[84] decision confirmed that administrative representations or assurances which seek to induce a specific investor to make an investment could give rise to legitimate expectations.

The claim arose out of the Canadian government's rejection of the investors' project to operate a quarry and marine terminal in the Canadian province of Nova Scotia, after a negative environmental assessment process. The claimant's expectations were created by multiple sources: (1) the official public policy of Nova Scotia in welcoming and strongly supporting investment in mining, (2) meetings with provincial natural resources officials discussing the availability of quarrying sites, (3) specific confirmation of support from the Nova Scotia's minister for natural resources and (4) the conduct of Canada's officials reinforcing the claimant's expectation that regulators' concerns could be addressed through a fair process.

The tribunal adhered to the reliance conception of legitimate expectation as it acknowledged that the investor needed to have 'reasonably relied' on the representations.[85] In this case, specific encouragements to pursue the investment project led the claimants to invest very substantive corporate resources. The tribunal therefore found a breach of Article 1105.[86]

Gold Reserve v. Venezuela

The *Gold Reserve v. Venezuela*[87] decision confirmed that consistent conduct could create expectations in the investor under the reliance conception. The tribunal had to consider whether the issuance of repeated and consistent certifications of claimant's compliance with its obligations under the concessions could give rise to the legitimate expectations that other delays or other failures to abide by the applicable rules would be accepted by the administration. The investor expected that the administration would tolerate the failure to observe certain rules and therefore continued to invest substantial amounts in the project. The tribunal held that the investor's legitimate expectations were reasonable and frustrated for the reason that:

84 *William Ralph Clayton, William Richard Clayton, Douglas Clayton, Daniel Clayton and Bilcon of Delaware Inc. v. Government of Canada*, UNCITRAL, PCA Case No 2009-04, Award on Jurisdiction and Liability (17 March 2015).

85 Ibid para 445.

86 The tribunal's finding focuses on the arbitrary actions of the Joint Review Panel (JRP) to a significant extent.

87 *Gold Reserve Inc. v. Bolivarian Republic of Venezuela*, ICSID Additional Facility Case No ARB(AF)/09/1, Final Award (22 September 2014).

> [r]espondent must have been aware that MIBAM's *repeated and consistent certifications of Claimant's compliance with its obligations under the concessions*, the mining rights and the mining contracts, as the case may be, *generated an expectation that delays or other failures to fully abide by the applicable rules had been and would continue to be accepted by the Administration.* Because of Respondent's consistent attitude, Claimant expected to be permitted to continue working on the project by investing substantial amounts to provide the necessary financing.[88]

From the quoted passage, we can conclude that repeated and consistent conduct could form the basis for legitimate expectations, as the tribunal pointed to 'repeated and consistent certifications of the compliance with obligations', the absence of any warnings or formal notice which 'reinforced' the expectations and the knowledge of the investor's reliance.[89]

The more pertinent question is whether the reliance on such expectation was reasonable. The tribunal's reasoning on this aspect focused on the acts that created the expectations in the first place, such as the absence of objections, the issuance of the permit and the assurance about the commitment to the project.[90] One could ask whether a reasonable investor in the position of the claimant would have expected and acted in the same way. In any case, the tribunal's reasoning seemed to be motivated by the relevant circumstances – namely, that the termination of the concession was due to the change of political priorities rather than the non-compliance with the rules.[91]

The tribunal's reasoning could be endorsed by the reliance theory because the tribunal acknowledged the effect of the certifications of compliance, the absence of objections or warnings or formal notices and most significantly the act of reliance of further investment. The analysis under the voluntarist conception of legitimate expectations might have led to a different outcome because it is not clear that 'consistent conduct' exhibits a manifestation of the will to undertake an obligation. Some scholars, however, assert that 'consistent state conduct displaying favourable treatment over a certain period of time may be considered as a promise that such treatment will continue in the future,

[88] Ibid para 605 (emphasis added).

[89] The absence of action on the part of the state could be justified by reference to the doctrine of acquiescence: D Bowett, 'Estoppel before International Tribunals and Its Relation to Acquiescence' (1957) 33 *BYIL* 176, 202.

[90] *Gold Reserve v. Venezuela* (n 87) paras 578–79.

[91] Ibid para 580.

provided the change in conduct is not predictable'.[92] Such use of the term 'promise' requires explanation and justification. It would be best to conceptualise 'consistent practice' as the conduct which creates the expectation that leads to detrimental reliance rather the act manifesting a will to undertake a legal obligation.

6.3.2 *Act of Reliance: Conception and Characteristics*

Detrimental reliance is the fundamental element for establishing responsibility under the reliance theory of legitimate expectations. However, some fundamental questions related to the concept of reliance need some clarifications. For instance, what does 'reliance' mean?[93] Is it only limited to intentionally or knowingly induced reliance or includes other types of reliance – carelessly induced reliance or reliance which could have been foreseen?[94] Is detrimental reliance required? These issues are addressed in the following paragraphs with reference to investment treaty decisions.

6.3.2.1 Conception of Reliance

An act of reliance means 'one's acting in response to another's statement'.[95] MacCormick explains the concept of reliance to mean 'not merely having expectations about others' conduct, but basing one's own conduct on such expectations'.[96] It can also be explained in terms of 'the promoting and proximate cause' of action.[97] Protection of reliance reflects a deeper concern with protection of decision-making autonomy of individuals, which explains why detrimental reliance is a predicate for liability and blame in morals and laws.[98] In different contexts, reliance has different meanings. In contractual context, it refers to acts of preparation to perform contractual duty.[99] In investment treaty arbitration,

92 F Dupuy and PM Dupuy, 'What to Expect from Legitimate Expectations? A Critical Appraisal and Look into the Future of the "Legitimate Expectations" Doctrine in International Investment Law' in Nassib G. Ziadé (ed), *Festschrift Ahmed Sadek El-Kosheri* (The Hague: Kluwer Law International 2015), 273, 292.

93 Conison 'Assurance, Reliance, and Expectation' (n 36).

94 Atiyah, *Promises, Morals and the Law* (n 20) 40.

95 S Stoljar, 'Promise, Expectation and Agreement' (1988) 47 *CLJ* 193, 207.

96 MacCormick, 'Voluntary Obligations' (n 12) 195.

97 Conison 'Assurance, Reliance, and Expectation' (n 36) 340 ('reliance on an utterance occurs where the utterance is 'a substantial factor in determining the course of conduct').

98 Ibid 341.

99 L Fuller and WR Perdue, 'The Reliance Interest in Contract Damage' (1936–1937) 46 *Yale LJ* 52.

it may refer to acts which incur expenditures related to investment projects, such as hiring of experts or feasibility studies.[100]

6.3.2.2 Characteristics of Reliance

This section addresses two main questions: (1) Is actual or probable reliance required? (2) To what extent does reliance have to be caused by the state's conduct, and is detrimental reliance required?

6.3.2.2.1 Actual or Probable Reliance Actual reliance is not necessary to create a promissory obligation because the actual reliance goes to the seriousness of the breach.[101] However, such view could be disputed because the probability of reliance is not equivalent to the actual reliance.[102] This difference has divergent practical implication in that under the probability paradigm, the promisor might be allowed to change his or her mind after the promise has been made but *prior to* any act of reliance. There is no actual loss because there is no reliance yet.

The latter view is preferable because logically, if we accept a representation to be binding in the absence of actual reliance, the bindingness must derive from grounds, such as the intention of the promisor or the expectation created, other than the act of reliance. The decision of *Mohammad Al-Bahloul v. Tajikistan*[103] supports the actual reliance paradigm. The claimant signed an agreement on oil and gas exploration with the State Committee. He invested certain funds in the operation, but the claimant believed the operation would not succeed because of inadequate technology and level of experience of the workforce. So after consultation, the joint venture entities were set up. The claimant argued that it had a legitimate expectation that licences would be issued based on the exploration agreements, the joint venture documents, presidential decrees and repeated assurances from the minister of energy and the president of the republic. The tribunal was satisfied that the earlier assurances of the committee in the first two exploration agreements and the subsequent issuance of the necessary

[100] See more details regarding reliance damages in Chapter 8.

[101] MacCormick, 'Voluntary Obligations' (n 12) 197 ('What matters is whether one side did in fact rely upon the other's representations about future conduct or present fact; *and whether that other intended that they should know or knew that they would*' [emphasis added]).

[102] Atiyah, *Promises, Morals and the Law* (n 20).

[103] *Mohammad Al-Bahloul v. Tajikistan* (n 25).

licences constituted a representation, which gave rise to expectations.[104] However, the tribunal rejected the claim for lack of evidence of 'actual reliance'.[105]

Furthermore, the tribunal in *Peter Allard v. Barbados*[106] also rejected the claim on legitimate expectations for the lack of actual reliance on the representation by the claimant. The claim arose out of the failure to take necessary environmental protection measures, which resulted in the contamination of the claimant's eco-tourism site (the sanctuary).

The claimants alleged to have relied upon the representations that Barbados would undertake to generally protect the environment at the sanctuary and to manage the sluice gate, which were based on the 1986 plan (Barbados' plan with respect to the patterning of land use), the official correspondence and various reports. The tribunal explicitly adopted the reliance conception of legitimate expectations, as it set out three cumulative conditions: (1) a specific representation, (2) reliance and (3) reasonableness of reliance. Although the tribunal was not convinced that the representations were capable of creating a legitimate expectation,[107] the tribunal placed emphasis on the lack of reliance on the assurances as a basis for rejecting the claim on legitimate expectations.[108] The tribunal found that the claimant had decided to acquire and develop the sanctuary as early as his first visit to the sanctuary in 1994 *prior to* the alleged representations of Barbados made during the period from 1995 to 2004, which the claimant sought to rely.

It can be observed that the tribunal's adherence to the reliance conception is unquestionable as it clearly recognised reliance by the investor on the host state's representations to be 'an essential element' of the notion of legitimate expectations.[109] However, the tribunal seemed to take the view that a specific representation which reflects 'the expression of an intention to create an obligation for the State' is also required.[110] This approach arguably narrows the scope of representations, which could give rise to legitimate expectations under the reliance conception.

[104] Ibid para 212.
[105] Ibid para 210.
[106] *Peter A. Allard v. The Government of Barbados*, PCA Case No 2012-06 (27 June 2016).
[107] Ibid para 199 ('The terms and context of these statements do not suffice to support the expression of an intention to create an obligation for the State. Nor is each reasonably amenable to be interpreted by an investor to create such an obligation.').
[108] Ibid para 226.
[109] Ibid para 217.
[110] Ibid para 199.

6.3.2.2.2 Causative Nature of a State's Promise and Detrimental Nature of Reliance On the first issue, the investor has to prove that its act of reliance has been caused by the specific representation made by the state. However, does such representation have to be a major factor or one of the factors for its investment decision? We could think of two different approaches. First, a 'but for' test would ask whether, but for the state's conduct, the investor would have taken the relevant detrimental action. Second, a 'substantial motivation' test would ask whether the state's conduct was a substantial motivation for the investor's detrimental action when considered in light of other motivating factors.[111]

In investment treaty arbitration, there is no requirement for a specific causation threshold. The only requirement is that the expectation must be taken into account at the time of initial investment.[112] The tribunal in *Micula v. Romania* required the expectation to be 'a determining factor' in the investment decision:

> The Claimants must also have relied on that expectation when they made their investments. *However, it is not necessary for the entire investment to have been predicated solely on such expectation.* Businessmen do not invest on the basis of one single consideration, no matter how important. In the Tribunal's view, *that expectation must be a determining factor* in an investor's decision to invest, or in the manner or magnitude of its investments.[113]

In other decisions, such as in *Duke Energy v. Ecuador*, the investor had the expectations created by the terms of the agreement, which were considered as *conditions precedent* to its investment; therefore, in such case it was obvious that the state's conduct was at least the determining factor if not the 'but for' factor.[114]

The second issue relates to whether detrimental reliance is required to establish a claim based on legitimate expectations. We could summarise three different approaches on this issue, as reflected in the jurisprudence.

The first view holds that detriment in terms of damages is required. The well-known decision of *Thunderbird v. Mexico* stated that reliance must lead to damages suffered: 'the concept of 'legitimate expectations' relates ... to a situation where a Contracting Party's conduct creates reasonable and justifiable expectations on the part of an investor (or

[111] A Robertson, 'Towards a Unifying Purpose for Estoppel' (1996) 22(1) *Mon LR* 1, 15.
[112] U Kriebaum and C Schreuer, 'At What Time Must Legitimate Expectations Exist?' (2012); available at www.transnational-dispute-management.com.
[113] *Micula v. Romania* (n 32) para 672 (emphasis added).
[114] *Duke Energy v. Ecuador* (n 43) para 363.

investment) to act in reliance on said conduct, such that a failure by the NAFTA Party to honour those expectations could cause the investor (or investment) *to suffer damages*'.[115]

The second view suggests that there is a change of position requirement. The tribunal in *AWG v. Argentina* advocated for 'change of economic position' as a result of the expectations.[116]

The third view states that there is no specific requirement for 'detrimental reliance' but only some sort of reliance. For instance, the tribunal in *EDF v. Romania* emphasised 'reasonable reliance' upon the representations.[117] Similarly, the tribunal in *Waste v. Management* stated that 'it is relevant that the treatment is in breach of representations made by the host State which were reasonably relied on by the claimant'.[118] The tribunal in *LG & E v. Argentina* viewed that the FET analysis involved consideration of the investor's expectations when making its investment *in reliance on* the protections to be granted by the host state.[119]

Divergent positions also exist in domestic administrative laws and international law.[120] There seems to be some disagreement on whether reliance is a necessary condition for the claim of legitimate expectations. In some municipal administrative laws, the courts have sought to distinguish two quite different meanings of the term 'rely upon': the weak sense of 'be aware of and believe to be true' and the strong sense of 'act upon to one's detriment'.[121]

The weak version of reliance requires the proof of knowledge of the representation on the part of the representee.[122] Professor Forsyth observes that it is 'self-evident and fundamental [that if someone] did not in fact expect something, that person's expectation, being non-

[115] *Thunderbird v. Mexico* (n 27) para 147 (emphasis added).

[116] A similar view is adopted by the tribunal in *Suez v. Argentina* (n 64) para 226.

[117] *EDF (Services) Ltd v. Romania*, ICSID Case No ARB/05/13, Award (2 October 2009) para 216; *Continental Casualty v. Argentina*, ICSID Case No ARB/03/9, Award (5 September 2008) para 258.

[118] *Waste Management v. Mexico*, ICSID Case No ARB(AF)/00/3, Award (30 April 2004) para 98.

[119] *LG & E Energy Corp. v. Argentine Republic*, ICSID Case No ARB/02/1, Decision on Liability (3 October 2006) para 127.

[120] See the discussion in Chapter 2.

[121] I Steele, 'Substantive Legitimate Expectations: Striking the Right Balance?' (2005) 121 *LQR* 300.

[122] *Minister of State for Immigration & Ethnic Affairs v. Ah Hin Teoh* [1995] HCA 20, 31; Lord Steyn *R v. Secretary of State for the Home Department, ex p Hindley* [2000] UKHL 21.

existence cannot be protected'.[123] However, some domestic courts have taken the opposite view. For instance, in *R (Rashid) v. Secretary of State for the Home Department*, the English Court of Appeal held that the applicant's lack of knowledge of the Home Secretary's settled policy on internal relocation within Iraq was not 'relevant' or 'material' on the question of legitimate expectations.[124] The High Court of Australia in *Minister of Ethnic Affair and Immigration v. Teoh* adopted a similar position that 'it is enough that the expectation is reasonable in the sense that there are adequate materials to support it'.[125]

The strong version of reliance holds the view that it is not necessary for a person to have changed his or her position as a result of a representation in order for an obligation to fulfil a legitimate expectation to arise because *the principle of good administration* prima facie requires adherence by public authorities to their promises.[126] The opposing view suggests that reliance is often required to show that it would be unlawful to go back on a representation.[127]

The different approaches may be explained by different ideologies underlying the doctrine of legitimate expectations. The conception of legitimate expectations which seeks to protect the rule of law or which promotes good administration does not necessarily require detrimental reliance. However, the conception that aims at compensating the harm suffered by the investor will necessarily require it.[128]

6.3.3 Reasonableness of Expectations: Resolving the Mystery Case of Reasonable Investor

Expectations created or acts of reliance alone do not create an obligation unless it is considered as 'reasonable'. The interpretation of this notion is crucial to the determination of liability. The notion of reasonableness is

123 CF Forsyth, 'The Provenance and Protection of Legitimate Expectations' (1988) 47 *CLJ* 238.

124 *R. (on the application a/Rashid) v. Secretary a/State for the Home Department* [2005] EWCA Civ 744.

125 *Minister of State for Immigration & Ethnic Affairs v. Ah Hin Teoh* [1995] HCA 20, joint judgement of CJ Mason and J Deane, 365.

126 *R. (on the application of Bibi) v. Newham LBC* [2001] EWCA Civ 607; [2002] 1 WLR 237 para 31.

127 P Craig, *Administrative Law* (London: Sweet and Maxwell, 4th edn, 1999), 619.

128 J Watson, 'Clarity and Ambiguity: A New Approach to the Test of Legitimacy in the Law of Legitimate Expectations' (2010) 30(4) *LS* 633, 649.

itself hard to define, as Julius Stone calls a 'legal category of indeterminate reference'.[129] Yet why do we depend on this concept?

The 'reasonableness' standard has been employed as an objective threshold for liability in many areas of laws.[130] HLA Hart famously has explained that 'the resort to a reasonableness standard is actually one of the law's clever devices to reopen a bit of space for ordinary moral reasoning in a rule that would otherwise be apt to level it away'.[131] Similarly, John Gardner has suggested that the reasonable person standard 'allows her [the judge] to pass the buck to the finder of fact, who is invited to use extra-legal standards to bridge the gap from legal rule to legal ruling'.[132]

This section aims to provide a conceptual analysis of the reasonableness requirement in investment treaty arbitration by postulating the 'reasonable investor' standard for assisting tribunals in determining which expectations should be legally protected.[133] This problem may be termed as 'the mysterious case of reasonable investor'.[134]

This framework is justifiable for two reasons. First, the reliance theory of legitimate expectations operates with reference to the investor's reasonable conduct, so it is right to determine the standard for evaluating the entitlements of the investor based on the purposes or social values embodied in the standard.[135] Second, the reasonable investor approach has the advantage of being less intrusive on the state's right to regulate, as it does not directly focus on the wrongfulness or blameworthiness of the act. Furthermore, the reasonableness standard offers a flexible framework in balancing the interests, through the imposition of duty of due diligence or contributory fault.

The concept of a reasonable investor in the context of investment treaty arbitration is not novel. In recent years, the investment treaty

[129] J Stone, *The Province and Function of Law: Law as Logic, Justice, and Social Control: A Study in Jurisprudence* (Cambridge, MA: Harvard University Press, 2nd edn, 1946).

[130] J Gardner, 'The Many Faces of the Reasonable Person' (2015) 131 *LQR* 563.

[131] HLA Hart, *The Concept of Law* (Oxford: Oxford University Press, 2nd edn, 1994) 132–33.

[132] Ibid 23.

[133] P Cane, *Anatomy of Tort Law* (Oxford: Hart Publishing, 1997) ('Reasonableness is not a question of what people actually do but of what courts think is a reasonable standard of conduct for society to enforce against its citizens through the mechanism of tort law').

[134] The term is adapted from J Gardner, 'The Mysterious Case of Reasonable Person' (2001) 51(3) *UTLJ* 273.

[135] D Kennedy, 'Form and Substance in Private Law Adjudication' (1976) 89 *HLR* 1685, 1688.

jurisprudence has incrementally elaborated the criteria for defining the objective expectations.[136] The problem with this development is that there has been a lack of principled justification for why these elements are relevant in the first place and how they relate to each other in a normative way. The tribunal in *Suez v. Argentina* has already posed this question: '*what would have been the legitimate and reasonable expectations of a reasonable investor in the position of the Claimants, at the time they made their investment . . . bearing in mind that country's history and its political, economic and social circumstances?*'[137] Nevertheless, we are unclear about the characteristics of the 'reasonable investor'.

The elaboration of the 'reasonable investor' standard in this section is based on insights from various sources, such as investment treaty decisions, political theories, notably John Rawls' theory of reasonable citizen and Gardner's concept of reasonable person as the 'justified person'[138] and other relevant principles. First, we should clarify one caveat for drawing from the reasonable standards as applied in other areas of laws. For instance, whilst the notion of reasonable person under law of negligence or the law of contract may lend some assistance, one should take note of different contexts. The reasonable person in tort law is the standard for the defendant,[139] whilst the reasonable investor is the claimant. The reasonable person standard in the law of contract, concerning the rule of remoteness of damage[140] or the interpretation of the contract,[141] functions in a mutual consent-based relationship.

136 *Duke Energy v. Ecuador* (n 43) para 340 ('The assessment of the reasonableness or legitimacy must take into account all circumstances, including not only the facts surrounding the investment, but also the political, socioeconomic, cultural and historical conditions prevailing in the host State. In addition, such expectations must arise from the conditions that the State offered the investor and the latter must have relied upon them when deciding to invest.').

137 *Suez v. Argentina* (n 64) para 209 (emphasis added).

138 Gardner, 'The Many Faces of the Reasonable Person' (n 130); Gardner, 'The Mysterious Case of the Reasonable Person' (n 134); A Ripstein, *Equality, Responsibility and the Law* (Cambridge: Cambridge University Press, 1998). For other useful reflections on the notion of the reasonable person, see G Fletcher, 'The Right and the Reasonable' (1984) 98 *HLR* 949; G Gaus, 'The Rational, the Reasonable, and Justification' (1995) 3 *JPP* 234.

139 *Blyth v. Birmingham Waterworks* (1856) 11 Ex 781 per B Alderson 784.

140 MA Eisenberg, 'The Principle of Hadley v. Baxendale' (1992) 80 *Cal L Rev* 563.

141 *Investors Compensation Scheme Ltd v. West Bromwich Building Society* [1998] 1 WLR 896 at 912–13.

6.3.3.1 'Reasonable Person' in Political Theories

We may elucidate the reasonable investor by using the concept of the reasonable citizen in Rawls' political theory of liberalism. The concept of reasonableness serves as the criterion for judging the legitimacy of the public conception of justice and political claims and decisions. The concept of a reasonable citizen is central to realising his vision of a well-ordered constitutional democratic society.[142] Only when individuals support this conception of public reasonableness and adhere to its demands, will it become possible to sustain the conditions required to preserve a well-ordered liberal democracy.

One could suppose that the investment treaty regime is *inspired* by the rule of law ideal and values of liberal democracy; therefore, Rawls' theory of a reasonable citizen can provide a conceptual framework for understanding certain characteristics or traits of 'a reasonable investor'. The starting point is to consider the definition of a reasonable citizen in Rawls' theory:

> Citizens are reasonable when, viewing one another as free and equal in a system of cooperation over generations, *they are prepared to offer one another fair terms of social cooperation ... and they agree to act on those terms, even at the cost of their own interests in particular situations*, provided that others also accept those terms. For those terms to be fair terms, citizens offering them must reasonably think that those citizens to whom they are offered might also reasonably accept them ... They must be able to do this as free and equal, and not as dominated or manipulated, or under the pressure of an inferior political or social position.[143]

From the quoted passage, we could deduce that the concept of reasonable citizens coheres with Gardner's concept of the reasonable person as a justified person[144] and with MacCormick's concept of a reasonable person who recognise other people's interests:

> Reasonable people are objective: *they are not so consumed with passion for their own interest or project (though they may indeed be very committed to*

[142] S Young, 'Rawlsian Reasonableness: A Problematic Presumption?' (2006) 39(1) *Can J Pol Sc* 159.

[143] J Rawls, 'The Idea of Public Reason Revisited' (1997) 64(3) *U Chi L Rev* 765, 770 (emphasis added).

[144] J Gardner, 'Justifications and Reasons' in A Simester and ATH Smith (eds), *Harm and Culpability* (Oxford: Oxford University Press, 1996) (This means that the actions or beliefs are taken, formed, held or experienced (as the case may be) 'for undefeated reasons – for reasons that are neither outweighed nor excluded from consideration by countervailing reasons'.).

> *it) as to be unable to stand back momentarily and see the situation from other persons' points of view.* Having done that, they are able to judge their own interests in competition with others' in an at least partly objective way.[145]

6.3.3.2 Clarifying Attributes of the Reasonable Investor

Based on the conceptual framework discussed, we can articulate three important attributes of the reasonable investor: (1) the reasonable investor would act with the state on fair terms of social cooperation, even at the cost of his or her own interests in some situations; (2) the reasonable investor holds the beliefs and makes decisions which display appropriate regard for both its interests and the interests of the state;[146] (3) the reasonable investor would show appropriate regard for a particular risk in making its decision or holding its belief.[147]

It must be reasonable to assume that both the state and the investor would like to attain 'the well-ordered society' which will be achieved only if the state and investor treat each other in a 'reasonable' manner, recognising the right of each other to develop, pursue and realise their own visions of the good life. It is therefore necessary that those attributes must form part of the analysis of the reasonable investor standard. We can analyse those three attributes of the reasonable investor based on the current jurisprudence: recognition of proper exercise of state power for public interests (Section 6.3.3.2.1), recognition of intensive exercise of sovereignty in times of crisis (Section 6.3.3.2.2) and the reasonable investor as a prudent investor (Section 6.3.3.2.3).

6.3.3.2.1 Recognition of Proper Exercise of State Power for Public Interests The reasonable investor recognises that a normal exercise of governmental function of public authorities may affect its investment. This norm finds its clear expression in the decision of *El Paso v. Argentina*. The tribunal reiterated that legitimate expectations cannot be solely the subjective expectations of the investor and correspond to the

[145] N MacCormick, 'Reasonableness and Objectivity' (1999) 74 *Notre Dame L Rev* 1575, 1579 (emphasis added).

[146] Ripstein, *Equality, Responsibility and the Law* (n 138) 192 ('the reasonable person in [the law's] sense is ... the person whose actions display appropriate regard for both her interests and the interests of others'.).

[147] Ibid 56.

objective expectations, which can be deduced from the circumstances and with due regard to the rights of the state.[148]

> If the circumstances change completely, any reasonable investor should expect that the law also would drastically change. It is reasonable to foresee that a small change in circumstances might entail minor changes in the law, while a complete change might entail major changes in the law'.[149]

In the highly regulated electricity or oil and gas sector, the government is normally empowered by statutory provisions to take appropriate regulatory measures for the circumstances. This should be relevant to the determination of the investor's legitimate expectations. The tribunal confirmed that 'any investor entering the oil and gas market had to include the real possibility of reasonable changes and amendments in the legal framework, made by the competent authorities within the limits of the powers conferred on them by the law'.[150]

Furthermore, the decision of *Spyridon v. Romania* affirmed that an investor's expectation which is affected by the proper exercise of state power for the public interests is unlikely to be considered as reasonable and legitimate, especially in the absence of the state's specific promise or representation.[151]

The dispute involved the normal exercise of governmental function of public authorities, in relation to tax inspection and food safety policies, which affect investors' expectations. Claimant's source of expectations was based on the share purchase agreement signed with Romanian state-owned enterprise to purchase shares in a state-owned company. Their detrimental act of reliance was further investment in the company. Its expectations as to the sale and disposal of Continent SA were breached when their investments were subject to a series of malicious and unjustifiable acts by governmental agencies. The claimant principally contended that the tax authorities carried out so many controls which deprived the claimant of its legitimate expectations. The tribunal held that the tax authorities duly exercised their powers within the laws;[152] therefore, the claimant could not have legitimately expected that the

[148] *El Paso Energy International Company v. The Argentine Republic*, ICSID Case No ARB/03/15, Award (31 October 2011) para 358.
[149] Ibid para 363.
[150] Ibid para 400.
[151] *Spyridon Roussalis v. Romania*, ICSID Case No ARB/06/1, Award (7 December 2011).
[152] Ibid para 504.

authorities would not fulfil their duty to verify the claimant's fulfilment of its tax obligations.

For the claim on food safety measures, the claimant similarly alleged that the measures were unjustifiable, disproportionate and discriminatory and deprived the claimant of its rights and legitimate expectations. Recognising food and safety policies to be within the domain of sovereign power,[153] the tribunal held that the investor could not have legitimate expectation that the authorities would refrain from exercising their duty in implementing regulations or taking measures which reflect a clear and legitimate public purpose.[154]

Furthermore, a reasonable investor should be aware of real possibility of reasonable changes in the legal framework, especially in highly regulated sectors and in the presence of specific regulatory powers provided by the laws. The decision of *Methanex Corporation v. United States of America* endorsed the view that the situations of the host state must be relevant in determining the level of liability: 'Methanex entered a political economy in which it was widely known, if not notorious, that governmental environmental and health protection institutions at the federal and state level . . . continuously monitored the use and impact of chemical compounds and commonly prohibited or restricted the use of some of those compounds for environmental and/or health reasons'.[155]

6.3.3.2.2 Recognition of Intensive Exercise of Sovereignty in Times of Crisis The reasonable investor recognises that in times of crisis, states may have to take draconian measures to protect public interests. This point is articulated in the decision of *Continental Casualty v. Argentina*:

> Stability of the legal framework is undoubtedly conducive to attracting foreign investments, especially direct investments where business plans can extend over a number of years; and even more so in respect of those where initial investments are substantial and are recouped only over a long period of time. On the other hand, it would be unconscionable for a country to promise not to change its legislation as time and needs change, or even more to tie its hands by such a kind of stipulation in case a crisis of any type or origin arose. Such an implication as to stability in the BIT's Preamble would be contrary to an effective interpretation of the Treaty; reliance on such an implication by a foreign investor would be

153 Ibid para 686.
154 Ibid para 691.
155 *Methanex Corporation v. United States of America*, NAFTA/UNCITRAL, Final Award of the Tribunal on Jurisdiction and Merits (3 August 2005) para 9.

> misplaced and, indeed, unreasonable. In any case, it is uncontested that the legal and regulatory regime for CNA's insurance business in general remained stable throughout the crisis.[156]

However, it is important to recognise that the exercise of sovereign power is not absolute. The abuse of regulatory right would lead to international responsibility. The discussions of two selected decisions illustrate this point.

In *Suez v. Argentina*, the tribunal considered the issue of legitimate expectations with regard to the acts of handling contractual relationship between the parties. The claimants' expectations were that the parties would work together in a cooperative manner to ensure that the relationship was mutually advantageous.

The acts of the state in refusing to revise the tariff and in pursing the forced renegotiation of the Concession Contract contrary to the legal framework were found to be in breach of the FET standard, bearing in mind two significant facts: (1) the crisis had abated and economic growth returned and (2) the failure to employ flexible means which would protect the interests of both parties.[157] The tribunal emphasised the particular manner in which the state induced and created expectations in the claimants and the subsequent act of investing capital in reliance on their expectations.[158]

We could make two observations in relation to the tribunal's reasoning. First, the tribunal set out the following characteristics of expectations of a reasonable investor by endorsing the statements of previous tribunals.[159] The reasonable investor would take into account various factors, such as business risk, the industry's regulatory patterns and the facts surrounding the investment including political, socioeconomic, cultural and historical conditions prevailing in the host state. In that respect, the tribunal explicitly confirmed that the claimants' expectations must include the possibility that the government would exercise its legitimate regulatory power in response to unpredictable circumstances within the rules of law.

Second, the tribunal did not allow the respondent to rely on its argument about the country's history of economic instability to avoid its responsibility. The tribunal placed emphasis on the fact that the

156 *Continental Casualty v. Argentina* (n 117) para 258.
157 *Suez v. Argentina* (n 64) para 215.
158 Ibid para 207.
159 *LG & E v. Argentina* (n 119) and *Duke Energy v. Ecuador* (n 43).

claimants requested the incorporation of the specific clauses on extraordinary tariff adjustment reviews, therefore, 'a country cannot persuasively allege its historic instability to avoid its responsibility to foreign investors, when it specifically endeavoured to remove this disincentive to foreign investment by providing specific assurances in a Concession Contract and in bilateral investment treaties'.[160]

In *AWG v. Argentina*, the tribunal confirmed that an abuse of regulatory discretion would constitute an international responsibility. The tribunal found state liability on the basis of the state's abuse of regulatory right. Persistent and rigid refusal to revise the tariff and the continued pursuit of measures despite the normality of event led the tribunal to conclude that 'such actions were outside the scope of its legitimate right to regulate and in effect constituted an abuse of regulatory discretion'.[161] Furthermore, many investment decisions and legal scholars affirm the principle that circumstances of the host state or the knowledge of regulatory risks on the part of investor are relevant to the reasonableness of expectations.[162]

6.3.3.2.3 The Reasonable Investor as Prudent Investor The reasonable investor shows appropriate regard for particular risk in making his or her decision or holding his or her belief. This attribute finds the support in legal notions of due diligence[163] and contributory fault.[164] The relevance of the investor's conduct is still the contentious issue.

On the one hand, the principle of due diligence provides a justification for considering the investor's conduct. Its rationale is based on the idea that people have the autonomy to make rational decisions and should minimise possible risks[165] as well as take care

[160] *Suez v. Argentina* (n 64) para 214.

[161] *AWG v. Argentina* (n 1) para 237.

[162] *Bayindir Insaat Turizm Ticaret ve Sanayi A S v. Pakistan*, ICSID Case No ARB/03/29, Award (24 August 2009); *Generation Ukraine v. Ukraine*, ICSID Case No ARB/00/9, Award (16 September 2003); *Parkerings Compagniet AS v. Lithuania*, ICSID Case No ARB/05/8, Award on Jurisdiction and Merits (14 August 2007).

[163] R Barnidge, 'The Due Diligence Principle under International Law' (2006) 8(1) *Int C L Rev* 81.

[164] DJ Bederman, 'Contributory Fault and State Responsibility' (1989–1990) 30 *Va J Int'l L* 335.

[165] N Gallus, 'The "Fair and Equitable Treatment" Standard and the Circumstances of the Host State' in C Brown and K Milles (eds), *Evolution in Investment Treaty Law and Arbitration* (Cambridge: Cambridge University Press, 2011), 223.

to prevent harm to themselves and to protect their own interests.[166] The law should not protect undue risks assumed by people.

The duty of due diligence has been endorsed in investment legal scholarship and some investment decisions.[167] One scholar argues that there is 'a duty on the foreign investor to make due diligence efforts to determine whether his expectations are legitimate, reasonable and well-founded' and 'a duty to have regard to the circumstances of the host State'.[168] The duty of due diligence is implicitly recognised as part and parcel of the right to legitimate expectations by the tribunal in the decision of *Parkerings v. Lithuania*:

> In principle, an investor has a right to a certain stability and predictability of the legal environment of the investment The investor will have *a right of protection of its legitimate expectations* provided it *exercised due diligence* and that its legitimate expectations were reasonable in light of the circumstances. Consequently, an investor must anticipate that the circumstances could change, and thus structure its investment in order to adapt it to the potential changes of legal environment.[169]

The investment treaty jurisprudence confirms that all circumstances have to be taken into account in the assessment of legitimate expectations, such as the facts surrounding the investment; the political, socioeconomic, cultural and historical conditions prevailing in the host state as well as business risk or industry's regular patterns,[170] 'political volatility',[171] 'post-civil war',[172] conditions of economy in transition,[173] 'energy crisis and national shortage',[174] 'vicissitude of the economy of the state'[175] and a 'highly regulated banking climate'.[176]

166 P Finn, 'Commerce, the Common Law and Morality' (1989) 17 *MULR* 87, 97–98.

167 P Muchlinski, '"Caveat Investor"? The Relevance of the Conduct of the Investor under the Fair and Equitable Treatment Standard' (2006) 55 *ICLQ* 527.

168 M Sornarajah, *Resistance and Change in the International Law on Foreign Investment* (Cambridge: Cambridge University Press, 2015), 278–80.

169 *Parkerings v. Lithuania* (n 162) para 333 (emphasis added).

170 *LG & E v. Argentina* (n 119) para 130.

171 *Bayindir v. Pakistan* (n 162) para 194.

172 *Toto Construzioni Generali SpA v. Republic of Lebanon*, ICSID Case No ARB/07/12, Award (7 June 2012) para 245.

173 *Parkerings v. Lithuania* (n 162), paras 335–36.

174 *Duke Energy v. Ecuador* (n 43) para 347.

175 *Generation Ukraine v. Ukraine* (n 162) para 20.37.

176 *Alex Genin and Others v. Republic of Estonia*, ICSID Case No ARB/99/2, Award (25 June 2001) para 370.

The opposing view doubts the rationale for and the extent to which circumstances or political history of the host state should be relevant for interpretation of fair and equitable treatment because it might undermine the object and purpose of an investment treaty in promoting or protecting foreign investment.[177] Should there be different levels of stringency in the application of the FET standard for different countries?[178] The purpose and objective of the treaties cannot be the reference point for determining a duty of due diligence. The application of the reliance principle for protection of legitimate expectations dictates that the investor's act of reliance must be assessed, which includes whether it has exercised its due diligence duty.

One important question of practical relevance is whether an investor is required to have actual or constructive knowledge of regulatory risks. Considering that the rationale of the due diligence principle is that investors must keep themselves informed about the risks and circumstances of a host country, the requirement of constructive knowledge will be more desirable than actual knowledge. The tribunal in the decision of *Nordzucker v. Poland* endorsed this position by suggesting that the claimant was or must have been aware of the threat that a national sugar company might be created and in the political context of Poland at the time, that political opposition could make the privatisation difficult if not impossible; therefore, this political situation could be a reason why the consent of the ministry might be withheld.[179]

The experience or the situation of the investor is relevant to the determination of the investor's reasonable expectations. For example, the tribunal in the decision of *Metalpar v. Argentina* considered the investor's business experience in the relevant industry in Argentina and concluded that it was 'unlikely that Claimants legitimately expected that their investments would not be subject to the ups and downs of the country in which they were made or that the crisis that could already

[177] R Dolzer, 'Fair and Equitable Treatment: Today's Contours' (2014) 12 *Santa Clara J Int'l L* 7, 27.

[178] *Eastern Sugar BV v. Czech Republic*, SCC Case No 088/2004, Partial Award (27 March 2007), Dissenting Opinion of Volterra, para 273 (he 'does not believe that for historical reasons the Czech Republic should be held to a less stringent [fair and equitable treatment] standard than other countries, say the Netherlands').

[179] *Nordzucker v. Poland*, UNCITRAL, Second Partial Award (Merits) (28 January 2009) para 88.

be foreseen would not make it necessary to issue legal measures to cope with it'.[180]

The investor's contributory negligence could be accommodated in the reasonableness test by asking the following question: 'how would a reasonable person, in the position of the claimant, react in reliance on the created expectation?' In this case, the conduct of the state might have created the expectation, but the investor's reliance on such expectation was not reasonable. The tribunal stated that 'a wise investor would not have paid full price up-front for land valued on the assumption of the realization of the Project; he would at least have staged future payments to project progress, including the issuance of the required development permits'.[181]

It is important to analyse the notion of contributory fault and its relevance to our discussion of the notion of the reasonable investor. The concept of contributory fault in international law is based on the principle that the injured party has to be responsible for its own negligence. There can be no issue of contributory fault if there is no internationally wrongful act. In other words, it comes into play at the stage of remedy. Whilst the contributory fault has the same philosophy as the duty of due diligence or prudence, its operation and function are different. Applying the concept of contributory negligence, the tribunal in *MTD v. Chile* reduced the amount of damages on the basis that the investor had contributed to the harm by failing to undertake reasonable due diligence before making the investment.[182] Moreover, in recent decisions concerning Yukos affairs, the concept of contributory fault played a significant role in reducing the damages awarded to the claimants by 25 per cent.[183] It concerned the blameworthy conduct of the investors engaged in the potentially abusive tax structure and the allegedly wilful and arbitrary confiscation of its investment by the host state acting for political reasons.

[180] *Metalpar v. Argentine Republic*, ICSID Case No ARB/03/5, Award (6 June 2008) paras 242–43.

[181] Ibid.

[182] *MTD Equity Sdn. Bhv. and MTD Chile S.A. v. Chile*, ICSID Case No ARB/01/07, Decision on Annulment (21 March 2007) 13 ICSID Rep 500 para 178 ('The Tribunal considers that the Claimants should bear the consequences of their own actions as experienced businessmen').

[183] W Sadowski, 'Yukos and Contributory Fault' (2015) 5 *TDM*.

The tribunal in *ECE v. Czech Republic*[184] affirmed that in determining the reasonableness of the investor's expectations, it must be in regard to specificity of assurances given by the competent authorities prior to or at the time of the making of the investment,[185] the factual circumstances of the specific situation[186] and the investor's own contributory conduct.[187]

The claim arose out of the government's revocation of a planned approval to the claimant for the construction of a shopping centre in Liberec, at the northwest of the Czech Republic. The claimants argued that the delays in the administrative actions and proceedings caused the obstruction and abandonment of the project. The claimants alleged a breach of the FET standard by invoking various elements: bad faith, due process, the failure to provide a transparent and predictable business environment and frustration of legitimate expectations.[188] Having set out the principle that the tribunal will assess the extent to which the investor might have caused or contributed to the delay, the tribunal held that the claimant could have been aware of the possibility that there could be delays in the decision-making process given that administrative authorities and the courts might have to deal with the competing claims raised by its competitor. This factor should be considered in the determination of the claimant's legitimate expectations.[189]

6.4 Critical Reflections on the Reliance Conception of Legitimate Expectations

The reliance conception of legitimate expectations can be recommended for two main reasons. First, the reliance conception provides a flexible conceptual framework for balancing the interests of the state and the investor. This balance can be achieved through the application of the reasonableness test.

The reasonable investor approach to assessment of legitimate expectations is consistent with the underlying principle of detrimental reliance. If the purpose of the rule is to protect the investor against suffered harm,

[184] *ECE Projektmanagement v. The Czech Republic*, UNCITRAL, PCA Case No 2010-5 (19 September 2013).
[185] Ibid para 4.762.
[186] Ibid para 4.765.
[187] Ibid para 4.766.
[188] Ibid paras 4.475–4.486.
[189] Ibid para 4.766 ('it is not the function of the doctrine of "legitimate expectations" to remove the risk element from commercial investment, including the risk of competitors or other parties resorting to domestic remedies').

it is only logical to focus on the investor's conduct in light of the state's representation. One might argue that the purpose of the investment treaty protection is to sanction the unlawful act of the state and not to remedy the plight of the aggrieved investor. These two rationales are not mutually exclusive. The adherence to one conception over the other has a significant implication. If the purpose of the doctrine is to sanction the unlawful or unconscionable conduct of the state, the rules on legitimate expectations should focus on the state's conduct.

The reliance conception of legitimate expectations offers a framework which determines state liability without being unnecessarily offensive. For example, the tribunal in *Continental Casualty* had to consider the issue of regulatory stability and the investor's expectation and stated that 'it would be *unconscionable* for a country to promise not to change its legislation as time and needs change, or even more to tie its hands by such a kind of stipulation in case a crisis of any type or origin arose . . . reliance on such an implication by a foreign investor would be misplaced and, indeed, unreasonable'.[190]

Under the reliance theory, the tribunal would not need to judge on the 'conscionability' of the state's conduct, which carries a significant moral stigma on the state's conduct. It could have asked the following question to avoid the unnecessary controversy: would a reasonable investor have expected the country to promise not to change its laws or tie its hands in case of crisis?

The second strength is its remedial implication of the reliance conception. The reliance conception would require an award of reliance damages as opposed to expectation damages or performance remedy. This remedy is better suited to the remedial structure of the investment treaty regime.

[190] *Continental Casualty v. Argentina* (n 117) para 258 (emphasis added).

7

In Search of the Most Suitable Conception of Legitimate Expectations

7.1 Introduction

Chapters 4–6 revealed three conceptions of legitimate expectations and their respective strengths and weaknesses, the summary of which is presented in Table 7.1 (Section 7.2). We could ask if these three conceptions should continue to be applied, as is the case at present. Or should one particular conception be articulated to promote the certainty and integrity of the rules and if so, which one?

This chapter argues for the reliance conception as the unifying conception (Section 7.3). The selection of the most suitable conception principally focuses on consideration of both macro and micro aspects of the investment treaty regime. The macro analysis is essentially concerned with the fundamental building blocks of the regime – namely, (1) the underlying balancing of regulatory interests of states and protection of investor's right and (2) remedial structure of the investment treaty regime (Section 7.3.1). The micro analysis is guided by the following analytical framework: which conception could protect legitimate expectations in addressing the assimilation of contract and expectation? Which conception of legitimate expectations should be adopted to protect legitimate expectations arising from non-contractually binding representations, administrative representations and legislative framework, considering the purpose of applying the principle of legitimate expectations in the interpretation of fair and equitable treatment (Section 7.3.2)?[1]

[1] S Fietta, 'Expropriation and the "Fair and Equitable" Standard: The Developing Role of Investors' "Expectations" in International Investment Arbitration' (2006) 23 *J Int'l Arb* 375; F Wennerholm, 'What Can You Expect? The Role of Legitimate Expectations in Investment Protection Disputes' in K Hobér et al. (eds) *Between East and West: Essays in Honour of Ulf Franke* (NewYork, NY: JurisNet, 2010).

7.2 Three Contending Conceptions of Legitimate Expectations

The voluntarist conception of legitimate expectations attributes the bindingness of a promise to the will of the promisor. Therefore, legitimate expectations would only be legally protected if they arise from a legal commitment. There are two fundamental flaws with this conception. First, contractual right is assimilated with contractual expectations, which can then be protected under the principle of legitimate expectations. This allows contractual obligations to be enforced by the fair and equitable treatment clause in investment treaties. Second, there is a challenge in identifying the state's intention to undertake a legal obligation, especially in non-contractual arrangements.

The bare expectations or assurance conception locates the obligation in the intention to provide assurance. In effect, this is a weaker version of the voluntarist conception as there is no need to prove an intention to assume a legal obligation. This conception suffers from the same drawback of conflating the contract-treaty breach distinction.

The distinctive reliance theory does not focus on the legally binding nature of the state's conduct but on the reasonable act of reliance by the investor upon the state's promise. The reliance theory provides a flexible conceptual framework for considering both the perspectives of the state and the investor. Table 7.1 summarises the connection among conceptions of legitimate expectations, constitutive elements for liability and remedy.

7.3 'Best-Fit' Criteria for Choosing the Unifying Conception of Legitimate Expectations

The reliance conception fits best with the current paradigm of investment treaty arbitration because it provides a normative framework for striking a delicate balance between states as the regulators and protectors of public interests and protection of investors' rights (Section 7.3.1.1). Furthermore, the reliance theory of legitimate expectations, which excludes the fulfilment of promises and expectation interests, fits best with the structure of remedial powers of tribunals (Section 7.3.1.2).

Table 7.1 *The Connections among Conceptions of Legitimate Expectations, Constitutive Elements and Remedies*

Conceptions of Legitimate Expectations	Constitutive Elements for Liability	Key Features	Remedies
Voluntarist conception	• 'The will' or 'intention' of the state to *undertake an obligation* (and not just an intention to perform an act), which is explicit or implicit from circumstances. • Full disclosure of information by a promise. • Intention communicated and received by the promise.	• The investor's sentiments or situations seem to have secondary importance. • The power to make a promise is protected in order to enable people to forge a special relationship as well as to garner respect for personal autonomy and trust. • 'Reasonableness' of expectation is assessed with reference to the conduct of the state (whether it makes a binding promise to do what the investor expects).	• Expectations damages (Charles Fried) • Possibility of reliance damages (Joseph Raz)
Assurance/bare expectation conception	• Voluntary or intentional creation of assurance or expectation in the promisee. • The expectation involves a future conduct.	• The 'value of assurance' in facilitating planning and coordination justifies a promissory obligation. • The notion of 'reasonableness' of expectation is assessed with reference to the	• Performance of a promised act • Expectation damages

	• The promisee desires assurance; the promisor is aware of that fact (mutual knowledge).	intentional creation of expectation and mutual knowledge of the parties.	
Reliance conception	• An act of intentionally or knowingly inducing reliance (MacCormick) or conduct which creates expectations. • An element of detrimental reliance. • Assessment of reasonableness of expectations.	• Liability is determined by reference to reasonableness of reliance (the investor's conduct). • The notion of 'reasonableness' is assessed with reference to various factors, including social values, conduct of the investor and circumstances of the host state.	• Reliance damages

Source: Based on the findings of the analysis carried out in Chapters 4–6.

7.3.1 Macro Aspect of the Investment Treaty Regime

7.3.1.1 Regulatory State Paradigm and Protection of Legitimate Expectations

The theory of legitimate expectations must take into account the fundamental characteristics of the current investment treaty regime – namely, the balancing of a state's and an investor's interests. States benefit from an investment treaty as a commitment device which can address concerns from investors and attract more investment. Investors can rely on the treaty as a mechanism for protecting their rights when the relationship with a state worsens.[2] Such theory must accommodate the primary duty of government in looking after the basic welfare of its people,[3] whilst adequately protecting the legitimate interests of investors. This consideration is necessary if the doctrine of legitimate expectations is to be a relevant and useful tool in enhancing the credibility of a government's contract and policy commitments.[4]

The recent trend of international investment rule-making is to duly recognise regulatory powers of the state,[5] known as the 'regulatory state paradigm'.[6] In such a paradigm, states actively exercise their regulatory powers in pursuit of public interests in different domains.[7] The regulatory state paradigm, as an analytical concept, arguably changes how regulatory measures alleged to be in breach of an investment treaty should be assessed with reference to the purposive dimension of such measure.[8] Sovereign states, as masters of investment treaties, have woken up to the reality of the intrusive effect of investment treaties on their regulatory powers, which are manifested in two ways: (1) some developed states find themselves as respondents and (2) states have discovered

[2] World Bank, *World Development Report 2005: A Better Investment Climate for Everyone*, Volumes 33–35, 179.

[3] J Raz, 'Liberty and Trust' in R George (ed), *Natural Law, Liberalism, and Morality: Contemporary Essays* (Oxford: Oxford University Press, 2001), 114.

[4] *International Thunderbird Gaming Corporation v. Mexico*, UNCITRAL Case, Final Award (26 January 2006) Separate Opinion of Arbitrator Waelde para 35.

[5] UNCTAD IIA Issues Note, *Taking Stock of IIA Reform*, No 1, March 2016.

[6] K Yeung, 'The Regulatory State', in R Baldwin, M Cave and M Lodge (eds), *The Oxford Handbook of Regulation* (Oxford: Oxford University Press, 2010).

[7] NK Dubash and B Morgan (eds), *The Rise of the Regulatory State of the South Infrastructure and Development in Emerging Economies* (Oxford: Oxford University Press, 2013).

[8] Yeung, 'The Regulatory State' (n 5) 80.

public policy implications of investment treaty arbitration.[9] Consequently, states have to calibrate substantive and procedural rules under the investment treaty regime to accommodate this emerging trend.[10]

The reliance conception provides a sophisticated normative framework, which allows adjudicators to consider both the conduct of a state and that of an investor in the determination of state liability. Such framework requires investors to take precautions to protect their own interests and to be sensitive to regulatory concerns pursued by the state. The voluntarist conception, by contrast, is very state-centric as the question of liability entirely depends on the state's intention to undertake a legal obligation and has no room for investor expectations, thus rendering notional the concept of 'legitimate expectations'. Similarly, the enquiry under the assurance conception focuses on the state's intention to create expectations in the investor and does not require an assessment of acts or conduct on the part of the investor. In the era of heightened regulation for the public interests, the reliance conception of legitimate expectations is likely to play the most significant role in fostering a relationship of trust and confidence between the host state and the investor. There can be no trust or confidence if the law does not seek to hold states accountable for their own conduct which causes harm to investors.

7.3.1.2 Remedial Structure of Investment Treaty Regime

The reliance conception of legitimate expectations is a preferable conception from a remedial perspective because an investment treaty tribunal possesses limited remedial tools to rectify a breach of obligation. The choice of conceptions is ultimately between an enforcement of expectations or promises and compensation for harm or loss caused by detrimental reliance on such promises. Therefore, the important criteria for choosing the conception of legitimate expectations should take into account the availability of remedial powers in achieving the purpose of the rule. If the expectation-based conception is to be adopted, the remedial consequence will be protection of expectation interests, which will require specific performance (of contractual obligations) or restitution. Not only does this type of remedy pose some practical difficulty for enforcement, it has the serious implication on the fettering of sovereign powers.

[9] A Roberts, 'Clash of Paradigms: Actors and Analogies Shaping the Investment Treaty System' (2013) 107(1) *AJIL* 45, 45–94.

[10] S Spears, 'The Quest for Policy Space in a New Generation of International Investment Agreements' (2010) 13(4) *J Int'l Econ L* 1037.

Unlike judicial review proceedings, in which courts may grant a quashing order, a mandatory order or a prohibiting order, as well as damages and restitutionary measures,[11] investment treaty tribunals can employ a more limited armoury of remedial powers. Investment treaty tribunals cannot order a specific restitution unless the investment treaty specifically gives them the power to do so. Moreover, an order of restitution is impractical because the tribunal has to ensure that there are specific legislative or executive acts of the host state to restore the antecedent legal position of the investor. Material restitution may pose some practical difficulty in enforcing a transfer of property between the disputing parties.[12]

7.3.2 Micro Aspect of the Investment Treaty Arbitration

This section analyses the practical implication of different conceptions of legitimate expectations applied to resolve concrete cases. First, we consider which conception of legitimate expectations can circumvent the assimilation problem of contractual right and expectations, which violates the well-accepted principle that a contract breach does not *per se* constitute a treaty breach. Second, we discuss the protection of expectations arising from non-legally binding representations. If the purpose of having the doctrine of legitimate expectations in investment treaty arbitration is to protect interests which would otherwise not be protected under other specific provisions of investment treaty, it would defeat the purpose to choose the conception which would leave those interests unprotected. Based on such assumption, I argue that the reliance conception is the most suitable because it can overcome the assimilation problem by treating a contractual breach as a delict (Section 7.3.2.1) and it can protect expectations which arise from non-contractual representations – namely, administrative representations and expectations created by specific legislative framework (Section 7.3.2.2).

7.3.2.1 Protection against Harm from a Breach of Contract and the Reliance Theory of Legitimate Expectations

The doctrine of legitimate expectations has been invoked to convert a mere contract breach into a treaty breach, whereby contractual provisions create legitimate expectations, a breach of which constitutes

[11] M Sunkin, 'Remedies Available in Judicial Review Proceedings', in D Feldman (ed), *English Public Law* (Oxford: Oxford University Press, 2004) 948–49.

[12] B Sabahi, *Compensation and Restitution in Investor-State Arbitration Principles and Practice* (Oxford: Oxford University Press, 2011) 63–71.

a breach of the FET standard. This approach is objectionable for two reasons.

First, it violates a well-established principle in international law that a breach of contract governed by municipal law does not *per se* constitute a treaty breach. The principle of distinctiveness of contract breach and treaty breach is well accepted.[13] The Commentary to the ILC Draft Articles on Responsibility of States for Internationally Wrongful Acts affirms this point: 'the breach by a State of a contract does not as such entail a breach of international law. Something further is required before international law becomes relevant, *such as a denial of justice by the courts of the State in proceedings brought by the other contracting party*'.[14] Furthermore, the investment treaty jurisprudence confirms that a breach of contract constitutes a breach of the FET standard only if some additional elements were proved, such as sovereign authority,[15] discrimination or denial of justice,[16] an outright and unjustified repudiation of the transaction[17] or a substantial breach under certain limited circumstances.[18]

Second, it raises the fundamental question of whether it is necessary to frame liability for a breach of contract in terms of legitimate expectations. If international responsibility for a breach of contract can and has

[13] S Schwebel, 'On Whether the Breach by a State of a Contract with an Alien Is a Breach of International Law' in A Migliazza, F Pocar, P Lamberti Zanardi and P Ziccardi (eds), *International Law at the Time of its Codification – Essays in Honour of Roberto Ago*, Volume 3 (Milan: A. Giuffrè, 1987), 401. For a critical view, see M Sornarajah, *The International Law on Foreign Investment* (Cambridge: Cambridge University Press, 3rd edn, 2010); CF Amerasinghe, 'State Breaches of Contracts with Aliens and International Law' (1964) 58 *AJIL* 881.

[14] International Law Commission, *Draft Articles on Responsibility of States for Internationally Wrongful Acts with Commentaries*. Report of the International Law Commission: 53rd Sess (2001) (United Nations Publications, 2008), art 4, 41 (emphasis added).

[15] *Impregilo S.p.A. v. Islamic Republic of Pakistan*, ICSID Case No ARB/03/3, Decision on Jurisdiction (22 April 2005) para 260; *Bayindir Insaat Turizm Ticaret VE Sanay A.S. v. Islamic Republic of Pakistan*, ICSID Case No ARB/03/29, Award (27 August 2009) para 180; *Consortium RFCC v. Royaume du Maroc*, ICSID Case No ARB/00/6, Award (22 December 2003).

[16] *Glamis Gold, Ltd v. United States of America*, NAFTA/UNCITRAL, Award (8 June 2009) para 620 ('a mere contract breach, without something further such as *denial of justice or discrimination*, normally will not suffice to establish a breach of Article 1105' [emphasis added]).

[17] *Waste Management v. Mexico*, ICSID Case No ARB (AF)/00/3, Award (30 April 2004) para 115.

[18] *Parkerings Compagniet AS v. Lithuania*, ICSID Case No ARB/05/8, Award on Jurisdiction and Merits (14 August 2007) para 316.

been established based on other tortious grounds, it is that additional element, such as denial of justice, which constitute the basis for the state's international responsibility.[19] What is the precise role, if any, of the investor's legitimate expectations in establishing state liability? How does the reliance conception articulate the role of legitimate expectations?

The reliance conception of legitimate expectations can circumvent the contract-treaty breach conundrum precisely because it treats a contractual breach as a delict, which is distinct from a contractual wrong to be governed by the applicable law of the contract. The reason for holding a state liable for a breach of contract is not based on the violation of an investor's contractual expectation *per se*. The basis for liability is that the state steps out of its role as a contractor and exercises its sovereign power to violate the contract and causes harm to the investor, which constitutes a tortious conduct.[20] Such action constitutes a contractual wrong as well as an international delict, which results in international responsibility. FA Mann elaborated on this nature of wrong, as follows:

> The breach of contract is alleged to result from the fact that the dependent state whose law governs the contract, has in the exercise of its legislative or executive powers, taken measures specifically designed to terminate or interfere with the particular contract in issue. Here the international tort consists in the confiscatory, discriminatory or arbitrary character of the exercise of the defendant state's sovereignty or, in short, in the abus de droit of which it is guilty and which is sufficient to attract its liability.[21]

The tribunal's reasoning in *Eureko v. Poland*[22] illustrates how legitimate expectations could be misused to convert a mere contract breach into an international responsibility without proving other delictual requirements. This case essentially concerns a breach of share purchase agreement (SPA) between the claimant and Poland's state treasury, whereby the state treasury undertook to sell off its shares in the country's leading insurance company (PZU) by way of initial public offering (IPO). The claimant's expectation

[19] R Jennings and A Watts (eds), *Oppenheim's International Law* (Harlow: Longman, 1996), 927.

[20] F Dunn, *The Protection of Nationals: A Study in the Application of International Law* (Baltimore, MD: Johns Hopkins Press, 1932) 165–67, 171.

[21] FA Mann, 'State Contract and State Responsibility' (1960) *AJIL* 572, 575; RY Jennings, 'State Contracts in International Law' (1961) 37 *BYIL* 156.

[22] *Eureko B.V. v. Poland*, UNCITRAL Case, Partial Award (19 August 2005) 12 ICSID Rep 335.

about the sale of share was important for its decision to invest in the first place. Such expectation was made concrete in the SPA and subsequent amendment. However, the IPO never took place. The key issue is whether the frustration of legitimate expectations grounded in contractual arrangement could constitute a breach of the FET standard.

The essence of the tribunal's reasoning is that a breach of contract (which embodied the investor's expectations as the basis for its decision to make investment) constituted a breach of the FET standard. The tribunal reasoned that

> Eureko's investments, its contractual rights to an IPO, which would have led it to acquire majority control of PZU, have been, in the opinion of the Tribunal, unfairly and inequitably treated by the Council of Ministers and Minister of the State Treasury. *Those organs of the RoP, consciously and overtly, breached the basic expectations of Eureko that are at the basis of its investment in PZU and were enshrined in the SPA, and, particularly, the First Addendum.*[23]

It was argued that the violation of the FET standard could have been exclusively based on Poland's conduct, which manifestly breached the claimant's basic expectations.[24] This view relied on the voluntarist conception of legitimate expectations, whereby these expectations were enshrined in the contractual instruments, which would assimilate contractual right and expectation. It is important to note that in this case, the tribunal also relied on arbitrary and discriminatory conduct of the state to establish the breach of the FET standard.[25] This would make it difficult to ascertain the precise role of legitimate expectations in the assessment of the FET standard.

One way of resolving this case is to treat it as a contract breach governed by Polish law.[26] The better view is for the reliance conception of legitimate expectations to provide the basis for liability under the investment treaty by focusing on the delictual wrong from causing harm through a breach of contract.

7.3.2.2 Protection of Expectations Arising from Non-legally Binding Representations

The discussions in the previous chapters have confirmed that non-contractual expectations are unlikely to meet the threshold for protection

[23] Ibid para 232 (emphasis added).
[24] Fietta, 'Expropriation and the "Fair and Equitable" Standard' (n 1) 390.
[25] *Eureko B.V. v. Poland* (n 21) para 233.
[26] Z Douglas, 'Nothing If Not Critical in Investment Treaty Arbitration' (2006) 22 *Arb Intl* 27 ('the unfair and inequitable treatment of a contractual right to an IPO is surely just a euphemism for a breach of the contractual right').

of legitimate expectations under the voluntarist conception. This outcome is not acceptable because the doctrine of legitimate expectations was introduced in investment treaty arbitration in order to provide legal protection to the types of interests which have not received legal protection under other treaty provisions. This provides a compelling reason for supporting the reliance conception, which attributes liability to the detrimental reliance on the part of the investor. Whether the state's act is legally binding is not determinative of the reasonableness of expectations. If the voluntarist theory were chosen, then non-contractual expectations are unlikely to be protected. Contractual expectations may well be protected under other rules of international law relating to state contracts.

7.4 Proposed Guidelines for the Application of the Reliance Theory of Legitimate Expectations

This chapter, which concludes Part III of this book, draws together the conclusions from the previous chapters and proposes guidelines for application of the reliance theory of legitimate expectations. These guidelines provide a normative framework for adjudication of cases for a breach of the FET standard. Following are the reformulated principle and its guidelines.

The Reformulated Reliance Principle for Protection of Legitimate Expectations

> 'A host State's sovereign power to regulate in the public interest is limited to the extent that it would cause harm to particular investors. Where a host State has, through its representation or conduct, created or induced expectations on the part of an investor, upon which the investor has reasonably relied, the host State has a duty to prevent the detriment resulting from such reliance, failure of which gives rise to a duty to compensate the investor for his reliance loss'.

Guidelines for the Application of the Reliance Theory of Legitimate Expectations

1. **The rationale or the fundamental purpose of protecting legitimate expectations** is protection/prevention against a detriment that the investor has suffered as a result of reasonable reliance on the expectation created by the state's conduct.

1.1 The law of legitimate expectations is concerned with compensation for harm or loss incurred by detrimental reliance on the state's conduct rather than with enforcement of sovereign promises or undertakings.

1.2 The basis for liability is detrimental or injurious reliance. The state's conduct alone does not provide the justificatory basis for liability, although it is highly relevant in the assessment of threshold requirements and reasonable expectations.

2. **General Conditions for Liability**

2.1 **The Threshold Requirement**

2.1.1 The act capable of precipitating legitimate expectations includes a representation or conduct which amounts to the creation or encouragement of an expectation of future action. It is not limited to a contractual undertaking, a binding or clear representation or a legal commitment.

i. The threshold question is *not* whether the state has made a promise or a representation but whether the state's conduct has created a relevant expectation for the investor.

ii. An intention to induce reliance is neither a requisite element nor a sufficient basis for establishing liability.

2.2 **The Reasonableness Requirement**

2.2.1 In order to assess the reasonableness of expectations, the tribunal may ask the following conceptual question: '*what would a reasonable investor in the position of the claimant have expected and would such investor have acted in reliance upon the State's conduct, taking into account various circumstances?*'[27]

2.2.2 The tribunal may take into account the following factors:

i. A reasonable investor would assess the nature of the state's conduct or representation in forming its expectation.

[27] There seems to be two distinct aspects of the reasonableness requirement: (1) Is it reasonable for the investor to entertain the expectation? and (2) Is it reasonable for the investor to act on such expectation? There may be a situation where it is reasonable to entertain an expectation but unreasonable in the circumstances to take such detrimental action. For example, when a state makes an informal commitment to cooperate with an investor in a project, it might be reasonable for the investor to incur modest expenditure in preparing to establish the business but 'unreasonable' to undertake substantial capital commitment before any formal arrangement.

ii. A reasonable investor would take into account a normal exercise of a state's sovereignty, in particular in times of emergency situations.

iii. A reasonable investor would take into account the circumstances of the host state.

2.3 **Detriment Requirement** To claim for protection of legitimate expectations, the claimant must prove that it has suffered some detriment. There can be no liability in the absence of reliance.

2.3.1 An investor must have relied on such expectation as a determining though not exclusive factor to make the relevant investment or change its position to its detriment.

2.3.2 The detriment must flow from the reliance upon the expectation created by the State's conduct. The frustration of the expectation has led to detriment.

2.4 **Relief Based on Detrimental Reliance**

2.4.1 The remedy must be determined by reference to the primary objective of preventing or reversing the investor's detriment and not of fulfilling the investor's expectations.

2.4.2 Reliance damages may be awarded.

PART III

Application of the Reliance Theory of Legitimate Expectations

8

Normative Consequences of the Reliance Theory of Legitimate Expectations

8.1 Introduction

This chapter examines three significant consequences of applying the reliance theory of legitimate expectations. First, the scope of protection of legitimate expectations is restrictive and will exclude the catchall or superfluous use of legitimate expectations (Section 8.2). Second, the reliance theory can be applied to protect legitimate expectations arising from both legally and non-legally binding sources (Section 8.3). In this regard, protection of legitimate expectations in case of a breach of contract, administrative representations or change of regulatory or legislative framework will be examined. Third, the complementary relationship between the reliance theory of legitimate expectations and other relevant rules, such as non-arbitrariness or the rules of umbrella clause will be examined (Section 8.4).

8.2 Restrictive Scope of Protection of Legitimate Expectations

The current jurisprudence has recognised that both explicit and implicit representation could give rise to legitimate expectations.[1] The reliance

[1] *Parkerings-Compagniet AS v. Lithuania*, ICSID Case No ARB/05/8, Award (11 September 2007) para 331 ('The expectation is legitimate if the investor received an explicit promise or guarantee from the host-State, or if implicitly, the host-State made assurances or representation that the investor took into account in making the investment'); *Grand River Enterprises Six Nations Ltd et al. v. USA*, NAFTA/UNCITRAL, Award (12 January 2011) paras 140–41 ('Ordinarily, reasonable or legitimate expectations of the kind protected by NAFTA are those that arise through *targeted representations or assurances made explicitly or implicitly* by a state party'); *Total S.A. v. Argentina*, ICSID Case No ARB/04/1, Decision on Liability (21 December 2010) para 120 ('an investor's legitimate expectations may be based on any undertaking and representations made explicitly or implicitly by the host State').

theory of legitimate expectations would invalidate the catchall conception of legitimate expectations as advocated by the tribunal in *Tecmed v. Mexico*[2] (Section 8.2.1). Furthermore, it would exclude the instances in which expectations do not arise from the state's conduct or where the concept of legitimate expectations is used as a conclusion rather than as a normative principle (Section 8.2.2). The selected decisions – *Saluka v. Czech Republic*,[3] *Charles Lemire v. Ukraine*[4] and *Rumeli v. Kazhakstan*[5] – are discussed to illustrate this point.

8.2.1 Rejection of the Catchall Conception of Legitimate Expectations

The expectation that would be protected under the reliance conception is a specific and narrow expectation – namely, that which has been created by the state's conduct and resulted in the investor's detrimental reliance. Consequently, the catchall concept of legitimate expectations elaborated in the decision of *Tecmed v. Mexico*, as stated here, could not be endorsed:

> The foreign investor expects the host State to act in a consistent manner, free from ambiguity and totally transparently in its relations with the foreign investor, so that it may know beforehand any and all rules and regulations that will govern its investments, as well as the goals of the relevant policies and administrative practices or directives, to be able to plan its investment and comply with such regulations . . . The foreign investor also expects the host State to act consistently, i.e. without arbitrarily revoking any preexisting decisions or permits issued by the State that were relied upon by the investor to assume its commitments as well as to plan and launch its commercial and business activities. The investor also expects the State to use the legal instruments that govern the actions of the investor or the investment in conformity with the function usually assigned to such instruments, and not to deprive the investor of its investment without the required compensation.[6]

So what kind of expectations would be protected? Let us analyse pertinent facts of the case. The claimant acquired investments relating to

[2] *Técnicas Medioambientales Tecmed, S.A. v. Mexico*, ICSID Additional Facility Case No ARB(AF)/00/02, Award (29 May 2003) 10 ICSID Rep 134 para 154.

[3] *Saluka Investments BV (The Netherlands) v. Czech Republic*, UNCITRAL Rules, Partial Award (17 March 2006).

[4] *Joseph Charles Lemire v. Ukraine*, ICSID Case No ARB/06/18, Award (14 January 2010).

[5] *Rumeli Telekom A.S. and Telsim Mobil Telekomikasyon Hizmetleri A.S. v. Republic of Kazakhstan*, ICSID No ARB/05/16, Award (29 July 2008).

[6] *Tecmed v. Mexico* (n 2) para 154.

a controlled landfill of hazardous industrial waste in 1996 with a renewable licence on a yearly basis. The licence was granted until 1998, when the government agency refused the renewal. According to the claimant, the refusal to renew the licence was largely due to political circumstances (the change of local administration and the encouragement of a movement of citizens against the landfill by the local government), the consequence of which led to the loss of the profits and income from the economic operation. The claimant argued that the refusal to renew the permit constituted a violation of the FET standard.

The frustration of the investor's legitimate expectations formed the core of the tribunal's assessment of the FET standard. The key question was whether the claimant's expectation that the permit's renewal would be granted to maintain the operation of the landfill until the relocation to a new site was reasonable.

Based on the reliance conception, the tribunal would have to determine whether the state has induced the investor to create such expectation and reasonably relied on it to its detriment. From the tribunal's passages, the investor might have been induced by a non-memorialised instrument with the provision stating that 'the current landfill operated by CYTRAR shall be closed as soon as the new facilities are ready to operate' as well as the resolution (which decided not to renew the permit), which itself stated to the effect that the claimant agreed with the different levels of the federal, state and municipal government that the landfill would be relocated and made this agreement public.[7] Furthermore, the visits to sites that were possible locations for the relocated landfill might reinforce that expectation. The pre-existing legal relationship and assurances by the authorities might have also contributed to the inducement of expectations.

With respect to the reasonableness of such expectation and the investor's reliance, it could be argued that the expectation was not reasonable because the cancellation was foreseeable in light of the circumstances. Based on the facts of the case, there were incidental statements as to the landfill's relocation in the correspondence between the parties – which suggested that the claimant might have been aware of a possibility of closing down the business without complying with the prior relocation. The tribunal did not regard this as 'a clear and unequivocal expression of the will of the Mexican authorities to change their position as to the extension of the Permit' nor 'an explicit, transparent and clear warning'

[7] Ibid para 160.

addressed to the claimant about the rejection of the relocation.[8] For the purpose of our analysis, this fact suggested that the risk of closing down was not unlikely in light of the circumstances.

Despite this uncertainty, the tribunal would have to take into account the pre-existing legal relationship between the parties, and certain 'assurances' by the authority on the continuation of the project. Therefore, the respondent should have prevented the detriment which would be caused to the claimant as a result of its action – for instance, providing clarity on the situation (renewal or withdrawal) so that the claimant could take necessary actions.[9] In any case, the claimant would have to prove detriment suffered and the remedy would not be a restitution of permit or loss of profits. Under the reliance theory, the liability, if established, would be based on the failure to prevent detriment or harm as a result of its own action rather than the failure to fulfil the claimant's expectation of renewal of the permit.

The analysis illustrates that the doctrine of legitimate expectations aims to provide protection in a specific type of situation. Consequently, the doctrine of legitimate expectations as articulated by the tribunal in *Tecmed* could not be endorsed under the reliance theory. Such conception has been rightly subject to numerous criticisms. Such an exquisite expression of the rule of law in action would have even surprised AV Dicey! The tribunal's reasoning would have better fitted the breach of non-arbitrariness standard because it focused on the delays,[10] ambiguity,[11] inconsistency and lack of transparency[12] or contradictions in the attitude and conduct of the agency.[13]

8.2.2 *Exclusion of Rhetorical Use of Legitimate Expectations*

In some instances, the doctrine of legitimate expectations is applied to give effect to expectations that are not based on a specific representation or is used in a superfluous manner. For instance, in the decision of *Rumeli v. Kazhakstan,* the tribunal employed the notion of legitimate

[8] Ibid.

[9] Ibid para 167 ('the Claimant was entitled to expect that the government's actions would be free from any ambiguity that might affect the early assessment made by the foreign investor of its real legal situation or the situation affecting its investment and the actions the investor should take to act accordingly').

[10] Ibid para 161.

[11] Ibid paras 164, 167.

[12] Ibid para 164.

[13] Ibid paras 162–64.

expectations as a conclusion rather than as a normative element for state liability. The tribunal held this breach to amount to a breach of the BIT on the ground that the unlawful act is attributable to the state (Investment Committee) and 'the decision was arbitrary, unfair, unjust, lacked in due process *and did not respect the investor's reasonable and legitimate expectations*'.[14] Another example of superfluous use is found in *LG & E v. Argentina*, whereby the tribunal held that 'the fair and equitable standard consists of the host State's consistent and transparent behavior, free of ambiguity that involves *the obligation to grant and maintain a stable and predictable legal framework necessary to fulfill the justified expectations of the foreign investor*'.[15] Such superfluous use of the doctrine cannot be endorsed under the reliance conception. Let us examine two arbitral decisions to illustrate the point.

8.2.2.1 *Saluka v. Czech Republic*

The rhetorical use of legitimate expectations falls outside the purview of the reliance theory. Let us recall pertinent facts and analyse the tribunal's reasoning. Against the background of the Czech banking crisis and the discriminatory provision of state financial assistance in favour of national banks, the tribunal relied on the notion of legitimate expectations in the assessment of the FET standard. Its conception was based on tautology when it referred to an expectation to be fairly and equitably treated:

> [T]he host State, in providing State aid, is clearly bound not to *frustrate an investor's legitimate and reasonable expectation to be treated fairly and equitably*. The host State is therefore obliged to provide financial assistance to firms or industries in a way that does not amount to an unfair or inequitable treatment of a foreign investor. In particular, the provision of State aid to specific firms or industries must not be discriminatory or unreasonably harmful for the foreign investor.[16]

Furthermore, the tribunal curiously suggested that the source of expectations does not necessarily have to come from the state's conduct, but it is sufficient that the investor could reasonably expect a state to behave in a certain manner.[17] These two aspects of the decision cannot be endorsed under the reliance theory of legitimate expectations because the source of

[14] *Rumeli Telekom A.S. and Telsim Mobil Telekomikasyon Hizmetleri A.S. v. Republic of Kazakhstan*, ICSID No ARB/05/16, Award (29 July 2008) para 615 (emphasis added).

[15] *LG & E Energy Corp. v. Argentine Republic*, ICSID Case No ARB/02/1, Decision on Liability (3 October 2006) (emphasis added).

[16] *Saluka v. Czech Republic* (n 3) para 446 (emphasis added).

[17] Ibid para 329.

expectation must come from the representation or conduct of the state. Moreover, this decision has been rightly criticised for going far 'beyond any previous authority on the relevance of legitimate expectations to the fair and equitable standard' and as well as 'the domestic public law origins of the legitimate expectations principle'.[18]

8.2.2.2 *Charles Lemire v. Ukraine*

The decision of *Charles Lemire v. Ukraine* reflects the tribunal's approach of conjuring up the investor's legitimate expectations rather than identifying a source of legitimate expectations from a particular conduct. The issue was whether the non-issuance of a licence by the respondent for business expansion breached the claimant' expectations.

The significant part of the tribunal's reasoning was the distinction between legitimate expectations 'on a general level' and 'on a more specific and personal level'. On a general level, the tribunal suggested that the claimant could expect

> a regulatory system for the broadcasting industry which was to be consistent, transparent, fair, reasonable, and enforced without arbitrary or discriminatory decisions ... [O]nce he had been awarded the necessary administrative authorization to invest in the Ukrainian radio sector, there would be a level playing field, and the administrative measures would not be inequitable, unfair, arbitrary or discriminatory.[19]

On a more specific and personal level, the claimant had the legitimate expectation that his investment would be allowed to expand in parallel with the growth of the private radio industry in Ukraine.[20] The tribunal emphasised that these legitimate expectations were not based on an individual negotiation between Mr. Lemire and the Ukrainian state; '*they represent the common level of legal comfort which any protected foreign investor in the radio sector could expect*'.[21]

Based on the reliance theory, such use of legitimate expectations could not be endorsed as it only uses the term 'legitimate expectations' in a rhetorical manner. The expectation which represents the level of legal

[18] S Fietta, 'Expropriation and the "Fair and Equitable" Standard: The Developing Role of Investors' "Expectations" in International Investment Arbitration' (2006) 23 *J Int'l Arb* 37.

[19] *Joseph Charles Lemire v. Ukraine*, ICSID Case No ARB/06/18, Award (14 January 2010) para 267.

[20] Ibid.

[21] Ibid (emphasis added).

comfort and does not arise from the state's conduct falls outside the scope of legitimate expectations.

However, on the facts of the case, it could have been established that the claimant's expectation had been based on the meetings and representations of the officials, in particular official letters.[22] The claimant argued that he had a legitimate expectation that he would be authorised to increase the size and audience of his radio company, and to establish three radio networks in Ukraine. This plan had been discussed with the National Council members and encouraged by them.[23] However, the facts of the case suggest that the claimant's expectation would be unreasonable given the ambiguous nature of the assurance based on the letters communicated between government agencies, far from any specific guarantee or commitment.

8.3 Application of the Reliance Theory of Legitimate Expectations in Different Situations

8.3.1 Protection of Legitimate Expectations Arising from Contract and the Reliance Theory

This section[24] examines selected arbitral decisions which addressed a breach of contract and protection of legitimate expectations. Using the reliance theory of legitimate expectations to adjudicate these cases would provide much clarity and coherence. The enquiry under the reliance theory focuses on the harmful conduct of the state resulting from the exercise of its sovereign power in breaching the relevant contract and thus preserves the role of the law applicable to the relevant contract for a contractual breach.

8.3.1.1 *EDF v. Romania*

The *EDF v. Romania*[25] decision illustrates the difficulty of applying the voluntarist conception of legitimate expectations, in particular whether contractual term is a sufficient basis for determining legitimate

[22] Ibid para 270.

[23] Ibid para 210.

[24] The discussion in this section and in Chapter 6 should complement each other, in particular the analysis of arbitral decisions, which clarifies the types of acts that can induce reliance. However, this section focuses on the unique contribution of the reliance conception in resolving uncertainties.

[25] *EDF (Services) Ltd v. Romania*, ICSID Case No ARB/05/13, Award (2 October 2009).

expectations in the context of contract breach. As a result, the tribunal seemed to take inconsistent approaches in two contract claims.

EDF v. Romania concerns an alleged breach of contract about the extension of a contract term between two entities whose contract acts were directed by the respondent in relation with the claimant. The key issue was whether the non-extension of the contract term in violation of the claimant's legitimate expectation would constitute a breach of the FET standard (given that the act was attributable to the respondent). The claims relating to the failure to extend the duration of (a) the ASRO contract and (b) the SKY and Constanta joint venture are considered.

On the first claim, the tribunal rejected the claimant's position that it had a legitimate expectation that the term would be extended for at least another ten-year term, based on the circumstances related to the negotiation and performance of the contract with AIBO.[26] The tribunal viewed that the fact that the contract provided for the *possibility* of an extension could not provide a valid basis for a legitimate and reasonable expectation or constitute a legal obligation to extend the term. The tribunal also did not find any 'arbitrary and improper motives' in the conduct of the two contracting entities and found no breach of contract. The fact that the acts may be attributed to the respondent does not change the contractual nature of the issue.[27]

On the second claim, the tribunal found no breach of the FET obligation because the legitimate expectations that one of the entities would continue the joint venture with the claimant were only based on the contract itself. The tribunal suggested that 'to validly claim a breach of the FET standard under the BIT, Claimant should have proven *not only a breach of the SKY contract, but also that such other assurances had been given by the Government and had been breached*'.[28] Those extra-contractual sources include specific assurances in writing from government representatives, statutes, regulations or other commitments by the government.[29]

The peculiar aspect of the tribunal's reasoning was that the contract was a sufficient basis for the determination of legitimate expectations in the first claim but not in the second claim. What is the rationale for this difference? The difference might be explained in terms of different conceptions of legitimate expectations.

[26] Ibid para 244.
[27] Ibid para 247.
[28] Ibid (emphasis added).
[29] Ibid para 298.

The tribunal employed the voluntarist conception on the first claim, which focused on the precise scope of contractual obligation as the basis for legitimate expectation. It suggested that the relevant provision only indicated the parties' 'willingness to consider an extension *rather than a legal obligation to extend the term*'.[30] By contrast, in the second claim, the tribunal denied legitimate expectations precisely because there was no assurance beyond the contract. The tribunal could not rely solely on the contractual provisions. It is unclear how a breach of those specific assurances may give rise to international responsibility; presumably those representations must be of a specific nature or the breach involved an exercise of sovereign power.

One might suggest that the tribunal's different stances were not based on any principled justification but rather motivated by the desire to achieve a particular outcome (i.e. to avoid imposing liability through the rules of legitimate expectations). The reliance conception could provide a more coherent conceptual framework, which would grant the tribunal some flexibility to assess all relevant factors and achieve the same outcome in a principled and coherent manner. The reasoning under the reliance theory could be stated as follows: the circumstances of the negotiation, the performance of the contract as well as such customary provision in the contract might have induced the expectation upon which the investor acted to its detriment. However, the tribunal might evaluate the reasonableness of such expectation with reference to the vague nature of the clause or the absence of detriment or change of position.

8.3.1.2 *Walter Bau v. Thailand*

The *Walter Bau v. Thailand*[31] case illustrates how the reliance theory of legitimate expectations could have led to a different outcome in case of a breach of contract. The tribunal relied heavily on the investors' legitimate expectations as a constitutive element for a breach of the FET standard.[32]

The dispute arose from an alleged breach of the concession contract between the government agency and the investor to build a toll way to the airport in Thailand.[33] The tribunal had to consider whether the government's lengthy refusal to raise tolls pursuant to the concession agreement and other acts, contrary to the investor's legitimate expectations,

[30] Ibid (emphasis added).
[31] *Walter Bau v. Thailand*, UNCITRAL Case, Award (1 July 2009).
[32] Ibid para 11.11.
[33] Note that the claimant had only a minority share in the concessionaire company.

constituted a breach of the FET standard. The tribunal upheld a breach of legitimate expectations on the ground that:

> [i]n spite of the fact that there was *no guarantee* by the Respondent of an explicit rate of return, the Tribunal considers that a reasonable rate of return – reasonable in all the circumstances, including *the signing of MoA2* – was part of the Claimant's legitimate expectations and *the failure to fulfill* such a reasonable expectation was *a breach* of the Respondent's FET obligations.[34]

The tribunal's reasoning was not based on any particular conception of legitimate expectations.[35] The tribunal did not focus on the contractual provisions as a reflection of the intention of the state to assume a legal obligation, nor its intention to create assurance nor the act of detrimental reliance by the investor. The tribunal recognised the importance of the concession agreement in assessing the claimant's legitimate expectations, in particular clause 25.1 of the concession agreement, which explicitly stated that it was the government's prerogative whether to increase the toll upon the request by the concessionaire.[36] However, the tribunal suggested that 'a reasonable rate of return' could be considered as a reasonable expectation of the investor, which forms a basis for a breach of the FET standard.

The tribunal opportunistically employed the notion of legitimate expectations as a basis for allowing acts contrary to the claimant's expectations to constitute international responsibility. For instance, the tribunal asserted that a reasonable rate of return was 'part of the understanding between the parties', in particular the claimant's legitimate expectations; therefore the decision to reject a toll increase breached the FET standard.[37] Some acts by the government, such as the short-

[34] Ibid paras 12.1–12.3 (emphasis added).

[35] Note however that the tribunal endorsed the summary of FET clause by *Biwater Gauff v. Tanzania*, which adopts the reliance-based conception: *Biwater Gauff v. Tanzania*, ICSID Case No ARB/05/22, Decision (24 July 2008) para 602 ('protection of legitimate expectations: the purpose of fair and equitable treatment standard is to provide to international investments treatment that does not affect the basic expectations that were *taken into account by the foreign investor to make the investment* as long as these expectations are reasonable and legitimate *and have been relied upon by the investor to make the investment*') (emphasis added).

[36] Ibid para 12.9.

[37] The tribunal agreed with the respondent's expert witness, which views that clause 25.1 only entitles Don Muang Tollway Co. Limited (DMT) in which the claimant had a 10 per cent stake to request the respondent to consider adjusting the tolls within the parameters contained in that clause and the agreement provided an arbitration as a form of dispute settlement under the governing law.

term total closure of a domestic airport or changes to the road network which went beyond the 'traffic management', and the toll reduction of 2004 (the decision taken by the main concessionaire) breached the contractual obligation. But these contractual breaches could not be transformed into international responsibility by simply frustrating the investor's legitimate expectations.

The following discussions illustrate that different conceptions of legitimate expectations could affect reasoning and outcomes of the case.

Suppose that there were three arbitrators who applied three different conceptions of legitimate expectations in resolving this case. The first arbitrator, who applied the voluntarist conception, identified a clear intention to undertake a legal obligation as a basis for establishing legitimate expectation about the toll increase. In this case, from the facts, it might be construed that the respondent did not make a specific promise to automatically grant a request for a toll increase but only to consider the request.[38] Therefore, the tribunal could not impute a specific undertaking by the respondent to grant a specific rate of return. The breach of contract principally determined a breach of legitimate expectations.

The second arbitrator, who applied the assurance conception, focused on an intention to create an expectation in the investor. It might be argued that there was no intention to create the type of expectation that the toll increase request would always be granted; otherwise the contractual provisions would have been drafted differently. It is precisely because the respondent wanted to retain the prerogative over the question of toll increases that the wording of Article 25.1 was included.

The third arbitrator, who applied the reliance conception, required proof of the respondent's inducement of the investor's expectation upon which the investor relied to its detriment. The inducing conduct could be the conclusion of the concession contract and the invitation of interested investors to participate in the construction project by the respondent. The key ingredient for liability would be an act of detrimental reliance in terms of capital investment that the investor made. Despite the absence of a guarantee, the conduct of the state and the context could have created the expectation that there would be no persistent refusal to increase the toll because the parties entered into the concession agreement believing there would be a reasonable rate of return. The respondent could not have expected any foreign investors to enter into an arrangement with

[38] Ibid para 12.9.

such a large commitment of capital without being fairly confident of a reasonable rate of return.

This analysis shows that different conceptions of legitimate expectations result in different reasoning and possibly different outcomes. The outcome in the decision of the first arbitrator might be viewed as favourable to the state, but it seems to totally ignore the context and other important factors, such as the detriment suffered by the claimant. The reliance conception provides a more sophisticated framework for taking into account all relevant factors. It seeks to compensate for the harm from relying on the state's conduct; therefore, the threshold for specificity of representation is not as strict as under the rule which seeks to enforce expectations. Furthermore, reliance damages should have been awarded as a result of the breach because the purpose of the rule is protection against the harm suffered by the investor.

8.3.1.3 *MTD v. Chile*

The case of *MTD v. Chile*[39] is often cited for the proposition that inconsistent acts between different organs of a state can breach the FET standard and that the duty of due diligence affects the level of protection for an investor. This case illustrates a close connection between inconsistency of a state's act and a breach of legitimate expectations.

The claimant contended that the respondent created and encouraged strong expectations that the investment project could be built in the specific proposed location and entered into a contract confirming that location. Subsequently, the local authority disapproved that location as a matter of policy after the claimant irrevocably committed its investment to build the project in that location.

Instead of addressing the parties' arguments on legitimate expectations, the tribunal relied on the principle of consistency as the basis for liability by emphasising the inconsistency of actions between different organs of the same government[40] based on the unitary nature of the state.[41] The tribunal held Chile responsible for the breach of fair and equitable treatment arising from the approval of an investment project by the Foreign Investment Committee which was inconsistent with the urban policy of the government.[42]

[39] *MTD Equity Sdn. Bhv. and MTD Chile S.A. v. Chile*, ICSID Case No ARB/01/07, Decision on Annulment (21 March 2007) 13 ICSID Rep 500.

[40] Ibid para 163.

[41] Ibid para 165.

[42] Ibid para 166.

Two questions are analysed here: (1) is the tribunal's reasoning based on the principle of consistency legally sound? and (2) what are the possible outcomes from the application of different theories of legitimate expectations?

First, the tribunal's reasoning on consistency is questionable as a matter of legal principle. Consistency is one of the central elements of the rule of law,[43] which allows investors to plan their investments according to the legal framework. In municipal public laws, courts apply the principle of consistency in requiring public bodies to adhere to their policies.[44] However, it is highly questionable whether the public law principle of consistency can form a basis for liability in international investment law.[45] Is there a duty to act consistently in international law? On that basis, the state should not be condemned for acting inconsistently when different agencies with different responsibilities are acting within their authority and legal powers. The tribunal's reasoning on consistency does not recognise the division of responsibilities by different agencies and seems to impose a 'one stop service' standard on the respondent.

Second, if the case were to be analysed through the lens of legitimate expectations, would the investor's expectation be protected on the facts of the case? The claim based on expectations would have failed under the voluntarist conception despite the existence of a contract or assurance. The contract did not cover the guarantee about the zoning permits and environmental approvals; rather, it stipulated explicitly that it was not without prejudice to other laws and regulations. Therefore, it is the responsibility of the investor to assure itself that it is properly advised.[46] Thus, the investor's expectations would have fallen outside the protected scope of protection. How about the expectation of consistency between governmental actions? The voluntarist conception would have regarded such a claim as unreasonable in the absence of a specific promise to that effect.

[43] S Schill, 'Fair and Equitable Treatment, the Rule of Law and Comparative Public Law' in S Schill (ed), *International Investment Law and Comparative Public Law* (Oxford: Oxford University Press, 2010).

[44] K Steyn, 'Consistency – A Principle of Public Law?' (1977) 2(1) *JR* 22; R Clayton, 'Legitimate Expectations, Policy, and the Principle of Consistency' (2003) 62(1) *CLJ* 93.

[45] Other arbitral decisions such as *Lauder v. Czech Republic* ruled that the fair and equitable treatment could be violated if domestic agencies acted inconsistently in applying domestic legislation.

[46] *MTD v. Chile* (n 39) para 119.

The assurance conception might have resulted in rejection of the claim on the ground that there was no specific assurance by government officials about the benefits, which the claimant expected. Under the reliance conception, the claimant might have entertained the expectation that the project could be built, but the claim might have failed because of the knowledge of regulatory risks. The tribunal might conclude that the investor should have exercised its due diligence in verifying the situation, especially when the contractual clause clearly stipulated that further approvals were required. It is important to note that the tribunal considered the knowledge of business risk and the investor's failure to observe due diligence to be relevant for the quantum of damages,[47] and not a bar to the liability of the state.[48]

8.3.1.4 *Occidental v. Ecuador (II)*

The reliance theory of legitimate expectations could add clarity and consistency to the tribunal's reasoning in *Occidental v. Ecuador (II)* [49] in resolving a breach of contract and claims for legitimate expectations. In *Occidental II*, the heart of the claimants' case pertains to whether the respondent's termination of the Participation Contract ('caducidad') was valid under the governing law as well as international law. The claimant argued that 'the *Caducidad* Decree was inconsistent with the Treaty and Ecuadorian law because, *inter alia*, it frustrated their legitimate expectations in the circumstances'.[50] The tribunal recognised that the claimants were in breach of the contractual obligation by the failure to observe this authorisation requirement.[51]

The tribunal rejected the claim based on frustration of legitimate expectations for the reason that considering the claimant's negligent failure to secure the required authorisation, 'the Claimants cannot be found to have had a legitimate expectation that the Minister would not

[47] Ibid para 164.

[48] Ibid para 178 ('The BITs are not an insurance against business risk and the Tribunal considers that the Claimants should bear the consequences of their own actions as experienced businessmen').

[49] *Occidental Petroleum Corporation and Occidental Exploration and Production Company v. The Republic of Ecuador*, ICSID Case No ARB/06/11, Award (5 October 2012).

[50] Ibid para 383.

[51] Ibid para 381 ('In conclusion, the Tribunal finds . . . that OEPC, by failing to secure the required ministerial authorization, breached Clause 16.1 of the Participation Contract and was guilty of an actionable violation of Article 74.11 of the HCL').

exercise his discretion and impose *caducidad*'.[52] The tribunal was right to reject the claim because the risk was foreseeable that following the claimant's negligent act, the respondent would and could exercise the right stipulated in the contract to terminate the arrangement.

Furthermore, the tribunal considered the principle of legitimate expectations in two further issues concerning Law 42 and the VAT Interpretive Law. The tribunal had to determine the lawfulness of these measures for the calculation of damages (in which legitimate expectations play an important part in judicial reasoning).[53]

First, the tribunal considered whether Law 42, which was in essence a windfall profits tax, taking 50 per cent of qualified extraordinary profits earned by oil companies from production activity, was in breach of the FET standard, in particular frustrating the investor's legitimate expectation. The tribunal concluded that Law 42, which was considered a unilateral decision of the Ecuadorian Congress to completely rewrite the contractual rights, flouted the claimant's legitimate expectations and breached the FET obligation.[54] The tribunal emphasised the effect of the respondent's representation in inducing the claimant's act of making investment. The tribunal relied on the contractual terms as the basis for determining the reasonableness of expectation:

> The considerable investments made by OEPC in Ecuador after the execution of the Participation Contract were based upon the explicit representations made by the Respondent during the negotiation of the Participation Contract which were then crystallized in the participation agreed by the parties in Clauses 8.1 and 8.5. The investor, OEPC, was justified in expecting that this contractual framework would be respected and certainly not modified unilaterally by the Respondent.[55]

The second claim relates to the Ecuadorian VAT Interpretative Law enacted by the Ecuadorian Congress, which excluded petroleum activities from the reimbursement of VAT.[56] The tribunal had to consider whether claimants' legitimate expectations were breached. The tribunal concluded without much analysis that 'the VAT Interpretative Law, unfairly and arbitrarily, frustrated the legitimate expectations of the Claimants in precisely the same way as the SRI's Decrees and is thus

52 Ibid; the main issue for the tribunal to consider was whether the termination was a proportionate response.
53 Ibid para 546.
54 Ibid para 525.
55 Ibid para 526.
56 Ibid para 558.

also in breach of the Treaty'.[57] Therefore, the VAT Interpretative Law is without legal effect and should not be considered as a factor which impacts the fair market value of the claimants' investment.

The tribunal's reasoning in the first claim could have been articulated more clearly by the reliance principle. The state caused harm to the investor through its failure to fulfil its representations during the negotiation and its contractual undertaking. The investor's act of detrimental reliance in the form of substantial investment provided the basis for the obligation to compensate for the reliance loss. The reasoning on the VAT interpretive law was questionable. Without much legal analysis of the tribunal, the use of legitimate expectations as merely a conclusion rather than a normative element should not be endorsed under the reliance conception.

8.3.2 Boundary of Legitimate Expectations of Legal Stability and the Reliance Conception

The legal framework provides an important basis for an investor to decide to invest in a country. Change of circumstances may require state to change its laws. To what extent the investor can expect stability of the legal framework is amongst the 'grey areas' in the law of legitimate expectations.[58] In the 'Guidelines for the application of the legitimate expectations doctrine', F Dupuy and PM Dupuy suggest three criteria for guiding tribunals in the assessment of expectations of stability of the legal framework as follows: 'The most decisive factor is whether there have been specific commitments by the host state to the effect that the rules applicable to the investment shall remain unaltered. Two other important elements . . . the state's margin of maneuver . . . the degree of change in the investment environment'.[59]

These guidelines, as a good starting point, are far from addressing some fundamental questions: how do the 'specific commitment' and the other two elements explain the reasonableness of the investor's expectation? (In other words, what is it about 'specific commitment' that justifies an obligation borne by the state?) What are the characteristics of the legal

[57] Ibid para 560.

[58] F Dupuy and PM Dupuy, 'What to Expect from Legitimate Expectations? A Critical Appraisal and Look Into the Future of the "Legitimate Expectations" Doctrine in International Investment Law' in Nassib G. Ziadé (ed), *Festschrift Ahmed Sadek El-Kosheri* (The Hague: Kluwer Law International, 2015), 273.

[59] Ibid 290.

framework which can give rise to legitimate expectations? What is the precise role, if any, of the investor's legitimate expectations, besides a label of conclusion, in the assessment of fair and equitable treatment in this context? How is the legal analysis under the reliance conception of legitimate expectations different from the existing rules?

This section shows that the reliance theory can provide a distinct basis for state responsibility arising from a change of regulatory framework. In recent jurisprudence, tribunals have considered the extent and manner of change as well as sovereign right to regulate in determining state liability.[60] For instance, a change must not be arbitrary, discriminatory, or must be in accordance with due process of law.[61] In *CMS v. Argentina*, the tribunal focused on the manner in which the regulatory framework was 'totally dismantled' contrary to the prior specific commitment made.[62] The tribunal in *El Paso v. Argentina* suggested that a 'total alteration of the legal framework' could give rise to a breach of fair and equitable treatment.[63] The tribunal in *Toto v. Lebanon* suggested that 'changes in the regulatory framework would be considered as breaches of the duty to grant full protection and fair and equitable treatment only in case of a *drastic or discriminatory* change in the essential features of the transaction'.[64] The *PSEG v. Turkey* decision emphasised the 'roller-coaster effect of the regulatory modifications' with 'endless' legislative changes.[65] Furthermore, the tribunal in *Impregilo v. Argentina* referred to 'unreasonable modifications of that legal framework'.[66]

By contrast, the reliance theory of legitimate expectations attributes liability to the inducement by the state through legislative framework and

[60] *Parkerings-Compagniet AS v. Lithuania*, ICSID Case No ARB/05/8, Award (11 September 2007) para 332 ('it is each State's undeniable right and privilege to exercise its sovereign legislative power. A State has the right to enact, modify or cancel a law at its own discretion.').

[61] *Franck Charles Arif v. Republic of Moldova*, ICSID Case No ARB/11/23, Award (8 April 2013) para 538 ('accordingly, an investor's legitimate expectations might be breached not only by a substantive change in policy, but also by the treatment of the investor during the process of the change of policy').

[62] *CMS Gas Transmission Company v. Argentine Republic*, ICSID Case No ARB/01/8, Award (12 May 2005) para 277.

[63] *El Paso Energy International Company v. The Argentine Republic*, ICSID Case No ARB/03/15, Award (31 October 2011) para 374.

[64] *Toto Construzioni Generali SpA v. Republic of Lebanon*, ICSID Case No ARB/07/12, Award (7 June 2012) para 244.

[65] *PSEG Global Inc. and Konya Ilgin Elektrik Üretim ve Ticaret Limited Sirketi v. Turkey*, ICSID Case No ARB/02/05, Award (19 January 2007) para 250.

[66] *Impregilo S.p.A. v. Argentine Republic*, ICSID Case No ARB/07/17, Award (21 June 2011) para 291.

detrimental reliance of the investor. The emphasis is whether the law in question could create the expectation in the investor on which the investor then relies to its detriment. A specific nature of legislative framework is therefore relevant because when a specific law grants specific benefits to a specific group of investors or a particular investor, it is likely to induce greater reliance. Through the specific legislative framework, a proximate relationship of trust and confidence between the investor and the state is established. Therefore, any adverse and detrimental change of the law, surrounding circumstances of the host state as well as the investor's own conduct would be all relevant to determine the 'reasonableness' of expectations.

8.3.2.1 Specific Commitment and 'Particular Relationship'

There must be a specific commitment and a particular relationship between the state and the investor in order to claim legitimate expectations.[67] There must be a specific legislative framework directed to a specific group of investors about a specific benefit, contractual undertaking in the form of stabilisation clause[68] or other forms of specific assurance.[69] However, the tribunal in the decision of *El Paso v. Argentina* confirmed that specific commitment could come in a variety of forms and does not need to be legally binding. The tribunal emphasised the detrimental reliance on the part of the investor as the basis for obligation in the following terms:

> First, in order to prevent a change in regulations being applied to an investor or certain behaviour of the State, there can indeed exist *specific commitments directly made to the investor* – for example in a contract or in a letter of intent, or even through a specific promise in a person-to-person business meeting – and not simply general statements in treaties or legislation which, because of their nature of general regulations, can evolve. *The important aspect of the commitment is not so much that it is legally binding* – which usually gives rise to some sort of responsibility if it is violated without a need to

[67] *El Paso v. Argentina* (n 63) para 404 ('There was no particular relationship between El Paso and the GOA before this arbitration, and no special commitment on which El Paso could reasonably rely').

[68] *Mobil Investments Canada Inc. and Murphy Oil Corporation v. Canada*, ICSID Case No ARB(AF)/07/04, Decision on Liability (22 May 2012) para 153.

[69] *Ioan Micula, Viorel Micula, S.C. European Food S.A, S.C. Starmill S.R.L. and S.C. Multipack S.R.L. v. Romania*, ICSID Case No ARB/05/20, Award (11 December 2013) para 673.

> refer to FET – *but that it contains a specific commitment directly made to the investor, on which the latter has relied.*[70]

The *Continental Casualty v. Argentina* decision is a case in point for the lack of a beneficiary for which there can be no particular relationship.[71] The decision concerns the claimant's expectation of a legal stability, which is affected by the respondent's measures in response to an economic crisis, such as bank deposit freezes and foreign exchange controls.[72] These measures fundamentally changed its exchange and currency regime and therefore frustrated the claimant's expectations. The claimant relied on specific legislative enactments and contractual undertakings of Argentina (the Intangibility Law and the terms of issuance of the Government Guaranteed Loans [GGL's], respectively) to support that its expectations were legitimate, rather than the convertibility regime of 1991.[73]

The tribunal rejected the claim because the representations based on the legal or contractual regime were not specifically addressed to the claimant but rather to the general public:

> In the present case, general pronouncements are mostly at issue, predominantly of a legislative type. Moreover, the features of the legal or contractual regime at issue here were applicable or addressed either to the generality of Argentina's public, or to a wide range of depositors and subscribers of certain financial instruments. Moreover, the general legislative 'assurances' were not the basis on which Continental had relied in making its investment in Argentina, since it had entered in that market before such assurances.[74]

Two observations can be made in relation to the tribunal's reasoning. First, the tribunal's finding of a breach of legitimate expectations depended on determination of specificity of both the promised entitlement and the promisee. In this case, the promised entitlement was addressed not just to the claimant but to the generality of the public. It is interesting to note that the tribunal sought to distinguish the facts of this case from the precedents, which involved specific undertakings, legislative, administrative or contractual, directed or agreed with the investor, on the basis of which and in reliance upon the aggrieved

70 Ibid para 376.
71 *Continental Casualty v. Argentina*, ICSID Case No ARB/03/9, Award (5 September 2008).
72 Ibid para 100.
73 Ibid para 257.
74 Ibid para 259.

investor had actually made its investment and committed long-term resources.[75] Second, the tribunal reinforced the importance of an act of reliance on the law by way of making an investment as a condition for liability.

By contrast, the decision of *BG v. Argentina* illustrates the existence of the 'particular relationship' because specific assurance was given to particular foreign investors in the gas sector. The tribunal had to assess whether various specific measures in the regulatory framework[76] could be a source of legitimate expectations of a stable and predictable investment environment. The measures in question were *specifically targeted* to *assure* investors about specific risks *and induce specific foreign investors to invest in gas sector.* The regulatory framework including the laws in gas sectors that represented specific commitments about calculation of tariffs in US dollars, semi-annual adjustment regime of tariffs according to the US PPI and the entitlement of the revision of the tariffs every five years.[77] The tribunal reasoned that:

> Argentina's derogation from the tariff regime, dollar standard and adjustment mechanism was and is in contradiction with *the established regulatory framework as well as the specific commitments represented by Argentina, on which BG relied when it decided to make the investment.* In so doing, Argentina violated the principles of stability and predictability inherent to the standard of fair and equitable treatment.[78]

Two observations can be made in relation to the tribunal's reasoning. First, the reliance rationale underpins the tribunal's reasoning on legitimate expectations by emphasising how the specific undertaking induces the claimant's reliance to invest.[79] However, it is unfortunate that the tribunal sought to strengthen its reasoning by simultaneously citing the principles of stability and predictability to support its reasoning. This has made it difficult to determine whether legitimate expectation is a decisive factor in the assessment of the FET standard. Second, the tribunal did not fully engage in the analysis of whether the reliance was reasonable, though it pointed out the fact that the incorporation of provisions relating to the stability of the regulatory framework in the licence made its reliance reasonable.[80]

[75] Ibid para 260.
[76] *BG Group Plc v. Argentina*, UNCITRAL Case, Final Award (24 December 2007) para 27.
[77] Ibid para 305.
[78] Ibid para 307 (emphasis added).
[79] Ibid para 306.
[80] Ibid.

The interesting question to consider is this: would the voluntarist conception produce a different result? One could argue that the claim might have failed for lack of a specific promise on absolute legal stability in the form of stability agreement or stabilisation clause. The state could argue that it never made a specific promise not to entirely alter the legal and business environment. The difference between the two conceptions is that the reliance conception focuses on the harm caused by the representation to the investor, whilst the voluntarist conception emphasises the clear intention of the state to undertake an obligation.

In recent cases, the tribunal has relied on the general nature of legislative framework as a basis for rejecting a claim based on frustration of legitimate expectations. The issue of regulatory stability and legitimate expectations has been discussed in a series of cases related to the regulatory reform implemented by Spain to roll back certain incentives and benefits to promote investment in the concentrated solar power (CSP) sector. The analysis of the claimant's legitimate expectations is the key issue in the determination of the FET standard. This section considers some selected cases.

The case of *Charanne v. Spain* concerned the enactment of legislative measures which reduced or withdrew economic support that had previously been given to investors in the renewable energy sector in Spain. The tribunal had to consider the claimant's argument that the respondent's adoption of the measures in 2010 infringed upon the legitimate expectations created by those regulations in light of the FET standard under the Energy Charter Treaty. The key question is whether the existing regulatory framework at the time of investment could give rise to a legitimate expectation that there would be no modification of the law.[81]

The tribunal relied on two elements in concluding that the claimants could not have legitimate expectations that the regulations would not change. First, the tribunal pointed to the lack of specific commitments in the form of a stabilisation clause or any kind of statement directed at the claimants.[82] The tribunal considered the regulations to be of a general nature as well as the campaign materials.[83] Second, the regulatory measures must not have been reasonably foreseeable at the time of the investment.[84] In this respect, the tribunal accepted the respondent's

[81] *Charanne and Construction Investments v. Spain*, SCC Case No V 062/2012, Award (21 January 2016) para 498.
[82] Ibid para 490.
[83] Ibid paras 496–97.
[84] Ibid para 505.

contention that the claimants should have made a diligent analysis of the legal framework for the investment in the analysis of legitimate expectations.[85]

The tribunal's adherence to the reliance conception can be questioned when it accepts the principle behind the claimant's submission that even in the absence of specific commitments, legitimate expectations could be frustrated when modifying the existing regulation on which the investment decision was relied, the state acted unreasonably, disproportionately or contrary to the public interest.[86] It is submitted that this part of the tribunal's reasoning reflects a rhetorical/tautological use of legitimate expectations,[87] which should not be endorsed under the reliance theory of legitimate expectations. The tribunal could have assessed the regulatory measures with reference to the norms of reasonableness, public interest and proportionality without employing the term 'legitimate expectations'. Nevertheless, the tribunal concluded that there was no violation of the FET standard.[88]

The case of *Eiser v. Spain* concerned different regulatory measures – namely, the regulations in 2013–2014,[89] which had more drastic economic consequences for the claimant compared with the regulations in the *Charanne* case.[90] The tribunal found the breach of the FET standard in Article 10 of the Energy Charter Treaty on the basis that there was a drastic and abrupt revision of the regime on which the investment depended.[91] Whilst the regulatory framework (RD 661/2007) at the time of initial investment did not give the claimants immutable economic rights that could not be altered by changes in the regulatory regime, the

85 Ibid para 507 ('at least that is the level of care that would be expected of a foreign investor in a highly regulated as the energy sector, where a preliminary and comprehensive legal framework applicable to the sector analysis is essential to proceed with the investment').

86 Ibid paras 513–14.

87 Ibid para 539 (the tribunal concludes that 'the Claimants have not demonstrated that the 2010 norms would *violate the legitimate expectations* under the ECT by being *unreasonable, arbitrary, contrary to public interest, or disproportionate.* Nor is there any proof that these norms were unfair or inconsistent'.).

88 Ibid para 540.

89 *Eiser Infrastructure Limited and Energía Solar Luxembourg S.à r.l. v. Kingdom of Spain*, ICSID Case No. ARB/13/36, Award (4 May 2017); Royal Decree-Law 9/2013, Royal Decree 413/2014 and Ministerial Order IET/1045/2014.

90 Ibid para 369 (the case addressed much less sweeping changes to the photovoltaic regulatory regime, changes that produced far less drastic economic consequences for the Charanne claimants).

91 Ibid para 387.

Energy Charter Treaty protects claimants against the 'total and unreasonable change'.[92]

The analysis of the FET standard in this case does not rely on the principle of legitimate expectations, but on a breach of an obligation to provide fundamental stability. In this case, liability was found on the basis of total change of regulatory framework.[93] The tribunal employed the term 'expectation' in a non-normative manner. The true basis for liability was the drastic and unreasonable manner of change of law.[94]

The dispute in *Blusun v. Italy*[95] arose out of Italy's regulatory reform in the solar energy sector. The tribunal faced a question that it considered in other solar power cases – namely, whether the regulatory changes which frustrated the foreign investor's legitimate expectations breached the FET obligation under the Energy Charter Treaty. The alleged measures reduced the level of feed-in tariffs available in the future, which affected the claimant's investment.

The tribunal adopted the reliance conception of legitimate expectations. Even though the tribunal attached importance to the absence of a specific commitment for rejecting the legitimate expectations claim,[96] the tribunal considered as pertinent the detrimental reliance of the investor:

> In the absence of a specific commitment, the state has no obligation to grant subsidies such as feed-in tariffs, or to maintain them unchanged once granted. But if they are lawfully granted, and if it becomes necessary to modify them, this should be done in a manner which is not disproportionate to the aim of the legislative amendment, and should have due regard to *the reasonable reliance interest of recipients* who may have committed substantial resources on the basis of the earlier regime.[97]

In the non-solar energy case *Teinver v. Argentina*,[98] the tribunal considered the general nature of the applicable legislation to be very pertinent in determining an objective legitimate expectation of the investor. The dispute arose out of Argentina's measures related to the claimants'

92 Ibid para 362.
93 Ibid para 389.
94 Ibid para 387.
95 *Blusun S.A., Jean-Pierre Lecorcier and Michael Stein v. Italian Republic*, ICSID Case No ARB/14/3, Final Award (27 December 2016).
96 Ibid para 374.
97 Ibid para 372.
98 *Teinver S.A., Transportes de Cercanías S.A. and Autobuses Urbanos del Sur S.A. v. The Argentine Republic*, ICSID Case No ARB/09/1, Award (21 July 2017).

investments in two Argentine airlines: Aerolíneas Argentinas S.A. and Austral-Cielos del Sur S.A. The claimants challenged Argentina's failure to set economically reasonable airfares, resulting in the airfares being too low, hence impairing their right to earn a reasonable return. For a breach of fair and equitable treatment, the claimants argued that the respondent frustrated their legitimate expectations grounded on clear rights, specific commitments and guarantees in the regulatory framework at the time of their investment and additional assurances and commitments during the period of their investment.[99]

The tribunal considered the doctrine of legitimate expectations as part of the FET standard provision even though the term is not found in the treaty language. The tribunal endorsed a broad reliance-conception of legitimate expectations:

> [T]he fair and equitable treatment language has been interpreted to oblige a State not to frustrate an investor's legitimate expectations, *either at the time of the investment or in the course of the investment*, as long as those expectations were objectively reasonable, created by the State (the State intended for the investor to rely upon them) and *relied upon by the investor.*[100]

The tribunal's conception of legitimate expectations extended to the course of investment and not just the initial stage of making an investment. It is clear that the tribunal did not subscribe to the voluntarist conception because the tribunal had to consider 'all of the circumstances of a case from an objective and reasonable point of view' for its interpretation of legitimate expectations.[101] The tribunal seemed to endorse the 'reasonable investor' concept.[102]

The tribunal concluded that the claimant could not have legitimate expectations with respect to airfares under the existing regulatory framework. The tribunal emphasised the very general nature of the applicable legislation in question which did not reflect any specific intention or commitment to protect tariffs.[103] Furthermore, the tribunal considered the prevailing circumstances of serious financial difficulties faced by the airlines as well as the Argentine economy and the little-performed due

[99] Ibid paras 654–55.
[100] Ibid para 667.
[101] Ibid.
[102] Ibid ('what would have been the legitimate and reasonable expectations of a reasonable investor in the position of the Claimants here at the time they made their investment?').
[103] The tribunal proceeded to analyse the regulatory framework whether it could provide an objective basis for expectations on the part of claimants.

diligence or the review of the regulatory framework. Most significant for our analysis was the lack of reliance on any representation or commitment by Argentina.[104]

It is interesting to note that the tribunal seemed to engage in a rhetorical use of legitimate expectations when it considered the expectations with regard to the respondent's conduct subsequent to claimants' investment. The tribunal accepted the claimant's 'expectation that the conduct of the Respondent ... would be fair and equitable' and that the claimants could expect that the respondent 'would comply with its laws and regulations and act transparently, grant due process and refrain from taking arbitrary or discriminatory measures or exercising coercion'.[105] This part of the tribunal's reasoning, it is submitted, should not be endorsed because the term 'expectation' serves as a conclusion as opposed to the normative criteria.

8.3.2.2 Detrimental Reliance as the Basis for an Obligation to Protect Legitimate Expectations

The reliance conception requires a connection between a specific representation and an act of detrimental reliance. This has the benefit of avoiding the difficulty of interpreting whether a representation is a promise or simply a policy objective or a statement. The discussions of *CMS v. Argentina*,[106] *Ulysseas v. Ecuador*[107] and *Occidental v. Ecuador*[108] illustrate how the reliance conception of legitimate expectations would provide for a specific scope of state liability for a change of regulatory framework.

8.3.2.2.1 *CMS v. Argentina* In *CMS v. Argentina*, the tribunal emphasised the causation of the guarantees on the subsequent investment decisions as the basis for state liability. Against the backdrop of the Argentinian crisis, the essence of the claimant's claim was that 'dismantling the whole legal framework of the gas industry is contrary to any reasonable expectation'.[109] However, the tribunal, in holding a breach of the FET standard, did not explicitly resort to legitimate expectations;

[104] *Teinver v. Argentina* (n 98) para 672.
[105] Ibid para 679.
[106] *CMS v. Argentina* (n 62) para 286.
[107] *Ulysseas, Inc. v. The Republic of Ecuador*, UNCITRAL, Final Award (12 June 2012).
[108] *Occidental Exploration and Production Co v. Republic of Ecuador*, LCIA Case No UN 3467, Award (1 July 2004).
[109] *CMS v. Argentina* (n 62) para 286.

rather, it focused on the total dismantling of the specific commitments[110] on the basis of which the investment was made.[111]

Whilst the reasoning is not framed in terms of legitimate expectations, the underlying rationale behind the tribunal's reasoning could be explained by the reliance conception. The tribunal focused on the effect of the specific law in inducing the foreign investor and the expectations created by the basic conditions for the licences to be granted to private operators. The investor's expectation that there would not be a total dismantling of the legal framework might be considered reasonable given that the investment in public utilities sectors would require a long-term commitment. Under the reliance theory, the tribunal would not have to ascertain whether the state had made a promise but how the change of the law that had induced the investor's decision to invest brought about the detrimental impact on the investor.

8.3.2.2.2 ***Ulysseas v. Ecuador*** The *Ulysseas v. Ecuador* decision illustrates the advantage of using the reliance theory to avoid the complex question of whether a 'promise' has been made. In this case, the dispute arose from the background of the privatisation scheme in the electricity sector. The specific regulatory framework, the Power Sector Regime Law, was enacted to provide a series of mechanisms to create a competitive electricity market which promoted efficiency and private participation in the sector. The tribunal had to determine whether certain measures taken, which affected profitability or price or collection of payments and which frustrated the claimant's expectations of the stability of electricity regulatory framework, constituted a breach of the FET standard.

The claimant's expectations of legal stability was based on the '*promises embodied*' in contractual arrangements, the 1998 Constitution and certain provisions of the Power Sector Regime Law as well as the general course of conduct of the respondent.[112] However, the respondent's positions were that these provisions were not '*purported representations*' and were merely general provisions which set forth policy objectives and offered no legal guarantee.

The tribunal ultimately denied the protection of legitimate expectations by invoking the knowledge of regulatory risk on the part of the investor about a process of constant evolution in the country.[113]

[110] Ibid para 277.
[111] Ibid para 275.
[112] *Ulysseas v. Ecuador* (n 107) para 216.
[113] Ibid para 253.

By implicitly applying the reliance theory, the tribunal did not need to determine definitively whether the state had made a promise through these provisions. It would suffice to determine that the specific regulatory framework must have induced the investor's expectations and detrimental reliance.

The tribunal was correct to conclude that the knowledge of past unstable situations in the country rendered the expectations of the immutable legal framework unreasonable. Furthermore, the tribunal's inclination for the reliance conception was reflected in its regard towards the relevance of the detrimental impact, whereby the tribunal suggested that the claimant had not proved that 'regulatory changes in payments to power generators made Claimant business prospects worse than in September 2006'.[114]

With the voluntarist conception, the reasoning becomes more complicated because the tribunal had to determine whether the state had assumed a legal obligation not to alter the regulatory framework. The tribunal might have reached a similar conclusion on the basis of the voluntarist conception as it did under the reliance conception – namely, that the state had never made a specific commitment to that effect.

Less consistent with the reliance conception is the tribunal's reasoning on the issue of fuel credits.[115] The tribunal held that the claimant could not have legitimately expected the fuel credits scheme to continue to be available because the state did not make a specific commitment in that regard.[116] In addition, the tribunal even suggested that the claimant had accepted a possibility of change in laws and regulations by the effect of Article 24 of the License Contract. One could suggest that the reasoning based on the absence of specific commitment for rejecting legitimate expectations might be guided by the voluntarist conception.

8.3.2.2.3 ***Occidental v. Ecuador (I)*** The case of *Occidental v. Ecuador (I)* illustrates the close relationship between an obligation to maintain legal stability and an obligation to protect legitimate expectations of legal stability – a thin line which can potentially blur the reasoning of the tribunal. The tribunal had recourse to the notion of stability of the legal framework rather than address the claimant's argument based on

114 Ibid para 256.
115 Ibid para 254.
116 Ibid.

legitimate expectations. The reliance conception of legitimate expectations would lead to a more rational and principled outcome.

The case concerned a dispute arising from an inconsistent interpretation of the tax law. The claimant was engaged in the exploration and production of oil in Ecuador under a 1999 contract with an Ecuadorian state-owned corporation. In 2000–2001, the claimant regularly received VAT reimbursements on purchases for its activities. However, the Ecuadorian tax authority subsequently issued resolutions denying all further applications by the claimant for VAT refunds and requiring the return of the amounts previously reimbursed on the grounds that VAT reimbursement was already accounted for in the contract.

The relevant issue on legitimate expectations was whether

> by revoking preexisting decisions that were legitimately relied upon by the investor to assume its commitments and plan its commercial and business activities, Ecuador has frustrated OEPC's legitimate expectations on the basis of which the investment was made and has thus breached the obligation to accord it fair and equitable treatment.[117]

The respondent asserted that there was no expectation of a VAT refund at the time the investment was made and denied any wrong-doing.

The critical point of this case is that the tribunal relied on 'an obligation not to alter the legal and business environment' as an essential element of fair and equitable treatment.[118] The tribunal left aside the estoppel-based argument for protection of legitimate expectations raised by the claimant and emphasised a change of legal and business environment as the underlying basis for liability:

> The Tribunal concludes on this matter that, as stated above, OEPC undertook its investments, including its participation in the pipeline arrangements, in a legal and business environment that was certain and predictable. This environment was changed as a matter of policy and legal interpretation, thus resulting in the breach of fair and equitable treatment. This breach relates to the effects of both revoking the Granting Resolutions and denying further VAT refunds. The rights of the Claimant are therefore protected under the fair and equitable treatment standard required by the Treaty and enforced by the Tribunal, independently of any estoppel. This last issue therefore becomes moot.[119]

[117] *Occidental v. Ecuador* (n 108) para 181.
[118] Ibid para 191.
[119] Ibid para 196.

Two critical observations can be made in relation to the tribunal's reasoning. First, the tribunal's reliance on an obligation not to alter the legal and business environment is questionable given that such obligation could be recognised only if the state has made a specific undertaking to that effect. It cannot be imputed into the notion of fair and equitable treatment as a legal standard for liability. One might argue that the principle of non-arbitrariness might have provided a more suitable standard of review given that, based on the facts of the case, the decision-making process seemed to lack proper reason, clarity and justification.[120]

Second, the case could have been analysed in terms of the reliance conception of legitimate expectations as follows: pre-existing decisions could fall within the broad meaning of 'conduct' which could give rise to legitimate expectations. An argument could be made to suggest that pre-existing decisions might have created an expectation that the VAT reimbursement would be continued. However, the claimant could not establish that it relied on this practice to its detriment (additional investment).[121] Furthermore, the tribunal would have to determine whether it was reasonable for the claimant to entertain such expectation in light of the surrounding circumstances, such as the lack of specific representation.

8.3.3 *Protection of Expectations Created by Non-legally Binding Representations*

The reliance conception of legitimate expectations is more likely to provide protection to expectations arising from non-legally binding representations than the other conceptions. The basis for liability is not a legally binding nature of the promisor's representation but the detrimental reliance on that representation.[122] Choosing the conception which would leave expectations based on administrative representations unprotected in all circumstances defeats the purpose of introducing the doctrine of legitimate expectation in investment treaty arbitration.

There are two parts to this section. The first part examines the relationship between 'right' and expectation and its relevance for the doctrine of legitimate expectations. I argue that under the reliance theory, legitimate expectations do not have to be based on a prior right (Section 8.3.3.1).

[120] Ibid para 184.
[121] Ibid para 195.
[122] The discussion on administrative representation as inducing acts in Chapter 6 supplements the analysis here.

This rationale provides the basis for analysing protection of expectations arising from administrative representations with reference to selected arbitral decisions (Section 8.3.3.2).

8.3.3.1 Reliance Theory of Legitimate Expectations and the Right versus Expectation Conundrum

The issue of the relationship between right and expectation has received increasing attention in scholarly commentary. The essential question is whether legitimate expectations have to be based on legally binding commitment or on right.[123]

8.3.3.1.1 Divergent Positions of Investment Treaty Jurisprudence

The current investment treaty jurisprudence diverges on the issue of the relationship between expectation and right. Several tribunals have taken the view that legitimacy of expectation depends on a prior legal right.[124] For instance, the dissenting opinion of Professor Abi-Saab in *Micula v. Romania* takes the view that legitimate expectations cannot 'transpire or be captured or condensed out of thin air' and must be based on 'some kind of *legal* commitments'. His reasoning is stated in the following term:

> Under general international law, responsibility cannot ensue without a prior breach of *a legal obligation*. The conduct or representation of the government has to bear the makings of *an identifiable legal commitment* towards the specific investor, before we can speak of a breach (or frustration) of legitimate expectations, calling for a remedy or compensation ... It can ensue from behaviour or conduct. But such conduct must be sufficiently concrete and specifically directed to the particular investor, to constitute *an objective 'representation' of a legal commitment*, that can be objectively seen as generating legitimate expectations.[125]

[123] J Paulsson, 'Can "Legitimate Expectations" Ever Be "Rights"?' *JOTWELL* (19 April 2016) http://lex.jotwell.com/can-legitimate-expectations-ever-be-rights (accessed on 30 May 2016). Dupuy and Dupuy, 'What to Expect from Legitimate Expectations' (n 58) (the authors do not seem to provide any deep insight, except an observation that 'the term "legitimate expectations" becomes interesting when it describes expectations recognised by law even though they are not directly derived from a rule of law').

[124] Some tribunals seem to suggest that legitimate expectations must be based on 'acquired rights'; see *M.C.I. Power Group L.C. and New Turbine, Inc. v. Republic of Ecuador*, ICSID Case No ARB/03/6, Award (31 July 2007) para 279 or 'quasi-contractual relationship' in *Glamis Gold, Ltd v. United States of America*, NAFTA/UNCITRAL, Award (8 June 2009) para 766.

[125] *Micula v. Romania* (n 69), Separate Opinion of Georges Abi-Saab para 3.

The opposite view contends that expectations do not necessarily arise from a legally binding act. The typical paradigm of this view is found in the case of administrative representations. For instance, in *PSEG v. Turkey*, an investor's expectation aroused by BOT policy is not based on a legal right because such policy document did not confer any legal right on claimants and there was no specific undertaking by other means to that effect. The tribunal rejected the claim – not on the basis that an investor did not have a legal right but because there was no specific representation by a state. In *White Industries v. India*, the tribunal rejected the claim on legitimate expectations because the representation was vague. In that case, the representations of a vague nature by Indian officials regarding the safety of investment and quality of the Indian legal system could not give rise to legitimate expectations.

These cases failed the threshold test of legitimate expectations because of the lack of specific representation rather than the absence of a prior legal right or commitment. A legal right can be non-specific, whereas a specific representation is not necessarily a legal commitment (i.e. a promise given in an informal setting).

8.3.3.1.2 The Reliance Conception and the Problem of Right and Expectation

The philosophical divide between these two approaches is underlined by different conceptions of legitimate expectations. The view which requires a representation of legal commitment adheres to the voluntarist conception that focuses on the will of the state to undertake a legal obligation. The view that adopts the reliance conception is neutral on the legally binding character of a representation but requires an act of detrimental reliance on the part of the investor. A state may or may not necessarily engage in a legally binding relationship with an investor; hence, the investor may not be in possession of any legal right until that created expectation is relied upon and subsequently crystallised into a legally protectable interest.[126]

According to the reliance conception, legitimate expectations are not necessarily contingent on a prior legal right because it is not the nature of interest but the conduct of the state and the subsequent act of reliance

[126] The similar operation is seen in the law of estoppel, which creates rights for the claimant: a claimant does not necessarily have a legal right but through the conduct of the representor and the detrimental reliance upon such conduct by the representee, the interest becomes legally protected: MP Thompson, 'From Representation to Expectation: Estoppel as a Cause of Action' (1983) 42(2) *CLJ* 257, 257–58.

which provide the basis for liability. However, the underlying right may be relevant for the assessment of reasonable expectations.

There is no clear line between 'right' and 'expectation' because rights are, in effect, legitimate expectations that are usually based on socially or legally recognised entitlements. Rights are 'legitimate expectations, arising from the adoption of authoritative rules and the institutions that support them, that identify the interests to be protected and furthered by the acts and forbearances of others'.[127] Joseph Raz suggests that 'rights themselves are grounds for holding others to be duty bound to protect or promote certain interests of the right-holder'.[128] The threshold question is whether the conduct in question has created expectations in the investor. When investors have a right, they have 'expectations' for those interests to be protected. However, the use of the term 'expectations' in that case does not add much to the legal analysis, such as the case of property right and expectations.

In English administrative law, the doctrine of legitimate expectations protects an entitlement less than a right. Some early cases characterise legitimate expectations as 'moral obligations'.[129] Some authors indicate that a legitimate expectation gives legal protection to interests, which by themselves do not attract legal protection.[130] The case law also confirms that the doctrine of legitimate expectations is 'capable of including expectations which go beyond enforceable legal rights, provided they have some reasonable basis'.[131] The doctrine is able to intervene where interests have crystallised into protectable rights by virtue of some action of the decision-maker. It is the 'legitimate expectation arising out of the conduct of the decision-maker' which provides the basis for protection and not the nature of the interest.[132]

[127] C McKinnon, *Issues in Political Theory* (Oxford: Oxford University Press, 3rd edn, 2014), 178.

[128] J Raz, 'Authority and Justification' (1985) 14 *Phil & Pub Aff* 1.

[129] See, for example, *O'Reilly v. Mackman* [1983] 2 AC 237, 275D-F per Lord Diplock; *Attorney-General of Hong Kong v. Ng Yuen Shiu* [1983] 2 AC 629, 636E-F; GCHQ, p 401A per Lord Fraser; *R v. Secretary of State for Health, ex parte United States Tobacco International Inc.* [1992] 1 QB 353, 369G-H per Taylor LJ.

[130] P Reynolds, 'Legitimate Expectations and the Protection of Trust in Public Officials' (2011) *PL* 330.

[131] *Att Gen Hong Kong v. Ng Yuen Shiu* [1983] 2 AC 629, 636.

[132] Some authors take the opposite view that it is the nature of the interest and not the conduct of the decision-maker which justifies judicial protection. P. Elias, 'Legitimate Expectation and Judicial Review' in J Jowell and D Oliver (eds) *New Directions in Judicial Review* (London: Stevens, 1988), 41.

8.3.3.1.3 Unlawful Representations: The Problem of Right and Expectation Illustrated The autonomy of expectations from rights is evident in the discussion of unlawful promise and legitimate expectations. The fundamental question considered here is this: can an investor's expectation be deemed reasonable or legitimate if it arises from an illegal or *ultra vires* representation (i.e. made beyond the powers of the representing authority)?

This issue was contested in the decision of *SPP v. Egypt.*[133] In that case, the claimant entered into agreements with Egypt to establish a joint venture with a view to develop an international tourist complex at the Pyramids Oasis. Subsequently, the government effectively cancelled the project, placing the joint venture enterprise in judicial trusteeship. The key issue is whether illegal acts by officials affect the legal protection of an investor's legitimate expectations. The tribunal took the view that even if certain acts of Egyptian officials were illegal under Egyptian law, such acts were performed by governmental authorities which created a legitimate expectation for the investor. The tribunal's estoppel-based reasoning reads as follows:

> These acts were cloaked with the mantle of Governmental authority and communicated as such to foreign investors who *relied on them in making their investments* . . . which are now alleged to have been in violation of the Egyptian municipal legal system, created expectations protected by established principles of international law.[134]

The tribunal invoked the notion of legitimate expectations underpinned by the reliance rationale. The tribunal emphasised the act of detrimental reliance on the government's representation as the basis for liability. The voluntarist conception of legitimate expectations might lead to different outcome because there might be a presumption that the state cannot be taken to exceed its powers in undertaking an obligation; therefore, the promise made beyond its power could arguably be deemed involuntary.

On the one hand, under the rules of international law, the state cannot invoke the illegality under the domestic law to abrogate from its international responsibility. From this view, a state cannot denounce that an act of the official who exceeds his or her authority is not an act of state,

[133] *Southern Pacific Properties (Middle East) Ltd v. Arab Republic of Egypt*, ICSID Case No ARB/84/3, Award (20 May 1992) (1994) 19 *Yb Comm Arb* 51.

[134] Ibid para 83.

which would attract international responsibility.[135] The principle of legality, which is often invoked as the basis for denying legal protection under domestic laws, would not be applicable in the context of international law.

This issue raised a similar concern in the context of domestic public law.[136] The prevailing view in English public law suggests that unlawful representations do not bind public authorities because the constitutional principle of legality prevails – namely, that to give protection to expectations is to allow public agencies to act beyond their legal powers.[137] However, the argument based on legality does not have absolute status because there is a possibility of estoppel argument where the individual has detrimentally relied on a representation which he or she reasonably believed to be reliable and authoritative. Furthermore, there are scholars who advanced an argument for compensation for *ultra vires* legitimate expectations on the ground that the bases of protecting legitimate expectations, such as fairness, legal certainty, abuse of power or trust, do not exclude *ultra vires* representations to be illegitimate.[138]

Given that the basis for protecting legitimate expectations is to protect against detrimental reliance, it follows that *ultra vires* representations should not preclude protection of an investor's expectations. Furthermore, the 'reasonableness' element provides a conceptual platform for tribunals to balance the need to safeguard the position of the individual and the lawful exercise of regulatory powers.

'Expectations' can become 'rights' by virtue of the conduct of the state in creating expectations upon which the investor has relied to its detriment. Expectation is not necessarily based on a right under the reliance conception. The paradigm of administrative representations best illustrates that expectation without a prior legal right can be protected because the conduct of an investor (and reliance thereupon) essentially

[135] ILC, 'Articles on Responsibility of States for Internationally Wrongful Acts' in *Yearbook of the International Law Commission, 2001, Volume II*, UN Doc A/CN.4/SER.A/2001 /Add.1. Article 7 ('the conduct of an organ of a State or of a person or entity empowered to exercise elements of governmental authority shall be considered an act of the State under international law if the organ, person or entity accts in that capacity, even if it exceeds its authority or contravenes instructions').

[136] S Hannet and L Busch, 'Ultra Vires Representations and Legitimate Expectations' (2005) *PL* 729.

[137] M Elliott, 'Unlawful Representations, Legitimate Expectations and Estoppel in Public Law' (2003) 8(2) *JR* 71.

[138] Y Vanderman, 'Ultra Vires Legitimate Expectations: An Argument for Compensation' (2012) *PL* 85, 86.

crystallises this interest into a legally protected interest. However, one might add that the importance of the underlying legal right on the legitimacy of expectations is more evident under the voluntarist conception. This is yet another reason to prefer the reliance conception over the voluntarist conception.

8.3.3.2 Reliance Conception and Administrative Representations: Arbitral Decisions Analysed

8.3.3.2.1 ***Metalclad v. Mexico*** The *Metalclad v. Mexico*[139] decision illustrates the point that the investor's expectations created by specific administrative representations of federal officials could be protected under the reliance conception.

The Mexican government issued federal construction and operating permits for a landfill but failed to obtain a necessary municipal construction permit because of the assurance to the contrary by the federal official. The claimant asserted that federal officials informed it that if it submitted an application for a municipal construction permit, the municipality would have no legal basis for denying the permit and that it would be issued as a matter of course.[140]

The tribunal had to consider whether the local government's act in refusing the project frustrated the claimant's expectations about its entitlement to continue its construction of the landfill and constituted a breach of the FET standard. The tribunal employed the language of reliance rationale by referring to the investor's reliance on the representations of officials:

> Metalclad was entitled to rely on the representations of federal officials and to believe that it was entitled to continue its construction of the landfill. In following the advice of these officials, and filing the municipal permit application on November 15, 1994, Metalclad was merely acting prudently and in the full expectation that the permit would be granted.[141]

However, in the subsequent paragraph, the tribunal confusingly used the concept of legitimate expectations in a tautological manner in the context of 'the failure to ensure a transparent and predictable framework'. The tribunal referred to the absence of a clear rule regarding a municipal construction permit, as well as the absence of any established

139 *Metalclad v. Mexico*, ICSID Case No ARB(AF)/97/1, Award (30 August 2000).
140 Ibid para 88.
141 Ibid para 89.

practice or procedure for handling applications for a municipal construction permit as the failure to ensure the transparency:[142]

> Mexico failed to ensure a transparent and predictable framework for Metalclad's business planning and investment. The totality of these circumstances demonstrated a lack of orderly process and timely disposition in relation to an investor of a Party acting in *the expectation that it would be treated fairly and justly* in accordance with the NAFTA.[143]

The reliance conception could provide a framework for resolving this case, as follows. The claimant's expectation was created and induced by the explicit assurance of the federal officials on the specific concern of the claimant. However, there might be an argument for suggesting that a reasonable and prudent investor might have verified that no further compliance with municipal regulations would be required, especially if the business operates in a federal state. The outcome of the case based on legitimate expectations would turn on this crucial aspect. The claim based on the voluntarist conception would have certainly failed because it would be difficult to establish a legal obligation on the part of the state to grant a permit.

8.3.3.2.2 ***Fuchs v. Georgia*** The *Fuchs v. Georgia*[144] decision also affirmed that administrative representation, especially made in light of the assurance given by the highest levels of government to a specific investor, could create legitimate expectations under the reliance conception. The decision concerned a specific representation about the compensation that the claimant was entitled to receive after the government took an expropriatory measure. Protection of legitimate expectations was the 'gravamen' of the claimant's claim;[145] the respondent created a legitimate expectation that it would compensate the claimant for the loss of his investment through the establishment of various commissions and other conduct.

The tribunal drew attention to the claimant's sources of expectations based on the joint venture agreement and the deed of concession which guaranteed reimbursement in case of expropriation.[146] However, the tribunal focused on the purported assurances by Georgian government

142 Ibid para 88.
143 Ibid para 99 (emphasis added).
144 *Ron Fuchs v. The Republic of Georgia*, ICSID Case No ARB/07/15, Award (3 March 2010).
145 Ibid para 434.
146 Ibid para 442.

officials that the claimant would be compensated for his losses, especially the compensation process, which was formed under the order of the president.

Whilst the tribunal's conclusion on the breach of the FET standard is correct, its reasoning on the analysis of legitimate expectations is unclear. The tribunal suggested that the specific assurances of compensation gave rise to a specific expectation of compensation that

> Georgia would conduct itself vis-à-vis his investment in a manner that was reasonably justifiable and did not manifestly violate basic requirements of consistency, transparency, even-handedness and nondiscrimination. This includes, in the view of the Tribunal, implementing a compensation process following the expropriation of GTI's rights that is both procedurally and substantively fair.[147]

The reliance conception could make the tribunal's reasoning on legitimate expectations more coherent and clearer. The investor's expectation could be considered reasonable in light of the specific assurance and the contextual circumstances.[148] It is important to emphasise that there is clear evidence that the assurances of compensation modified the claimant's behaviour in taking the step of foregoing private law claims in reliance on those assurances about the compensation process.

Alternatively, the tribunal could have chosen to articulate the procedural unfairness of the compensation process rather than recourse to the frustration of legitimate expectations basis for liability. The tribunal observed that 'the process which ultimately unfolded following constitution of the compensation commission in 1997 can only be described as non-transparent, arbitrary and unfair',[149] taking into account the facts of lengthy delays, refusals by various government officials to address the matter and internal disputes, reshuffling of responsibility, etc. Treating these two aspects distinctly also indicate that legitimate expectations and non-arbitrariness address two aspects of the unlawful act.

8.3.3.2.3 ***Gold Reserve v. Venezuela*** The *Gold Reserve v. Venezuela*[150] decision illustrates that the reliance conception could protect the

[147] Ibid para 441.

[148] Ibid para 449 ('throughout this period, the evidence discloses that senior members of the Georgian Government believed that the State was responsible for the Claimants' losses and that some amount of compensation was owed to them').

[149] Ibid para 446.

[150] *Gold Reserve Inc. v. Bolivarian Republic of Venezuela*, ICSID Additional Facility Case No ARB(AF)/09/1, Final Award (22 September 2014).

expectations arising from the consistent conduct of the state in a way that the other two conceptions could not. In this case, the tribunal had to consider whether the governmental act in the issuance of repeated and consistent certifications of the claimant's compliance with its obligations under the concessions could give rise to the legitimate expectations that other delays or other failures to abide by the applicable rules likewise would be accepted by the administration.[151] The tribunal held that the investor's legitimate expectation was reasonable by considering the value and effect of the certifications of compliance, the absence of objections or warnings or formal notices and most significantly the act of reliance of further investment.[152]

The voluntarist conception of legitimate expectations would lead to a different outcome because it has to be established that 'consistent conduct' exhibits a manifestation of the will to undertake a legal obligation. Some scholars have asserted that 'consistent state conduct displaying favourable treatment over a certain period of time may be considered as a promise that such treatment will continue in the future, provided the change in conduct is not predictable'.[153] Such assertion requires explanation as to how the notion of 'promise' can explain the basis for obligation. It is best to conceptualise consistent conduct as an act which can induce the expectation on which the investor relies to its detriment under the reliance theory.

8.4 Relationship between the Reliance Theory and Other Relevant Rules

In investment treaty arbitration, the doctrine of legitimate expectations has been applied in conjunction with other rules, such as non-arbitrary standard or umbrella clause, especially in case of a breach of contract. It is important to clarify the relationship between the reliance theory and the umbrella clause and the non-arbitrariness principle for two reasons. First, these rules provide legal protection in different categories of circumstances. Second, these two rules are often raised to undermine the importance of the principle of legitimate expectations. The essence of the claim is that in the domain of contractual breach, existing rules such as the umbrella clause or the principle of *pacta sunt servanda* provide

151 Ibid para 605.
152 Ibid paras 578–79.
153 Dupuy and Dupuy, 'What to Expect from Legitimate Expectations' (n 58) 292.

a perfectly adequate legal standard. Applying the doctrine of legitimate expectations to convert a breach of contract to a treaty breach would be equivalent to introducing the umbrella clause by the backdoor.[154]

Furthermore, some legal scholars contend that the non-arbitrariness principle is a more appropriate, adequate and sophisticated framework, which renders unnecessary the recourse to the principle of legitimate expectations[155] partly because the doctrine of legitimate expectations introduces 'the subjective perception of the normative beholder'.[156]

The argument advanced here is that the reliance theory of legitimate expectations provides a legal standard for reviewing sovereign conduct in a distinctive manner from the umbrella clause (Section 8.4.1), the principle of non-arbitrariness (Section 8.4.2) and the estoppel principle (Section 8.4.3).

8.4.1 *Umbrella Clause and the Reliance Theory of Legitimate Expectations*

This section analyses the scope of application, conditions for establishing liability and the rationales of the umbrella clause and the reliance doctrine of legitimate expectations. It argues that these two rules are distinct and complementary.

On the scope of application, the reliance doctrine of legitimate expectations includes contractual and non-contractual undertakings, such as administrative representations, consistent conduct and laws and regulations.[157] However, there is a strict threshold for a unilateral undertaking, which requires a specific obligation.[158]

[154] C Schreuer, 'Fair and Equitable Treatment: Interactions with Other Standards' (2007) 4(5) *TDM* 18. This view was endorsed by the tribunal in *Hamester* v. *Ghana*, para 337.

[155] C Campbell, 'House of Cards: The Relevance of Legitimate Expectations under Fair and Equitable Treatment Provisions in Investment Treaty Law' (2013) 30(4) *J Int'l Arb* 361.

[156] M Paparinskis, *The International Minimum Standard* (Oxford: Oxford University Press, 2013) 259. See also Emmanuel Gaillard, 'CIRDI, Chronique de sentences arbitrales' (2008) *J de droit Intl* 332 (warning against the 'exacerbated subjectivism' associated with legitimate expectations).

[157] M Cristina and G Salias, 'Do Umbrella Clauses Apply to Unilateral Undertakings?' in C Binder et al. (eds), *International Investment Law for the 21st Century: Essays in Honour of Christoph Schreuer* (Oxford: Oxford University Press, 2009).

[158] *Enron Corporation & Ponderosa Assets, L.P. v. Argentina*, ICSID Case No ARB/01/3, Award (22 May 2007) para 264 (the tribunal pointed out that the regulatory framework provided several specific guarantees to foreign investors, such as calculation of tariffs in US dollars, semi-annual adjustment of tariffs in accordance with the US Producer Price Index (PPI) as well as exemption from freezing or price controls without compensation).

On the conditions for liability, the reliance conception of legitimate expectations treats detrimental reliance of the investor as the basis for the obligation. It must be established that the investor has suffered detriment as a consequence of its reliance on the state's commitment. Furthermore, such reliance is subject to a reasonableness assessment in light of other relevant factors.

There are three main approaches to conditions for liability under the umbrella clause. First, the restrictive approach advocated by *SGS v. Pakistan* rejects the far-reaching interpretation which would accept the ordinary meaning of the clause, requiring a state to comply with its undertakings towards investments, including all contractual obligations, thus transforming any contract breaches into treaty breaches. It is suggested, however, that this highly restrictive interpretation of the duty of observance remains an isolated position. The reliance conception of legitimate expectations would play a distinct and relevant role in comparison with the umbrella clause.

Second, the literal approach adopted in *SGS v. Philippines* accepts that the umbrella clause requires an observance of undertakings specific to the investment and without changing their proper law. Other arbitral decisions have imposed certain conditions for claiming the umbrella clause, – for instance, compliance with a forum selection clause, and an exercise of sovereign power in concluding or breaking a contract, the privity of contract condition and the specificity of legislative obligations.

Third, the middle ground approach supported by *Joy Mining v. Egypt* makes a distinction between commercial and governmental breaches of contract. The tribunal rejected that mere commercial breaches of contract, as opposed to governmental types of breaches, would create international responsibility for breaches of the observance of undertakings clause.

However, in the subsequent case of *SGS v. Paraguay*, the tribunal found that the umbrella clause would turn a contract breach into a treaty breach regardless of a forum selection clause. There is a very compelling argument for supporting the contention that the umbrella clause should cover commercial breaches – namely, that protection against sovereign conduct is already covered by expropriation and fair and equitable treatment, so it is superfluous to limit the scope of an umbrella clause to just a sovereign breach. Therefore, the scope of application of the umbrella clause (covering both sovereign and commercial breaches) would be very different from the reliance conception of legitimate expectations.

Regardless of any approach of the umbrella clause, it is the 'inducing' effect of the representation and detrimental reliance which would distinguish the umbrella clause and the doctrine of legitimate expectations. These two principles are underlined by different rationales. Whilst the reliance doctrine of legitimate expectations seeks to protect against detrimental reliance of the investor upon the state's conduct, the core purpose of the umbrella clause, underlined by the principle of *pacta sunt servanda*, is protection of contracts or enforcement of expectations interests.[159] Andrew Newcombe and Lluís Paradell highlighted the rationale of the umbrella clause as follows:

> The [umbrella] clause thus enshrines the principle of 'pacta sunt servanda,' a cornerstone of the legal security of economic transactions and the basis for contract law in national and international law. In this context, the rationale for the clause lies in the liberal internationalist approach that developed in the 1950s: namely, *that there should be effective international protection of contracts in order to achieve peace and prosperity through international trade, investment and economic integration.*[160]

Another significant difference is the relevance of the applicable municipal law. The existence, nature and scope of an undertaking under the umbrella clause is, in principle, the law of the host state or the law applicable to the contract. In contrast, determination of legitimate expectation is not contingent on the characterisation of a right under municipal law.

In conclusion, both an umbrella clause and the doctrine of legitimate expectations can serve as a legal tool in investment treaty arbitration in a distinct and complementary manner. The umbrella clause has limits to mitigate the effect of its application,[161] just as the 'reasonableness' notion can limit the scope of legitimate expectations.

159 S Schill, 'Contracting with Foreigners: International Investment Law Implications' in R Noguellou and U Stelken, *Comparative Law on Public Contracts* (Brussels: Bruylant, 2010), 78.

160 A Newcombe and L Paradell, *Law and Practice of Investment Treaties: Standards of Treatment* (The Netherlands: Wolters Kluwer, 2009) 437 (emphasis added).

161 The tribunal has set out limits to the scope of umbrella causes, which include municipal law doctrines of *force majeure*, changed circumstances (*rebus sic stantibus*), non-compliance by the investor with some of the corresponding contractual obligations, commercial impracticability or frustration, police powers, 'imprévision,' or any other prerogative of the state to disregard administrative law contracts or to renegotiate those contracts.

8.4.2 *Principle of Non-arbitrariness and the Reliance Theory of Legitimate Expectations: Two Different Principles*

Some scholars have argued that the principle of non-arbitrariness provides an adequate standard for reviewing sovereign acts and hence no need to resort to the doctrine of legitimate expectations. Such view is based on two misconceptions: (1) non-arbitrariness and the principle of legitimate expectations apply to the same types of situations[162] and (2) non-arbitrariness offers 'the sophisticated criteria' for the legal assessment of sovereign conduct.[163]

This section seeks to illustrate that (a) the reliance conception of legitimate expectations applies in different situations from the non-arbitrariness principle and (b) the application of non-arbitrariness is problematic, confusing and far from being 'sophisticated' due to its multiple meanings and multiple sources of obligation.

First, the vague notion of 'arbitrariness' has been given a variety of definitions and interpretations.[164] The term 'arbitrary' exhibits a certain level of ambiguity, as illustrated in the *ELSI* case: 'arbitrariness is not so much something opposed to a rule of law, as something opposed to the rule of law . . . it is a wilful disregard of due process of law, an act which shocks, or at least surprises, a sense of judicial propriety'.[165] The notion of arbitrariness is associated with basing decisions on prejudice or preference, lacking clarity or rationality.[166] Professor Schreuer usefully summarised the characteristics of 'arbitrariness' based on the analysis of jurisprudence as follows: a measure is arbitrary if it inflicts damage on the investor without any apparent legitimate purpose; a measure that is not based on legal standards but on discretion, prejudice or personal preference, a measure taken in wilful disregard of due process and proper procedure; and a measure taken for reasons that are different from those suggested by the decision-maker.[167]

Second, the confusion and complexity also come from the fact that non-arbitrariness is a legal standard whose justifications can be found in

162 J Stone, 'Arbitrariness, the Fair and Equitable Treatment Standard, and the International Law of Investment' (2012) 25 *LJIL* 77.

163 Paparinskis, *The International Minimum Standard* (n 156) 259.

164 Stone, 'Arbitrariness' (n 162) 85.

165 *Elettronica Sicula SpA (ELSI) (United States v. Italy)* [1989] ICJ Rep 15 161 para 128.

166 *MTD v. Chile* (n 39); *LG & E v. Argentina* (n 15) para 158.

167 C Schreuer, 'Protection against Arbitrary or Discriminatory Measures' in CA Rogers and RP Alford (eds), *The Future of Investment Arbitration* (Oxford: Oxford University Press, 2009), 183–98.

three important sources. First, it is found in investment treaties in the stand-alone clauses, which explicitly prohibit 'arbitrary or discriminatory' measures,[168] or an obligation to avoid arbitrariness is an interpretive element or a stand-alone obligation under the FET standard.[169] The NAFTA tribunal tends to consider the concept of arbitrariness as part of the fair and equitable standard because there is no separate treaty provision on the non-arbitrary treatment, and the arbitrary conduct often leads to a breach of the FET standard.[170] Second, it is recognised as a general principle of law by virtue of Article 38 of the Statute of the International Court of Justice.[171] Third, non-arbitrariness is an international customary law standard, as reflected in the international minimum standard of treatment.[172]

The complexity of applying the non-arbitrariness standard is reflected in the issue of whether non-arbitrariness in the FET provision and in the non-impairment provision should be conceptually different. There are two arguments for treating them as different. First, there is a strong assumption that the treaty drafters purposively use two different terms.[173] Second, it is possible to violate one standard without violating the other.[174] This conundrum illustrates the practical difficulty of applying the non-arbitrariness standard.

Whilst it is difficult to ascertain the 'core' element of non-arbitrariness because it is concerned with different aspects of an unlawful conduct, the notion of arbitrariness generally pertains to the manner or the conduct of handling a situation.[175] By contrast, the essence of the reliance conception of legitimate expectations is concerned with protection against detrimental reliance upon the state's conduct.

Therefore, it is perfectly possible to envisage a situation where a certain conduct does not infringe the principle of arbitrariness but may breach the principle of legitimate expectations. Such decision might be well-reasoned, well-grounded and it might comply with due process of law, but it is contrary to its specific undertaking, which the

[168] P Dumberry, 'The Prohibition against Arbitrary Conduct and the Fair and Equitable Treatment Standard under NAFTA Article 1105' (2014) 15 *JWIT* 117.
[169] Ibid.
[170] Ibid.
[171] Stone, 'Arbitrariness' (n 162) 86.
[172] Dumberry, 'The Prohibition against Arbitrary Conduct' (n 168).
[173] Schreuer, 'Protection against Arbitrary or Discriminatory Measures' (n 167).
[174] *LG & E v. Argentina* (n 15) para 162 ('characterizing the measures as not arbitrary does not mean that such measures are characterized as fair and equitable').
[175] Newcombe and Paradell, *Law and Practice* (n 160) 247.

state has made to induce the investor's reliance to its detriment. Some arbitral decisions, in the assessment of the FET standard, treat 'frustration of legitimate expectations' as an act of reneging on the previous undertaking and 'arbitrary conduct of state', as conceptually different.[176]

From the preceding analysis and the current jurisprudence,[177] the assertion that non-arbitrariness offers 'the sophisticated criteria' whilst the principle of legitimate expectations deconstructs 'the progress of the twentieth century back to the subjective perception of the normative beholder'[178] is untenable.

There is another difference between the two principles. The enquiry under non-arbitrariness looks at the unlawful conduct of state, whilst the reliance principle of legitimate expectations considers the perspectives and expectations of individuals. This different perspective goes to the existential question of the investment treaty regime: whether it is about sanctioning an unlawful conduct of the state or about protecting the plight of individuals. If it is the latter, there is a strong case for defending the reliance principle of legitimate expectations. From the theory of expressive function of law, which regards law as 'public affirmation of social values and norms',[179] recognising legal protection of legitimate expectations shows that the investment treaty regime cares about protection of an individual's autonomy or the importance of trust and confidence between the state and the investor as well as the imperative to correct injustice done to the individual from the promise-breaking.

8.4.3 The Reliance Theory of Legitimate Expectations and Estoppel Principle

The author takes the view that the reliance principle of legitimate expectations is distinct from the international law principle of estoppel[180] at least in two significant aspects.

[176] *Metalpar v. Argentine Republic*, ICSID Case No ARB/03/5, Award (6 June 2008) para 187 ('there is no arbitrary governmental conduct nor is there a contractual situation of any kind leading Claimants to entertain legitimate expectations that were violated by such conduct, the Tribunal concludes that Argentina did not violate the provision that requires it to afford fair and equitable treatment to Claimants' investments').

[177] The discussion on 'reasonable investor' in Chapter 6 suggests the objective standard.

[178] Paparinskis, *The International Minimum Standard* (n 156).

[179] C Sunstein, 'On the Expressive Function of Law' (1996) 144 *U Pa L Rev* 2021.

[180] The analysis on the direct or analogous application of the rule of estoppel is carried out in Chapter 2.

First, the principle of legitimate expectations requires proof of detrimental reliance because the purpose of the rule is concerned with protection against harm that results from the reliance on the state's representation; therefore, no responsibility can be established without the detriment. By contrast, there is still divergence of opinions on the detriment requirement in the international law of estoppel.

Second, the reliance conception of legitimate expectations requires the reasonableness of expectations. In assessing the notion of reasonableness, arbitral tribunals consider the perspectives and conduct of an investor, including his or her knowledge of regulatory risk. Such requirement does not exist in the application of the interstate rule of estoppel.

Furthermore, the different context in which the international law of estoppel and the principle of legitimate expectations operate is relevant. The concept of estoppel operates between equal actors, whilst the investor–state relationship is qualitatively different.[181] The reliance conception of legitimate expectations and the estoppel principle may not share the same fundamental moral principle or rationale.[182] The international law of estoppel is primarily concerned with the promotion of consistent conduct of states. The underlying purpose of the reliance doctrine of legitimate expectations concerns a relationship between a state and an investor who have made and received an undertaking from each other in pursuit of their mutually advantageous discourse of investment. The law seeks to protect the investor from the harm suffered as a consequence of relying on the expectations created by the state's conduct. The principle of legitimate expectations should not be a legal standard under which ideal administrative values could be subsumed. Nor is it the mechanism to enforce a sovereign promise. It is not a catchall principle through which

[181] Paparinskis, *The International Minimum Standard* (n 156) 253.

[182] I Samet, 'The Morality of Proprietary Estoppel' in J Penner and H Smith (eds), *The Philosophical Foundations of Property Law* (Oxford: Oxford University Press, 2013) (the author identifies the loss-prevention principle, as elaborated by Thomas Scanlon, as the underlying rationale for the rules of proprietary estoppel); for competing rationales for the rule on estoppel, see A Robertson, 'Towards a Unifying Purpose for Estoppel' (1996) 22(1) *Mon LR* 1 (the author discusses three competing purposes of estoppel – protecting against detrimental reliance, preventing unconscionable conduct and fulfilling expectations).

adjudicators insert whatever fundamental values which societies believe well-behaved, liberal democratic states should have.

Therefore, for those reasons, it is best to develop the set of rules for protection of legitimate expectations in the context proper to the investor–state relationship by relying on the reliance theory of legitimate expectations to guide the interpretation of key issues.

9

Rethinking Remedies for a Breach of Legitimate Expectations

Corrective Justice and Reliance Damages

9.1 Introduction

This chapter reconsiders the issue of remedies for a breach of an obligation to protect legitimate expectations under the FET standard. It might be an obvious proposition to state that the laws should furnish remedies to the aggrieved investor whose legitimate expectations have been breached. This rationale is about more than the expressive role of law showing that the law takes violations seriously.[1] It is a matter of principle that investors are entitled to seek remedy when their right to be fairly and equitably treated is infringed. The reason for this chapter is predicated on the axiom that where there is a right there is a remedy.[2] This principle is widely recognised in domestic laws. Chief Justice Holt in *Ashby v. White* stated that '*it is a vain thing to imagine a right without a remedy*; for . . . want of a right and want of remedy are reciprocal'.[3] Justice Holmes acknowledged that 'a legal right (and a legal duty) is nothing but a prediction that if a man does or omits certain things he will be made to suffer in this or that way by judgment of the court'.[4] The investment treaty tribunal in *Charles Lemire v. Ukraine* also confirmed that 'a wrong committed by a State against an investor must always give rise to a right for compensation of the

[1] S Puig, 'No Right without a Remedy: Foundations of Investor-State Arbitration' (2014) 35 *U Pa J Int'l L* 829, 831.

[2] FA Mann, 'The Consequences of an International Wrong' (1976) 48(1) *BYIL* 1; *Factory at Chórzow Case (Germany v. Poland)* (Jurisdiction) [1928] PCIJ Rep Series A No.17 at 29 ('it is a logical consequence flowing from the very nature of law and is an integral part of every legal order'). Chen concurs with the statement; B Cheng, *General Principles of Law as Applied by International Courts and Tribunals* (London: Stevens & Sons, 1953), 170.

[3] *Ashby v. White*, 92 Eng. Rep. 126 (K.B. 1703).

[4] OW Holmes, 'The Path of Law' (1897) 10 *Harv L Rev* 457, 458.

economic harm sustained'.[5] The question is how should the infringed right be remedied?

Remedy for a breach of legitimate expectations is either the making good of the investor's expectations (expectation interests) or the compensation for the detriment suffered by the investor for reliance on the state's conduct (reliance interests).[6] The purpose of this chapter is not to address the topic of remedy in international investment law[7] but to focus on the appropriate remedy for a breach of legitimate expectations in light of the proposed reliance theory.

Why rethink the remedies? The situation of remedy in investment treaty arbitration is rather curious. How can the investment treaty tribunals award expectation damages by the application of the *interstate* rules on remedies to the investor–state context when there is no specific standard for compensation for the breach of the FET standard?

Can this be the correct approach given that those interstate rules are meant to apply to a totally different context in terms of the wrong suffered and the injured party? How can these rules be compatible with the reliance theory of legitimate expectations? Does the paradigm of investment treaty arbitration pose a particularly unique moral dimension, whereby the respondent state is condemned for taking measures to protect the public interests and using the public resources to pay damages? Should these moral complexities influence how we should 'rethink' the remedial rules rather than just apply the interstate rules 'lock, stock and barrel'[8]?

One scholar was right to point out that 'the law on damages has so far received the least theoretic attention despite its enormous practical

[5] *Joseph Charles Lemire v. Ukraine*, ICSID Case No ARB/06/18, Award (14 January 2010) para 147.

[6] D Barak-Erez, 'The Doctrine of Legitimate Expectations and the Distinction between the Reliance and Expectation Interests' (2005) 11(4) *EPL* 583 (the author argues that the distinction between expectation interests and reliance interests could be applied in the context of public law concept of legitimate expectations).

[7] There are some learned scholars who treat this topic in great detail: B Sabahi, *Compensation and Restitution in Investor-State Arbitration: Principles and Practice* (Oxford: Oxford University Press, 2011); S Ripinsky and K Williams, *Damages in International Investment Law* (London: British Institute of International and Comparative Law, 2008).

[8] *International Status of South-West Africa Case*, ICJ Reports, Advisory Opinion, Judge McNair Opinion, 1950, 148 ('The way in which international law borrows from this source is not by means of importing private law institutions "lock, stock and barrel", ready-made and fully equipped with a set of rules.').

importance'.[9] This chapter does not intend to remedy that theoretic deficit. Rather, it addresses the specific issue of the appropriate remedy for the breach of legitimate expectations in light of (a) the reliance theory and (b) the current remedial framework based on the ILC's Articles on States Responsibilities.

The argument advanced in this chapter – that the determination of relief for the breach of legitimate expectations should be based on a detrimental reliance – is justified on the bases of principle, policy and authority (Section 9.2). It reinforces and substantiates the remedial implication of the reliance theory of legitimate expectations proposed in Chapter 6, which states that 'the host State has a duty to prevent the detriment from such reliance, the failure of which incurs a duty to compensate the investor for his reliance loss'.[10] The next part of this chapter (Section 9.3) provides a critique of the current remedial regime, which is based on the interstate rules, applicable to the breach of fair and equitable treatment. It concludes by suggesting that either a new set of rules should be formulated or the current rules should be applied in light of the framework established in the first part.

9.2 Argument for Detrimental Reliance-based Relief

The main point in this section is that the principle of corrective justice provides the underlying basis for the state's duty to compensate the investor who suffers from harm as a result of its conduct. However, there are relevant factors which should be considered for the application of the 'modified' principle of corrective justice. This chapter identifies three sets of relevant factors. The first concerns the principles at play – namely, the reformulated reliance principle (which articulates that it is the 'reliance' interest at stake) and the so-called correlativity of right and duty, which suggests that remedy should match an infringed right

[9] SW Schill, 'Damages in International Investment Law. S. Ripinsky, K. Williams (Book review)' (2010) *TDM* 1.

[10] The main focus of that chapter is the normative implication on conditions for liability and does not discuss the implication for the remedy in detail. For that reason, the reliance damages need further justification from other theoretical aspects of the corrective justice as well as policy considerations. MacCormick's and Atiyah's reliance theories of promise do not directly address the remedial question but are concerned with the basis for obligation. This is confirmed in R Craswell, 'Against Fuller and Perdue', (2000) 67 *U Chi Law Rev* 99, 134 ('Atiyah's work is more directly concerned with the question of which promises ought to be enforced, as distinct from the question of what remedies are available when an enforceable promise is breached').

(Section 9.2.1). The second set concerns policy considerations, such as the special position of the state and public resources (Section 9.2.2). The third set looks at how investment treaty tribunals have sought to protect the 'reliance' interests (Section 9.2.3).

9.2.1 *'Principle' Considerations*

Before considering the underlying theory of corrective justice, let us examine the provenance of the 'modified' principle of corrective justice by reviewing the relevance of public and private laws as the sources of guidance on remedy.

9.2.1.1 Public and Private Laws as Sources of Guidance

The logical starting point is to draw insights from the theory of tort laws – namely, the theory of corrective justice, which concerns redress sought by an individual against another individual. Like the public law paradigm, the individual seeks redress against the state in investment treaty arbitration. The core idea of the corrective justice is that a person who injures another has a personal duty to put that person back in the position that he or she was in before the injury occurred. Whilst acknowledging that the theory of corrective justice underlying the tort law is largely concerned with the legal relationships between individuals, the corrective justice can be modified to provide the basis for the duty to compensate for loss as a result of a breach of legitimate expectations. The 'modification' aspect is where the public law considerations can provide the source of guidance.

In public law, a range of available remedies include mandatory orders, prohibitory orders, quashing orders, substitutionary orders, declarations and recommendations.[11] Contrary to the position in investment treaty arbitration, the award of damages is generally not a remedy available on judicial review. Judicial review does not, therefore, provide an avenue for compensation to an applicant who has suffered loss as a result of an unlawful administrative act. The claimant has to bring a claim in tort law for claiming damages or other limited grounds.[12] The limited use of damages has been criticised by some scholars.[13] It is interesting to note

[11] P Cane, 'Remedies Available in Judicial Review Proceedings' in D Feldman (ed) *English Public Law* (Oxford: Oxford University Press, 2004).

[12] M Fordham, 'Monetary Awards in Judicial Review' (2009) *PL* 1.

[13] Cane, 'Remedies Available in Judicial Review Proceedings' (n 11) 949 ('the absence of a right of damages for losses sustained as a consequence of public law wrongs is widely

that whilst municipal public law is expanding the scope of damages for public law wrong,[14] in investment treaty arbitration, there is the case made for including the primary remedies.[15]

The 'public law considerations' for award of damages provide a useful source of guidance for our context. The rationale for limited availability of damages lies with the concern that the liability would cripple the public authority. This aspect pays special attention to the unique position of the state. Furthermore, there is the issue with the moral aspect of using public resources on compensating individuals. These two aspects are elaborated in the next section on policy considerations.

9.2.1.2 Modified Corrective Justice and Protection of Legitimate Expectations

The state's obligation of reparation finds support in philosophical theories, which can be explained in terms of the corrective justice theory. Grotius contends that damage should be made good in private injuries: 'By nature a man's life is his own, not indeed to destroy, but to safeguard; also his own are his body, limbs, reputation, honor and acts of his will'.[16] Similarly, MacCormick has advanced a justification for obligations of reparation based on individual security: 'the justifying ground of *obligations of reparation*, from a moral point of view, is that individuals have as a matter of principle *a right to reasonable security* in their persons and possessions, and accordingly *a right to be compensated* when that reasonable security is infringed'. Ross has suggested 'a duty of reparation' as a duty to act to right a previous wrong we have done.[17] Fuller and Perdue

recognised as one of the most serious of the remaining gaps in our remedial system. It is a gap that does not exist in more developed systems'); M Fordham, 'Reparation for Maladministration: Public Law's Final Frontier' (2003) 8 *JR* 104 (the author argues that the absence of a public law reparation remedy for maladministration is a deficiency).

[14] The International Law Commission; P Cane, 'Damages in Public Law' (1999) 9 *Otago LR* 489 ('adding damages to the catalogue of public law remedies would add significantly to the range of functions performed by public law remedies. Excluding damages from the public law remedial repertoire puts victims of public law wrongs at a significant disadvantage which requires justification').

[15] A Aaken, 'Primary and Secondary Remedies in International Investment Law and National State Liability: A Functional and Comparative View' in S Schill (ed) *International Investment Law and Comparative Public Law* (Oxford: Oxford University Press, 2010).

[16] H Grotius, *De Jure Belli ac Pacis Libri Tres*, FW Kelsey (trans) (London: Oxford Clarendon Press, 1925), vol. II, ch. XVII, 430–31.

[17] D Ross and P Stratton-Lake, *The Right and the Good* (Oxford: Oxford University Press, 2002).

have made the argument for protection of reliance interest in the following terms:

> The promisee who has actually *relied on the promise*, even though he may not thereby have enriched the promisor, certainly presents *a more pressing case for relief* than the promisee who merely demands satisfaction for his disappointment in not getting what was promised him. In passing from compensation for change of position to compensation for loss of expectancy we pass, to use Aristotle's terms again, from the realm of corrective justice to that of distributive justice . . . with the transition, the justification for legal relief loses its *self-evident quality*.[18]

From the quoted passage, there are two important points to make. First, Fuller and Perdu have defined reliance damages as the amount needed to put the promisee in the position he or she would have occupied if the promise had never been made.[19] This might also mean restitution to the status quo. Second, some scholars have argued that 'it is fallacious to suppose that defining the relevant right is itself sufficient to define the appropriate remedy'.[20] In particular, Craswell has questioned Fuller and Perdue's argument for reliance damages based on the corrective justice on the basis that the argument assumed that

> the relevant baseline was *the position the promisee would have occupied if the promise had never been made, from which it followed that only departures from that baseline could count as injuries and required compensation.* And while there are of course arguments that can be advanced in favour of each of these baselines, those arguments all rest on some other normative theory, not on corrective justice itself.[21]

Craswell has further stated that 'while corrective justice theory can give us a way of talking about what to do when the relevant baseline is infringed, *it cannot tell us what baseline ought to be selected as relevant*'.[22] This is significant for our discussion because the argument for reliance damages in this chapter does not entirely rely on the corrective justice principle; it also takes into account policy consideration which will assist us in defining the proper baseline.

[18] L Fuller and WR Perdue, 'The Reliance Interest in Contract Damage (Parts 1 and 2)' (1936–37) 46(52) *Yale LJ* 373.

[19] R Craswell, 'Against Fuller and Perdue', (2000) 67 *U Chi Law Rev* 99, 127 (Craswell criticised Fuller's classification of reliance interest, and to speak of only a single reliance 'interest' obscures these differences among the various reliance cases).

[20] Ibid 126.

[21] Ibid 127.

[22] Ibid.

However, one should bear in mind that the important implication of the corrective justice principle is that the purpose of a remedy is compensatory[23]. The remedy should not be for retributive purpose.[24] Whilst deterrence is not the main purpose of investment treaty arbitration,[25] compensation has a deterrent effect.[26] This consideration may play against compensation which goes beyond addressing the injustice or the harm done to the aggrieved investor. In this regard, one can draw support for reliance damages from Raz's suggestion that 'compensating individuals for harm resulting from reliance on voluntary obligations is . . . a proper goal for the law'; thus reliance damages could be a standard legal remedy for breach of contract.[27] However, for 'practical' reasons, he has cautioned that reliance damages might lead to expensive litigation and judicial mistakes in the calculation of reliance damages.[28] On that basis, one could argue that investment treaty tribunals could consider awarding reliance damages. This should be the case in particular because the principle of legitimate expectations seeks to protect 'reliance interest' (based on the thesis) and the principle of correlativity of right and duty demands that the remedy match the infringed right.

[23] D Shelton, 'Righting Wrongs: Reparations in the Articles on State Responsibility' (2002) 96 *AJIL* 833 (remedial justice is the rationale of the ILC Articles which provides the current remedial framework for investor–state disputes).

[24] J Cottingham, 'Varieties of Retribution' (1979) 29 *Phil Q* 238.

[25] The rules of international law on remedies are deterrent in nature, meaning the injured have a right to provide for their future security and to chastise the offender and deter future wrongdoing. See E de Vattel, *The Law of Nations* (Philadelphia: Philadelphia, 7th edn, 1849), bk. II, s.52.

[26] G Harten and M Loughlin, 'Investment Treaty Arbitration as a Species of Global Administrative Law', (2006) 17(1) *EJIL* 121–50 ('although awards are compensatory and usually do not include exemplary or punitive damages, the award of damages, by imposing a retrospective sanction, has a deterrent effect on the state'); FV Garcia-Amador, *The Changing Law of International Claims* (New York: Oceana Publications, 1984), 559 [the concept of reparation in international law has included both a compensatory element (restitution or damages) and a punitive one (satisfaction)].

[27] J Raz, 'Book Review: Promises in Morality and Law' (1982) 95 *Harv L Rev* 916, 934 ('As far as this argument goes, supporters of the harm principle should favor reliance damages rather than expectation damages as a standard legal remedy for breach of contract. Contrary to often expressed views, the belief that the proper role of contract law is the protection of the practice of undertaking voluntary obligations does not necessarily lead to endorsement of an expectation-value measure of the legal protection of contracts'.).

[28] Ibid 938 ('it may be wise legal policy to provide for expectation damages on the ground that to leave it to the courts to determine in every case whether reliance on the contract caused harm would lead to expensive litigation and frequent judicial mistakes').

9.2.1.2 Correlativity of Right and Duty

The analysis draws from Ernest Weinrib's conception of corrective justice – namely, 'the reason conception of remedies', which states that the wrongful act is *the reason for the remedy* because it is an injustice that the judge, as the embodiment of justice, must reverse.[29] The determination of the appropriate remedy ultimately depends on an *appreciation of the nature of the infringed right.* For example, if protection of legitimate expectations concerns the right not to be harmed, then reliance damages should be the appropriate remedy, whereas if it concerns the right to performance of the promised act, then expectation damages or specific performance should be awarded. In our context of legitimate expectations, the reliance principle enables us to appreciate the nature of infringed right – the reliance interest – which defines the nature of the remedy.

The correlativity of an infringed right and duty is endorsed in Daniel Friedmann's analysis of the rights–remedies relations.[30] The so-called primacy of the right model posits that the legal right precedes the remedy both in time and in importance.[31] Remedies are merely derivative from the legal rights. Legal rights have an independent existence, and it is possible to conceive of legal rights unsupported by legal remedies.[32] However, in the absence of defined remedy, as is the case with the FET standard, could we infer that remedy is available on the ground that 'where there is a right there must be a remedy'?

Such inference is reasonable because without remedy, the right to fair and equitable treatment cannot be vindicated. The principle that remedy is derivative from a substantive right because remedy provides the means to vindicate such right is well accepted in municipal laws. Chief Justice Marshall in *Marbury v. Madison* stated that 'the very essence of civil liberty certainly consists in the right of every individual to claim the

[29] E Weinrib, 'Two Conceptions of Remedies' in Charles EF Rickett (ed), *Justifying Private Law Remedies* (Oxford: Hart Publishing, 2008).

[30] D Friedmann, 'Rights and Remedies' in N Cohen and E McKendrick (eds), *Comparative Remedies for Breach of Contract* (Oxford: Hart Publishing, 2005); D Friedmann, 'Rights and Remedies' (1997) 113 *LQR* 424.

[31] Ibid 4 (The opposite model is the primacy of the remedy model, which suggests that the effectiveness and availability of remedy determines the nature of the legal right and its existence. Friedmann suggested that 'the right derives from the remedy and as a matter of sequence the remedy precedes the right. Consequently the absence of a remedy points to the non-existence of a legal right.').

[32] Ibid 8.

protection of the laws, whenever he receives an injury. One of the first duties of government is to afford that protection'.[33] However, further justification has to be made for arguing that an investor has the right of his or her own which gives rise to a remedy. The analysis on the theoretical foundation of the investor's right in investment treaty arbitration is necessary.

In investment treaty arbitration, the theoretical foundation of the investor's remedial right is often conceptualised in terms of the state's obligation to remedy an infringement of right. This is the consequence of applying the current remedial rule based on the interstate rules in the ILC Articles on State Responsibility. Under the ILC Articles the focus is on '*the duty of the injuring State to compensate*' rather than '*the right of the injured party to remedy*' for the reason that it avoids the difficulties where the same obligation is owed simultaneously to several, many or all states, only a few of which are specially affected by the breach. It is important to emphasise that the general obligation of reparation arises automatically upon commission of an internationally wrongful act and is not, as such, contingent upon a demand or protest by any state.[34]

This conception of reparation is not the same as the paradigm whereby the injured state has *a right to remedy* because *an obligation to compensate* only arises upon the demand of the injured party. This means that investors can choose to exercise their right at their own discretion or waive their remedial right. The 'right' paradigm is more suitable with the cases of legitimate expectations when the state has caused harm to a particular investor within a proximate relation upon the representation or promise.

The remedial right of the investor for a breach of legitimate expectations can be founded on the substantive right that the investor has as *its own right*. This analysis draws from the theory of direct right of investor,[35] which states that when an investor brings a claim against a state, it exercises a right of its own.[36] This contrasts with the

[33] *Marbury v. Madison*, 5 U.S. (1 Cranch) 137, 163 (1803).

[34] Commentary (4) to Article 31 (emphasis added).

[35] Z Douglas, 'The Hybrid Foundations of Investment Treaty Arbitration' (2003) 74 *BYIL* 151.

[36] Z Douglas, *The International Law of Investment Claims* (Cambridge: Cambridge University Press, 2009) 36 ('In the investment treaty context, the investor is master of its own destiny and keeper of its own rights. Logic would seem to dictate that an investor can sign away its substantive rights under an applicable investment treaty in a contract with the host state'). R Volterra, 'International Law Commission Articles on State

'derivative' model,[37] which posits that where there is a breach of treaty obligation, an investor merely steps into the shoes of its national state without being privy to their interstate legal relationship. The investor acts as an agent to enforce treaty obligations before investment tribunals. The injury caused to the investor, which the state of the investor vicariously conceives, provides the basis for state responsibility. The very recognition of a legal right entails some consequences regarding the remedy.[38]

If we accept that the goal of protecting legitimate expectations is preventing detrimental reliance rather than protecting expectations interests, it follows that reliance damages should be the remedy for rectifying the injustice caused by the state's conduct. MacCormick's observation reinforces the point: 'the remedial right is indeed an exact correlative of the obligation of reparation. If we did not insist upon fulfilment of that in relevant cases, we would show that our original assertion of the primary right was insincere'.[39]

9.2.2 Policy Considerations

There is a compelling argument for suggesting that the principle of corrective justice, which aims at compensation for private parties, should be modified in the context of investor–state relationship. Some scholars have questioned the applicability of corrective justice theories where the respondent is a public body on the ground that taxpayers money should not be used to pay out for the wrong committed by the public authority because taxpayers are not responsible for the wrong. Levinson has raised this objection:

Responsibility and Investor-State Arbitration: Do Investors Have Rights?' (2010) 25(1) *ICSID Rev* 218, 219 ('therefore, it is arguable that any rights thereby accruing to investors *must surely be derivative rights*, rights derivative of the overarching rights and obligations under international law of the investors' State of nationality and the host State').

37 Volterra, 'International Law Commission Articles on State Responsibility and Investor-State Arbitration: Do Investors Have Rights?' (n 36) ('therefore, it is arguable that any rights thereby accruing to investors *must surely be derivative rights*, rights derivative of the overarching rights and obligations under international law of the investors' State of nationality and the host State' [emphasis added]).

38 D Shelton, 'Remedies in International Human Rights Law' 38 ('in most legal systems, including the international legal system, the philosophy of remedial justice provides the foundation for the law of remedies').

39 N MacCormick, 'The Obligation of Reparation' in N MacCormick (ed), *Legal Right and Social Democracy: Essays in Legal and Political Philosophy* (Oxford: Clarendon Press, 1982), 219.

> Compensation ultimately comes from the pockets of taxpayers [which] ... attenuates the connection between moral responsibility and the burden of rectification. Corrective justice theories ground the duty to rectify in the causation of moral harms. But taxpayers do not 'cause' constitutional violations in any intuitive sense of causation, nor are they morally responsible for constitutional wrongdoing.[40]

In the context of investment treaty arbitration, a similar argument could be made that the citizens of host states do not cause treaty violations, yet their tax money has to contribute to the compensation made to foreign investors. However, the counterargument is that taxes belong to the government; there is no legal sense in which taxpayers own the taxes they have had to pay. To assert otherwise is to deny that the state has its own legal personality. But that is just a technical argument because from the standpoint of political theory, the state's capacity to perform its duty owed to its citizens is undermined by the burden of compensations. Therefore, this reality should not be ignored.

Related arguments have been raised about the adverse impact of compensation on the performance of duties by the public authorities. Public finance is not unlimited and state liability incurs diversion of public resources to the claimant, which may affect the general public welfare. Furthermore, states do not disappear or become insolvent, which makes them an attractive target for compensation claims.[41] The imposition of liability may encourage host states to change their priorities and become more risk averse and lead them to adopt administrative practices or policies that are not optimally in the public interest.[42] States are subject to competing demands; therefore, state liability could adversely affect a host state's regulatory powers.

All of these factors should be relevant to the 'baseline' of applying the theory of corrective justice. The different nature and function of a state also means that this should be reflected in the remedial rule.

[40] D Levinson, 'Making Government Pay: Markets, Politics and the Allocation of Constitutional Costs' (2000) 67 *U Chi Law Rev* 345, 408.

[41] The recent UNCTAD publication suggests a record high of 70 ISDS cases filed in 2015 and the overall number of publicly known cases reached 696. UNCTAD IIA Issues Note, *Investor-State Dispute Settlement: Review of Developments in 2015* (8 June 2016) http://investmentpolicyhub.unctad.org/Publications/Details/144 (accessed on 12 June 2016).

[42] K Tienhaara, 'Regulatory Chill and the Threat of Arbitration: A View from Political Science', in C Brown and K Miles (eds), *Evolution in Investment Treaty Law and Arbitration* (Cambridge: Cambridge University Press, 2011).

Peter Cane elaborated this point in the context of municipal public law:

> Government is different from its citizens in having power which they do not have and, in having responsibilities to the community as a whole which they do not have ... [I]n order to control the exercise of the legitimate coercive powers of the government we may be justified in imposing certain liabilities on government which do not also rest on citizens and in order to enable it to fulfil its responsibilities to society as a whole, we may be justified in relieving government of certain liabilities to which its citizens are subject.[43]

In international law, there is some evidence to suggest that the public nature of the state is relevant in the determination of damages.[44] In the context of investment treaty arbitration, the Separate Opinion of Professor Brownlie in *CME v. Czech Republic* endorses the argument that the special role and character of the state should be relevant in the consideration of remedy.[45] The opinion has a wider implication for our conception of investment treaty protection. The tribunal has to consider the special character and responsibilities of the state.[46] It is not 'reasonable' that by signing investment treaties, the country should accept the risk of national economic disaster and 'catastrophic repercussion for the livelihood and economic well-being of the population'.[47] Investment treaties are not 'an insurance against business risk'.[48] Raz's concept of

[43] P Cane, 'Damages in Public Law' (1999) 9 *Otago LR* 489.

[44] Ripinsky and Williams cited some examples to show this. For instance, they discussed the earlier drafts of the ILC Articles which included a provision stating that reparation must not 'result in depriving the population of a State of its own means of subsistence'. However, this provision was dropped. Second, the authors also discussed the case of *Himpurna v. PLN*, whereby the tribunal suggested that awarding the *lucrum cessans* in full would be an abuse of right and 'would tend to impoverish the host State' – 'intolerable' – 'like stepping on the shoulder of a drowning man' – *Himpurna v. PLN*, Final Award of 4 May 1999, (2000) *XXV Yearbook of Commercial Arbitration* 13 para 343. Ripinsky and Williams, *Damages in International Investment Law* (n 7).

[45] *CME v. Czech Republic*, UNCITRAL Case, Partial Award (13 September 2001) 9 ICSID Rep 121, Separate Opinion on the Issues at the Quantum Phase of Ian Brownlie CME QC para 76 ('the resources of a corporation entail considerable flexibility in changing the location of assets and in changing the organisation of assets. The resources of a country, its human and natural resources, are a given: they are necessarily fixed.').

[46] Ibid paras 75–79.

[47] Ibid para 78.

[48] *MTD v. Chile*, ICSID Case No ARB/01/07, Decision on Annulment (21 March 2007) 13 ICSID Rep 500 para 178; *Maffezini v. Spain*, ICSID Case No ARB/97/7, Award (13 November 2000) para 64 ('Bilateral Investment Treaties are not insurance policies against bad business judgments').

the duty of government towards its own people underlines the core of Professor Brownlie's reasoning.[49]

It can be argued that the rules for damages proper to the context of investment treaty arbitration should consider the burden of compensation which will be borne by the whole population and bear a significant adverse impact on the welfare of the state. The 'social costs' of imposing an imperfect duty (over-compensation or under-compensation) should be avoided. If the aggrieved investor is under-compensated, other investors may be reluctant to engage in foreign direct investment in the future. However, over-compensation could mean 'catastrophic repercussion' and undermine the political legitimacy of investment arbitration.

9.2.3 *Authority (Case Law) Considerations*

It may be difficult to discern any instructive jurisprudence from ICSID cases regarding awards of actual investment costs. The trend suggests that actual investment costs are more likely to be implemented when future profits are highly indeterminate.[50] Reliance damages are readily discernable or estimable and do not involve prediction of uncertain future profits. An award of reliance damages ensures that tribunals can minimise error costs or the risk of adjudicative errors. The following discussion of selected cases provides useful insights into what the 'reliance interests' entail in the context of investment treaty arbitration.

The reliance measure is best seen in awards representing actual or direct investment costs incurred by the investor, including 'sunk costs,' 'wasted costs' or 'out-of-pocket expenses'. The head of damages for breach of contract in international law, *damnum emergens*, is conceptually similar to the reliance measure, which compensates an injured party for any actions it undertook to its detriment in anticipation of the other party's contractual performance, resulting in a loss because of

[49] J Raz, 'Liberty and Trust' in R George (ed), *Natural Law, Liberalism, and Morality: Contemporary Essays* (Oxford: Oxford University Press, 2001) ('The primary duty of government is to see to it that conditions prevail in which all its citizens enjoy physical and mental health, avoid severe physical pain and suffering and enjoy a level of education making them capable of availing themselves of the options available in their society, and that they enjoy a decent standard of living, i.e., are provided with the resources necessary to pursue options of sufficient range and variety to enable them to develop all aspects of their personality if they so choose.').

[50] D Collins, 'Reliance Remedies at the International Center for the Settlement of Investment Disputes' (2009) 29 *Nw J Int'l L & Bus* 195.

breach. The notion of 'out of pocket expenses' is elaborated on by the tribunal in *Southern Pacific Properties v. Egypt:*

> [C]onsiderable amounts of time and money were spent on negotiating, planning and implementing the project. [The Claimant] made capital contributions and loans [to its affiliate] . . . these amounts must be reimbursed as part of . . . fair compensation . . . [W]hen the project was cancelled, construction was under way and considerable marketing activity had been carried out. Most of the detailed engineering design and specifications for the first phase . . . had been completed. A construction contract had been concluded for the infrastructure, construction had begun and lot sales had commenced. To the extent that the expenses associated with this activity have been proven, reimbursement of such expenses is also part of . . . fair compensation.[51]

PSEG v. Turkey provides useful insights into the notion of reliance damages with regard to the pre-investment expenditures.[52] In this case, the claimants argued for compensation for their legislative interference. The tribunal found a breach of the FET obligation for the way the government handled negotiations with the investor and the changes to the legal framework[53], for abuse of authority[54] and inconsistent acts.[55] The expectation damages were denied in this case because the calculation of these would be highly speculative given that PSEG's proposed power plant and coal mine never commenced. The tribunal rejected the fair market value because no expropriation claim was established.[56] The tribunal's articulation of a general conception of reliance damages is useful to note:

> An investment can take many forms before actually reaching the construction stage, including most notably the cost of negotiations and other preparatory work leading to the materialization of the Project, even in

[51] *Southern Pacific Properties (Middle East) Ltd v. Arab Republic of Egypt*, ICSID Case No ARB/84/3, Award (20 May 1992) (1994) 19 Yb. Comm. Arb. 51; (1995) 3 ICSID Rep. 189, para 384.

[52] *PSEG Global Inc. and Konya Ilgin Elektrik Üretim ve Ticaret Limited Sirketi v. Turkey*, ICSID Case No ARB/02/05, Award (19 January 2007).

[53] Ibid (while the tribunal found that there was in this case a breach of fair and equitable treatment, this breach related not to damages to productive assets but to the failure to conduct negotiations in a proper way and other forms of interference by the respondent government).

[54] Ibid para 247.

[55] Ibid para 249.

[56] Ibid para 305 (since the tribunal had found that there was no expropriation in this case, either direct or indirect, the fair market value did not appear to be justified as a measure for compensation in these circumstances).

> connection with *pre-investment expenditures*, particularly when, like in this case, there is a valid and binding Contract duly executed between the parties.[57]

The particular out-of-pocket expenses included costs of preparing the power plant project as well as mine studies, contract negotiations and financing, environmental costs, permits and licence. This award should be construed to suggest that subsequent expenses (even those preceding a formal contract) constitute a recoverable loss, once a host state approves a particular investment decision.

Contrary to *PSEG v. Turkey*, the tribunal in *MTD v. Chile*[58] adopted a different approach to determining pre-investment expenditures. The tribunal adopted the classic standard formulated by the PCIJ in the *Chórzow Factory* case and awarded the claimant's wasted expenditure on the initial investment. The tribunal held that the project expense made *prior to* the execution of the investment contract was not legitimate for the purpose of the calculation of damages. The tribunal viewed that prior to the contract, the claimants had no legitimate expectations in relation to the project; therefore, pre-contract expenses could not be recovered. This case is also notable for the relevance of the 'contributory fault' which is implicitly applied by the tribunal to discount 50 per cent of the damages. The tribunal held that claimants should be responsible for the lack of oversight, diligence and business awareness.

The tribunal in *Metalclad v. Mexico* relied on reliance damages as a proxy to determine the 'fair market value' of an investment. The tribunal held that the same standard of compensation ('fair market value' of the lost investment as provided for in the NAFTA article on expropriation) applied to both breaches of NAFTA because both situations involved the complete interruption of the landfill operation and negated the possibility of any meaningful return on the claimant's investment. In other words, the claimant's investment was lost completely.[59] The claimant proposed two alternative methods for calculating damages: (1) a discounted cash flow (DCF) analysis of future profits to establish the fair market value of the investment (approximately US$90 million) and (2) valuation of Metalclad's actual investment in the landfill (approximately US$20 million–US$25 million).[60]

57 Ibid.

58 *MTD v. Chile* (n 48).

59 Para 113.

60 Paras 114–16.

The tribunal adopted the fair market value of the investment but declined to use the DCF analysis[61] on the ground that it is highly speculative because the claimant could not provide any realistic estimate of lost profits and the landfill had never been in operation.[62] Therefore, the compensation was made '*by reference to Metalclad's actual investment in the project*'.[63] The tribunal also viewed that the award of actual investment in the landfill was consonant with the principle set out in the *Chórzow* case.[64]

It is interesting to note that the recoverable actual investment costs would not be too far removed from the investment for which damages are claimed. It is therefore reasonable for tribunals to take into account certain factors, such as connection with the investment, connection with the investor, reasonableness of expenses and sufficient evidence, to avoid over-compensation in case of reliance damages. However, as with most investment treaty decisions, the motivation behind awarding reliance damages seems to be explained by the difficulty of calculating future profits rather than goal of protecting the underlying reliance interests. This is attributable to the fact that the thinking on remedies is dominated by the interstate rules.

9.3 A Critique of the Current Remedial Framework Based on the Interstate Rules

This section analyses the current remedial framework for the breach of the FET standard, which finds its source in the interstate remedial rules. Whilst fair market value is often prescribed as a standard of compensation

[61] *Metalclad v. Mexico*, ICSID Case No ARB(AF)/97/1, Award (30 August 2000), para 119 ('Normally, the fair market value of a going concern which has a history of profitable operation may be based on an estimate of future profits subject to a discounted cash flow analysis').

[62] Ibid para 120 ('where the enterprise has not operated for a sufficiently long time to establish a performance record or where it has failed to make a profit, future profits cannot be used to determine going concern or fair market value').

[63] Ibid para 113.

[64] Ibid para 122 ['The award to Metalclad of the cost of its investment in the landfill is consistent with the principles set forth in *Chórzow Factory* (Claim for Indemnity) (Merits), *Germany v. Poland*, P.C.I.J. Series A., No. 17 (1928) at p. 47, namely, that where the state has acted contrary to its obligations, any award to the claimant should, as far as is possible, wipe out all the consequences of the illegal act and reestablish the situation which would in all probability have existed if that act had not been committed (the status quo ante)'].

for a breach of expropriation provision in investment treaty,[65] no specific standard for remedy is stipulated for a breach of the FET provision (which includes an obligation to protect legitimate expectation).[66]

The legal lacunae has been filled by the customary international laws, as reflected in the ILC's Articles on State Responsibility, which are designed for the interstate relationship. Some scholars have observed that the customary rule of full reparation is vague and depends on the tribunal's discretion to choose the calculation method; therefore, flexibility comes at the cost of subjective application of the legal principles.[67] Should this approach be questioned?

The wisdom of the theory of the judicial borrowing would caution against uncritical transplantation of interstate rules of remedies to the context of investor–state dispute.[68] The scholars' views on this issue are far from unanimous,[69] whilst the tribunals' views are less sceptical.[70] On the one hand, Professor Douglas has argued that 'uncritical transplantation of secondary rules that govern, inter alia, the consequences of a diplomatic protection claim between two state parties is inappropriate'.[71] His argument relies on the fact that Part Two, Article 33(1) states that the provisions apply only in relation to injuries caused by a wrongful act of a state to another state, several states or the international community as a whole.[72]

65 MH Mendelson, 'Compensation for Expropriation: The Case Law' (1985) 79(2) *AJIL* 414.

66 C Smutny, 'Principles of Compensation in Investment Treaty Arbitration' (2007) 22 *ICSID Rev – FILJ* 1.

67 Ripinsky and Williams, *Damages in International Investment Law* (n 7) 90 ('the customary rule of full compensation is of a very general nature and it does not offer a conceptual framework for the recovery of damages that would be comparable in specificity to the value approach in expropriation cases').

68 This theory is discussed in Chapter 2.

69 S Hindelang, 'Restitution and Compensation: Reconstructing the Relationship in Investment Treaty Law' in R Hoffman and C Tams (eds), *International Investment Law and General International Law: From Clinical Isolation to Systemic Integration?* (Baden-Baden: Nomos, 2011) (the author suggests that the rules from the ILC Articles can be directly relied on because invocation by investors is not different).

70 This issue is very little discussed by arbitral tribunals. Some tribunals seem to overlook the different nature of legal relationship between state and individual. For instance, the Ad Hoc Annulment Committee in *MTD v. Chile* suggests that the ILC Articles concern diplomatic protection claims which are brought by states on behalf of individuals; therefore, there is no reason not to apply these rules to treaty breaches brought by individuals. *MTD v. Chile* (n 48) para 99.

71 Douglas, 'The Hybrid Foundations of Investment Treaty Arbitration' (n 35) 189.

72 Ibid.

For the opposing view, some scholars, such as Ripinsky and Williams, have argued that the ILC Articles should be 'a starting point for analysing the rules on compensation in a State-private party dispute'.[73] Similarly, David Caron has suggested that the ILC's rules should continue to apply because it is 'a valuable tool to promote clarity and uniformity in the international law of remedies' and 'there is no better available source of guidance'.[74] Ripinsky and Williams' arguments rely on the drafting history as well as the commentary to suggest that the rules do not exclude investor–state relationships. For instance, Ripinsky and Williams argue that the drafting history suggests that the limitation on the scope of application at the time has less relevance now – that is, whether private entities could possess international legal personality and private persons could bring claims against states. There is no drafting history of the ILC Articles, which suggests that the rules governing compensation owed to private parties are different from those applicable in the interstate context. Furthermore, Ripinsky and Williams rely on Article 33(2) to support the claim that the ILC Articles do not negate the relevance of the principles set out in Part Two for the relationship between private parties and states.[75]

The main point here is that the current remedial regime applicable to the breach of legitimate expectations based on the ILC's Articles is not satisfactory for three main reason: (1) the nature of the wrong and the aggrieved party under investment treaties are different from those in the ILCs Articles, (2) the prescription of restitution as a primary remedy is incompatible with the compensatory justice and (3) the award of expectation damages as a default position is inconsistent with the protected interest by the principle of legitimate expectations. The argument – if sustained – does not imply that the ILC's Articles should no longer be the reference framework, but that the rules should be tailored to the particular context of investor–state dispute, which has been analysed in the preceding section.

[73] Ripinsky and Williams, *Damages in International Investment Law* (n 7) 30.

[74] D Caron, 'The ILC Articles on State Responsibility: The Paradoxical Relationship between Form and Authority' (2002) 96 *AJIL* 857

[75] 'Article 33: Scope of International Obligations Set Out in This Part ... (2) This part is without prejudice to any right, arising from the international responsibility of a State, which may accrue directly to any person or entity other than a State'. The commentary to Article 33(2) (Comment 4) mentions investors' rights under BITs as one of the examples of state responsibility to non-state entities.

9.3.1 *Fictional Notions of Damage and Victim*

The application of the current remedial regime for a breach of legitimate expectations might proceed as follows. The fundamental principle that states are obligated to make 'full reparation' for any injury caused by an internationally wrongful act is set out in Article 31 of the ILC's Articles on State Responsibility.[76] Article 2 stipulates that 'an internationally wrongful act' occurs when there is state conduct that constitutes 'a breach of an international obligation of the State'. Therefore, a breach of legitimate expectations under the FET standard in investment treaties constitutes an internationally wrongful act giving rise to the obligation to make full reparation under Article 31.[77] Most investment treaty decisions, which deal with remedy for the breach of fair and equitable treatment, implicitly or explicitly proceed with a similar reasoning. Can the interstate rules, which are underlined by the logic that the state is asserting that its own right has been violated, be the framework of reference for the investment treaty paradigm, whereby the injured party is the investor who asserts its own right?

The well-cited principle of full reparation seeks to 'as far as possible, wipe-out all the consequences of the illegal act and re-establish the situation which would, in all probability, have existed if that act had not been committed'.[78] The ILC mainly followed the *Chórzow Factory* approach by adopting the duty of full reparation for internationally wrongful acts in Article 31. Article 34 of the ILC Articles specifies the form of reparation, which include restitution, compensation and satisfaction[79] with the primacy of restitution as the form of reparation preferred over compensation.[80]

The existing remedial rules aim to rectify the injury vicariously caused to the state of the investor. It is therefore inappropriate to apply the

[76] 'Article 31: Reparation. 1. The responsible State is under an obligation to make full reparation for the injury caused by the internationally wrongful act. 2. Injury includes any damage, whether material or moral, caused by the internationally wrongful act of a State'.

[77] Article 36 provides that compensation shall cover 'any financially assessable damage including loss of profits insofar as it is established'.

[78] *Factory at Chórzow (German v. Poland)* (Merits) [1928] PCIJ Rep Series A No 17.

[79] Article 37(2) of the ILC's Articles on Responsibility of States for Internationally Wrongful Acts sets out a list of forms that satisfaction may assume, such as acknowledgement of the breach, an expression of regret, a formal apology, a guarantee or assurance of non-repetition of the wrongful act.

[80] ILC Articles on Responsibility of States for Internationally Wrongful Acts, Commentary to Article 31, para 5. The reparation includes both material and moral losses.

interstate rules to the different paradigm in which investors bring *their own claims* under investment treaties because they themselves suffer from harm. Different rules are required to address the rectification of the infringed right of an investor. The damage suffered by the investor is never identical to that of the injured state. The nature of rules governing interstate relations is different from the rules governing investor–state relation.[81]

The *Chórzow Factory* case emphasised that the *rights of an investor* under an investment treaty are different from the *rights belonging to a state*, and the *nature of damage suffered* by an individual is not analogous to that suffered by a state:

> The rules of law governing the reparation are *the rules of international law in force between the two States concerned, and not the law governing relations between the State which has committed a wrongful act and the individual who has suffered damage. Rights or interests of an individual the violation of which rights causes damage are always in a different plane to rights belonging to a State*, which rights may also be infringed by the same act. The damage suffered by an individual is never therefore identical in kind with that which will be suffered by a State; it can only afford a convenient scale for the calculation of the reparation due to the State.[82]

Furthermore, the Separate Opinion of Thomas Wälde in *International Thunderbird Gaming v. Mexico* also emphasised the different contexts in which the interstate rules of remedy and the investor–state rules function. In the investor–state context, it concerns the right of a private person to bring a claim against a foreign government for governmental conduct affecting the investor. This contrasts with the interstate disputes between sovereigns. Analogies from such interstate international law have therefore to be *treated with caution.*[83]

[81] H Lauterpacht, *The Function of Law in the International Community* (Oxford: Clarendon Press, 1933) 425 (on *pacta sunt servanda*) ('The rules governing the relations of States are fundamentally different from those governing the relations of persons with the State. Within the State ... there obtains a relation of supremacy and subordination, and the creation of legal rules is exclusively, or almost exclusively, left to organs exercising power over the people of the State so that the legal rule appears as a command issuing from above, whereas the legal rules among States cannot be anything else except agreements and promises between equals.').

[82] *Factory at Chórzow (German v. Poland)* (Merits) [1928] PCIJ Rep Series A No 17, para 28.

[83] *International Thunderbird Gaming Corporation v. Mexico*, UNCITRAL Case, Final Award (26 January 2006) Separate Opinion of Arbitrator Waelde, para 13 (emphasis added).

9.3.2 *Restitution as a Primary Remedy in Conformity with Protection of Reliance Interest*

The *primary* remedy of restitution, which is prescribed in the inter-state context, is not appropriate for the reality of the enforcement of remedies in the investor–state context. This remedy is not absolute because there are conditions in which compensation should be awarded. There is no principled reason why, in the context of the breach of legitimate expectations, the starting point should be the restitution when the primary objective or fundamental purpose of the rule is to compensate for the harm. This argument is buttressed by the lack of supervisory power or enforcement mechanism as well as the constraining effect on the exercise of the state's regulatory power, especially the legislative power.

The consequence of applying the interstate rules is that restitution should be the primary remedy[84] and in principle is most adequate for fulfilment of the claimant's expectations.[85] The *Chórzow Factory* judgement confirmed that the state was under 'the obligation to restore the undertaking and, if this be not possible, to pay its value at the time of the indemnification, which value is designed to take the place of restitution which has become impossible'.[86]

There are two meanings of 'restitution'.[87] First, the narrow view adopted by Article 35 of the ILC Articles is to return to the situation which existed before the wrongful act was committed (status quo). The broader, 'hypothetical' view is to reestablish the situation that would have existed if the wrongful act had not been committed. The commentary to the ILC Articles suggests that the narrow view of restitution may have to be supplemented with compensation to satisfy full reparation for the damage caused. The restitution can be material

[84] Article 35; the general rule expressed in *Chórzow Factory* suggests that the primary and preferred remedy is restitution. The ILC Articles on State Responsibility impose certain conditions of application – notably, that restitution may be awarded only if it 'is not materially impossible' and if it 'does not involve a burden out of all proportion to the benefit deriving from restitution instead of compensation'.

[85] Restitution in kind, or, if this is not possible, payment of a sum corresponding to the value which a restitution in kind would bear; the award, if need be, of damages for loss sustained would not be covered by restitution in kind or payment in place of it.

[86] ILC Commentary to Article 35, para 3.

[87] B Sabahi, *Compensation and Restitution in Investor-State Arbitration: Principles and Practice* (Oxford: Oxford University Press, 2011).

(return of property) or juridical.[88] This rule in effect seeks to protect expectation interests.[89]

There are three problems with the application of restitution as a remedy for a breach of legitimate expectations. First, restitution may not be an appropriate remedy in the situation where the investment relationship broke down and the investor wanted to exit the country.

Second, restitution lacks an effective enforcement mechanism. Monetary awards are easier to enforce. The lack of supervisory power is a very important reason for rejecting restitution remedies in the context of investment treaty arbitration. This underlines the tribunal's rationale for refusing the performance remedy in *Amco Asia v. Indonesia*.[90] The tribunal questioned whether the state could be ordered to restore the licence.[91] In addition, restitution damages may not benefit from the strong enforcement provisions in the ICSID Convention, which only concerns monetary awards.[92]

The decision in *Franck Charles Arif v. Moldova*[93] reinforced the concern with lack of supervisory powers. This dispute arose from breach of contractual arrangement, whereby the claimant sought damages covering either loss of profits or wasted costs, including capital expenditure (such as installing escalators at the airport), operating expenditures

[88] The commentary to ILC Article 35 explains: 'the term "juridical restitution" requires or involves the modification of the legal situation either within the legal system of the responsible State or in its legal relations with the injured State. Such cases include the revocation, annulment or amendment of a constitutional or legislative provision enacted in violation of a rule of international law, the rescinding or reconsideration of an administrative or judicial measure unlawfully adopted in respect of the person or property of a foreign or a requirement that steps be taken ... for the termination of a treaty'. ILC, 'Articles on Responsibility of States for Internationally Wrongful Acts' in *Yearbook of the International Law Commission, 2001, Volume II*, UN Doc A/CN.4/SER. A/2001/Add.1.

[89] Some arbitral tribunals awarded restitution as well as compensation. In *Goetz v. Burundi*, which involved a breach of indirect expropriation, the tribunal gave the parties four months to agree on compensation and asked the government to consider reissuing the certificate. The government did both things.

[90] *Amco Asia v. Indonesia*, ICSID Case No.ARB/81/1, Award (20 November 1984) 1 *ICSID Rep* 413.

[91] Ibid para 202 ('it is obvious that this Tribunal cannot substitute itself for the Indonesian Government, in order to cancel the revocation and restore the license: such actions are not even claimed, and it is more than doubtful that this kind of *restitutio in integrum* could be ordered against a sovereign State'.).

[92] ICSID Convention Art. 54(1), C Smutny 'Principles of Compensation in Investment Treaty Arbitration' (2007) 22 *ICSID Rev – FILJ* 1, 6.

[93] *Franck Charles Arif v. Republic of Moldova*, ICSID Case No ARB/11/23, Award (8 April 2013).

related directly to the airport (such as advertising, payroll expenses and rent) and stock purchases, as well as moral damages for the pain, stress, shock, anguish, humiliation and shame suffered as a result of Moldova's acts and omissions in relation to Mr Artif's investments.

The tribunal noted the absence of confirmation by the state of the effective possibility of restitution and the absence of any supervisory powers of the tribunal, so the tribunal awarded compensation as an alternative remedy. The tribunal considered damages in respect of the airport stores but not the border stores in which there was no breach.

The interesting feature of this case is that the tribunal considered restitution to be a preferred remedy and more consistent with the objectives of bilateral investment treaties, as it preserved both the investment and the relationship between the investor and the host state. Nevertheless, the tribunal decided to award damages in light of the circumstances.[94] Restitution would require the respondent to allow and to enable the claimant to open and operate his duty-free store at Chisinau International Airport without undue interruption. All relevant licences and authorisations would have to be reissued by the respondent and its organs, as well as a new lease agreement, at identical or essentially similar terms as the former lease agreement.

However, the tribunal recognised the drawback of restitution for the lack of supervisory power and decided to adopt the compromised approach in ordering restitution *with the remedy of compensation suspended for a period of ninety days*.[95] It is important to note that the tribunal rejected the loss of profit but accepted wasted costs (reliance interest), which is consistent with the protected reliance interest that it adopted as the basis for liability.[96]

Third, restitution can be considered as intrusive on state sovereignty. In the context of domestic law, the reluctance to award specific performance is explained by the reason that specific performance represents an excessive interference with personal freedom[97] or state sovereignty in the context of international law. This adverse impact on sovereignty may be

94 Ibid para 569.

95 Ibid para 572.

96 Ibid para 576 ('the Tribunal considers that the DCF methodology is not appropriate for a business that never operated and where a satisfactory basis for its projected revenues has not been demonstrated. Use of a DCF methodology in these circumstances gives an excessively speculative outcome.').

97 D Kimel, *From Promise to Contract: Toward a Liberal Theory of Contract* (Oxford: Hart Publishing, 2003), 99.

mitigated by the rule that if it is 'materially impossible' to grant restitution in kind (i.e. the property is destroyed) or if the burden is disproportionate to the benefit, restitution will not be accepted. In *Tecmed v. Mexico*, the tribunal addressed the issue of restitution in kind of the licences, which the claimant only claimed secondarily after the primary claim for damages.[98] The tribunal viewed such restitution measure to be 'impossible' and given that the compensation is adequate for the claimant's claim, it did not consider further the admissibility of restitution.

Nevertheless, restitution would involve a measure which interferes with a sovereign right to regulate. For instance, the tribunal in *CMS Gas v. Argentina* pointed out the challenge of restoring the previous regulatory framework.[99] In the absence of confidence between the foreign investor and the host state, restitution may not be practically possible. Similarly, the tribunal in *LG & E* expressed the concern of undue interference with state sovereignty through restitution measures.[100]

9.3.3 *Expectation Damages as Default Rule and the Reliance Interests*

The third argument is concerned with the fact that the current remedial rules seek to protect expectations interest as the *default* position because it is considered the most adequate means to achieve full compensation. The remedy of reliance damages would be residually awarded only when there is difficulty and uncertainty in proving the amount of lost profit. The damages based on the DCF method would put the injured party in as good a position as *if the promised act had been performed.* Furthermore, Article 36(2) of the ILC Articles provides that 'compensation shall cover any financially assessable damage including loss of profits insofar as it is established'.

Therefore, in the context of a contractual breach, the 'full compensation' principle would favour the award of expectation damages: 'in order to wipe out the consequences of the breach, the injured party must be compensated for the expenses already incurred and must be awarded the

[98] *Técnicas Medioambientales Tecmed, S.A. v. Mexico*, ICSID Additional Facility Case No ARB(AF)/00/02, Award (29 May 2003) 10 ICSID Rep 134 para 183

[99] *CMS Gas Transmission Company v. Argentina*, ICSID Case No ARB 01/08, Decision of the ad hoc Committee on the Application for Annulment (25 September 2007) 14 *ICSID Rep* 251, para 406 ('it would be utterly unrealistic for the tribunal to order the Respondent to turn back to the existing regulatory framework existing before the emergency measures were adopted').

[100] *LG & E Energy Corp. v. Argentine Republic*, ICSID Case No ARB/02/1, Decision on Liability (3 October 2006) para 87.

profits lost – as those two elements would be the equivalent of substituting for *contract performance*'.[101] The key criticism of expectation damages is that it creates an intense financial burden on the state because the amount of expectation damages is usually much higher than reliance damages.

Furthermore, the remedy of expectation damages could be criticised from the theory of over-reliance perspectives. The essence of the over-reliance theory is that the expectation measure provides an incentive to a promisee to rely on a contract to a greater extent than is efficient by selecting a level of reliance as if performance of the contract is certain when in fact there is always a chance that the promisor will breach.[102] Scholars have argued that the expectation measure gives excessive assurance of performance and thus leaves the promisee without sufficient incentive to limit his or reliance. The promisor therefore bears liability in excess of the value of his or performance, leaving society as a whole less well-off and less efficient, in economic terms.[103] This criticism should be moderated because, in reality, tribunals could adopt a variety of methodologies to avoid or mitigate that problem, for instance the notions of contributory fault and failure to mitigate as the compensation-reducing factors.[104]

In defence of the expectation damages, there are basic rules for determining recoverable lost profits to ensure that it will not have an unduly adverse impact. For instance, lost profits have to be established with reasonable certainty.[105] The ILC's Articles also stipulate that lost profits are recoverable 'where an anticipated income stream has attained sufficient attributes to be considered a legally protected interest of sufficient certainty to be compensable'.[106] In addition, the jurisprudence has developed the criteria to limit the scope of expectation damages. For instance, there is a tendency to reject the lost profits claim for a start-up business or

[101] C Smutny 'Principles of Compensation in Investment Treaty Arbitration' (2007) 22 *ICSID Rev – FILJ* 1, 15–16 (emphasis added).

[102] M Eisenberg and B McDonnell, 'Expectation Damages and the Theory of Overreliance' (2002) 54 *Hastings LJ* 1335.

[103] W David Slawson, 'Role of Reliance in Contract Damages' (1990) 76 *Cornell L Rev* 197, 199.

[104] S Ripinsky, 'Assessing Damages in Investment Disputes: Practice in Search of Perfect' (2009) 10(1) *JWIT* 15.

[105] *Amoco International Finance v. Iran*, Award (14 July 1987), 15 Iran-US CTR 189, para 238 ('one of the best settled rules of the law on international responsibility of States is that no reparation for speculative or uncertain damage can be awarded').

[106] Commentary to Article 36, para 27.

at the time of breach it was not a going concern. A tribunal would require a sufficiently long record of past profitability to support a lost profits claim. Furthermore, the extent of completion of the investment project can be relevant for determining the lost profits claim.[107] The record of the investor's successful experience with similar projects can be a factor which tribunals consider.[108] Furthermore, there are ways to prevent unmeritorious claims for speculative loss or lessen the harshness and adverse consequence of expectation damages. The fundamental objection is that the ILC's Articles has the protection of expectations damages at its heart.

From the standpoint of the reliance theory, the existing remedial framework could not be endorsed because the fundamental purpose of the primary rule is to protect the investor's reliance interest. The application of the ILC's Articles does not identify the type of infringed interests.[109] Insofar as the breach of legitimate expectations is concerned, the reliance damages should be the default position. However, expectation damages could be a residual option if it is impossible to calculate the relevant detriment and the award of expectation damages (only to the extent necessary to achieve the objective) is the only way to correct injustice. This approach to the fulfilment of the investor's expectations is consistent with Fuller and Purdue's observation regarding the occasional coincidence between protection of the reliance and expectation interests.[110]

The analyses of expectation damages in the following selected decisions[111] illustrate that the tribunals applied various methods of

[107] *Autopista Concesionada de Venezuela, C.A. v. Bolivarian Republic of Venezuela,* ICSID Case No ARB/00/5 (23 September 2003) para 360.

[108] *Compañiá de Aguas del Aconquija S.A. and Vivendi Universal v. Argentina*, ICSID Case No ARB/97/3, Award (20 August 2007) para 8.3.4 ['a claimant might be able to establish clearly that an investment, such as a concession, would have been profitable by presenting sufficient evidence of its expertise and proven record of profitability of concessions it (or indeed others) had operated din similar circumstances'].

[109] Ripinsky and Williams, *Damages in International Investment Law* (n 7) 107 ('the framework based on protected interests has so far not taken root in international jurisprudence').

[110] Fuller and Purdue, 'The Reliance Interest in Contract Damage (Parts 1 and 2)' (n 18) 373–75. This approach is similar to that provided in Section 90 of the Restatement of Contracts (2d), whereby the promise is binding if injustice can be avoided only by enforcement of the promise.

[111] It is important to recognise the difficulty of attributing the reasoning on the remedy exclusively to the breach of legitimate expectations. In most cases, the decisions address the remedy for a breach of the FET standard, which might include other components than legitimate expectations, as a basis for liability. Therefore, we pay special attention

calculation for damages which sought to protect the investor's expectation interests – that is, to put the investor in the position which he or she would have occupied had the state not departed from the representation. The purpose of this analysis is not to present the details and technicality of the methodologies of calculation, but to reinforce the argument that the remedial framework based on the ILC's Articles is not a good starting point because it sets to protect the expectation interests, contrary to the proposed reliance theory of legitimate expectations.

The analysis of the decision of *Walter Bau v. Thailand* in this context is appropriate for the reason that the tribunal principally relied on the breach of legitimate expectations as the basis for breach of the FET standard.[112] Therefore, the tribunal's decision on remedy for the breach of the FET standard directly informs us about the remedy for the breach of legitimate expectations. Furthermore, this case confirms the key point in this thesis that the conception of legitimate expectations, which determines the type of infringed right, has consequence on the remedy.

On the issue of liability,[113] the tribunal was in essence motivated by the voluntarist conception when they conflated the contract breach with the treaty breach in the vocabulary of legitimate expectations in order to enforce the contractual expectations of the investor. It is no surprise that the tribunal came to favour the DCF method to calculate damages in order to achieve the results 'most closely to what the Parties effectively *expected* to occur for the duration of the concession'. In other words, the tribunal tried to estimate the fair value of the claimant's shares had the respondent fulfilled its obligations under the concession contract.[114]

The tribunal attempted to distinguish other precedents, which involved highly speculative profits, from this present case and confirmed

here to the decisions, which the tribunal accorded the significant role of legitimate expectations in the assessment of fair and equitable treatment.

112 *Walter Bau v. Thailand*, UNCITRAL Case, Award (1 July 2009) para 12.3 ('the Tribunal considers that a reasonable rate of return – reasonable in all the circumstances, including the signing of MoA2 – was part of the Claimant's legitimate expectations and *the failure to fulfil such a reasonable expectation was a breach of the Respondent's FET obligations*' [emphasis added]).

113 See the analysis of this case in Chapter 7.

114 *Walter Bau v. Thailand* (n 112) para 14.26 ('But, in the present instance, the Tribunal is convinced that the application of the traditional DCF Approach is the one which leads to results corresponding most closely to *what the Parties effectively expected to occur for the duration of the concession*') (emphasis added); para 14.28 ['The Tribunal is of the view that the best way to assess damages is to: (a) Estimate what would have been the fair value of the Claimant's shares on 3 December 2006 (the date of the sale of those shares) had the Respondent fulfilled its obligations under MoA2'].

that the present claim was based on far more than 'inherently speculative elements' for the reason that the concession agreement was accompanied with elaborate and sophisticated studies prepared by independent experts at the request of one or the other party or by lenders, and these studies were clearly used by those parties as the bases for the determination of the terms of those various agreements. Therefore, the tribunal was 'convinced' that it would be possible to calculate damages owing to the claimant in the present case based on the DCF method.[115]

Whether or not the analysis on the speculative nature of the loss is correct is not the ground for objection for the present purpose. From the analytical framework guided by the reliance theory of legitimate expectations, the tribunal's reasoning on liability was wrong and its decision on remedy was also questionable in light of the identified interest protected by the principle of legitimate expectations. The tribunal's reasoning on the remedy might be correct had it not been for the breach of contractual claim, in which the protection of contractual expectation would be at stake. But that claim should be litigated under the applicable law of the concession contract. The pertinent fact that the claimant in this case were the minority shareholders in the local company (so could not directly sue the government but could bring the shareholders claim) was significant. It manifests the undesirable effect of applying the wrong conception of legitimate expectations, which leads to undeserved entitlements: the minority shareholders could enforce the contractual obligation of the state to recover its expectation interests, which otherwise it would not have had under the concession agreement governed by the law of the host state. The outcome would have produced less injustice had the tribunal calculated the damage with reference to the investor's reliance interests in terms of actual investment or investment expenditures.

The second decision of *Micula v. Romania* on the remedy is notable for two reasons. First, the tribunal specifically employed the term 'expectation damages' in the context of the 'full compensation' principle articulated in the *Chórzow Factory* case:

> The Tribunal does not see any reason to deviate from the Claimants' *primary expectation damages approach* which, in the Claimants' own submission, should place them in the position that they would have been but for Romania's breach of the BIT, and is thus consistent with

[115] Ibid para 14.211.

the full compensation principle articulated in the *Chórzow Factory* case.[116]

This is significant because contrary to scholars' view that the distinction between expectation and reliance interests was not adopted in international law,[117] the explicit confirmation that *Chórzow Factory* formulation aims to protect the 'expectation interests'. One can question if the tribunal was correct to suggest that this return to status quo would have to be supplemented by compensation to put the investor in the position as if the relevant obligation was performed.

Second, the tribunal categorically rejected reliance damages because it viewed the reliance approach to not be in compliance with the full compensation and endorsed expectation damages approach which would have put the claimant in a situation without the respondent's breach of the obligation.[118]

The tribunal analysed three methods of calculation presented by the claimants: two expectation damages computations (methods A and B) and one reliance damages computation (method C). Methods A and B would be appropriate for the contractual remedy but not for the remedy for 'delictual' wrong under the reliance conception of legitimate expectations. Therefore, method A, which seeks to grant the increased costs and lost profits that the claimants would have made had they been allowed to develop their business the way they allege they had planned to do, in particular, by implementing incremental investments and the sale of sugar containing products (SCPs) to third parties, should be rejected. Method B covers the increased costs and lost profits that the claimants would have made had they continued operating their existing platform.

The tribunal's reasoning on liability for a breach of legitimate expectations indicated its adherence to the reliance conception when it insisted that the claimants 'must have relied on that expectation when they made their investment'.[119] Yet, the tribunal sought to protect expectations

[116] *Ioan Micula, Viorel Micula, S.C. European Food S.A, S.C. Starmill S.R.L. and S.C. Multipack S.R.L. v. Romania*, ICSID Case No ARB/05/20, Award (11 December 2013) para 948.

[117] S Ripinsky, 'Assessing Damages in Investment Disputes: Practice in Search of Perfect' (2009) 10(1) *JWIT* 15; D Collins, 'Reliance Remedies at the International Center for the Settlement of Investment Disputes' (2009) 29 *Nw J Int'l L & Bus* 195.

[118] *Micula v v. Romania* paras 944, 948.

[119] Ibid para 672 ('The Claimants *must also have relied on* that expectation when they made their investments. However, it is not necessary for the entire investment to have been predicated solely on such expectation. Businessmen do not invest on the basis of one single consideration, no matter how important. In the Tribunal's view, that expectation

interest rather than reliance interest. Had the liability issue been considered properly from the reliance theory of legitimate expectations, method C should have been the preferred method of calculation – namely, 'the value of the losses incurred by the Claimants in investing in reliance on their expectation that the incentives would remain in place for ten years'.[120]

Although the claimant's legitimate expectations formed a very significant part of the tribunal's analysis on the FET standard, it was not a decisive element as it found the breach with reference to other components of the FET standard.[121]

The decision of *Lemire v. Ukraine* is under analysis here for the reason that despite the fact that the tribunal awarded the expectation damages, it imposed 'a diligent and reasonable investor' standard in the calculation of damages. The tribunal applied the hypothetical scenario standard in the determination of damages. The claimant submitted that the difference between the actual ('as is') and the hypothetical ('but for') value of Gala Radio represents the damage caused by the respondent to the claimant. The claimant suggested that the calculation of damages should place the claimant in the position he should have been in had there not been a breach by the respondent.

There are two notable aspects about the reasoning in this case. First, the tribunal confirmed that the absence of standard compensation for the FET standard does not mean no redress.[122] Second, in the calculation of damages, the tribunal was reluctant to endorse the fair market value method as the claimant's business still exists and has not been deprived of an asset. Therefore, it endorsed the *Chórzow Factory* principle of placing the investor in the same pecuniary position in which it would have been if respondent had not violated the BIT.[123]

In essence, the tribunal granted expectation damages by trying to calculate the value of the business if there had been no breach, rather than focus on the amounts invested. This is reflected in the following passage:

must be a determining factor in an investor's decision to invest, or in the manner or magnitude of its investments'. [emphasis added]).

120 Ibid para 944.

121 Ibid para 726.

122 *Joseph Charles Lemire v. Ukraine* (n 5) para 147 ('a wrong committed by a State against an investor must always give rise to a right for compensation of the economic harm sustained').

123 Ibid para 149.

> Although the amounts invested do not constitute a ceiling to the compensation, there must, with respect to most enterprises, be a common-sense correlation between both concepts: the amounts invested influence the size of the enterprise, and the size of the enterprise, together with the investor's activities and skills, *define the earning expectations and the value of the business.*[124]

One could argue that the reliance damages would be the amounts invested rather than the earning expectations and the value of the business. The 'but for' standard that the tribunal adopted operates under a hypothesis of no breach, which would still be based on uncertain factors. The tribunal itself admitted the weakness of this approach.[125] The notable feature of the tribunal's reasoning is its reference to the 'diligent and reasonable investor' standard[126] in the calculation. It may seem a sensible approach to take into account the investor's conduct. However, it is challenging to quantify the amount of 'diligence' and 'reasonableness' in the calculation of damages.

From the review of other investment treaty decisions in which the breach of legitimate expectations was involved, one could make the observation that in most cases, tribunals adopted the full compensation principle in the ILC's Articles and as reflected in the customary international law as the starting point. In those cases, tribunals often adopted the DCF method for the market value as the appropriate measure of compensation.[127] It is true that the impact of the protection of expectation interests is contained and checked. The tribunals have adopted a variety of methods to ensure that the compensation would not be granted for the

[124] Ibid para 300 ('Investment and damages are of course separate concepts: investment refers to the resources which Claimant brought into Ukraine in order to create and fund Gala Radio, and damages to the loss of value which Gala Radio suffered as a consequence of the breaches in the BIT').

[125] Ibid para 248 ('The Tribunal has no crystal ball and cannot claim to know what would have happened under a hypothesis of no breach; the best any tribunal can do is to make an informed and conscientious evaluation, taking into account all the relevant circumstances of the case, not unlike that made by anyone who assesses the value of a business on the basis of its likely future earnings').

[126] Ibid.

[127] *CME v. Czech Republic*, UNCITRAL Case, Partial Award (13 September 2001) 9 ICSID Rep 121 para 618 ('payment of a sum corresponding to ... the fair market value of claimant's investment as it was before consummation of the Respondent's breach of the Treaty'); *El Paso Energy International Company v. The Argentine Republic*, ICSID Case No ARB/03/15, Award (31 October 2011) paras 701–03 [the fair market value standard shall therefore be adopted to determine the value of the loss suffered by the claimant by comparing the fair market value of El Paso's investment with and without the GOA measures (respectively, the actual and the 'but for' scenarios)].

highly speculative loss. For instance, the test of 'reasonable certainty' would exclude claims for future gains or loss of profits which are too uncertain and speculative.[128] The idea of allocating risk to the investor through the principles of contributory negligence and the duty to mitigate is another instance of easing the harsh effect of the full compensation principle. From the principled perspective, the current remedial framework provides the wrong start by focusing on 'expectation' interest as the default position rather than focusing on the reliance interest which is the core of legitimate expectations.

9.4 Conclusion

As a result of these conceptual foundations, the reliance damages should be the prevailing standard for remedy in case of a breach of legitimate expectations under the FET standard. Reliance damages are compatible with the protection of the infringed right under the reliance conception of legitimate expectations. They are more discernable than expectation damages, which are often predicated on hypotheses. Furthermore, performance or restitution remedy is impractical from the point of view of enforceability and intrusiveness on the state's regulatory powers. The expectation damages seek to protect expectation interest, which is not the interest protected by the reliance theory of legitimate expectations.

The critique of the principles of international law regarding the full compensation presented in this chapter does not mean that the principles should no longer be applied. The main point is that the application of those rules in the case of the breach of legitimate expectations should take into account the different context in which the investor–state dispute functions, by taking into account the nature of infringed right and the special position of the state. For these reasons, it is time to rethink the remedies.

[128] Some tribunals have disallowed claims for lost profits when they are 'too uncertain and speculative' [*Nykomb v. Latvia*, Award (16 December 2003) para 41] or 'wholly uncertain' [*PSEG v. Turkey*, Award (19 January 2007) para 313].

BIBLIOGRAPHY

Aaken A van, 'Primary and Secondary Remedies in International Investment Law and National State Liability: A Functional and Comparative View' in S Schill (ed), *International Investment Law and Comparative Public Law* (Oxford: Oxford University Press, 2010)

Akehurst M, 'Equity and General Principles of Law' (1976) 25 *Int'l & Comp L Q* 801

Alexandrov SA, 'Breaches of Contract and Breaches of Treaty – The Jurisdiction of Treaty-based Arbitration Tribunals to Decide Breach of Contract Claims in SGS v. Pakistan and SGS v. Philippines' (2004) 5 *JWIT* 555

Allan TRS, *Law, Liberty and Justice: The Legal Foundations of British Constitutionalism* (Oxford: Clarendon Press, 1994)

Alvik I, *Contracting with Sovereignty: State Contracts and International Arbitration* (Oxford: Hart Publishing, 2011)

Amerasinghe CF, 'State Breaches of Contracts with Aliens and International Law' (1964) 58(4) *AJIL* 881

Aquinas T, *The Summa Theologica of St. Thomas Aquinas*, English Dominicans (trans) (London: Burns, Oates and Washbourne). Repr (New York, NY: Christian Classics 1981)

Ardal P, 'And That's a Promise' (1968) 18(72) *Phil Q* 225

'Promises and Reliance' (1976) 1 *Dialogue: CPhRev* 54

Aristotle, *Nicomachean Ethics*, Jonathon Barnes (ed) (Princeton, NJ: Princeton University Press, 1984)

Ashley C, 'What Is a Promise in Law?' (1903) 16(5) *Harv L Rev* 319, 320

Atiyah PS, 'Contracts, Promises and the Law of Obligations' (1978) 94 *LQR* 193

Promises, Morals and the Law (Oxford: Oxford University Press, 1981)

The Law of Contract (Oxford: Oxford University Press, 1961)

The Rise and Fall of the Freedom of Contract (Oxford: Clarendon Press, 1979)

Baetens F, 'No Law Is an Island, Entire of Itself: How International Investment Law Interacts with Other Fields of Public International Law' in F Baetens (ed), *Investment Law within International Law: Integrationist Perspectives* (Cambridge: Cambridge University Press, 2013)

Baler A, 'Trust and Antitrust' (1986) 96 *Ethics* 231

Bamforth N, 'Legitimate Expectation and Estoppel' (1998) 3(4) *JR* 196

Barak-Erez D, 'The Doctrine of Legitimate Expectations and the Distinction between the Reliance and Expectation Interests' (2005) 11(4) *EPL* 583
Barnett R, 'A Consent Theory of Contract' (1986) 86 *Colum L Rev* 269
Barnidge R, 'The Due Diligence Principle under International Law' (2006) 8 *Int C L Rev* 81
Benson P, 'Grotius' Contribution to the Natural Law of Contract' (1985) 6 *CJNS* 1
Bilder R, 'The Role of Trust in International Law' (1981); available at http://ssrn.com/abstract=912741 (accessed on 10 June 2016)
Bix B, 'Theories of Contract Law and Enforcing Promissory Morality: Comments on Charles Fried' (2012) 45(3) *Suffolk U L Rev* 719
Bowett D, 'Estoppel before International Tribunals and Its Relation to Acquiescence' (1957) 33 *BYIL* 176, 202
Brown C, 'A Comparative and Critical Assessment of Estoppel in International Law' (1995) 50 *U Miami L Rev* 369, 410–12
'The Protection of Legitimate Expectations as a "General Principle of Law": Some Preliminary Thoughts' (2009) 6(1) *Transnational Dispute Management*
Byers M, *Custom, Power and the Power of Rules* (Cambridge: Cambridge University Press 1999)
Calmes S, *Du principe de protection de la confiance légitime en droits allemand, communautaire et français* (Nouvelle bibliothèque de thèses) (Paris: Dalloz 2001)
Campbell C, 'House of Cards: The Relevance of Legitimate Expectations under Fair and Equitable Treatment Provisions in Investment Treaty Law' (2013) 30(4) *J Int'l Arb* 361
Cane P, *Anatomy of Tort Law* (Oxford: Hart Publishing, 1997)
Caron D, 'The Interpretation of National Foreign Investment Laws as Unilateral Acts under International Law' in MH Arsanjani et al. (eds), *Looking to the Future: Essays on International Law in Honor of W Michael Reisman* (Leiden: Nijhoff 2010)
Chayes A, 'The Role of the Judge in Public Law Litigation' (1976) 89 *Harv L Rev* 1281
Chitty J (ed), *Emmerich de Vattel, The Law of Nations or Principles of the Law of Nature, Applied to the Conduct and Affairs of Nations and Sovereigns* (Cambridge: Cambridge University Press, 2011)
Cholbi MJ, 'A Contractualist Account of Promising' (2002) 40(4) *SJPH* 475
Clayton R, 'Legitimate Expectations, Policy, and the Principle of Consistency' (2003) 62(1) *CLJ* 93
Cohon R, 'Hume on Promises and the Peculiar Act of the Mind' (2006) 44(1) *JHPH* 25
Collins D, 'Reliance Remedies at the International Center for the Settlement of Investment Disputes' (2009) 29 *Nw J Int'l L & Bus* 195
Collins H, *The Law of Contracts* (London: Weidenfeld & Nicolson 1986)

Conee E, 'The Moral Value in Promises' (2000) 109(3) *Phil Rev* 411

Conison J, 'Assurance, Reliance, and Expectation' (1998) 6 *S Cal Interdis LJ* 335

Connolly W, *The Terms of Political Discourse* (Princeton, NJ: Princeton University Press, 3rd edn, 1993)

Cottingham J, 'Varieties of Retribution' (1979) 29 *Phil Q* 238

Coyle S and Morrow K, *The Philosophical Foundations of Environment* (Oxford: Hart Publishing 2004)

Craig P, *EU Administrative Law* (Oxford: Oxford University Press, 2nd edn, 2012)

'Grounds for Judicial Review: Substantive Control over Discretion' in D Feldman (ed), *English Public Law* (Oxford: Oxford University Press 2004)

'Substantive Legitimate Expectations in Domestic and Community Law' (1996) 55(2) *CLJ* 289

Craswell R, 'Against Fuller and Perdue' (2000) 67 *U Chi Law Rev* 99, 127

'Treaty and Contract in Investment Arbitration' (2009) 6(1) *Transnational Dispute Management*

Crawford J, *Brownlie's Principles of Public International Law* (Oxford: Oxford University Press, 8th edn, 2012)

'Treaty and Contract in Investment Arbitration' (2008) 24(1) *Arbitration Int'l* 374

Cristina M and Salias G, 'Do Umbrella Clauses Apply to Unilateral Undertakings?' in C Binder et al. (eds), *International Investment Law for the 21st Century: Essays in Honour of Christoph Schreuer* (Oxford: Oxford University Press, 2009)

Cuniberti G, 'Enhancing Judicial Reputation through Legal Transplants – Estoppel Travels to France' (2012) 60(2) *Am J Comp L* 383

Cupit G, 'How Requests (and Promises) Create Obligation' (1994) 44(177) *Phil Q* 439

D'Aspremont J, *Formalism and the Sources of International Law: A Theory of the Ascertainment of Legal Rules* (Oxford: Oxford University Press, 2011)

Daujotas R and Audzevičius R, 'The Concept of Legitimate Expectation in Investor-State Arbitration and the European Court of Human Rights' (2012) 6(2) *Bulletin of the International Commercial Arbitration* 11

De Brabandere E, 'Arbitral Decisions as a Source of International Investment Law' in T Gazzini and E De Brabandere (eds), *International Investment Law: The Sources of Rights and Obligations* (Leiden: Martinus Nijhoff Publishers, 2012)

Dolzer R, 'Fair and Equitable Treatment: Today's Contours' (2014) 12 *Santa Clara J Int'l L* 7

Dolzer R and Schreuer C, *Principles of International Investment Law* (Oxford: Oxford University Press, 2008)

Dotan Y, 'Why Administrators Should Be Bound by Their Policies?' (1997) 17(1) *OJLS* 23

Douglas Z, 'Can a Doctrine of Precedent Be Justified in Investment Treaty Arbitration?' (2010) 25 *ICSID Rev – FILJ* 104

'Concepts of Property' in Z Douglas, J Pauwelyn and JE Viñuales (eds), *The Foundations of International Investment Law – Bringing Theory into Practice* (Oxford: Oxford University Press, 2014)

'Nothing If Not Critical in Investment Treaty Arbitration' (2006) 22 *Arbitration Int* 27

'The Hybrid Foundations of Investment Treaty Arbitration' (2003) 74 *BYIL* 151

The International Law of Investment Claims (Cambridge: Cambridge University Press 2009)

Douglas Z, Pauwelyn J and Viñuales JE (eds), *The Foundations of International Investment Law – Bringing Theory into Practice* (Oxford: Oxford University Press, 2014)

Downie RS, 'Three Accounts of Promising' (1985) 35(140) *Phil Q* 259

Dubash NK and Morgan B (eds), *The Rise of the Regulatory State of the South Infrastructure and Development in Emerging Economies* (Oxford: Oxford University Press, 2013)

Dumberry P, 'The Prohibition against Arbitrary Conduct and the Fair and Equitable Treatment Standard under NAFTA Article 1105' (2014) 15 *JWIT* 117

'The Protection of Investors' Legitimate Expectations and the Fair and Equitable Treatment Standard under NAFTA Article' (2014) 31(1) *J Int'l Arb* 47

Dunn J, 'The Concept of "Trust" in the Politics of John Locke' in R Rorty, JB Schneewind and Q Skinner (eds), *Philosophy in History: Essays in the Historiography of Philosophy* (Cambridge: Cambridge University Press, 1984)

Dupuy F, La protection de l'attente légitime des parties au contrat – Etude de droit international des investissements à la lumière du droit compare [Thèse: University of Paris (Panthéon-Assas) and Berlin: Humboldt Universität, 2007]

Dupuy F and Dupuy PM, 'What to Expect from Legitimate Expectations? A Critical Appraisal and Look into the Future of the "Legitimate Expectations" Doctrine in International Investment Law' in NG Ziadé (ed), *Festschrift Ahmed Sadek El-Kosheri* (The Hague: Kluwer Law International, 2015)

Dworkin R, 'In Praise of Theory' (1997) 29 *Ariz St LJ* 353

Earl Childress, III, D, *The Role of Ethics in International Law* (Cambridge: Cambridge University Press, 2014)

Eisenberg MA and McDonnell B, 'Expectation Damages and the Theory of Overreliance' (2002) 54 *Hastings LJ* 1335.

Elias P, 'Legitimate Expectation and Judicial Review' in J Jowell and D Oliver (eds), *New Directions in Judicial Review* (London: Stevens, 1988)

Elliot M, 'Judicial Review's Scope, Foundations and Purposes: Joining the Dots' (2012) *NZ L Rev* 75

'Legitimate Expectations, Consistency and Abuse of Power: The Rashid Case' (2005) 10 *JR* 281

'Unlawful Representations, Legitimate Expectations and Estoppel in Public Law' (2003) 8(2) *JR* 71

Feinberg J, 'The Nature and Value of Rights' (1970) 4(4) *JLS* 243

Fietta S, 'Expropriation and the "Fair and Equitable" Standard: The Developing Role of Investors' "Expectations" in International Investment Arbitration' (2006) 23 *J Int'l Arb* 375

Finn P, 'Commerce, the Common Law and Morality' (1989) 17 *MULR* 87

Finnis J, *Natural Law and Natural Rights* (Oxford: Clarendon Press, 1980)

Fitzmaurice G, 'The General Principles of International Law Considered from the Standpoint of the Rule of Law' (1997) 11 *Collected Courses of the Hague Academy of International Law* 1

Flanagan R, 'Legitimate Expectation and Applications – An Outdated and Unneeded Distinction' (2011) 17 *Canta LR* 283

Fletcher G, 'The Right and the Reasonable' *Harv L Rev* 98 (1984) 949

Fordham M, 'Legitimate Expectation II: Comparison and Prediction' (2001) 6 *JR* 262

'Monetary Awards in Judicial Review' (2009) *Public Law* 1

'Reparation for Maladministration: Public Law's Final Frontier' (2003) 8 *JR* 104

Forsyth CF, 'Legitimate Expectations Revisited' (2011) 16(4) *JR* 429

'The Provenance and Protection of Legitimate Expectations' (1988) 47 *CLJ* 238

'Wednesbury Protection of Substantive Legitimate Expectations' (1997) *PL* 375

Francioni F, 'Equity in International Law' *Max Planck Encyclopedia of Public International Law* (Oxford: Oxford University Press, 2013)

Franck T, 'Word Made Law: The Decision of the ICJ in the Nuclear Test Cases' (1975) 69 *AJIL* 616

Fried C, *Contract as Promise: A Theory of Contractual Obligation* (Boston, MA: Harvard University Press, 1981)

Friedman LM, 'Legal Culture and Social Development' (1969) 4(1) *L & Soc Rev* 29

Friedmann D, 'Rights and Remedies' (1997) 113 *LQR* 424

'Rights and Remedies' in N Cohen and E McKendrick (eds), *Comparative Remedies for Breach of Contract* (Oxford: Hart Publishing, 2005)

Friedrich D and Southwood N, 'Promises and Trust' in H Sheinman (ed), *Promises and Agreements: Philosophical Essays* (Oxford: Oxford University Press, 2011)

Fuller L and Perdue WR, 'The Reliance Interest in Contract Damage (Parts 1 and 2)' (1936–1937) 46(52) *Yale LJ* 373

Gallus N, 'The "Fair and Equitable Treatment" Standard and the Circumstances of the Host State' in C Brown and K Milles (eds), *Evolution in Investment Treaty Law and Arbitration* (Cambridge: Cambridge University Press, 2011)

Garcia-Amador FV, *The Changing Law of International Claims* (New York, NY: Oceana Publications, 1984)

Gardner J, 'Justifications and Reasons' in A Simester and ATH Smith (eds), *Harm and Culpability* (Oxford: Oxford University Press, 1996)

'The Many Faces of the Reasonable Person' (2015) 131 *LQR* 563

'The Mysterious Case of Reasonable Person' (2001) 51(3) *UTLJ* 273

'What Is Tort Law For? Part 1. The Place of Corrective Justice' (2011) 30(1) *L & Phil* 33

Gaus G, 'The Rational, the Reasonable, and Justification' (1995) 3 *JPh* 234

Gautier D, *Morals by Agreement* (Oxford: Oxford University Press, 1987)

Gehne K and Brillo R, 'Stabilization Clauses in International Investment Law: Beyond Balancing and Fair and Equitable Treatment' NCCR Working Paper, No 2013/46

Geller PE, 'Legal Transplants in International Copyright: Some Problems of Method' (1994) 13 *PBLJ* 199

Gilbert M, 'Scanlon on Promissory Obligation: The Problem of Promisees' Rights' (2004) 101 *JPh* 83

Goldberg V, 'Protecting Reliance' (2014) 114(4) *Colum L Rev* 1033

Gordley J, *The Philosophical Origins of Modern Contract Doctrine* (Oxford: Clarendon Press, 1991)

Grotius H, *De Jure Belli ac Pacis Libri Tres*, FW Kelsey (trans) (London: Oxford Clarendon Press, 1925)

Gutteridge HC, 'The Meaning and Scope of Article 38 (1) (c) of the Statute of the International Court of Justice' (1952) 38 *Transactions of the Grotius Society* 125

Habermas J, 'On the Internal Relation between the Rule of Law and Democracy' (1995) 3(1) *Eur J Int Law* 12

Hannet S and Busch L, 'Ultra Vires Representations and Legitimate Expectations' (2005) *PL* 729

Hardin R, *Trust and Trustworthiness* (New York, NY: Russell Sage Foundation, 2002)

Hart HLA, 'Are There Any Natural Rights' (1955) 64 *Phil Rev* 175

Harten GV and Loughlin M, 'Investment Treaty Arbitration as a Species of Global Administrative Law' (2006) 17(1) *Eur J Int Law* 121

Hellman D and Moreau S, *Philosophical Foundations of Discrimination Law* (Oxford: Oxford University Press, 2013)

Hieronymi P, 'The Reasons of Trust' (2008) 86(2) *AJP* 213

Hirsch M, 'Between Fair and Equitable Treatment and Stabilization Clause: Stable Legal Environment and Regulatory Change in International Investment Law' (2011) 12 *JWIT* 783

Hirsch M, 'The Sociology of International Investment Law' in Z Douglas, J Pauwelyn and JE Viñuales (eds), *The Foundations of International Investment Law - Bringing Theory into Practice* (Oxford: Oxford University Press, 2014)

Hlophe J, 'Legitimate Expectation and Natural Justice: English, Australian and South African Law' (1987) 104 *SALJ* 165

Hogg M, *Promises and Contract Law, Comparative Perspectives* (Cambridge: Cambridge University Press, 2014)

Holmes OW, 'The Path of Law' (1897) 10 *Harv L Rev* 457

Hume D, *A Treatise of Human Nature* (Oxford: Oxford University Press, 2000)

Janis MW, 'Equity in International Law' in R Bernhardt (ed), *Encyclopedia of Public International Law* Volume II (Amsterdam: North-Holland)

Jennings RY, 'State Contracts in International Law' (1961) 37 *BYIL* 156

Jensen D, 'In Defence of the Reliance Theory of Equitable Estoppel' (2001) 22 *Adel L Rev* 157

Jones DH, 'Making and Keeping Promises' (1966) 76 *Ethics* 287

Kahn-Freund O, 'On Uses and Misuses of Comparative Law' (1974) 37 *MLR* 1

Kaufmann-Kohler G, 'Is Consistency a Myth?' in E Gaillard and Yas Banifatemi, *Precedent in International Arbitration: IAI Seminar*, Paris - December 14, 2007

Kelly PJ, *Utilitarianism and Distributive Justice: Jeremey Bentham and the Civil Law* (Oxford: Oxford University Press, 1990)

Kennedy D, 'Form and Substance in Private Law Adjudication' (1976) 89 *Harv L Rev* 1685

Kimel D, *From Promise to Contract: Toward a Liberal Theory of Contract* (Oxford: Hart Publishing, 2003)

Kingsbury B and Schill S, 'Investor–State Arbitration as Governance: Fair and Equitable Treatment, Proportionality and the Emerging Global Administrative Law' (2006) IILJ Working Paper 2009/6 24–30

Klager R, 'Fair and Equitable Treatment: A Look at the Theoretical Underpinnings of Legitimacy and Fairness' (2010) 11(3) *JWIT* 435

Fair and Equitable Treatment in International Investment Law (Cambridge: Cambridge University Press, 2011)

Knight CJS, 'Expectations in Transition: Recent Developments in Legitimate Expectations' (2009) *PL* 15

Kolb R, 'Principles as Sources of International Law (With Special Reference to Good Faith)' (2006) 53(1) *NILR* 1

Kolodny N and Wallace RJ, 'Promises and Practices Revisited' (2003) 31(1) *Phil & Pub Aff* 119

Kriebaum U and Schreuer CH, 'At What Time Must Legitimate Expectations Exist?' (2012); available at www.transnational-dispute-management.com

Kuklin B, 'The Justification for Protecting Reasonable Expectations' (2001) 29(3) *Hofstra L Rev* 863

'The Plausibility of Legally Protecting Reasonable Expectations' (1997) 32 *Val U L Rev* 19

Laird I and Askew R, 'Finality versus Consistency: Does Investor-State Arbitration Need an Appellate System' (2005) 7 *J App Prac & Process* 285

Lang J, 'Legal Certainty and Legitimate Expectations as General Principles of Law' in U Bernitz and J Nergelius (eds), *General Principles in European Community Law* (The Hague: Wolters Kluwer, 2000)

Langer M, 'From Legal Transplants to Legal Translations: The Globalization of Plea Bargaining and the Americanization Thesis in Criminal Procedure' (2004) 45(1) *Harv Int'l L J* 1

Lauterpacht H, *The Function of Law in the International Community* (Oxford: Clarendon Press, 1933)

Legrand P, 'Legal Traditions in Western Europe: The Limits of Commonality' in AJ de Roo, E Örücü and RW Jagtenberg (eds), *Transfrontier Mobility of Law* (The Hague: Wolters Kluwer, 1995)

'The Impossibility of "Legal Transplants"' (1997) 4 *Masst J Eur & Comp L* 113

Levinson D, 'Making Government Pay: Markets, Politics and the Allocation of Constitutional Costs' (2000) 67 *U Chi Law Rev* 345

Locke J, *Two Treatises of Government* (1689), P. Laslett (ed) (Cambridge: Cambridge University Press, 1988)

Loughlin M, *Foundations of Public Law* (Oxford: Oxford University Press, 2012)

Political Theory and Public Law (Oxford: Clarendon Press, 1992)

MacCormick N, 'The Obligation of Reparation' in N MacCormick (ed), *Legal Right and Social Democracy: Essays in Legal and Political Philosophy* (Oxford: Clarendon Press, 1982)

'Voluntary Obligations' in N MacCormick (ed), *Legal Right and Social Democracy: Essays in Legal and Political Philosophy* (Oxford: Clarendon Press, 1982)

'Voluntary Obligations and Normative Powers' (1972) 46(Supplement) *Proceedings of the Aristotelian Society* 59

MacGibbon IC, 'Estoppel in International Law' (1958) 7 *ICLQ* 468

Mairal HA, 'Legitimate Expectations and Informal Administrative Representations' in S Schill (ed), *International Investment Law and Comparative Public law* (Oxford: Oxford University Press, 2010)

Mann FA, 'State Contracts and State Responsibility' (1960) 54(3) *AJIL* 572

Mbengue MM, 'National Legislation and Unilateral Acts' in T Gazzini and E de Brabandère (eds), *The Sources of Rights and Obligations in Transnational Investment Law* (Leiden: Martinus Nijhoff Publishers, 2012)

McLachlan C, Shore L and Weiniger M, *International Investment Arbitration: Substantive Principles* (Oxford: Oxford University Press, 2007)
McNair A, 'The General Principles of Law Recognized by Civilized Nations' (1957) 33 *BYIL* 1
McNeilly FS, 'Promises De-moralized' (1972) 81 *Phil Rev* 63
Mendelson M, 'Compensation for Expropriation: The Case Law' (1985) 79(2) *AJIL* 414
'The Subjective Element in Customary International Law' (1995) 66 *BYIL* 177
Mill J, *On Liberty, Utilitarianism and Other Essays* in M Philip and F Rosen (eds), (Oxford: Oxford University Press, 2nd edn, 2015)
Millett P, 'Equity's Place in the Law of Commerce' (1998) 114 *LQR* 214
Mitchell C, 'Leading a Life of Its Own? The Roles of Reasonable Expectation in Contract Law' (2003) 23(4) *OJLLS* 639
Momirov A and Fourie AN, 'Vertical Comparative Law Methods: Tools for Conceptualizing the International Rule of Law' (2009) 2(3) *Erasmus L Rev* 292
Moules R, *Actions against Public Officials: Legitimate Expectations, Misstatements and Misconduct* (London: Sweet and Maxwell, 2009)
Muchlinski P, '"Caveat Investor"? The Relevance of the Conduct of the Investor under the Fair and Equitable Treatment Standard' (2006) 55 *ICLQ* 527
Müller JP and Cottier T, 'Estoppel' in Rudolf Bernhardt (ed), *Max Planck Encyclopedia of Public International Law* (2003)
Narveson J, 'Promising, Expecting and Utility' (1971) 1 *CJPh* 207
Nelken D, 'Comparatists and Transferability' in P Legrand and R Munday (eds) *Comparative Legal Studies: Traditions and Transitions* (Cambridge: Cambridge University Press, 2003)
'The Meaning of Success in Transnational Legal Transfers' (2001) 19 *Windsor Yrbk Acc Jus* 350
'Towards a Sociology of Legal Adaptation' in D Nelken and J Feest (eds), *Adapting Legal Cultures* (Oxford: Hart Publishing, 2001)
Newcombe A and Paradell L, *Law and Practice of Investment Treaties: Standards of Treatment* (The Netherlands: Wolters Kluwer, 2009)
Ngugi J, 'Promissory Estoppel: The Life History of an Ideal Legal Transplant' (2007) 41(2) *U Rich L Rev* 425
Nickel PJ, 'Trust and Obligation-Ascription' (2007) 10(3) *Ethical Theory and Moral Practice* 309
Oppenheim L, 'The Science of International Law: Its Tasks and Methods' (1908) 2 *AJIL* 313, 336
Örücü E, 'Law as Transposition' (2002) 51 *ICLQ* 205
Owen D, 'Expectations in Tort' (2011) 43 *Ariz St LJ* 1287, 1291
'Foreword Why Philosophy Matters to Tort Law' in D Owen (ed), *The Philosophical Foundations of Tort Law* (Oxford: Clarendon Press, 1997)
Owens D, 'A Simple Theory of Promising' (2006) 115(1) *Phil Rev* 51

'Promising without Intending' (2008) 105(12) *J Phil* 737

Shaping the Normative Landscape (Oxford: Oxford University Press, 2012)

Paley E, *The Works of William Paley, D. D. and an Account of the Life and Writings of the Author*, Volume III (London: Longman and Co, 1838)

Pandya A and Moody A, 'Legitimate Expectations in Investment Treaty Arbitration: An Unclear Future' (2010–2011) 15 *Tilburg L Rev* 93

Paparinskis M, 'Analogies and Other Regimes of International Law' in Z Douglas, J Pauwelyn and JE Viñuales (eds), 'Good Faith and International Economic Law' in A Mitchell, M Sornarajah and T Voon (eds), *Good Faith and International Economic Law* (Oxford: Oxford University Press, 2015)

The Foundations of International Investment Law – Bringing Theory into Practice (Oxford: Oxford University Press, 2014)

The International Minimum Standard (Oxford: Oxford University Press, 2013)

Patterson D, 'The Value of a Promise' (1992) 11(4) *L & Phil* 385

Paulsson J, 'Can "Legitimate Expectations" Ever Be "Rights"?' (19 April 2016) *JOTWELL*

'The Power of States to Make Meaningful Promises to Foreigners' (2010) 1(2) *JIDS* 341

Pink T, 'Promising and Obligations' (2009) 23(1) *Philos Perspect* 389

Pitson AE, 'Hume on Promises and Their Obligation' (1988) 14(1) *HumeS* 176

Popelier P, 'Legitimate Expectations and the Law Maker in the Case Law of the European Court of Human Right' (2006) *EHRLR* 10

Popper K, *Objective Knowledge: An Evolutionary Approach* (Oxford: Oxford University Press, 1972)

Posner R, 'The Concept of Corrective Justice in Recent Theories of Tort Law' (1981) 10 *J Leg St* 187

Postema GJ, *Philosophy and the Law of Torts* (Cambridge: Cambridge University Press, 2001)

Potesta M, 'Legitimate Expectations in Investment Treaty Law: Understanding the Roots and the Limits of a Controversial Concept' (2013) *ICSID Rev – FILJ* 1

Pound R, *Social Control through Law* (New Haven, CT: Yale University Press, 1942)

Pratt M, 'Defeating Reasonable Reliance' (1999) 18 *U Tas LR* 181

'Identifying the Harm Done: A Critique of the Reliance Theory of Estoppel' (1999) 21 *Adel L Rev* 209

'Promise, Contracts and Voluntary Obligations' (2007) 26(6) *L & Phil* 531

'Scanlon on Promising' (2001) 14 *Can J L & Jurisprudence* 143

Prichard HA, 'The Obligation to Keep a Promise' in Jim MacAdam (ed), *Moral Writings* (Oxford: Clarendon Press, 2002)

Pufendorf S, *De Jure Nature et Gentium* (1672) [On the Law of Nature and Nations], CH Oldfather and WA Oldfather (trans) (New York, NY: Hein Press, 1995)

Puig S, 'No Right without a Remedy: Foundations of Investor-State Arbitration' (2014) 35 *U Pa J Int'l L* 829

Rawls J, *A Theory of Justice* (Cambridge, MA: Harvard University Press, 1971)

'The Idea of Public Reason Revisited' (1997) 64(3) *U Chi L Rev* 765

'Two Concepts of Rules' (1955) 64(1) *Phil Rev* 3

Raz J, 'Authority and Consent' (1981) 67 *Va L Rev* 103

'Authority and Justification' (1985) 14 *Phil & Pub Aff* 1

'Book Review: Promises in Morality and Law' (1982) 95 *Harv L Rev* 916

'Is There a Reason to Keep Promises' (2012) No 12–320, Research Paper Series, Columbia University Public Law and Legal Theory, Columbia Law School

'Legal Principles and the Limits of Law' (1972) 81 *Yale LJ* 823

'Liberty and Trust' in R George (ed), *Natural Law, Liberalism, and Morality: Contemporary Essays* (Oxford: Oxford University Press, 2001)

'On the Nature of Rights' (1984) xciii(370) *Mind* 194 [reprinted in Morton Winston, ed], *The Philosophy of Human Rights* (Belmont, CA: Wadsworth, 1989)

'Practical Reason and Norms' (Oxford: Oxford University Press, 1999)

'Promises and Obligations' in PMS Hacker and J Raz (eds), *Law, Morality and Society: Essays in Honor of H.L.A. Hart* (Oxford: Clarendon Press, 1977)

'Reply to MacCormick' (1972) 46(Supplement) *Proceedings of the Aristotelian Society* 80

'Voluntary Obligations and Normative Powers II' (1972) 46 Proceedings of the Aristotelian Society. Supplementary, Volume 80

Reisman WM and Arsanjani MH, 'The Question of Unilateral Governmental Statements as Applicable Law in Investment Disputes' (2004) 19 *ICSID Rev – FILJ* 328

Reynolds P, 'Legitimate Expectations and the Protection of Trust in Public Officials' (2011) *PL* 330

Riggs RE, 'Legitimate Expectation and Procedural Fairness in English Law' (1988) 36 *Am J Comp L* 395

Ripinsky S, 'Assessing Damages in Investment Disputes: Practice in Search of Perfect' (2009) 10(1) *JWIT*

Ripinsky S and Williams K, *Damages in International Investment Law* (London: British Institute of International and Comparative Law, 2008)

Roberts A, 'Clash of Paradigms: Actors and Analogies Shaping the Investment Treaty System' (2013) 107(1) *AJIL* 55

'Power and Persuasion in Investment Treaty Interpretation: The Dual Role of States' (2010) 104 *AJIL* 179

Robertson A, 'Reasonable Reliance in Estoppel by Conduct' (2000) 23 *UNSW Law Journal* 87

'Reliance and Expectation in Estoppel Remedies' (1998) 18 *Leg Stud* 360, 365

'Towards a Unifying Purpose for Estoppel' (1996) 22(1) *Mon LR* 1

Robins M, 'The Primacy of Promising' (1976) 85(339) *Mind* 321

Promising, Intending and Moral Autonomy (Cambridge: Cambridge University Press, 1976)

'Promissory Obligations and Rawls's Contractarianism' (1976) 36 *Analysis* 190

Ross WD, *Foundations of Ethics* (Oxford: Clarendon Press, 1939)

Rubin AP, 'The International Legal Effects of Unilateral Declarations' (1977) 1 *AJIL* 1

Sabahi B, *Compensation and Restitution in Investor-State Arbitration: Principles and Practice* (Oxford: Oxford University Press, 2011)

Sadowski W, 'Yukos and Contributory Fault' (2015) 5 *TDM*

Salacuse J, 'The Emerging Global Regime for Investment' 2010 51(2) *Harv Int'l LJ* 427

Sales P and Steyn K, 'Legitimate Expectations in English Law: An Analysis' (2004) *PL* 564

Samet I, 'The Morality of Proprietary Estoppel' in J Penner and H Smith (eds), *The Philosophical Foundations of Property Law* (Oxford: Oxford University Press, 2013)

Scanlon T, 'Promises and Practices' (1990) 19(3) *Phil & Pub Aff* 199

'Reasons, Responsibility, and Reliance: Replies to Wallace, Dworkin, and Deigh' Symposium on T. M. Scanlon's What We Owe to Each Other' (2002) 112(3) *Ethics* 507

What We Owe to Each Other (Cambridge, MA: Harvard University Press, 1998)

Schill S, 'Contracting with Foreigners: International Investment Law Implications' in R Noguellou and U Stelken, *Comparative Law on Public Contracts* (Brussels: Bruylant, 2010)

'Crafting the International Economic Order: The Public Function of Investment Treaty Arbitration and Its Significance for the Role of the Arbitrator' (2010) *LJIL* 401

'Damages in International Investment Law. S. Ripinsky, K. Williams (Book Review)' (2010) 1 *TDM*

'Fair and Equitable Treatment, the Rule of Law and Comparative Public Law' in S Schill (ed), *International Investment Law and Comparative Public Law* (Oxford: Oxford University Press, 2010)

'Fair and Equitable Treatment under Investment Treaties as an Embodiment of the Rule of Law' IILJ Working Paper 2006/6, Global Administrative Law Series

Schønberg S, *Legitimate Expectations in Administrative Law* (Oxford: Oxford University Press, 2000)

Schreuer C, 'Fair and Equitable Treatment in Arbitral Practice' (2005) 5 *JWIT* 357

'Protection against Arbitrary or Discriminatory Measures' in CA Rogers and RP Alford (eds), *The Future of Investment Arbitration* (New York, NY: Oxford University Press, 2009)

'Travelling the BIT Route: Of Waiting Periods, Umbrella Clauses and Forks in the Road' (2004) 5 *JWIT* 231

Schroeder M, 'Administrative Law in Germany' in R Seerden and F Stroink (eds), *Administrative Law of the European Union, Its Members and the United States* (Gronigen: Intersentia, 2002)

Schultz T, 'Against Consistency in Investment Arbitration' in Z Douglas, J Pauwelyn and JE Viñuales (eds), *The Foundations of International Investment Law - Bringing Theory into Practice* (Oxford: Oxford University Press, 2014)

Schultz T and Dupont C, 'Investment Arbitration: Promoting the Rule of Law or Over-empowering Investors? A Quantitative Empirical Study' (2014) 25(4) *Eur J Int Law* 1147

Schwarze J, *European Administrative Law* (London: Sweet & Maxwell, 1992)

Schwebel SM, 'On Whether a Breach by a State of a Contract with an Alien Is a Breach of International Law' in A Migliazza, F Pocar, P Lamberti Zanardi and P Ziccardi (eds), *International Law at the Time of Its Codification - Essays in Honour of Roberto Ago*, Volume 3 (Milan: A. Giuffrè, 1987)

'On Whether a Breach by a State of a Contract with an Alien Is a Breach of International Law' in SM Schwebel (ed), *Justice in International Law: Selected Writings* (Cambridge: Cambridge University Press, 1994)

Schwehr B and Brown P, 'Legitimate Expectation - Snuffed Out?' (1991) *PL* 163

Sheinman H, 'Promising, Intimate Relationships and Conventionalism' (2008) 177 (4) *Phil Rev* 481

Shelton D, 'Righting Wrongs: Reparations in the Articles on State Responsibility' (2002) 96 *AJIL* 833

Shiffrin S, 'Promising, Intimate Relationships, and Conventionalism' (2008) 117(4) *Phil Rev* 481

'The Divergence of Contract and Promise' (2007) 120 *Harv L Rev* 708

Sinclair A, 'The Umbrella Clause Debate' in AK Bjorklund et al. (eds), *Investment Treaty Law: Current Issues III* (London: BIICL, 2009)

Sinclair I, 'Estoppel and Acquiescence' in V Lowe and M Fitzmaurice (eds), *Fifty Years of the International Court of Justice: Essays in Honour of Sir Robert Jennings* (Cambridge: Cambridge University Press, 1996)

Slaughter AM, 'A Typology of Transjudicial Communications' (1994) 29 *U Rich L Rev* 99

Slawson WD, 'Role of Reliance in Contract Damages' (1990) 76 *Cornell L Rev* 197

Smith M, 'The Value of Making and Keeping Promise' in H Sheinman (ed), *Promises and Agreements: Philosophical Essays* (Oxford: Oxford University Press, 2011)

Smutny C, 'Principles of Compensation in Investment Treaty Arbitration' (2007) 22 *ICSID Rev – FILJ* 1

Snare F, 'The Definition of Prima Facie Duties' (1974) 24(96) *Phil Q* 235

Snodgrass E, 'Protecting Investors' Legitimate Expectations – Recognising and Delimiting a General Principle' (2006) 21 *ICSID Rev – FILJ* 1, 25–30

Sohn LB and Baxter RR, 'Responsibility of States for Injuries to the Economic Interests of Aliens' (1961) 55 *AJIL* 545

Sornarajah M, *Resistance and Change in the International Law on Foreign Investment* (Cambridge: Cambridge University Press, 2015)

The International Law on Foreign Investment (Cambridge: Cambridge University Press, 3rd edn, 2010)

Southwood N and Friedrich D, 'Promises beyond Assurance' (2009) 144(2) *Philosophical Studies: An International Journal for Philosophy in the Analytic Tradition* 261

Spears S, 'The Quest for Policy Space in a New Generation of International Investment Agreements' 2010 13(4) *JIEL* 1037

Steele I, 'Substantive Legitimate Expectations: Striking the Right Balance?' (2005) 121 *LQR* 300

Steyn K, 'Consistency: A Principle of Public Law?' (1977) 2(1) *JR* 22

Stoljar S, 'Promise, Expectation and Agreement' (1988) 47 *CLJ* 193

Stone J, 'Arbitrariness, the Fair and Equitable Treatment Standard, and the International Law of Investment' (2012) 25(1) *LJIL* 77

Stone J, *The Province and Function of Law: Law as Logic, Justice, and Social Control: A Study in Jurisprudence* (Cambridge: Harvard University Press, 2nd edn, 1946)

Sunkin M, 'Remedies Available in Judicial Review Proceedings' in D Feldman (ed), *English Public Law* (Oxford: Oxford University Press, 2004)

Sunstein C, On the Expressive Function of Law (1996) 144 *U Pa L Rev* 2021

Suy E, 'Unilateral Acts of States as Source of International Law: Some New Thoughts and Frustrations' in *Droit du Povoir, Pouvoir du Droit. Mélanges offerts à Jean Salmon* (Brussels: Bruylant, 2007)

Teubner G, 'Legal Irritants: Good Faith in British Law or How Unifying Law Ends Up in New Divergencies' (1998) 61(1) *MLR* 11

Thirlway H, *The Sources of International Law* (Oxford: Oxford University Press, 2014)

Thomas R, *Legitimate Expectations and Proportionality in Administrative Law* (Oxford: Hart Publishing, 2000)

Thompson MP, 'From Representation to Expectation: Estoppel as a Cause of Action' (1983) 42(2) *CLJ* 257

Tienhaara K, 'Regulatory Chill and the Threat of Arbitration: A View from Political Science' in C Brown and K Miles (eds), *Evolution in Investment Treaty Law and Arbitration* (Cambridge: Cambridge University Press, 2011)

Tognazzini NA, 'The Hybrid Nature of Promissory Obligation' (2007) 35(3) *Phil & Pub Aff* 203

Tudor I, *The Fair and Equitable Treatment Standard in the International Law of Foreign Investment* (Oxford: Oxford University Press, 2008)

Urmson JO, 'The Interpretation of the philosophy of J.S. Mill' (1953) 3 *Phil Rev* 33

Vadi V, *Analogies in International Investment Law and Arbitration* (Cambridge: Cambridge University Press, 2015)

'Critical Comparisons: The Role of Comparative Law in Investment Treaty Arbitration' (2010) 39(1) *Denv J Int'l L& Pol'y* 89

Vanderman Y, 'Ultra Vires Legitimate Expectations: An Argument for Compensation' (2012) *PL* 85

Vandevelde K, 'A Unified Theory of Fair and Equitable Treatment' (2010) 43(1) *NYU J Int'l L & Pol* 43

Vasciannie S, 'The Fair and Equitable Treatment Standard in International Investment Law and Practice' (1999) 70 *BYIL* 99

Vicuna F, 'From Preston to Prescott: Globalizing Legitimate Expectation' in S Charnovitz, D Steger and P Van den Bossche (eds) *Law in the Service of Human Dignity: Essays in Honour of Florentino Feliciano* (New York, NY: Cambridge University Press, 2005)

'Regulatory Authority and Legitimate Expectations: Balancing the Rights of the State and the Individual under International Law in a Global Society' (2003) 5 *Int'l LF D Int'l* 188

Vitek W, 'The Humean Promise: Whence Comes Its Obligation' (1986) XII(2) *Hume Studies* 160

Volterra R, 'International Law Commission Articles on State Responsibility and Investor-State Arbitration: Do Investors Have Rights?' (2010) 25(1) *ICSID Rev – FILJ* 218

Waelde TM and Ndi G, 'Stabilizing International Investment Commitments: International Law versus Contract Interpretation' (1996) 31 *Texas Intl L J* 215

Wagner M, 'Jurisdiction by Estoppel in the International Court of Justice' (1986) 74 *Cal L Rev* 1777

Walter A von, 'The Investor's Expectations in International Investment Arbitration' in A Reinisch and C Knahr (eds), *International Investment Law* (Utrecht: Eleven International Publishing, 2009)

Watson A, 'Aspects of Reception of Law' (1995) 44 *Am J Comp L* 335

Comparative Law and Legal Change' (1978) 37(2) *CLJ* 313

Legal Transplants: An Approach to Comparative Law (Athens, GA: University of Georgia Press, 1993)
Legal Transplants and Law Reform (1976) 92 *LQR* 79
Watson G, 'Asserting and Promising' (2004) 117 *Philos Stud* 57
Watson J, 'Clarity and Ambiguity: A New Approach to the Test of Legitimacy in the Law of Legitimate Expectations' (2010) 30(4) *LS* 633
Wehberg H, 'Pacta Sunt Servanda' (1959) 53 *Am J Int'l L* 775, 786
Weiler JHH and Trachtman JP, 'European Constitutionalism and Its Discontents' (1997) 17(1) *Nw J Int'l L & Bus* 355
Weinrib E, 'Private Law and Public Right' (2011) (2) *UTLJ* 191
'Toward a Moral Theory of Negligence Law' (1983) 2 *L & Phil* 38
'Two Conceptions of Remedies' in Charles EF Rickett (ed), *Justifying Private Law Remedies* (Oxford: Hart Publishing, 2008)
Wennerholm F, 'What Can You Expect? The Role of Legitimate Expectations in Investment Protection Disputes' in K Hobér et al. (eds) *Between East and West: Essays in Honour of Ulf Franke* (New York, NY: JurisNet, 2010)
Wiener JB, 'Something Borrowed for Something Blue: Legal Transplants and the Evolution of Global Environmental Law' (2001) 27 *Ecology LQ* 1297
Wongkaew T, 'The Transplantation of Legitimate Expectations in Investment Treaty Arbitration: A Critique' in S Lalani and R Polanco (eds), *The Role of the State in Investor-State Arbitration* (Leiden: Brill Nijhoff, 2015)
Woolf H, 'The Role of the English Judiciary in Developing Public Law' (1986) 27 *Wm & Mary L Rev* 669
Yeung K, 'The Regulatory State' in R Baldwin, M Cave and M Lodge (eds), *The Oxford Handbook of Regulation* (Oxford: Oxford University Press, 2010)
Young S, 'Rawlsian Reasonableness: A Problematic Presumption?' (2006) 39(1) *Can J Pol Sc* 159
Zeyl T, 'Charting the Wrong Course: The Doctrine of Legitimate Expectations in Investment Treaty Law' (2011) 49 *Alberta L Rev* 203

INDEX